START UP

A PRACTICE BASED GUIDE
FOR NEW VENTURE CREATION

INGE HILL

START UP

A PRACTICE BASED GUIDE
FOR NEW VENTURE CREATION

 macmillan education · palgrave

First published 2016 by
PALGRAVE

Palgrave in the UK is an imprint of Macmillan Publishers Limited, registered in England, company number 785998, of 4 Crinan Street, London, N1 9XW.

Palgrave Macmillan in the US is a division of St Martin's Press LLC, 175 Fifth Avenue, New York, NY 10010.

Palgrave is a global imprint of the above companies and is represented throughout the world.

Palgrave® and Macmillan® are registered trademarks in the United States, the United Kingdom, Europe and other countries.

ISBN 978–1–137–42583–6

This book is printed on paper suitable for recycling and made from fully managed and sustained forest sources. Logging, pulping and manufacturing processes are expected to conform to the environmental regulations of the country of origin.

A catalogue record for this book is available from the British Library.

A catalog record for this book is available from the Library of Congress.

Typeset by MPS Limited, Chennai, India.

To Ian
For everything

CONTENTS

LIST OF FIGURES

LIST OF TABLES

LIST OF BOXES

PREFACE

Start Up **is a practice-led process guide** to starting a new venture for all those young and not-so-young people with very little or no enterprise knowledge, which focuses on the processes *before* start-up. The readers may be:

▶ Students on business degrees in year 1, those in other degree courses such as education, health, creative industries, hospitality, sports or engineering aiming to start up, and everyone who is interested in starting a new venture using their skills and/or passion, be they based at college or university;

▶ Master's or MBA students who do not have a business degree can discover new links between actions and business contexts they might only have encountered in an isolated way while working;

▶ Professionals keen to start their venture, part-time or full-time.

Start Up is written in a very accessible style, avoiding jargon where possible, and explaining academic and business terms where needed to allow access to one possible outline of the journey from business idea to launching a new venture. You will find that there is no clear-cut way to start a new venture. There are many ways, and this book presents one of them, plus plenty of insights on how to adapt it for your own purposes.

So many start-ups do not survive the first two years and have to close down. Many of the reasons come down to not fully understanding the processes and costs involved. I hope this book can address these challenges in a way that more of you continue trading, hence I am talking about the *sustainable start-up*.

What makes this book different are the following features:

▶ A focus on the processes of creating the start-up, and not just creating the product or the value proposition, and the repetitions of activities over the process, such as customer development, research and business modelling;

▶ An exploration of starting a social enterprise next to starting a for-profit venture – so many of the social enterprise start-ups I worked with told me that they wished they had learned about social enterprise when still at college or university;

▶ The international examples of start-ups and relevant links to national organizations throughout (including examples from the Netherlands, Sweden, Norway, Hong Kong, the US and Romania);

▶ Only student and graduate case studies are used to illustrate the venture creation process, showing that everybody can do what they do;

▶ A suggestion of one process as a blueprint which you can adapt for your own needs;

▶ Additional tools that can help to implement the practical suggestions the business model cube offers;
▶ Processes discussed are suitable in many countries.

Why I wrote this book: Within the next 15 to 20 years, the portfolio career, a combination of phases of employment and self-employment or team business start-ups, will be more the norm rather than the exception. Employability increasingly means not only the ability to work in teams, across borders, time zones and cultures, but also to be able to gain a living for a period of time in an independent way when industries restructure and new jobs are created with different skills sets while others are destroyed. In this context, starting a new venture is most likely an enterprising activity many more who are in their 20s now will be engaging with – be it as a freelancer or through starting a business with employees. These developments are matched by requests made by Lord Young (2013) and others to offer a more integrated approach to equipping young people for self-employment.

The most important factors responsible for this change in career paths and increasing number of new ventures include:

▶ Technological change that allows for a large variety of ways of working remotely, online and across borders with relative ease;
▶ Economic recessions creating a stronger need to reduce overheads, of which permanent staff are one large cost factor;
▶ Change in the international division of labour between countries, in the way that there are less places in the world that can be used as cheap "labour banks";
▶ Reduction of trade barriers between countries and trading blocs worldwide;
▶ Increasing demands for a more personalized way of working with greater amounts of freedom when and where to work from men and women.

My passion for empowering men and women to lead happier confident lives has been the main motivation to write this book. One way of realizing this aim so many have is through a *sustainable start-up*. Too many start-ups fail or are closed down, as those creating a venture do not fully understand how to go about it. I poured 15 years of start-up support and starting service ventures combined with over ten years of training and coaching into the form of a book, supported by my research on the pre-start-up phase.

Being out there building your venture profile and selling successfully to clients is an exciting project, with lots of ups and downs, often more downs, it sometimes feels, than ups. But for nothing in the world would the majority of people who have done it and are still doing it miss the experience, and that includes me. I thoroughly enjoyed the excitement of doing it myself and supporting others in setting up their own ventures.

Who else can gain from *Start Up*? This book is also essential for lecturers in Further and Higher Education institutions who are given the role to teach entrepreneurship or business start-up and have themselves not started and run a business or whose business experience is a while back. Similarly, **staff working in job centres** and organizations offering labour market services, and **career advisers** advising on introductions to business start-up can also benefit from reading this book and working their way through the chapters, realizing on paper a business idea.

If you have any feedback or stories you would like to share, contact me and the growing mystart-up community: ingehill@mystart-up.info.

Good luck with your sustainable Start Up!
Inge Hill , PhD

ACKNOWLEDGEMENTS

Over the years, many colleagues in academia have shared their gems of insight with me. It is impossible to point out a particular publication or individual. My thanks go to all of you!

I have met many start-ups and established entrepreneurs on the way while creating and running my own ventures and when working as an adviser, and so many left their mark on my learning journey. It would be difficult to name some and not the many others I have learned from. Thank you to all of you for sharing your learning and challenges with me, and encouraging and inspiring me. My most recent engagement on a business start-up programme in 2013 as an adviser is sticking in my mind, the Enterprise Catalyst Programme in Birmingham, co-funded by Birmingham City Council and ERDF funding. The individuals I supported during that programme from a wish or a necessity to earn a living through self-employment inspired me to write up my insights and share my learning with a wider audience while adding the academic gems of knowledge where appropriate.

I am most grateful to my former students who allowed me to support them in their endeavours to plan for a start-up in their countries in India, China, Vietnam, Romania, Thailand and Hong Kong since 2009; it helped me to realize that the processes and research suggested by me work outside the UK as well. Two of those former students kindly agreed to be included in this book, Vivek George, with Serratomo in Hong Kong, and Alexandru Damian with AMD Nobel in Romania. Thank you to all the start-ups I interviewed for the book and all the professionals and young people I worked with since 2000, in particular the Prince's Trust clients I had the pleasure to mentor.

Authors are only part of the team that produces a book! I would like to thank the production team at Palgrave, and in particular the editorial team with Jenny Hindley and Holly Rutter, for their great support and enthusiasm.

Finally, I would like to thank you, the reader, for your interest in this exciting field of business start-up. If you would like to share your story and experiences that could be included in the next edition of this book, or any feedback, please do get in touch at ingehill@mystart-up.info. I would love to hear from you.

ABOUT THE AUTHOR

Inge Hill started businesses between 2002 and 2012 and is passionate about inspiring others to start new ventures. She is a small business expert and offers 14 years of business support experience in London and the West Midlands. Inge saves clients time and money in start-up and business growth while improving their processes, business models and marketing strategies. Her clients included public sector providers such as Business Link, Birmingham and Wolverhampton City Council, SMEs and social enterprises. Inge worked as a business adviser for a number of government agencies such as Business Link for London and Business Link West Midlands, and on a number of government or EU-funded programmes working with start-ups, pre-start-ups and established SMEs. Awards won include a High Impact Award for a SME networking event during Entrepreneurship Week in 2010 with her own client base, an innovation voucher and a HEFCE/UnLtd award between 2010 and 2012.

Her UK academic career started as a Visiting Researcher and Visiting Lecturer at the London School of Economics, after which she took her first full-time job at Kingston University. She left academia in 2007 to focus full-time on her research and strategy consultancy. Teaching and working with students remained a passion and she continued to work as a Visiting Lecturer with West Midlands universities from 2008 until recently taking up an appointment as Senior Lecturer at Birmingham City University.

Inge has been twice selected to represent the UK on EU-funded Transversal Study Visits to discuss the international experiences in enterprise education and lifelong learning. At the International Enterprise Educator Conference (IEEC) 2014 conference she was selected to run one of the Provocateur sessions, an innovative way to lead the exchange of practice learning amongst peers. In her leisure time she shares her insights and passion with Prince's Trust start-up clients as volunteer mentor and is responsible for strategic planning on the board of the Black Country charity and social enterprise Access2Business since late 2014.

1

ENTERPRISE AND INDIVIDUALS IN SOCIETY AND THE ECONOMY

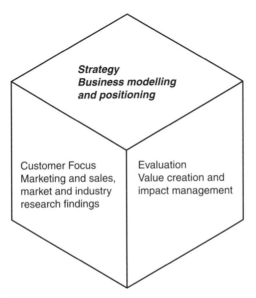

Figure 1.1   The Cube Strategy
Source: © Hill, 2012.

Summary

Chapter One introduces the book's structure and focus, including the language that the book uses and the symbols. The symbol of the Cube serves to illustrate the six most important areas for a *sustainable start-up*, and principles and practices needed to realize this *start-up* (Figure 1.2). A discussion of the basics of business functions and business in the economy is followed by an introduction to the most important young entrepreneur case studies who are referred to throughout the book.

The chapter aims to create a common base to start from for all readers. Thus, the chapter's discussions are aimed at those who may have little or no understanding of how a business works, what functions it needs to have to operate profitably and how it fits into society and the economy. It aims to include all readers who might not have read about basic business issues at all or not for a long time. Additionally, it outlines the structure of industries and illustrates with recent UK and international statistics, the situation of businesses in the economy, the role of start-ups and small and medium-sized enterprises.

CONTENTS

1.1 About this book

1.1.1 What this book offers

This book aims to be a **process guide**. Using the image of the Cube, it offers guidance on six facets of the start-up process, with associated principles and practices. There is not much academic research published yet that portrays in detail the pre-start-up phase and its success factors; and the research that is available has only been done for limited sectors. Similarly, there is not sufficiently useful guidance in drawing conclusions and decision-making during the pre-start-up process. The sequences of activities suggested in *Start Up* are only one possibility of how you could develop a start-up. They are based on my own experience of starting service businesses, alongside lessons gleaned from my involvement with hundreds of start-ups through my business support practice as well as my research. The good (or bad) news is that there is no one definite way or process that applies to all individuals, all business types and all sectors. It is possible, however, to identify a number of activities that ideally should be carried out, sometimes more than once, to create a *sustainable start-up*. In each chapter I briefly discuss when to carry out the suggested activities, how often and for what reasons. By exploring the pre-start-up process through the activities in this book, you will progress more quickly to the start-up launch. If you have created a new venture before, and as you feel familiar with some of the activities, you will be more confident in carrying them out.

Throughout this book I have included specific differences between for-profit and social enterprise start-ups. The social enterprise model is an exciting opportunity for more and more young people; I have been told over and over again that they wished they had learned more about it while at college or university.

1.1.2 Who should read *Start Up*?

Start Up offers an introduction to the most important processes and associated activities undertaken when exploring a business idea and preparing for new venture creation. It will take you on a journey from various starting points via finding and focusing a business idea and onward to actually getting up and running. *Start Up* is aimed squarely at first-timers deciding to engage in new venture creation and those with very little or no background in business. All the case studies are themselves students or recent graduates. Everybody, independent of age and education, can carry out the processes suggested.

While the processes themselves are suited to all sectors, they may need to be adjusted to the specific sector and national environment you are living and working in. It should be noted, however, that for manufacturing start-ups some additional processes are needed that are indicated only rather than described in detail, that being beyond the scope of this process outline. Other avenues for starting up in business include taking on a franchise or purchasing an existing business. If you follow the franchise start-up route, the journey and its processes are very different. Chapter Three contains a brief outline of using a franchise to start your first business (see Section 3.1.4). However, this process is largely beyond the scope of the book, as is entering into business by buying an existing business.

The book is also a great guide for newcomers to business advice or mentoring and career advisers, as it outlines one set of the processes an adviser can guide a mentee through. I have successfully used the processes and activities or variations of them many times since 2000; it is a joy to see a young person grow and develop their own venture.

1.1.3 Language used in *Start Up*

Throughout this book the word "product" is assumed to always include services as well. Similarly, when the word "goods" is used, this always includes services. Goods may also be called tangible goods, whereas services may be called intangible goods. In some chapters, services are addressed explicitly, where processes differ for services from those for tangible goods.

Throughout *Start Up* I write about my own experiences as a start-up business adviser and businesswoman using "I". When I use "we", then I am referring to you, the reader, and me, the author.

The language in *Start Up* tries to remain accessible by using as much commonly known terminology as possible and explaining business jargon wherever its use is worthwhile. I have tried to use the expanded form of phrases that are subsequently abbreviated even where it may be fairly commonly known. I prefer to lean toward the side of accessibility and ease of understanding.

1.1.4 Structure of *Start Up*

There are 16 chapters altogether in this book. While you are welcome to read the book from start to finish in sequence, I have written each chapter in such a way that you do not

> **Box 1.1   Symbols and their meanings**
>
>   Activity – here you are asked to engage in an exercise, from research to writing
>
>   Think and reflect – here you are invited to reflect on an issue
>
>   Case study – here a case study is presented to you in more detail

have to have read the previous chapters in order to be able to understand any one chapter. There are plenty of references to other chapters to show how the discussions link to each other, which may inspire you to follow up in that direction. I highly recommend reading the chapters that present most interest and relevance to your situation in the sequence that suits you. I would also recommend going back to the research chapters (Chapter Four and Chapter Five) as well as the business model chapter (Chapter Seven) and re-reading them before you get up and running. However, I do recommend reading every chapter at some point on your pre-start-up journey.

As pointed out earlier, this book aims to be a stand-alone resource and "process bible". I want to bridge the gap often left by how-to-start-a-business books and university textbooks and offer a unique combination of practical insights, including both lists of practical ready-to-use resources, real-life tips and "how-to's" and insight from recent research. It is therefore helpful, for example, to do all activities within chapters and within the revision sections at the end of each chapter, even if you do not read the whole chapter.

All chapters are structured in a similar way: they start with a brief content summary and an overview of the section main subheadings. This way, you can easily identify which section you would like to go to.

The last section in each chapter is always entitled "Concluding remarks and application of new insights". It offers some conclusions, highlights key learning points, lists revision questions and invites you to apply new insights to your own venture explorations. Tasks under revision questions and activities in the main text invite you to apply what you learned to a business idea you are exploring; and, regularly, you are invited to create entries into a start-up diary and take notes of any decisions you have made. The companion website offers a list of all activities (see www.palgrave.com/companion/hill-start-up).

This diary allows you to keep track of what you read, what you find out, ideas you have, decisions you make or insights you gain while reading this book and carrying out the exercises. This written reflection is important, as you might forget what you had an insight about if you do not capture it.

Each chapter has plenty of activities, insights and research findings, tools and points for consideration and application to your business idea. Box 1.1 explains the meaning of three symbols that guide you to find activities and case studies more easily.

All references used are listed at the end of the book. There is also a companion website to this book, which contains suggestions for further reading organized by themes, such as finance, social enterprise and women in business.

1.2   Why a Cube?

I have found in my work with students, clients and associates that very often using a visual metaphor can help create a stronger mental image and lead to better understanding when discussing complicated or inter-linked processes. For *Start Up* that image is a Cube (see Figure 1.2). The Cube provides a visual model of the areas that need to be addressed to achieve the goal – a *sustainable start-up*.

Each of the six faces presents the primary processes to be explored and developed. Each face is directly linked with four others through the sides and corners they share, and indirectly linked with the sixth area on its opposite face. All six areas are equal in size, equal in importance. The six faces of the *Start Up* Cube are Business Processes, Financial Circuits, Frameworks, Customer Focus, Strategy and Evaluation.

To take the idea of the *Start Up* Cube further, we can think of rolling the Cube like a dice so that each time another face lands on top. The randomness of this process links to the idea that there is no set sequence of activities you have to engage with to create a *sustainable start-up*. The length in time and sequence of steps varies by business type, sector and the individual; if you engage in your second or even third start-up you will get to the launch in a quicker way. The more often you throw a dice, eventually you will get all numbers to be on top at least once. And this is similar to the pre-start-up process; whatever business you start, and however you go about it, eventually you will have to address all of the areas the Cube highlights.

There are a number of steps in six areas that need to be done before being truly up and running, summarized by the six areas of the Cube. These steps are not stages in the sense that completion of one stage creates the basis for the next stage, but rather processes and activities that allow you to collect information and gain experiences; the sequence is variable, and you have to engage in several activities more than once.

Each of the six Cube faces is divided into two sections, these are:

1) Business Processes: operations and process management
2) Financial Circuits: spending and making money (including pricing)
3) Frameworks: internal frameworks (governance) and legal issues
4) Customer Focus (and environment): marketing and sales, and market and industry research
5) Strategy: business modelling and positioning
6) Evaluation: value creation and impact management.

If we imagine the Cube as a glass box, we may wonder: what is inside? The venture founder(s) (juggling the data, information and finances), the people – staff, networks – and resources are inside the Cube.

The steps for each process area in the pre-start-up phase are explained throughout this book. It is not a linear process; on the contrary, it is an iterative process, that means that many steps have to be done again when new insight and new knowledge have been gained.

Where does the start-up journey begin? The pre-start-up journey in my view starts with an idea you have that can make a big enough change to people's lives, either business people or consumers. Even if the idea is a material or tool for a machine, at the end of that machine is a person using the machine, pressing a button or using a keyboard.

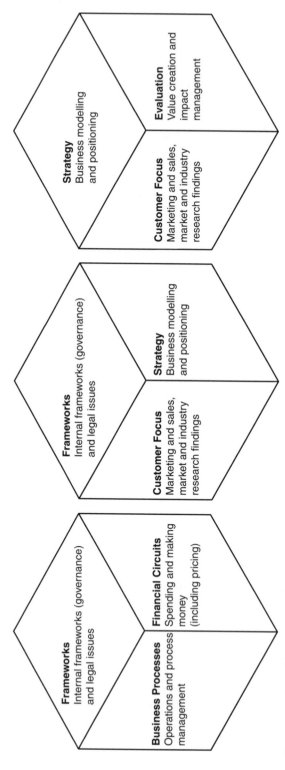

Figure 1.2 Views of the *Start Up* Cube

If that is where the start-up journey begins, where does it end? What is meant by a *sustainable start-up*? I perceive the lifetime of a start-up as sustainable if the founder(s) can freely make a decision whether to close the venture and when to do so, without being forced. It does not mean that the *sustainable start-up* has to exist forever. But it allows the founder(s) to close the business down or sell it when it is right for them and not being forced to close it, for example, due to lack of money. Reasons for closure could include that it is time in their lives to move on and do something else, or nobody wants to continue the business (succession planning is often not done early enough before a founder/business-owner has found the next owner/manager). Another reason could be that sometimes the market or industry conditions only allow for a business to thrive for a limited period of time; we come to those types of situations later. And it can mean that the founder(s) have simply learned enough with and from this kind of business activity and would like to start another business. Researchers call the closure of a business independent of the reasons "entrepreneurial exit".

In the fast-moving environment we live in, the shorter life of a business is acceptable; this is similar to the patchwork careers many of us have and more will have over the coming years. The stable one-job career (or two jobs in a working life) of previous generations is becoming rarer and will be much more rare; we discuss this further in Chapter Two. Many men and women aim for a better work–life balance and prefer self-employment and running a small business over a career in the corporate world. And because of the rapid changes through the impact of technologies not all businesses are built to last for decades.

Box 1.2 summarizes some of the limited findings of research done on the pre-start-up process. The limitations of the existing research lie in the fact that most studies are based on reports by entrepreneurs looking backwards on what they did. Even the act of recounting actions verbally or writing them down imposes a sequence on events that may have been performed simultaneously or in overlapping time frames or repeated at different times. We also create links to events in the past that were not necessarily there at the time, thus creating connections, justifying decisions or rationalizing actions in retrospect instead of acknowledging that so much of what we do is not directly related to a conscious process of decision-making and evaluating possible strategic directions. The large majority of studies published (over 90% in 2011) focus on large datasets such as the Panel Study of Entrepreneurship Dynamics in the US and other countries, and the GEM reports (Markova et al., 2011). The tools used to gather these data sets limit answer options and rarely allow the respondents to contextualise what an answer means to them and how it relates to other answers given, reducing the reality of experiences to fit into answer options offered. This means the complexity of how a business is started and what it means to the founder(s) could not be captured adequately.

Other limitations lie in the focus on technology-related start-ups and those for tangible products, which differ from those for services, and again from fully online businesses. Many of these research articles do not consider different resources and experiences of those starting up sufficiently and are often team focused while many start-ups are in fact carried out by individuals.

Similarly, some academic research takes the employment of staff as an "end-point" indicator for successfully being up and running – however, as statistics show (see Sections 1.3 and 1.4 of this chapter), many sustainable SMEs do not employ staff for a number of months, sometimes years, or not at all. Instead, associates and subcontractors are used. This means that the processes leading to sustainable micro-businesses may be overlooked in the body of research.

The suggested processes in *Start Up* realize a non-linear iterative process (this means that some parts of the process need to be repeated until the desired result is reached). While presented as a list of activities, always remember that they do not need to be carried out in sequential order.

Box 1.2 Selected research findings on the pre-start-up phase

While there is no agreement on the process of new venture creation, research findings seem to agree that the start-up process is a staged one. Research from the 1990s even discussed a linear process with predictable stages (Aidzes, 1988, came up with ten distinct stages, see also Miller and Friesen, 1983).

The phases before start-up, pre-start-up and the actual start-up phase are often summarized as the "start-up" phase (see for example Low and McMillan, 1988, McCline and Bhat, 2012). The following phases put the focus on various aspects of the time before and during "growth" and maturity, with growth defined primarily through units of sale. Idea generation and opportunity identification are summarized as "pre-start-up" as the logical starting point in that view. McCline and Bhat identify readiness activities such as noting market trends in the process of environment scanning, developing responses to market opportunities, business plan preparation and securing licenses, using the academic term of "nascent entrepreneurs" (see also Davidsson, 2006, Low and McMillan, 1988, McCline and Bhat, 2012) for those who have not yet launched the business. The start-up stage is the actual venture creation, yet indicators for being in that phase and clear starting points are not agreed upon in the research findings. Networks of family and friends are essential at this stage.

Recent research on "user entrepreneurs" identified those that start off as users of a product solution who are unhappy with the current situation and develop their own better solution, which they first sell within their networks and user communities before selling outside of their networks. Sectors that were studied included online games, sporting equipment and products for young people (Baldwin et al., 2006, Haeflinger et al., 2010, Shah and Tripsas, 2007). In these contexts, actual firm foundation and commercialization follows comparatively late, after industry entry and initial sales. Further exploration and development of improved versions of the product and further sales happened within user communities. The staged model does not apply in those contexts in the same way.

Researchers believed for too long that the activities leading to start-up were a linear process, with a clear starting point (idea generation and/or opportunity identification) and end-point marked by the first sales or even the first hiring of staff (Carter et al., 2003, Liao et al., 2005, McCline and Bhat, 2012). The two main approaches that influenced business support and policy so long were a developmental process model, which assumed that an identified number of stages had to be encountered (numbers range from four to 65 stages), and an activity-based model, which assumed that a number of activities would have to be carried out within a time frame, and key milestones had to be reached (Low and MacMillan, 1988, Reynolds and Miller, 1992). Only very few researchers identified that preparing for start-up is a feedback-driven non-linear process, which is rather chaotic and repeats some steps, and is really a learning process (Bhave, 1994,

McCline and Bhat, 2012). Influences of context were neglected, such as the environment, the traits of the individual doing the start-up, the industry sector or the market.

More recently, the "lean start-up" approach addresses the repetitive nature of the processes and integrates the aspect of trying, learning and trying again differently or in lean terminology build, measure and learn (Ries, 2011). It describes a sequence of action, reflection and learning, geared towards identifying quickly if there is a scaleable product under consideration and reducing the time in getting to market to finding out. Using the concept of a minimal viable product, this approach suggests focusing early in the idea exploration process on learning from customer reactions what kind of product and what kind of features will be of interest. Criticism for the lean approach points out that it is far too much technology start-up focused and that running "fat" – adding in non-essential features to gain a competitive edge – can be very successful and save time in taking product features out.

These above mentioned "lean" approaches or practices are not new; they have been used by many start-ups for years. Bootstrap start-ups with very little money, in particular, follow this iterative process, as they do not have sufficient money to do everything at once. Yet, the processes had not been described in that way or widely published before. The value of the "lean approach" lies in making several known and tried processes available to a larger audience. However, its emphasis on developing "scaleable" products belies the fact that even products or services that are not scaleable are of great value for many start-ups who are happy to build a business on a non-scaleable product/service.

But I am getting ahead too quickly. To learn more about the insights behind *Start Up* go on to 1.3, the next section. It talks about some principles and associated practices you will learn about in this book. If you first want to brush up on some basic business functions and industry sectors, Sections 1.5 to 1.7 do exactly that. They also unpack some of the assumptions and myths associated with being in business that may constitute barriers to your start-up success.

1.3 Principles and practices to create the *sustainable start-up*

1.3.1 Background to principles and practices for the *sustainable start-up*

The social and economic developments and changes in society that have occurred in the last 20 years have been well-rehearsed elsewhere and will only be briefly outlined here in order to remind you of some of the themes that have influenced the development and application of the practices and principles that follow.

We live in a fast-changing world, in fact it can be said that change is our only constant. Change can be seen in the rapid technology advancement that has changed our lives over the last decade through smartphones, tablet computers and social media. We need to be ready for further change, for example in increasingly mobile workplaces, and support the development as entrepreneurial change-makers. Development and further change should be to advance our safety, comfort, health, ease of living, wealth, etc. Real insight into our future needs as consumers can only come from close contact with all stakeholders, not just customers or business buyers.

Another driver of significant change is the impact of economic recession and scarcity of some resources, which requires re-thinking the way we use them and seeking alternative materials and methods to produce the same or different products and services.

Environmental changes due to different industrial production methods and diminishing of some resources require different ways of using resources and waste production, but also waste management and re-use of waste outputs. These developments have created an increasing demand for technology to use natural resources differently, for example.

Social changes, such as the increased levels of employment and education of women, have modified the way households are run and daily activities are carried out. Different services and products are needed alongside recognition of the changed profile of con-sumer markets. Overall, never before did women have that much money they can spend and make decisions about and demand products and services suiting their lives.

As another example, the ageing population also drives change, bringing different demands for products and services for the phases of their lives as "the young old" or the "helpless old". The needs are likely to change rapidly with the different work experience and levels of stress experienced by the baby boomer generation and will be different again for the Y-generation when they age.

There is no escape from change, so we must cultivate helpful principles and practices to adapt and succeed in the environment we live in. A *sustainable start-up* will itself embrace change. These principles and practices are explained in Section 1.3.2.

1.3.2 Six principles for a *sustainable start-up*

1) ALERTNESS. Be alert to change and stay light on your feet.

In order to be a *sustainable start-up* and keep up with constant changes, you need to con-stantly check in with your stakeholders, to find out how they feel, what they do and what they wish to see happening or changing. Only then can you react to them quickly and swiftly.

2) RESPONSIBILITY. You make decisions and are responsible for everything you create.

This touches on the fact that nothing moves in your world unless you move. The employee attitude of "I do what I am asked to do", or even "... do as little as I can get away with" does not work when you are self-employed or run a business yourself.

You will create many processes and have to take responsibility for their effects. Creating a supplier relationship means that you are responsible for providing the appropriate infor-mation and specification for what you need, and pay on time. The attitude is to be alert to the effect you have – even if it is not intentional. Using rare resources or having to end an employment contract may be decisions you have to make – keep an eye on the intended and unintended effects of all of your decisions.

Commitment to your goals and values means that you alone have the responsibility to make the effort to get to where you want to, to get the kind of support, funding or clients you desire. Patience with others, self and situations is part of that. And the tenacity to continue what you do and adapt it until you have the outcome you are looking for or change the outcome you thought you needed is important.

Lewis Barnes, the student entrepreneur introduced in Section 1.8.2, illustrates commitment in the following way:

> People were saying that nine 'til five wasn't for them, that time structure, they said, "ah I can't do that, I need to be my own boss". But then when [it was] alluded to them that, "actually, you'll be working probably twice the hours you would be working nine 'til five".... But you don't realise how much goes into it, it's – you need the commitment [...] it's huge to realise that. And then execute it.

3) RESOURCEFUL IMPACT. *You manage your resources to have the best possible impact on the economy and society.*

Building on principle 2, being a decision-maker, alone or in a team, brings the responsibility to acquire, allocate and distribute resources to projects. It is cost effective for you and the business to use as few resources as possible to achieve the best possible results for your customers and other stakeholders. At the same time, the impact your resource use has on society and the wider economy is worth monitoring. For example, if you pollute the environment, you will contribute to creating higher costs both for society and yourself in the form of taxes or fees (business rates in the UK, value-added tax (VAT), corporation tax, to name only a few).

4) INTERCONNECTEDNESS. *You know you are dependent on other organizations or individuals as much as they are on you.*

Demonstrating your respect, integrity and focus on your stakeholders shows that you know how much you need them and they need you. Without customers there is no business, and without suppliers supporting you by choosing to do business with you your business cannot operate either. This principle is linked to the above-discussed Responsibility principle – you need to be aware of the effect you have as you are connected with others and the environment.

The many co-working spaces popping up over the world follow this principle to create synergy effects between often competing start-ups or micro-businesses. Awareness of the value of your interconnectness does not mean losing your competitive edge or the profit orientation, but it is helpful realizing that there is abundant space for interaction and sharing without stealing ideas.

5) CO-CREATION. *You are part of an on-going value creation dynamic or system.*

You are committed to achieve the best possible outcomes for you and other stakeholders and start every interaction not only thinking of what value you can get out of them but also what value you can give to them. Similar to the fourth principle, such a mindset allows you to actively communicate with suppliers, customers and other stakeholders such as associations, unions, pressure groups etc. and board members where they exist. The attitude that you can and should give value where possible for you, opens your mind up to opportunities for your own business, for service or product changes. For that reason, choosing to follow this principle makes economic sense.

6) SUSTAINABILITY. You make a decision early if the idea you are pursuing is worth investing more time and money into.

This principle is essential to ensure you pursue only those ideas that both fit who you are and where you are in your life and that you can actually make money with. Too many start-ups jump off with an idea and buy large amounts of stock or rent an office (fixed with a contract for a year) without first checking out a few things necessary for longer term sustainability, such as collecting all costs for running the operations, potential future tax obligations, etc. Equally, sometimes an economically viable good idea is just not the right business opportunity for you. (See Chapter Three for more detail.)

1.3.3   Practices for the *sustainable start-up*

Each of the principles described above must be associated with practices or actions to be of any real-world usefulness. Examples of just some of the associated practices with each of the principles are listed below:

1) ALERTNESS.

   Associated practices include:

▶ Regularly consulting with suppliers on what they see happening in their networks;
▶ Carrying out industry research, customer research, employee research regularly;
▶ Actually listening to the findings and acting on the insights gained;
▶ Keeping up-to-date with technological developments, new products or services in your area;
▶ Learning new skills.

These practices are addressed in the Cube under Customer Focus, Business Processes and Strategy.

2) RESPONSIBILITY.

   Associated practices include:

▶ Monitoring the effect of your decisions on people, organizations, society and the environment (POSE);
▶ Actively asking for feedback from customers, staff and other stakeholders;
▶ Proactively seeking opportunities/contacts/links;
▶ Never giving up on achieving your objectives; having the insight to adjust them is not giving up, but showing flexibility;
▶ Seeking advice and listening; understanding you have to make the decision to follow it or not;
▶ Asking questions to all stakeholders what they think and want to do.

These practices are addressed in the Cube under Customer Focus, Evaluation and Strategy. As student entrepreneur Lewis advises:

   Speak to as many people as you can, even if it's as silly as stopping people in the street and pitch them an idea, just say "what do you think of this?" Feedback is feedback, it's priceless. Read, whether it be online, whether it be books, whether it be autobiographies, you can never read and know enough from other people's stories ... the main thing I would say was just talk to as many people, you know, hear their criticisms and try and act on it.

3) RESOURCEFUL IMPACT.

 Associated practices include:

▶ Proactively forecasting what you need and when you need it so that staff or suppliers have what they need to make things happen. Do not make your lack of planning their problem.
▶ Considering using those regarded as disadvantaged in the labour market, such as workers over 50 years of age or young people – they not only add value to your organization, but employing even one member of those groups also has a wider impact on society in many ways (such as less benefits have to be paid, less health expenses, less violence and destruction of public property, less public expenses). It makes economic sense to employ them; often there are even employer incentives to do so.
▶ Selecting local suppliers where possible and economically viable;
▶ Using resources that impact less on the environment where possible;
▶ Being efficient in your use of resources: do not pile up stock, do not take premises if you do not have to; do not purchase a vehicle as a start-up if hiring one does the job – this is called bootstrapping. This helps you to spend less money and have a higher profit as well as protect the environment.

These practices are addressed under Evaluation, Strategy and Financial Circuits in the Cube. Always ask yourself the question, "Can I do online what I feel I need to do face-to-face?" The effect of online meetings, workshops, learning or working is that you use fewer resources and thus money, save time and have more available for the activities that really do have to be done face-to-face. We discuss this in more detail in various chapters on business processes and operations.

4) INTERCONNECTEDNESS.

 Associated practices include:

▶ Demonstrating respect, integrity and professionalism in your treatment of customers, suppliers, staff, associates and other stakeholders alike;
▶ Remaining flexible in the way you can do things;
▶ Trusting that the right kind of business relations will develop as long as you do all you can;
▶ Constantly learning and adapting what you do to respond to changes you observe in your networks.

You are part of an on-going value creation dynamic. Showing flexibility in the way you act, within limits, is a requirement to be successful in business, and even more so for start-ups, while you are building a reputation and establishing networks. These practices are addressed under Evaluation and Customer Focus.

5) CO-CREATION.

 Associated practices include:

▶ Looking for leads for your suppliers and other stakeholders. For example, if you cannot provide a service to potential customers, proactively seek to recommend someone in your networks who can help them. The value of that recommendation will be appreciated and stick in their mind. It is more likely they will mention you in return if the situation arises.

▸ Offering services or products for free at professional association meetings, to potential customers or at networking meetings. Give first and do not worry about what comes back, as value given always attracts value. Why do you think Cadbury gave out free tasters samples or full chocolate bars when they came out with the most recent taste near shopping centres and in large supermarkets?

Learn as much as you can and actively seek feedback. (Read again the quote from Lewis under practice 2 in this section). These practices are addressed in the Cube under Evaluation and Strategy.

6) SEEK SUSTAINABILITY.

   Associated practices include:

▸ Researching customers, products and competitors early on;
▸ Keeping track of the information you collect on the industry and market;
▸ Gaining clarity of your goals and values early on;
▸ Drawing conclusions as early as possible, if and how much profit can be made;
▸ Deciding if that idea matches your life and values at this point in time;
▸ Deciding early if the idea you explore is worth investing more time and money into.

Even if you do not want to try out the principles offered, this book has a wealth of practical insights any start-up can benefit from, for most areas of a start-up process. It brings together experiences that can make your life as a start-up much easier and hopefully let you avoid saying, "If only someone had told me that at the beginning!" These practices are addressed in the Cube under all six themes.

The next three sections in this chapter provide the basics on business functions and terminology and discuss the role of businesses in the economy and society. If you know that already, you might still want to consider quickly reading over it to catch up on the latest statistics and see how various business sectors compare in terms of employment and turnover (see Section 1.6). I highly recommend learning about social enterprise and how it differs from for-profit enterprise – this type of enterprise is increasing in numbers and making a big difference to our lives – did you know that most universities are social enterprises? And that Jamie Oliver is running one? Find out more in Section 1.7 below.

If you follow the franchise start-up route, the journey and its processes are very different. Section 3.1.4 briefly outlines starting the first business using a franchise. There are pros and cons that need consideration, in particular the initial investment cost, money you have to pay out – 1000s of dollars or pounds – to buy a franchise. These processes are briefly addressed in Chapter Three, section 3.1.4. You can also buy an existing business; this way of a personal start-up is not addressed in this book.

1.4   Describing and defining "business"

1.4.1 What defines a business?

A business is an entity, run by one or more individuals, that engages in commercial activity, including providing services. Commercial activity here means selling tangible goods or services in exchange for money.

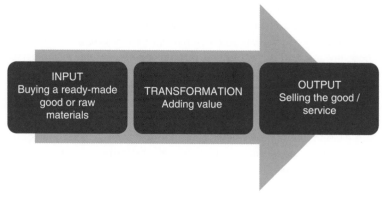

Figure 1.3 Most basic business activities

The most basic business activities, as illustrated in Figure 1.3, include:

⯈ Buying or creating a good/service;
⯈ Transforming and adding value to an existing good/service;
⯈ Selling a good/service.

The concept of creating, purchasing or selling of goods/services is relatively straightforward to understand. The process of transformation or adding value deserves a little more consideration. This process can have many shapes and forms, and examples include:

⯈ Buying raw materials and turning them into a product, such as transforming leather into shoes;
⯈ Buying parts and assembling them into a final product;
⯈ Buying ready-made parts and (re)packaging them, for example, importing toys in bulk from China or India and packaging them into attractive boxes with English text for sale to a new market;
⯈ Buying ready-made parts and adjusting their design, for example importing mobile phone cases and adding customized images to them;
⯈ Buying tools, including computers and software, and creating a service (online or face-to-face);
⯈ Using human resources in service creation: this may involve specialist training and skilful interaction with customers, such as provision of therapy or collection, collation, analysis and presentation of data for a client.

The basic functions a business may carry out show through through the examples above. They are commonly divided into:

a) *Buying (the technical term is purchasing) goods, tools or other services.* Large businesses often have various departments dealing with this function. A technical expression associated with it is "purchasing".

b) *Managing human resources.* A specific division or individual may be responsible for selecting and recruiting staff and looking after the business's valuable (and complicated) human resources – assessing and encouraging performance, ensuring their development, training and retention, and meeting the business's obligations (legal or moral) regarding their well-being and safety.

c) *Running the operations of the business*. For manufacturing businesses, this department or role is often fairly large and includes the functions of production planning, research and development, actual production, production management and supervision, managing the flow of goods inwards and outwards, and maintaining equipment, including sometimes even the IT department, etc.

d) *Marketing and PR*. Communicating with the public and buyers.

e) *Sales*. Actually selling the product and maintaining relationships with customers or potential customers.

f) *Finance*. A division whose responsibilities include cost management and control, financial planning, payroll – organizing payments to staff and pension payments. The last two functions may also be included in the responsibilities of the human resources division/role.

g) *Management and administration*. Senior management at director level spend a lot of time on strategy development and implementation and staff management.

This is a long list and might be intimidating, especially to the many "one-person bands" which exist, individuals running a business, who carry out most of the tasks. However, most "outsource" at least some of these business functions to other professionals for a fee. For example, many small businesses have an external bookkeeper, who does the accounts on a monthly basis.

1.4.2 How can we describe or classify businesses?

There are two primary areas of classification that are used when describing a particular business: its size, and the particular industry division it operates in. We will look at these each in turn.

A term often heard in relation to business is "small and medium-sized business/enterprise" or SME. What then *is* a "small" or "medium-sized" business? There are a number of definitions, used officially within the UK, the European Union, or more generally worldwide. For our purposes, we will follow the EU definition based on staff headcount or employee numbers (European Commission, 2006):

Businesses with staff of less than 10 are called micro-businesses.
Businesses with 10 to 49 staff are called small businesses.
Businesses with 50 to 249 staff are called medium-sized businesses.
Businesses with 250 or more staff are corporations, or corporates.

A more complex EU definition focuses on three criteria: annual turnover (that is, the amount of money that is coming into the business, or revenue), staff headcount and ownership, and annual balance sheet. This means for example that micro-businesses at the same time as having up to nine staff should have either a turnover or balance sheet of less than two million euro. Small businesses should have an annual turnover of less than 10 million euro and the annual turnover or balance sheet of medium-sized businesses should remain under 50 million euro (European Commission, 2003).

Across all 28 EU member states, micro-businesses account for over 90% of all businesses: Of all SMEs in 2013 that was 92.5% (or 19.97 million), whereas 6.4% (1.4 million) were small businesses, and only 1.1% were medium-sized (220,000) (European Commission, 2014).

In addition to their size, all businesses can be classified as belonging to an industry. An industry is often defined as a group of businesses that either produce or contribute to producing the same or similar products/services, such as a cars or legal services. Businesses in the same industry often use similar or the same raw materials, techniques of transformation, technology, specialist knowledge, etc.

Industries are often grouped in "sectors":

- Primary sector – it makes direct use of natural resources, including agricultural and extracting businesses, farming, mining and fishing.
- Secondary sector – it produces finished, usable products primarily through the manufacturing, production and construction industries.
- Tertiary sector – it is also known as the "service sector". Services can provide hairdressing, transport, entertainment or caring (childcare, elder care) to other businesses and consumers.
- Quaternary sector – this sector is also primarily concerned with provision of services that are mainly information based (sometimes described as the "knowledge economy"). Intellectual services include the traditional "professions" (medical, legal, accountancy, etc.), the so-called FIRE industries (i.e., financial services, insurance industry and real estate), as well as consultancy, education, research and development and media, cultural and political services.

There are a number of classifications that subdivide all industries into subsectors. Each country classifies industries in their own way. The UK government has identified 99 industry classifications, called UK Standard Industrial Classification of Economic Activities 2007 (Office for National Statistics, ONS, 2009). The year indicates the last year changes to the classification were carried out. Identifying subgroups of businesses or official classifications for industry sectors is of great benefit when analysing the environment businesses operate in. Identifying the industry sector your potential business opportunity is located in is essential as it helps to identify the category keywords you need to use for searching for industry sector data.

There are additional classification systems used by the United Nations applicable to all countries, International Standard Industrial Classification of All Economic Activities (ISIC, http://unstats.un.org/unsd/iiss/International-Standard-Industrial-Classification-of-all-Economic-Activities-ISIC.ashx), and one for the EU, the Statistical Classification of Economic Activities in the European Community (NACE, http://ec.europa.eu/competition/mergers/cases/index/nace_all.html, accessed 4 August 2013).

 Activity 1.1 Practice identifying industry classifications

Discover ...

- What does classification A1.4.6 refer to in the NACE system?
- In what year was the last version of ISIC published?
- How many digits does a classification in the UK SIC 2007 have?
- What is the SIC code for accountancy services?

In addition to "industry", there is another term used a lot when describing business: trade. What is a "trade" then? Trades or occupations or professions often require a particular skill or craft, often linked to an accreditation or exam in order to be carried out and/or a particular material and/or resources; one example is the jewellery making trade.

This should not be confused with "trading", two or more units taking part in the voluntary exchange of goods and services often through the exchange of goods for money.

For a comparison of many countries' trading activities worldwide you can find excellent data on the website of the World Trade Organization; this organization's website also offers quality data on UK trading activity.

The next section outlines the important relationships between government/state, citizens and businesses in society and the economy and explains their various core roles.

1.5 What is the role of business in the economy and society?

Businesses have many roles for the economy, the main important ones are:

▶ Employing staff;
▶ Generating profit and income for owners/shareholders;
▶ Paying taxes to the government;
▶ Buying goods;
▶ Selling goods;
▶ Innovating – coming up with new services or products;
▶ Contributing to national volume of import and export;
▶ Providing solutions to social, economic and environmental problems.

Businesses are distributed unevenly across a country, with a focus in urban areas. In the UK for example, London has the largest number of businesses that have employees and pay VAT (17.2% or 372,000 businesses in 2013 compared to approximately 12% of the population of the UK being located in London) whereas the Northeast of England had only 2.6% (56,000 businesses, and approximately 4% of the total UK population). Businesses are also distributed unevenly across industry sectors in different countries or regions. The largest industry group in the UK is professional, scientific and technical professional services with 16.9% (366,000) of all registered businesses operating in this sector. Table 1.1 lists the numbers of businesses in a selection of sectors for March 2013.

At the start of 2014 in the UK, there were a total of 5.2 million private sector businesses: 99.3% of these were micro-businesses (see Section 1.5.2 above for size definitions) and 99.9% were SMEs. In nearly all countries, the large majority of businesses do not have employees, this means there is either one person or two partners running the business. In the UK, this situation applied to 71% of all private businesses or 3.7 million in 2014. These were made up of 3.3 million sole traders (individuals running a business as self-employed by themselves), and 460,000 business partnerships. The remaining businesses had at least one employee (ONS, 2014). These 5.2 million businesses accounted for 48% of all private sector employment or 12.1 million jobs (Department for Business, Innovation and Skills (DBIS), 2014a). About 70% of all UK businesses operate not from external business premises but from home (DBIS, 2014b). Moreover, 6% of all SMEs were social enterprises (this term is explained in the next chapter) (DBIS, 2014b).

Trends for EU countries are similar. Across the 28 EU member states, there were 21.6 million SMEs in the non-financial business sector; they employed 88.8 million people. This means that 99 out of 100 businesses in this sector are SMEs and two-thirds of all employees work in SMEs.

Table 1.1   Number of businesses in selected industry sectors in 2013, UK

Industry sector	Number of businesses in 000s
Agriculture, forestry and fishing	144
Mining, quarry and utilities	10
Manufacturing	126
Construction	257
Wholesale	103
Retail	188
Accommodation and food services	129
Professional, scientific and technical professional services	**366**
Health	89
Information and communication	166
Finance, insurance and property	126
Education	35
Arts, entertainment and recreation and related services	146

Source: Office for National Statistics for the UK (ONS, 2014).

In 2013, in both Denmark and the UK, SMEs accounted for between 60% and 75% of all businesses in the five most important non-financial sectors (these five sectors are manufacturing and construction; accommodation and food services; professional, scientific and technical activities; wholesale and retail trade; and repair of motor vehicles). In Romania, other Eastern European countries and Italy, SMEs accounted for 70% of all businesses in these sectors (European Commission, 2014).

In the Netherlands and Sweden (34% and 36% respectively), the share of SME enterprises in business services is higher than other EU countries, while in Sweden and Denmark the relative share of SME employment in retail and wholesale is over 30% (32% and 38% respectively) whereas the UK's wholesale/retail sector only accounts for 29% of employment (European Commission, 2014).

Economies need a certain number of business start-ups on a regular basis, to bring in fresh ideas – not only for products, but also for ways of doing business. The numbers of new businesses starting up is also distributed differently across sectors. Examples of industries that have grown from 2012 on are technology, health services, education, professional services and creative industries.

While some industries see more new businesses being launched than others, it is a common insight that many start-ups do not survive the first three years, as Table 1.2 shows for selected areas of the UK. Of all businesses that were started in 2009, less than two-thirds were still trading in 2012 (only 62%), in some regions of the UK even fewer (ONS, 2013a). Some were just closed down as the owners decided to move on and/or had a new business they wanted to pursue or went into employment. Others experienced enforced closure as they had financial problems: reasons behind the financial difficulties are manifold and include lack of market knowledge, lack of funding, financial mismanagement or lack of appropriate human resources.

Table 1.2 Survival rates of start-ups by region

Proportion of 2009 start-ups that were still trading in 2012 in %	Region in England
62.5	England
58.0	Greater Birmingham and Solihull
59.7	London
68.4	Oxfordshire
60.5	Black Country

Source: Office for National Statistics, ONS, 2013.

The relatively high failure rate of new businesses means there is a case to do something to improve start-up survival rates, isn't there? This is one of the aims of this book: to support start-ups not having to close down before the owner wishes and remain sustainable and profitable for as long as the owner(s) wants. The issue of profitability is the topic of the next section which discusses another core point of differentiation between business models – for-profit or not-for-profit.

1.6 Business, charity or social enterprise – what is the difference?

So far we have discussed ways to describe business activity based on their size or the primary good or service produced. Another helpful differentiation of enterprises is based on their core purpose:

 ▸ Privately owned, profit-focused businesses are said to be located in the *first sector.*
 ▸ State-owned or publicly financed enterprises are located in the *second sector.*
 ▸ The *third sector* comprises voluntary and community groups, charities and social enterprises. These types of organizations are said to operate in the "social economy".
 ▸ What is increasingly described as a *fourth sector* is emerging and is not yet clearly defined, but practitioners and policy-makers are using the term to identify those organizations and individuals that are comfortable with operating in, between and beyond the established for-profit, governmental and non-profit sectors. Fourth sector organizations are focused on achieving specific social outcomes that are measurable and profitable.

In the previous section, the word social enterprise was introduced. But what does this term really mean? There are some enterprises in the economy that, as a matter of principle, will use the profits in different ways, with only very little or even none of the profit being taken away from the business by owners or as shareholder dividends.

As you may expect, there are a number of definitions of what a social enterprise is. The definition below is still widely used by government and social enterprises in the UK even though it is over 12 years old.

A social enterprise is a business with primarily social objectives whose surpluses [profits] are principally reinvested for that purpose in the business or in the community, rather than being driven by the need to maximise profit for shareholders and owners. (DTI, 2002)

It is important to keep in mind that while sometimes described as "non-profit" or "not-for-profit", these enterprises do make profits. For the UK, ideally at least 26% of the operating income needs to be generated through trading and not grants (money given to an organization it does not have to pay back) or donations in order for an organization to be classified as a social enterprise (see Teasdale, 2010).

Another definition used by the European Union goes wider:

> A social enterprise is an operator in the social economy whose main objective is to have a social impact rather than make a profit for their owners or shareholders. It operates by providing goods and services for the market in an entrepreneurial and innovative fashion and uses its profits primarily to achieve social objectives. It is managed in an open and responsible manner and, in particular, involves employees, consumers and stakeholders affected by its commercial activities. (European Commission, 2011)

From these two definitions we can see that the key characteristics of types of businesses that are included in the third sector are:

▶ The social objective is the reason for commercial activity;
▶ All or a majority of the profits are reinvested to achieve an agreed social objective or mission;
▶ The method of ownership, management and governance reflects their social mission.

"Social enterprise", then, is a label that is applied to a wide range of organizations with varying purposes that can be summed up as making a difference either to people, society and/or the environment. At least in the UK, that is. In other countries, in the EU and North America, different definitions exist.

The problem of finding agreement on what a social enterprise is and means in Europe alone has led to some confusion, added to the fact that terms being developed in the national language may not translate directly to the English term and sometimes the English term may be used as an adopted word in the national language. For Scandinavian countries the term "community enterprise" in translation is much more widely in use and understood, and community enterprise itself has a long tradition. A similar situation occurs in the Netherlands. Finland developed the term *Yhteiskunnallinen yrittajyys* which translates more to "societal entrepreneurship"; Germany increasingly uses the English terminology social enterprise and social entrepreneurship, as the connotations and the use of the German terms (*Sozialunternehmen, Sozialunternehmertum*) are too narrow to capture the changing meaning younger people under 35 years of age in particular want to see.

Table 1.3 lists the various national umbrella organizations for social enterprises in the UK, selected European countries and the US, if you want to learn more about what social enterprises do in your country.

In the US, the label "social enterprise" is applied to market-based initiatives that address social problems but can be making a profit for owners, and/or organizations that provide public or social goods, the social sector. The academic debate differentiates two schools of thoughts in the US (see Austin et al., 2006; Defourny and Nyssens, 2012):

1) The "earned income" school of thought includes under social purpose in the broader version all for-profit and non-profit ventures that address social problems. Income is generated in order to fulfil a social objective or mission (Defourny and Nyssens, 2012).

Table 1.3 Selected national and international social enterprise associations and bodies

UK	• Social Enterprise UK
US	• Social Enterprise Alliance • ASHOKA – Innovators for the Public
Netherlands	• Social Enterprise Netherlands
Finland	• Sosiaalinenyritys
Sweden	• Coompanion (advisory organizations supporting social enterprise start-ups) • SKOOPI (association of social work cooperatives) • Famna (non-profit health and social service organizations)
Hong Kong	• Hong Kong Social Enterprise Challenge (social venture business plan competition) • Centre for Entrepreneurship, Chinese University of Hong Kong (functions as an incubator offering support and mentoring)
International	• Social Economy Europe • Euclid Network, Third Sector Leaders (European network to connect change-makers in civil society in Europe)

2) The "social innovation" school of thought includes entrepreneurs in the non-profit sectors who are regarded as change-makers offering new solutions to existing problems through innovative resource leverage and/or resource combinations. Social innovation is at the core of this approach and can come to the light in new services and new qualities in services, new products or production methods, or new markets to name the most important ones.

More generally, social enterprises have been identified showing the following features:

▶ Having a primary social purpose with a secondary commercial activity;
▶ Achieving that purpose by engaging in trade;
▶ Reinvesting profits in the enterprise or new social ventures or providing free services to those in need;
▶ Democratically involving members in governance;
▶ Demonstrating open accountability.

A couple of examples of social enterprises, many in the UK will be familiar, with are Jamie Oliver's restaurant Fifteen (see below) and the Big Issue (homeless men and women selling the magazine called *The Big Issue* near railway stations and in city centres). Box 1.3 lists some other examples of social enterprises in the UK, US and other European countries. Some social enterprises specialize in employing people who otherwise would not get employment, called social firms. Others donate all their profits to a charity that offers free services to those in need.

British chef Jamie Oliver has a number of successful restaurants and other businesses. Three of his restaurants are run on the social enterprise model, the first opened with the name of Fifteen in London (2002), followed by similar restaurants in Amsterdam (2004) and Cornwall (2006). Through these restaurants, Jamie realizes his commitment to making a difference for disadvantaged young people, some of whom have been in prison, and offers a path to employment as a chef through an apprenticeship training programme. The profits made through the restaurant are donated to a charity he founded that provides training free of charge to a selection of young people each year.

> ## Box 1.3   Social enterprise examples in the UK, Netherlands, Sweden and the US
>
> ### UK
> ▸ Jamie Oliver Restaurant Fifteen http://www.jamieoliver.com/the-fifteen-apprentice-programme/about/story
> ▸ Beacon Centre for the Blind www.beacon4blind.co.uk - a charity and social enterprise offering services for those with sighting problems and blindness
> ▸ The Big Issue – helping the homeless to redevelop an independent life http://www.bigissue.org.uk/about-us.
>
> ### Netherlands
> ▸ Taxi Electric and Green Wheels – both social enterprises are aiming to make transport in the Netherlands more environmentally friendly.
>
> ### Sweden
> ▸ Mattecentrum founded by Johan Wendt – help for children who want to improve their maths skills through after-school online learning forums, free of charge.
>
> ### US
> ▸ ASHOKA – supporting social entrepreneurs and building an infrastructure for a society with lots of social enterprises www.ashoka.org/approach.

Social enterprises are of great value to all economies, not only because they are offering many jobs. Some data from the UK can illustrate the important role social enterprises play in all economies:

In 2012 there were 70,000 social enterprises in the UK (Social Enterprise UK, 2014):

▸ They employed about one million staff.
▸ There were three times as many social enterprise start-ups than for-profit businesses.
▸ They grew quicker in turnover than SMEs (38% compared to 29%).
▸ Just over 25% were led by members of black and ethnic minorities (compared to 11% for for-profit businesses).
▸ 91% had at least one woman in its leadership team, compared to 51% of for-profit SMEs.
▸ The sectors most-often chosen by all UK social entrepreneurs were education and consultancy followed by employment skills and housing, retail, culture and leisure and health services.
▸ 72% of all social enterprises generated income through trading, with the remaining number delivering their services on grants and donations only.

Finally, we should address the question, "What is social entrepreneurship, and does it differ from entrepreneurship?"

Entrepreneurship has been defined in many ways. For the purpose of this book we define it as the successful acquisition and combination of resources that allows one or more persons to create an income for themselves through an entity, which is separate from themselves. This can be realized through self-employment, formally operating as a sole trader or sole proprietor, as well as through registering a company.

A sole trader is the simplest form of business structure; it can be any business that is owned and controlled by one individual who is fully, personally, responsible for the business's activity.

The sole trader may employ staff. A company limited by shares is a formal legal entity that is registered with Company's House in the UK. The "shares" addition indicates that shares exist and that the liability of the company is limited to the capital originally invested for the share. For more details on these and other company forms see Chapter Eight on legal issues.

Social entrepreneurship has been defined in many ways as well (Fayolle and Matlay, 2012a, 2012b). For us, the following definition is helpful: "Social entrepreneurship is a process of creating value by combining resources in new ways. Resource combinations are intended primarily to explore and exploit opportunities to create social value by stimulating social change or meeting social needs" (Mair and Marti, 2006).

In the view of the social innovation school of thought, the social entrepreneur is acting as a change agent (Defourny and Nyssens, 2012, Dees, 1998), implementing changes in society that improve people's lives. Features of the social entrepreneur are further discussed in Section 2.4.1 of Chapter Two.

 Case study

> Since 2010, another term and concept of "social business" has been promoted by Muhammad Yunus and his followers (Yunus, 2010). This promotes a mission-driven approach to business that can have any legal form, however, does not pay any dividend to investors, but reinvests all profits into the organization to fulfil the mission. This approach is similar to the "earned income" school of thought discussed above for the US. Most of these social businesses are owned by investors; one well-publicized example is the joint venture of Grameen Bank and Danone, the dairy product producer, to provide yoghurt at very low prices to poor populations in Bangladesh (Defourny and Nyssens, 2012).

Lastly, there are *charities*, such as Oxfam and the Prince's Trust, based in the UK, or Greenpeace, for example, that operate internationally. But what is the difference? Charities exist to benefit the public, not specific individuals. In the UK, charities are restricted in what they can do, and are closely regulated by the Charity commission (http://www.charitycommission.gov.uk/, accessed 20 June 2014, and https://www.gov.uk/government/organisations/charity-commission, accessed 4 January 2015). They need to:

▶ Only do things that are charitable according to the law;
▶ Be run by trustees who do not usually personally benefit from the charity.

Did you know that in the UK most universities are charities? Check out the website of your local university and college.

Before we introduce the case studies, we need to dispel some myths that have been created around start-ups and new ventures in the next section.

1.7 Myths about start-ups and social enterprise

1.7.1 Sixteen myths about start-ups

 There are many limiting beliefs people tell others about what is needed or how you have to be to start a new venture. The most common ones that I have heard include:

1) A business has to be a full-time occupation.

If you are in a full-time job and want to see how, for example, selling a certain product goes, you do not have to immediately leave your job. With many start-ups it is possible to stay in the job and try out how it feels being out there selling a product or giving a service in your remaining spare time. The same applies if you are a student, or if you have a hobby that you want to retain. Everyone has the same 168 hours in a week. You choose how you spend them.

2) It takes a lot of time to start a new venture.

This might apply to more complicated ventures, particularly those that involve developing new technology or manufacturing. But not all new ventures are tech-based. And then you need to consider – what does a lot really mean? If you are passionate about and committed to starting even a technology-based or manufacturing company, you will do it and bring the funding in that is needed.

3) Starting a new venture needs a lot of money.

About 70% of all businesses are started from home, in a garden shed, garage or bedroom. Creative industries and service industries are growing, and many services can be offered mobile and online now. It can be surprising, in fact, how very little money is needed to start an enterprise.

4) You need a great idea, something truly innovative to start a new venture.

Sir Richard Branson re-organized existing markets with many of his ventures, such as the airline industry, and made millions. The majority of new ventures started are focused on doing something in a different way or in a new location or selling an existing product to a different customer group. Do something that is already out there, but do it better.

5) You have to be young to do it.

The statistics show that most new ventures are founded by those over 35. You can start a new venture at any age.

6) You have to know people with influence to become successful.

Networks can be built and developed; take the case study of Frinter Ltd, founded by two young men who met at university in the UK. Both founders came as students from abroad and only made contacts with other students to start with. While they founded their venture they gained support and contacts with business executives. Equally, Richard Rodman from the US knew nobody when he went to university in Ohio and is now networked to many influential business people (see Section 1.9 for more details on their stories).

7) You need supportive parents/partner to start a new venture.

While it helps if family members are supportive and might give you a loan or act as a mentor, many young and not-so-young people have become successful without that support. Similarly, while it helps to have a partner you can talk to about the business and who is supportive and understands you might have to work some weekends and evenings, you can be successful without that.

8) Consultancy is not a real business activity.

Business services is a growing sector that offers value to small and large businesses, and consultancy is part of that sector. While the business and technology world continues to change and businesses seek advice to adjust and adapt to these changes, consultancy will remain an important growing sector.

9) There are too many people already out there doing what you want to do.

Many markets that might look saturated can be re-organized, or re-segmented. There are a lot of beauticians or hairdressers already operating, yet there is still money to be made by those working mobile, going into offices and private homes. Similarly, mobile pet grooming services have also developed well.

10) You have to have formal education and intelligence to run a business.

While a formal education is always helpful, a practical intelligence, or a streetwise sense of how to get things done can be just as helpful for a *sustainable start-up*. Several successful entrepreneurs do not have any formal qualifications.

11) You have to be creative to be in business.

The type of creativity needed in business such as problem solving and opportunity- or trend-spotting can be learned. You do not have to create something completely new in order to be successful in business.

12) You have to be fully abled physically to start a business.

People with physical disability can easily run all sorts of businesses, including online ones. Many business activities can be organized flexibly around daily activities. People with mental health issues can equally build a business activity in an area they are passionate about and may find that doing so allows them to enrich their lives while undertaking treatment and recovering.

13) You have no time for a hobby when starting a business.

You can start and run a business part-time, around caring responsibilities, studies, or a part-time job and have time for a hobby.

14) You are too nice for being in business, you have to be ruthless.

People buy from people, and trust is an important part in the decision to purchase. Building relationships is important in business as well, and the best business relationships are honest ones, where you show true interest in someone's working or personal life and offer the support and information they need. Being ego-driven and ruthless is not helpful and will affect the reputation of any business, and many negatively affect its bottom line.

15) Starting a venture is a lonely process.

Even if you are self-employed and work from home, you do not have to be lonely. You can go to face-to-face networking meetings, socialize with other people online, and phone, just to catch up.

16) "Me-too" start-ups are not valuable and cannot make a lot of money.

Opening a venture that does more or less the same as other existing businesses is often called the "me-too" venture. An example may be opening another Indian restaurant or hair salon where there are already several, or developing another crowd funding platform after three have already been launched in your country. As long as you can demonstrate there is a demand for this kind of service or product, this kind of business can earn a living. And if while establishing itself the owner(s) might develop a distinctive offering, such as a dish combined with excellent service and successful marketing, then there is every chance this kind of business can go beyond simply returning a profit to making a real impact in the market.

 Why do people tell these myths? Here are some possible reasons:

▸ Lack of trust in the abilities of the potential start-up;
▸ Lack of knowledge of real-life start-ups;
▸ Personal agendas including the two outlined below;
▸ Negative associations with making money;
▸ Projection of their own fears onto others;
▸ Repeating old views without having looked into new venture creation for a while.

It is always worth considering the "messenger" as well as the "message". Negative comments received from someone you have a work relationship with, such as a line manager, might reflect their position more than yours. For example, a line manager discouraging employees from branching out into their own start-up may reflect the fact that the manager does not want to lose a staff member – after all recruitment takes time and costs money – rather than reflecting their opinion on the employee's ability to launch a product or on the value of the offering.

Similarly, at home some people may have concerns regarding the impact their partner starting a business will have on their relationship, balance of family care responsibilities or household income. As with any aspect in your relationships, honest communication and arriving at solutions you both agree with may relieve those concerns.

There are some additional myths told about social enterprise start-ups, which are unpacked in the next section.

1.7.2 Six myths about social enterprises

 ### 1) You have to be a group to start a social enterprise.

In recent years, plenty of social enterprises were started by one or two people and not a community group. While it may help to gather other people around you who share your vision, that is not a necessary requirement to building a social enterprise.

2) A social enterprise has to be community led.

While this is one successful way to start a social enterprise, it is not the *only* way to do it. A single student started an online support platform for parents of schoolchildren whose English is not very good, to offer help and support in Asian languages.

3) You cannot make a profit or earn a decent living.

Social enterprises are for-profit because, like other enterprises, they need to build reserves for emergencies and growth and have to make a profit to do so. The *distribution* of profits may be to members or in limited cases to shareholders or reinvested into the organization. Salaries are part of the enterprise's costs.

4) You have to employ disabled people.

Some social enterprises exist specifically with the social purpose of increasing employment opportunities for those with a disability or from disadvantaged backgrounds. In the UK they are often called "Social Firms". However, only some social enterprises engage that way. Many social enterprises have the same recruitment practices and staff profiles as other enterprises.

5) You have to give things away for free.

A social enterprise is an enterprise that generates some income or all its income from trading. It can use part of this income to provide services for free to those who need it the most, but can still charge some fee if it wishes to do so from clients who can afford to pay that fee.

6) Social enterprises do not pay normal salaries.

Social enterprises pay salaries at the same rates as some small businesses do, and salaries for CEOs can be in the six-digit figures. Start-up social enterprises might not do that, but neither do for-profit start-ups.

The next section introduces you to the main case studies we will discuss throughout the book. The case studies have been selected for inclusion for several reasons:

▸ To illustrate the *sustainable start-up* approach mapped in this book in its diversity;
▸ To demonstrate that the processes discussed apply to most industries and many countries;
▸ To choose types of start-ups students and young graduates commonly get involved in, in the industries that appeal to them;
▸ To indicate the large variety of approaches, reasons and ways of starting a new venture after graduation.

The companies include three online businesses, two creative industry businesses, three business service ventures, two product-focused businesses, one mature student start-up who started a social enterprise.

The ventures span a number of countries: the majority is based in the UK, one in Romania, one in Hong Kong and two in the US. The case studies are *not* compared to each other, but used as illustrations for the *sustainable start-up*, and the associated processes discussed in this book.

1.8   Meet the start-ups featured in this book

1.8.1 Photographer Alison Barton, Dudley, UK

Passion is at the heart of everything that I do. My passion and enthusiasm for photography as an art form, combined with my commitment to capturing beautiful memories for my clients that will last a lifetime and beyond. (www.alisonbarton-photography.co.uk, accessed 4 August 2014)

Alison was born in Stourbridge in the West Midlands, UK, where she went to school. Inspired by her father who was an enthusiastic amateur photographer, she grew up surrounded by photographs. Her father nurtured her interest in photography as a young girl.

While still at school and college, Alison worked as an assistant to a female, local photographer. Starting as a placement for work experience in Year Nine, she was subsequently offered paid work on Saturdays where she remained for about four years. Alison experienced first-hand how exciting and challenging self-employment in her area of interest and passion was. She saw her role-model making mistakes, which she remembered and was able to ensure she avoided when she set up her own photography business. She also gained first-hand insight into one of the key advantages of being your own boss, "the freedom to do the work she wanted to do, rather than being told by an employer what to do".

Since that time it was always in the back of her mind that one day she really wanted to be her own boss and run her own business. It was significant to Alison that the photographer she worked for was a woman, she points out:

> I think in a way [the fact] that she was a woman, yes – it was important, because I think photography is a really, or it was, a very male-dominated industry, particularly when she started, and I think she broke the mould a little bit really with what she was doing, how she was running her business, and she was so hugely passionate and still is, you know she really sort of injected that into me going forward and like I said had I not worked for her I wouldn't have probably pursued a self-employed career in that sense in photography I don't think at all.

At University College Falmouth, Cornwall, she studied general photography and gained a BA with Honours in Photography. While initially having no intention to start her own business immediately after university, Alison worked on her start-up once she had returned from university to her hometown. Today Alison is still running her business from home, nearly five years after officially registering it.

1.8.2 Lantyx Consulting Ltd by Lewis Barnes, UK

Lewis was born in Bradford and spent his first years there. At the age of eight he started playing tennis, and at twelve he left home to go to a tennis academy at Loughborough University (LTA), which gave him the foundation to eventually represent the UK in a number of international tennis tournaments before 2008.

His tennis achievements included:

2004 World Champion (under-14) Prestejov, Czech Republic
2008 Member of the England team, Junior Commonwealth Games in Pune, India
2008 Quarter-finalist at Junior Wimbledon (doubles)

In his view, competing in tennis at the highest level has given him focus, discipline and determination to succeed. It has also developed his teamwork skills, the ability to perform under intense pressure and to thrive in a competitive environment.

While doing his Higher National Diploma in London and working part-time for a promotional gift company, Lewis gained important insight into business and started his first venture which centred on importing a travel device. This start-up was not as successful as he had hoped for, and he closed it after 11 months.

As tennis had been at the centre of his life until 2008, he started talking to his many contacts in other clubs about developing young players. When one tennis club put into practice what he had discussed socially with a member and made a success of it, Lewis was encouraged to put his own experiences to use to support clubs in developing small academies for talented young tennis players, and in 2009 Lantyx Consulting Ltd was born. Lewis completed his studies with a Bachelor in Business and Management at Birmingham City University. Lewis is actively engaged with a number of charities as ambassador, including Cancer Research UK and the Prince's Trust.

1.8.3   Ben Smith, UK, Frumtious Ltd, fruit jelly lover

Ben was born in Leicester and enjoyed his first 18 years of education in this East Midlands city. After his A-levels he went to Birmingham to study International Business and French at Aston University. The structure of the degree course required him to spend a year on a work placement abroad. Ben went to France and worked with a large multinational firm in Paris, working in HR.

After his return to Birmingham he finished his studies. Following this, committed to making a difference to student lives, he applied to become Vice-president of Education and Welfare and was elected to a salaried position he held for two years. He worked as part of a team on the student newspaper and won Journalist Personality of the Year. His idea for his first venture developed while being a student himself. During that time he had the idea of a student magazine with features and bite-size reviews of local independent entertainment venues in Birmingham. Due to the lack of money to invest and the risks of getting a new print magazine into the market and make it sustainable, he started *Access Regional* with a friend as an online magazine, accessible through QR codes. He and his friend ran the magazine part-time for two-and-a-half years until October 2013.

During Ben's time at university, his aim had been to work in the corporate world and make his career there. For that reason, after his graduation and the years as vice-president at the Student Union he worked for a small commercial consultancy company for ten months. During that time he realized that the commercial consultancy world was not the business environment he would thrive in and left. Although Ben viewed this period as a valuable experience and financially very rewarding, working with larger established organizations to develop strategies to reduce costs and increase profits did not make the personal impact and give Ben the satisfaction that he had hoped for.

The idea for Frumtious came when he talked to a friend about how she taught chemistry to her primary school class. Frumtious is a health-conscious natural food company, producing fruit-based snacks suitable for all diets and ages. The product is a pot of real fruit jelly, made from blended fruits and a vegan setting agent. It is aimed to be a great way to enjoy fruit on the go, or to add to porridge or yoghurt. Specifically targeting health-conscious young adults and parents, Frumtious is committed to using only natural ingredients to create its range of products.

1.8.4   Frinter – Muhammad Ali and Shivam Tandon, UK

University friends Muhammad Ali and Shivam Tandon both worked for a short period of time for other employers before they came up with the idea of providing free printing services for students at colleges and universities, Frinter. The founders are originally from

© Alison Barton

© Ben Smith

© Frinter

© Kathryn Kimbley

Picture 1.1   Meet the case studies I: *(left to right)* Alison and Ben, Shivam and Muhammad, and Kathryn Kimbley

Pakistan and India and came to the UK to study at Birmingham City University. After graduating in 2011 with an engineering degree, Shivam started his first business helping students to sell their books after having finished university, which he did for two years in his leisure time while working full-time. Muhammad Ali worked for a research consultancy for three years after completing his degree in business and marketing. He also started his first business by himself in 2013, trading in the commodities market.

While the idea was born in late 2012, it took a while to design a workable business model; after a long development time Frinter was registered in August 2013 in Birmingham. Shivam left a well-paid job to focus full time on starting up Frinter with seed funding from E4F (Entrepreneurs for the Future), a technology incubator in Birmingham, UK.

Frinter helps students save money on printing by providing free-of-charge printing with adverts and high quality paid printing without adverts at lower prices than copy shops and university libraries. Users register with a short profile of themselves; for free printing, users enter their login details at the printer that then selects from the available advertisers those that want to target this type of customer with ads or special offers. Users can pay for ad-free printouts directly through their Frinter account.

Shivam's dream is to be "free financially, to basically have that financial freedom, because life is too short to just work, 9 to 5".

1.8.5 Social enterprise HumAnima CIC, mature graduate Kathryn Kimbley, UK

HumAnima Community Interest Company (CIC) (www.humanima.co.uk) was formed in January 2010. Kathryn is a professional counsellor, with a degree at Master's level from Keele University, who wanted to combine finding work reflecting her passion with addressing certain social issues and social needs within the local area. Wolverhampton, UK, is a very diverse city with a very high level of deprivation, low-income families and areas in which lots of people are on benefits. There is a link between increased economic deprivation and increased problems with mental health, depression and anxiety. The increased demand for mental health service provision creates a need that is not being fulfilled when people want and need to address their mental health problems.

Kathryn initially worked in various administrative roles, eventually going on to work in different charities like Wolverhampton Service User Involvement Team, the Thomas Pocklington Trust and as a Mental Health Advocate with Making Space in Chelmsleywood, where she led and managed the local advocacy service.

Kathryn has a lifelong passion for the human–animal bond and human–animal relationships. She has qualified with a Professional Certificate in Animal Assisted Therapy and a Foundation Certificate in Animals and Horticulture as Therapy. As a mature student without a first degree she was invited to do a Master's in Counselling Psychology at Keele University where she graduated in 2009. This allowed her to develop a service offer using her knowledge and dedication in her area of passion – counselling with the option of animal assisted therapy. Kathryn won a number of awards, including the Social Enterprise West Midlands Prima Award for Innovation sponsored by Price Waterhouse Cooper and an award from the School of Social Entrepreneurs in 2013, the latter providing her with specialist support in further developing her social enterprise for one year.

1.8.6 Alexandru Damian, MSc, Romania – AMD Nobel Pharmaceuticals SRL

During his studies for a Master's in Business and Management at Aston University, Birmingham, Alexandru went on a study visit to a UK company – MacuVision Europe Ltd. During this visit he half-jokingly asked the CEO if he was interested in selling his products in Romania, and the CEO's answer was, "Yes". A few days later Alexandru had set up a meeting with him to discuss the potential business opportunity in more detail. Following this meeting, Alexandru carried out more research and decided to focus his Master's dissertation on starting a business in Romania that imports a specific eye-care product from MacuVision to sell to eye professionals and the wider public. I had the pleasure of supervising this excellent dissertation, which was a lot more than just a feasibility study and a business plan. Immediately after graduation, Alexandru went back to Romania to start the business, which was registered in August 2013.

© Lewis Barnes

© Lillie Ranney

© Vivek George

© Richard Rodman

© Alexandru Damian

Picture 1.2   Meet the case studies II: *(left to right)* Lewis, Lillie, Vivek, Richard and Alexandru

After 15 months, the company was breaking even and providing a decent salary for Alexandru. It was during the in-depth and extensive market research and stakeholder interviews that he found his current business associate and now business partner for the company. Impressed by his passion, diligence and commitment, a medical doctor working in the pharma industry in Romania joined Alexandru in his business.

Alexandru's parents have been running small businesses for two decades, and Alexandru grew up with their experiences and insights on what it means to be in business, including the financial and emotional ups and downs that can bring. "Always move on, always go further – whatever life throws at you" is an insight he learned from his parents and lives himself now. You can see his website on www.amdnobel.ro.

Alexandru states "the highest benefit I consider having gained from studying is how to learn, and learning how to research" was the most important insight he gained from his studies for his business degree, and in particular through writing his dissertation.

1.8.7 Vivek George, MSc, Serratomo, Hong Kong

Vivek registered Serratomo in March 2013 in Hong Kong. The online marketing consultancy is run as a sole proprietor and offers low-cost solutions for small and large businesses in website design and development, marketing, social media design and development, search engine optimization and app development. Vivek got the idea for Serratomo when he needed a website of his own for his first planned start-up, a wine bar, and found that many companies in the UK and Hong Kong charged a lot of money for not a lot of output.

He graduated with a first class Master's in Project and Programme Management from Warwick University, Warwick Manufacturing Group, where he wrote his dissertation on applying project management tools to starting a wine bar in Hong Kong. I had the great pleasure of supervising him in this Master's project. He planned this start-up after his degree and successfully took part in a business plan competition at Warwick University. The most important learning points from his studies were gained through his dissertation, for which he already researched the business environment in Hong Kong and the excellent business support infrastructure available for start-ups though training, advice, incubators and organized networks.

1.8.8 Lillie Ranney, Foleeo, USA

Portfolio entrepreneur Lillie is a recent graduate from Ohio University, US, in Communications Studies from Scripps College of Communications, and is on her second start-up. Being her own boss and running her own business has been a clear goal for Lillie since she was a teenager. During university studies she took part in some entrepreneurship modules. While working on her portfolio for one module in 2011, she developed a wish to be able to showcase her work online in a great way, but no software or Internet platform she could find offered what she had in mind. Once she had finished the module, she started researching and planning an Internet platform that could realize her vision of an online portfolio. For about a year the lecturer for this module mentored her, she met him nearly weekly, to discuss aspects of the potential start-up. Once she had graduated in 2013, she applied successfully to the university-based Innovation Engine Accelerator programme (for digital media start-ups) and was accepted. In September 2013 her first start-up was born: Foleeo.biz, a free-to-use online platform initially aimed primarily at students, start-ups and SME professionals.

1.8.9 Richard Rodman, USA – Crowdentials

Richard is at time of writing a student at Ohio University, studying entrepreneurship and business management, a four-year degree. At 23 years old, he has already achieved a lot and knows for certain that a traditional 9-to-5 job is not for him. He is currently on his second business, Crowdentials. Crowdentials offers compliance software and wider services that assist crowdfunding platforms to comply with the changing legal environment, in particular the 2014 US Jumpstart Our Business Startups Act (JOBS Act); currently he is only operating in the US. Towards the end of his first year at university he started his first venture, FlashCrop LLC, releasing a mobile application that allows everyone to create flashcards quickly by taking pictures of notes, slides and other paper-based information. At that time, he was president of the student entrepreneurship society and was accepted for Ohio University's own accelerator, the Innovation Engine Accelerator programme for digital start-ups. This business is still running; however, he sold his shares in it in order to focus full-time on Crowdentials, for which he interrupted his studies at the insistence of the investor team who wanted him and his team to focus full-time on it. Richard won numerous prizes for start-ups and entrepreneurs, such as the first prize in the Athens Start-up Weekend, and Ohio University Idea Pitch, both in 2012, and first places for start-ups in Cleveland by Cleveland.com and The Plain Dealer.

1.9   Concluding remarks and application of new insights

Chapter One introduced you to the Cube business model and the six main areas to consider when starting a business, as they are guiding the structure of the book. The six areas of the Cube represent:

1 Business Processes: Operations and process management
2 Financial Circuits: Spending and making money (including pricing)
3 Frameworks: Internal frameworks (governance) and legal issues
4 Customer Focus and Environment: Marketing and sales, market and industry research findings
5 Strategy: Business modelling and positioning
6 Evaluation: Value creation and impact management.

The main insights behind the Cube, principles for the sustainable business and associated practices, are discussed in detail, as they inform the approach to discussing the six areas of the Cube, and the overall twelve areas.

Finally, Chapter One gave basic background information on what a business actually does and how the variety of businesses is sorted into industry sectors and subsectors. It then differentiated all enterprising organizations as charities, social enterprises and for-profit businesses. The discussion of myths and false beliefs about the nature and purpose of business showcased some further insights about the wide range of ways of doing and running a business; part-time, home-based and short-term are all legitimate aspects of conducting business.

Now you have the basic understanding what business is all about and what the book offers you on your journey to creating the *sustainable start-up*.

1.9.1 Personal reflection and development: begin a start-up diary

Start a pre-start-up journey map and diary. The map is a visual presentation of what you did first, second, third, etc., whereas the diary is a place to notice and record your thoughts, ideas and feelings. It is important to acknowledge that the journey can be an emotional one, and it is common to experience uncertainty, frustration, fear or feelings of being limited or not good enough to start a new venture. These emotional barriers are normal for everyone starting for the first time on a journey into the unknown world of new venture creation, the diary will help you to recognize and progress through them.

Include your answers to questions eight and nine (below) in your start-up diary. If you want to use a standard form for each diary entry, a sample format can be found on the companion website to this book (www.palgrave.com/companion/hill-start-up).

1.9.2 Revision questions and application of new insights

1 What are the 12 areas essential to consider when starting a business?
2 What is a social enterprise? What is the UK definition of social enterprise?
3 What role do businesses have in every economy?
4 How many principles does the book suggest as essential for the *sustainable start-up*? Name the principles and explain them in your own words.
5 What practices are suggested for the *sustainable start-up*?
6 Why did Kathryn and Lewis start their businesses?
7 What are the guiding mottos for Shivam and Alexandru?
8 What are the two most important insights you have gained after reading this chapter and introduction? Write them into your start-up diary.
9 Have you considered starting a business or becoming self-employed? If yes, what was your idea? Briefly outline it in your start-up diary. If you have not done so, why not? Have you been told stories/myths that prevent you from considering it as an option for you? Or what are your reasons for discounting it? Have you got a career plan at this moment in time? Note your answers in your start-up diary.

2

PERSONAL CAREER PATHS AND MOTIVES TO START AN ENTERPRISE

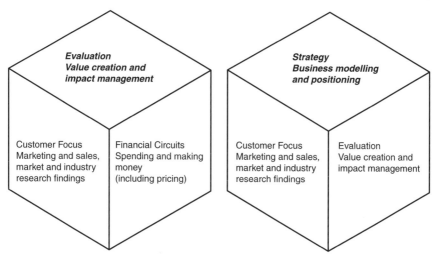

Figure 2.1   The Cube Evaluation and the Cube Strategy
Source: © Hill, 2012.

Summary

Chapter Two sheds light on changing career paths and the changing face and operations of business activities over the last decade. It then explores motives to start and close businesses and the changing trends in operations of business activities over the last decade. For the *sustainable start-up* journey it helps to see that your own personal reasons for considering a start-up are often shared by a number of other people in similar or even different situations and age groups. The wide variety of support available for starting a venture is introduced and illustrated with some examples from the UK, Northern European countries and the US. This chapter illustrates how to address the sixth Cube face Evaluation and the principle and practice of sustainability through increasing your awareness of where your skills and traits for start-up activities lie (Figure 2.1).

CONTENTS

2.1   Who starts new ventures?

Before going into detail and developing the tools and activities for developing a *sustainable start-up*, it is useful that we familiarize ourselves with the information available on people who start new ventures, and who does not.

According to the most recent UK and international GEM report, in the UK 7.6% of the population started a business in 2013 (total early stage entrepreneurial activity rate, GEM 2014a, that is the sum of owner managers and those actively trying to start a business). This is lower than for 2012, but higher than the average for the years 2002 to 2010, which was around 6%. The UK's statistic is higher than in France (4.6%) and Germany (5%), but lower than in the US with 12.7%. Only 3.8% of the population in the UK in 2013 were actively starting a business, or in other words were in the pre-start-up phase. Those who expected to start a business over the next three years measured much lower in the UK with 5.4% than in Germany (8.9%), France (13.7%) and the US (16.6%) (GEM, 2014a).

Between 2011 and 2013 the UK population started an increasing number of new ventures amounting to more than 500,000 start-ups in 2013 (440,600 in 2011, 484,224 in 2012; Department for Business, Information and Skills, 2014a). There is no general trend over longer periods of a trend of continuously rising number of start-ups in all countries studied.

In the UK in 2012 the highest number of 18- to 24-year-olds became self-employed since 2001, 3.2% (Department for Business, Information and skills, 2014a). After which it decreased to 2.9% at the end of 2013.

Did you know that women are still under-represented amongst start-ups? In 2013, only 5.8% of all adult women started businesses in the UK, compared to 7.6% of all men (see Table 2.1, GEM, 2014b). In most high income and industrialized countries, men are more likely to be entrepreneurially active than women. Female entrepreneurial activity rates are about two-thirds that of men. Table 2.1 shows what is called total early entrepreneurial activity, that is, all those involved in activities prior to start-up and those up to 42 months after start-up (GEM, 2014a). The Netherlands, Norway and Sweden have proportionately the lowest female rates of entrepreneurial participation.

The main reasons for the different activity rates between men and women include the social construction of roles for men and women in the labour force, stereotypical family commitment roles, the different resources women and men have available due to the different

Table 2.1 Total early stage entrepreneurial activity rate by gender in 2013, 18–64 years of age

Gender / Country (rounded figures in %)	UK	Netherlands	Romania	Norway	Sweden	Germany	Finland	US
Male	9	12	12	9	10	6	7	15
Female	6	7	8	4	6	4	4	10

Source: GEM, 2014b.

Table 2.2 Total nascent entrepreneurship rate and perception of failure in 2013, 18–64 years of age

Country / indicator in %	UK	Romania	Netherlands	Sweden	Finland	Norway	Germany	US
Nascent entrepreneurship rate	3.6	6.2	4.7	5.9	2.7	2.9	3.1	9.2
Perception of failure	36.4	37.3	36.8	36.6	36.7	35.3	38.6	31.1

Source: GEM, 2014a.

roles and participation in the labour force, as well as the perception and creation of business opportunities in a variety of industry sectors. For many women in typical women's roles, choosing self-employment is perceived as an act of disintegration of a role in society many do not want to take (Klyver et al., 2013).

Is fear of failing in business something you have thought about? Perception of business failure is one factor that influences some people's decision regarding whether or not to start a business. The ways different societies regard closing down a business and actual business failure vary across the world and are a factor in the way business opportunities are perceived by those considering a start-up, as shown in Table 2.2. However, the data do not show what kind of business individuals have in mind or are starting when they consider the importance of fear of failure. There are relatively similar data for European countries, with over a third of all interviewees indicating that the fear of failure is a factor in their decision to start a new venture, with Germany showing the highest fear of failure and Norway the lowest, but there is only little difference between 35.3% and 38.6%. The US has the lowest rate with only 31% and is also the country with the highest start-up rate (GEM, 2014a).

Table 2.2 also provides insight into those individuals who are actively engaged in preparing a start-up, have committed their own resources to the start-up and have been trading less than three months. This is called the nascent entrepreneurship rate. In the 2013 data from selected European countries, Sweden had the highest rate with nearly six in 100 individuals compared to Finland, which has the lowest rate with less than three in 100. However, there is no conclusive link between level of perception of failure and the level of nascent entrepreneurial activity (GEM, 2014a).

2.1.1 Who starts social enterprises or social ventures?

We defined social enterprise in the UK (see Chapter One) as an enterprise that is constitutionally formed to generate social (including environmental) impact for society and/or communities. For the UK the following trends can be found:

Young people under 30 years of age are the most likely group in the UK population to start up a social enterprise (27% compared to 20% of the general population) and more likely to support social causes (70% compared to 63% of the general population) (RBS 2013, second quarter). Reasons for the increased interest in social enterprise start-ups amongst the younger population may lie in the economic recession and the way traditional boundaries between private, public and voluntary sectors started to blur.

In the UK, women lead 38% of all social enterprises, and 41% of all start-ups under three years old. The large majority of leaders are between 44 and 65 years of age (58%), while 13% are over 65. The largest group across all ages leave a private sector job to start a social enterprise (38%), followed by those with a public sector career background.

For other countries it is more difficult to get exact numbers, as the definition is different to the UK and the boundaries between a social business and a business that just donates some of its profits to a social cause are more blurred. As pointed out in Chapter One, in countries such as in Scandinavia, the term community entrepreneur or societal entrepreneur is much more common (see Vestrum, 2014 for a case study on community entrepreneurs using a music festival as a vehicle for change in a remote rural Norwegian community). In addition, many countries simply do not collect data on social enterprises in a similar way to the UK.

2.1.2 Why businesses fail or are closed down

Many start-ups and businesses fail or are closed down, even after so many decades of experience and learning about business development support and business start-up. Discontinuation is the technical term for all types of voluntary closure. The main reasons given across all countries include (GEM, 2014a):

▶ The business not being profitable;
▶ Problems obtaining finance (yet not for the US);
▶ Other jobs or business opportunities (US and Europe).

Other reasons include retirement, other personal reasons or a pre-planned exit from the business.

The three reasons particular to exit from start-up that have been identified for student and graduate *start-ups* include (1) deciding to explore other opportunities such as another job, another business regarded as more interesting or profitable, or turning towards more formal education, (2) making calculated considerations regarding the likelihood of achieving set goals (and closing down if the assessment made is that the goals cannot be achieved) and (3) acting on social concerns including the negative perception of family and friends regarding the business opportunity (Yusuf, 2012).

Table 2.3 shows some statistics on active businesses in the UK in a number of sectors, and the rates of births and deaths in 2013 (Office for National Statistics, 2014 (ONS)). Sectors with the highest *start-up* or birth rate were business administration and support, and the ones with the highest death rate were finance and insurance. Further analysis by the ONS finds that only in 2009–10 the business death rate was higher than the birth rate, as an effect of the economic recession.

Table 2.3   Number of firms active in selected sectors in the UK in 2013 and business birth and death rates

Industry sector	Active businesses in 1000s	Business birth rate	Business death rate
Production	158	11.4	8.5
Construction	309	12.4	10.6
Wholesale	117	10.1	9.1
Retail	220	12.4	10.2
Transport and storage	82	15.1	10.3
Accomodation and food services	166	15.3	12.7
Information and communication	200	16.8	9.8
Finance and insurance	36	16.9	13.1
Property	95	11.1	7
Professional, scientific and technical	453	17	9.3
Business administration and support	216	20.7	10.6
Arts, entertainment, recreation and other services	180	10	8.7

Source: Office for National Statistics, 2014.

Reasons for failure are complex and include:

- Not paying taxes;
- Limited knowledge of financing and experience in record-keeping;
- Living too expensively for the business;
- Lack of pricing knowledge and emotional pricing;
- Starting up for the wrong reasons;
- Lack of planning of business activities;
- Not anticipating the time and resources needed to start and run the business;
- Poor market understanding and lack of adequate market research;
- Growing too quickly and unsuitable borrowing practices;
- Poor financial awareness, in particular not understanding cashflow;
- Lack of industry or sector experience and/or knowledge;
- Ignoring competitive threats;
- Being in the wrong location for retail businesses;
- Lack of appropriate skills in the founding team and/or staff;
- Personal burnout.

 The risks in starting trading too early and not investing sufficient time into research and planning, and having to close are manifold: money can be invested into activities not leading to success, and thus be wasted. The risks can include:

- Loss of personal savings;
- Loss of money lent by friends and family, thus straining and even destroying personal relationships;
- Gaining a low credit rating;
- Losing personal confidence and self-esteem.

These many failures and risks are the reason that this book puts great emphasis on feasibility research before engaging in a real start-up. Sufficient planning and research, including market testing, validation and a feasibility study – the exploration if there actually is a business opportunity, a chance to make money, behind an idea – can prevent all of the above from occurring, to a large extent. These activities illustrate the principles and practices implemented under the sixth Cube area of Evaluation and why they fail.

Now that we have identified who typically starts new ventures, their reasons need exploring. The next section gives an overview of why some people start new ventures and the role the broader socio-economic context plays.

2.2 Changing and fast-moving economies – changing career paths and places of work

2.2.1 Portfolio careers – just a new trend?

Knowing how to start and run a business, developing the skill to work flexibly in an organized way, is practical knowledge and experience needed to get a job and be prepared for the constantly changing conditions in the economy. These changes will lead to redundancies for many. Participation in the start-up experience can truly increase both employability and the repertoire of choices young millennials can make. In particular, it includes the choice of leaving an employer when values are not met, helping to turn that option from a wish to reality. Do you know why? The trends explored in the next sections provide contextual reasons why some people start a new venture.

 Most people over the age of 20 in 2014, often called the Y-generation or the millennials, will not have just one job for their working life. Rather, they are more likely to have phases of full-employment, self-employment and/or part-time employment mixed with phases of unemployment, often involuntarily, and contract working. These careers are often called portfolio careers. A recent survey of employers shows that they expect in the next 10 years most of the staff they employ will have had at least two jobs and a growing number to have been self-employed or run their own business (Right Management, 2014).

In a UK survey of HR directors in 2013, 80% expect the majority of their employees to have portfolio careers within the next five years. These HR professionals find that some employers see an advantage in having only a small number of core staff who share their values, while the remaining workforce will consist of contract workers and freelancers that are brought in if and when needed (Right Management, 2014). This means that project-focused freelancing will increase over the next years. With smaller budgets and the increasing wish of employees to work more flexibly, technology enables various forms of mobile working, using cloud and the Internet for meetings, document sharing and simultaneous working on documents.

Similarly, the millennial generation has different demands towards work and employers than the currently middle-aged work force: (PricewaterhouseCoopers, 2011, data for 2011, all interviewees were under 31 years of age):

▸ Work–life balance is much more important to them than financial rewards.
▸ Personal learning and development opportunities rank highest followed by flexible working hours.

- Personal values need to be matched by company values for just over half of the interviewees, and 56% would leave an employer if it did not meet their values (a decrease since 2008 by 22%).
- Having grown up with smartphones, technology and digital communication are central to the way lives are led and communication is done, with 41% preferring communicating electronically over face-to-face or phone.

2.2.2 Technological change and flexible ways of doing business

The face of work has changed over the last decades, most recently through cloud computing combined with using smartphones as working tools with office software. There is a great number of applications that can be used to communicate wherever you are (or nearly, where there is coverage) and to continue working on your documents without having to carry a tablet or laptop, just using a smartphones.

The *sustainable start-up* looks for all possible ways to use technology for smart(er) working. Some established micro-businesses have been doing it for a while.

Box 2.1 illustrates the way a consultancy business with an annual turnover of about £300,000 operates. This company is illustrating a possible realization of a *sustainable start-up* that matured: the company avoids having too many fixed costs (costs that occur even if no income is generated) and operates in a very flexible way (illustrating the principles and practices of alertness, responsibility, resourceful impact and co-creation, see Chapter One):

- They have only 2.5 paid staff.
- They rarely travel to meetings with associate staff members and keep meetings with clients to a minimum; most meetings are done online and/or via phone.
- They use very little stationery or sundries as a lot of work is created and shared electronically.
- Associates work on a contractual basis only; they are invited to bring business in and then lead on projects and are part of the business-planning activities (co-creation and interconnectedness are illustrated through these two practices).

Box 2.1   Taking advantage of mobile working

A consultancy company with focus on research services is a micro-business operating very leanly for over 25 years. For the last ten years the owner has been living in France in a mountain village. The company offices are in the south of the UK in a small town. The office is run by one full-time operations manager and one part-time administrative support staff. The only other full-time staff member is the sole director living in France.

The company has a network of associates. These are all self-employed professionals or individuals running micro-enterprises. When a project meets their requirements, and they want to work as a team under one company to gain the contract, they apply together under the one consultancy name to win the contract. Applying as an individual for a contract of higher value than £30,000 is rarely successful. For an application to gain a project or contract, teams are formed by the owner, and once the contract is won, the teams work together remotely.

Face-to-face meetings between team members happen twice a year in the offices of the company. All other meetings take place online between team members. They will meet with clients face-to-face, and will have face-to-face team meetings before or after client meetings.

Technology is used in many ways, including Skype, software for online meetings and workshops, and shared workspaces. For research, software for surveys and open interviews is used. Travel costs are minimized and overall fixed costs as well. When the sole director has client meetings she flies into the UK and stays in a hotel. These travel costs are not charged to the client.

In 2014, the business decided to abandon its physical office space completely and have everybody work remotely from home.

The above outlined contextual changes provide reasons why some individuals start businesses. Motivations are discussed in more detail in the next section.

2.3 Why individuals start new ventures – motivations and contexts

2.3.1 Motivations to start businesses – research findings

What is motivation then? It is commonly regarded as the driving force behind human actions. It consists of a unique combination of an individual's goals, needs and desires. Motive is similar in meaning; however, it is more often defined as the reason for doing something, the purpose.

Some individuals start businesses because they either have no other options for work, or no better options (in the academic literature called "necessity entrepreneurship", see for example, GEM, 2014a; see also Cassar, 2007, Taormina and Lao, 2007). There is a link between rises in necessity-driven start-ups and unemployment rates in most countries.

Most other reasons are summarized under the heading of opportunity driven, that means that the start-up is perceived as a positively different way to earn a living. "Opportunity" refers to identifying and exploiting market opportunities with the expectation of a material gain.

More recently, a subcategory has been created that identifies improvement-driven opportunity motivations as those motivations that are driven by the aim to earn more money or gain more independence (GEM, 2014a).

Classic research on motivation lists a number of motivational factors that might or might not occur together with the same individual (Birley and Westhead, 1994, Carter et al. 2003, Cassar, 2007, Kauanui et al, 2010, Rindova et al., 2009, Shane et al., 1991, Wu et al., 2007, Cardon, 2009):

- Economic gain;
- Desires for achievement, independence and control;
- Personal development;
- Improving social status;
- Opportunity to innovate and create new products;
- Mirroring role models;
- Realizing a passion;

- Achieving greater contentment at and through work;
- Contribution to community welfare.

Other authors differentiate between push and pull factors in setting up a business, for example. "Push" refers to factors in the business environment as much as the person of the entrepreneur that propel the man or woman away from what they are currently doing, to do something else such as starting a business; pull factors are those related to a particular prospect or characteristics of a situation regarded as favourable that attract an individual towards starting a new venture (Birley and Westhead, 1994, Moore and Buttner, 1997, Kirkwood, 2009). In Table 2.4 you can find the most common pull and push factors (based on research findings and my own business support and business start-up support experiences).

In *Start Up*, we see motivation as a combination of factors of *three* different types (based on Jayawarna et al., 2011) going beyond the push/pull dichotomy (a differentiation of factors in only two seemingly opposing types of reasons). These factors relate to four contexts, as described in the motivation profiles below. Motivation is therefore often a combination of

Table 2.4   Push and pull motivation factors

Push factors	Pull factors
Unemployment	Urge to mirror a role model
Difficult personal situation at home: death of partner/parent; divorce; illness of a parent	Wish to become rich
Dissatisfaction with current work situation (salary, boss, location, etc.)	Urge to make a difference
Young children and the wish to combine flexible working and income generation	Urge to make more money
Job insecurity	Desire to become independent and autonomous ("want to be my own boss")
Underpaid work/low pay	Spotting a business opportunity and the ability to seize it
Discrimination in the labour market and/or reaching a glass ceiling	Better work–life balance
Boredom/too much time	Attraction of a new challenge
Retirement and lots of time	Trying out something new that is fun
No work placement for students and the long-term unemployed	Retirement and lots of time to fill with a fun activity
Personal values regarding working with people (or animals) are not met by the work place	Desire to develop some practical skills instead of a work placement
	Personal development opportunity
	Passion for a particular area of work
	A particular talent and the wish to use it to earn a living
	Work activities can be organized around existing care commitments for children and/or elderly or disabled relatives
	Values around how to treat people can be realized in a unique way in the venture

both pull and push and contextual factors. Why is it important to know these factors and findings, you might wonder? Being aware of what influences your choices might inform and help to make a different choice in terms of work experience and/or sector to start a business in, and ultimately in your own chances to make a profit or a difference to people's lives.

The first context is shaped by the individual's family origin: the norms and values created in the family context regarding running businesses, work experience and education within the family, level of wealth or the lack of it. This family context impacts on perceptions of occupational choices and actual resources brought to entrepreneurship. Culturally influenced values, whether based in the local community or the community of ethnic origin, also play a role.

The second context – described as "household life course" – addresses the consumption and provision of reproductive resources, which impact on labour capacity and economic motivation. For example, if you are a parent you might want to create a way to generate income that fits flexibly around other parenting responsibilities; or if you are the sole earner in a relationship you may decide you do not want to risk starting a business.

The "business life course" context focuses on an individual's experience in mobilizing resources to achieve given outcomes: if you are a mature student with some work experience you have learned how to structure your time (time is a resource) to be effective (achieve higher education outcome); or if you have some experience in, for example, selling books or used toys to other people, you have learned about selling goods (a tangible resource) to make money (and/or reduce environmental waste, achieving a specific outcome).

A fourth context looks at an individual's belonging to social structures – along the lines of gender, ethnicity, age – which influence access to resources that shape pathways. The importance of these contexts changes over the lifetime of a person and shapes their motivation and access to resources. One example is that people under 25 years old are often regarded by banks as a credit risk, when they have no credit history, no or very little work experience and little or no savings.

In this context there are specific findings on gender and motivation. Social gender roles have an influence on motivation and the selection of start-up as a viable career choice, and also impact on the choice of sector for the start-up. There are contrasting findings in studies of motivation between men and women starting businesses: some studies find similarities in the motivation of women and men. These include achieving growth or striving for personal freedom, independence and higher job satisfaction (OECD, 2013a, Scheiner et al., 2007). Other findings point out differences including the way different goals such as personal fulfilment, flexibility and autonomy are prioritized (Carter et al., 2003, Humbert and Drew, 2010, Morris et al., 2006, OECD, 2013a,), or observe gender differences in motivation through external influences. Some examples found were that women were more influenced by a desire for independence; women considered their children as motivators more so than did men; men were influenced more by job dissatisfaction than were women. Reasons also differed by the phase of life a woman is in and her socio-economic context (young and independent, mother and single parent, wife and mother with a high-earning husband or partner, mature professional with a high income and personal savings and a passion to make a difference) (Klapper and Parker, 2010).

Women who are in the mother phase have other reasons for starting up their own business, often to be able to combine earning an income with providing/organizing childcare and to have the largest level of flexibility. All research indicates that women still have more responsibility for household work than men in industrialized and developing countries alike. This external environment influences their choice of career and consequently work experience.

Women are predominantly starting businesses in lower income sectors such as retail, crafts, wholesale, human health and beauty, social work, education, professional, scientific and technical activities and consultancy services (OECD, 2013a). This has, unsurprisingly, an effect on financial performance and possible profit-making.

Beyond specific gender-based contexts, people from ethnic minority backgrounds have many of the same motivations to start businesses. Additional reasons for them to start a new venture can include the experience of discrimination and lack of career progression or the wish to provide employment for community members that otherwise would have difficulties in getting a job and/or developing a career.

 Case study

These are the motivations of four of our case studies illustrating the *Start Up* approach (see Section 1.9 for details). The urge to mirror a role model was one of the many reasons for Ben Smith to start Frumtious, his fruit jelly manufacturing business (see Section 1.8.3). He wants to become the next Jamie Oliver, who is best known to young people in the UK for improving school meals and pupils' lives (pull factor) and for founding a social enterprise restaurant that provides chef training to disadvantaged young men. Ben is also escaping the experience of working as an employee in the for-profit sector, which is of secondary importance (push factor, career life course context). Ben is involved as second partner in starting a social enterprise supporting disadvantaged young people to start their own enterprises, which illustrates the importance he places on social impact while making a living, as did working for the Student Union of his former university, a charity (career life course context); his feeling of comfort in those environments is not surprising, as his parents brought him up to act socially responsible while having their careers in the social and education sector (family context). His first student start-up of an online magazine allowed him to gain experience in resource mobilization for a self-selected outcome (business life course).

The most important motivation for Alison Barton (see Section 1.8.1) for starting up her own photography business was her passion for photography combined with the fact that she did not find a job after completing her degree. While Alison always wanted to start her own business at some stage, the time for that was planned to be a few years after getting some more work experience (career and business life course). She clearly points out that without her early part-time work experience with a female photographer while still at school, she might not have regarded photography and self-employment as a viable option. One reason she mentions is that photography is a male-dominated sector (social structures context).

Damian Alexandru, another start-up case study in this book (see Section 1.8.6), was motivated by the attraction of the challenge of introducing a new product to Romania and by trying out something that has not been done for and in his country before (both pull factors), but these motivations have to be seen in the context of his role in the household; he is in a relationship in which he has taken on the role as the main earner. His parents are both self-employed and ran businesses, thus motivating him to follow his inclinations to try something independent and new (family context).

Richard Rodman, founder of Crowdentials (see Section 1.8.9), is mainly motivated by the opportunity to become rich while young (pull factor) and gain financial independence,

> supported by the push factor having seen his father being made redundant after over 30 years of loyalty to employers, and struggling with gaining a living afterwards (family context).

The next section outlines reasons found for starting social enterprises, which also indicates the main social missions chosen as a strong motivator.

2.3.2 Motivations to start social ventures

 Increasingly, many social start-ups try to find a different balance between the economic demands of earning a living and realizing a social mission. The reduction of social services and the welfare state benefits in many countries have led to an increase in the number of individuals with a variety of motives for starting a social enterprise. Recent marketization of society, bringing a number of services that previously were predominantly carried out by the state, is one contextual factor that has motivated different types of people to engage with social enterprise start-ups. While academic research sees a tension and conflicts (Battilana and Dorado, 2010), the new social entrepreneurs constantly find ways of balancing profit-making with social impact, and create new balances with different partners in different projects, which can be temporary in nature, to realize their social mission. We already discussed the joint venture between Muhammad Yunus and the large corporate Danone to sell yoghurt to the masses in Bangladesh; this kind of partnership is relatively new and illustrates a different type of individual and how he balances the social mission to improve the lives of the poor in a country with money-making and partnership with a large corporation in the dairy industry.

Particular motives for starting social ventures in all countries include:

▶ Identification of a need in society, of a particular group of people (for example, those with vision problems or orphans), a particular type of organization (for example, charities) or the environment (protecting a particular type of animal or plant);
▶ Spotting a market failure by commercial ventures that needs addressing to promote social equality, for example providing low-cost solutions to those with mobility difficulties and limited financial resources;
▶ Creating social wealth for local and other communities;
▶ Creating benefits and/or wealth for a specified group of people, members of the founded organization;
▶ Creating change in society;
▶ Making a quality of life difference for a particular group of people (for example, children in hospitals).

The main motivations for starting social enterprises in the UK in 2013 include improving a particular community, followed by improving health and well-being, creating employment, supporting vulnerable people. Supporting vulnerable young people and children was the motivation for 13% of social enterprises, protecting the environment follows after supporting other social enterprises (Social Enterprise UK, 2014).

As outlined in Chapter One, the concept and reality of non-profit organizations and social enterprise varies greatly across countries. Only when we understand the socio-economic context and even traditions in a country can we identify more clearly why numbers and types of social venture start-ups differ so markedly between countries.

Box 2.2 outlines some context for Sweden and the political and social tradition of dealing with social problems, which historically were the responsibility of institutions and were regulated through policy-making and many public institutions. The reduction in the number of local authorities in the last century, and reduced public funding led to a movement of societal or community entrepreneurs keen to maintain or revitalize the local communities. It is rooted in the country's strong civil society and cooperative movements. The latter have a strong tradition in job training and job integration to reduce unemployment.

Box 2.2 Societal instead of social entrepreneurship in Sweden and Denmark

As early as the 1970s Swedish individuals and groups took the initiative to found community-led social ventures to address local issues. As the state became unable to cater for all social needs in the same way as in the past, Swedish individuals and groups increasingly developed social enterprise-type organizations, often referred to as community enterprise and societal enterprises, to address the most urgent local problems, such as provision of care for older people, childcare and early learning and support for disabled citizens. Public-private partnerships between local authorities and social entrepreneurs are rising quickly to address these social problems. The term social enterprise is not widely accepted and understood in its translation to Swedish.

A starting point for finding out more is the Swedish national forum for social innovation and social entrepreneurship (see http://www.socialinnovation.se/en/?lang=en to find out more, in Swedish and English).

For further information on social enterprises in Denmark, it is worth checking out the Danish website of the Danish umbrella organization for social enterprises (http://www.VFSA.dk).

 Case study

For social entrepreneur Kathryn Kimbley (see Section 1.8.5) the passion to make a difference for disadvantaged people in the Black Country was her main reason for starting a social enterprise (social context and career life course). She has worked in a number of jobs working with and supporting the target beneficiaries of her services; she can also use her passion for the relationship between animals and humans to improve the mental health of the beneficiaries of her social enterprise (pull factors).

 Activity 2.1 What would motivate you to start a business, now or later in your career?

Reflect for a moment about your career plans. What do you want to do after university or college? How are you earning money right now, if you are working? Is there something you are passionate about and want to spend more time doing? Could others be interested in that hobby or skill? Have you ever thought about starting a business? Record your answers in your start-up diary.

The next section explains some traits of start-ups and entrepreneurs, leading to activities that will support you in identifying what traits and skills you have.

2.4 Who is an entrepreneur? What is an entrepreneur?

2.4.1 Entrepreneurial traits

Why is it helpful to find out what the traits of other business people are? It might help in your consideration if a start-up is for you to find out if you share some of these traits. Traits of entrepreneurs most often include (see for example Baron and Tang, 2009, Patel and Thatcher, 2014, Stewart and Roth, 2007):

- Internal locus of control;
- Need for independence;
- Need for achievement;
- Tolerance of some uncertainty;
- Willingness to take calculated risks;
- Self-efficacy;
- Social skills;
- Determination;
- Drive;
- Proactiveness;
- Decisiveness;
- Flexibility;
- Self-motivated.

Internal locus of control refers to the belief that someone is largely able to control their own destiny; this includes having luck now and again. *Self-efficacy* is the self-confidence to be able to carry out the tasks needed in business to achieve the set goals; this includes the ability to leverage or bring in resources (money, materials, the help of others) to achieve the set goals. The other attributes listed are self-explanatory.

Researchers cannot yet agree on what are the most important and typical personality traits of entrepreneurs; one reason is that most research has been carried out on men, used secondary data and mainly surveys and rarely differentiates data by a number of socio-demographic factors.

Social entrepreneurs are a very diverse group, similar to for-profit entrepreneurs, with a number of types that have different or additional traits. For social entrepreneurs the following additional traits were identified (see for example Dorado and Ventresca, 2013, Zarah et al., 2009):

- Social entrepreneurs are individuals with innovative solutions to society's most pressing social problems.
- They have been found to be ambitious and persistent, tackling major social issues and offering new ideas for wide-scale change. Social entrepreneurs often seem to be possessed by their ideas, committing their lives to changing the direction in their chosen field; they are passionate.
- They are often visionaries, but also realists at the same time, and are ultimately concerned with the practical implementation of their vision to make a difference to society.

- They are change agents who engage in a process of continuous innovation, adaptation and learning.
- They act boldly without being limited by resources currently in hand.
- They show a heightened sense of accountability to the key beneficiaries and the outcomes created.

Social entrepreneurs measure success with financial *and* social return; financial success is sufficient if they are able to cover their costs, have sufficient money to realize the social mission and run a sustainable organization. The impulse for engaging in trading comes from the social mission, not to become personally rich. Some seek profit in seemingly unprofitable fields, where solely profit-seeking business people would not start a new venture.

While the for-profit entrepreneur may donate money to charity, or even create a charity or foundation, that often only happens once the primary goal – wealth creation for personal gain – has been achieved; the latter is still at the forefront of being in business.

Few typologies of social entrepreneurs exist that capture the variety of types that are active across the world (based on Zarah et al., 2009):

1) *Social bricoleur*
This individual is addressing small-scale social needs, based on his or her detailed knowledge of local people and conditions and resources. These entrepreneurs excel in combining existing resources to solve problems, they do not need large amounts of money and investment, which enables them to act more independently and freely and respond to changes more quickly.

2) *Social constructivist*
These social entrepreneurs are serving clients whose social needs are not adequately or not at all addressed within the current system. Their overarching aim is to introduce reforms and innovations to the broader social system. They have a desire for social change on a large scale, they are ambitious, and share more traits with for-profit entrepreneurs than other types. They have to manage complex stakeholder networks – donors, employees, volunteers, government or other organizations. They have limited competition in what they do, yet find strong competition in getting the resources they need. Finally, they are keen to scale up the venture, driven by a mission for complex social change in the societies they live in.

3) *Social engineer*
This type of social entrepreneur introduces revolutionary change and reforms; the best-known example is Mohammad Yunus, the founder of Grameen Banking, Nobel Prize winner for peace. The reforms they seek are often regarded as threatening, illegitimate or subversive by ruling powers in society and government. Social engineering entrepreneurs are often the very first to do something radically different or new and need the support of the population to gain legitimacy for their ideas. They are often charismatic leaders and missionaries for a social purpose, but they can become too egocentric, focused on having the only or right view of how to do things; they can become manipulative and might violate dominating norms to achieve their goals. This can create more conflict at times than prosperity.

These descriptions can help to identify social venture leaders you might know; some of the traits listed will also apply to for-profit entrepreneurs.

Are there any distinctive traits that entrepreneurial leaders have, significantly different to other leaders? That has been discussed most recently by researchers, without a conclusive list of traits (see for example Roomi and Harrison, 2011). However, some traits most researchers can agree on include the following leadership skills *all* entrepreneurs need to show:

▶ A passionate belief in the vision of the product or service idea of the organization;
▶ The ability to communicate that vision;
▶ The capability to give direction and motivate others through the vision;
▶ The ability to give clear and easy to follow instructions;
▶ The capacity to mobilize resources and apply knowledge to the transformation of those resources into goods/services;
▶ The capacity for problem spotting and solving;
▶ The capability to develop a strategy and implement strategic activities.

2.4.2 Entrepreneurial skills, knowledge and business roles

There seems to be widespread agreement on the core skills entrepreneurs need to have, even if later on they might engage an expert in one or more of these skills areas, for example a bookkeeper or accountant to monitor and manage finances. All of these skills can be acquired through learning and training.

▶ Financial skills and knowledge;
▶ Marketing skills and knowledge;
▶ Administration skills;
▶ Communication skills;
▶ Networking skills;
▶ Industry knowledge and research skills;
▶ Sales skills;
▶ Leadership skills;
▶ People management skills;
▶ Self-management skills.

In each start-up, there are a number of roles or functions that need fulfilling: the **manager** of the business who keeps on top of everything, the **administrator** managing the administrative function that ensures all records are created and receipts kept, customer contacts stored and contacted regularly, the **innovator** who comes up with new ideas for services and products that will increase revenue, the **marketeer** who develops a marketing strategy and plan and markets the product, the **sales person** that ensures that products/services are sold, the **researcher** who collects and analyses market information, the **bookkeeper** who keeps track of expenses and money coming in and the **financial planner** who ensures that there is always enough cash in the "kitty" to pay the bills and/or staff where appropriate.

For the individual person who starts on his or her own that might feel daunting, yet again, there is plenty of training and support available to master many of those skills and roles, or to outsource them to someone else or to bring in staff and delegate.

2.5   Have you got what it takes to start and run a business?

 Based on my years of experience working with start-ups and established businesses and my own start-ups there are seven areas that are essential to consider before start-ing a business, be it part- or full-time: (see Figure 2.2), I call them in short WAASSIP:

▶ Working with other people;
▶ Attitudes and beliefs;
▶ Actions;
▶ Skills;
▶ Self-awareness and self-management skills;
▶ Insight by experience;
▶ Personality traits.

If you do not know yourself well enough, you might be overconfident in making assumptions of what you can achieve, which factors influence your projections for sales and ultimately how much money you can make. With this in mind, the most important element on the list might be self-awareness. Attitudes and beliefs are the second most important area.

 "Attitudes and beliefs" sums up the guiding principles governing how you go about working with other people, working in general and going about your life. This section also includes your norms and values, which influence how you select what skills you develop, what knowledge you choose to take on and integrate into what you already know and how you work with other people. And they influence who you think you are and would like to be.

Figure 2.2   Areas to reflect on when considering a start-up – WAASSIP

One example: The attitude that is symbolized by the "glass is always half full" and not half empty indicates the ability to see a positive aspect in the same situation whereas others will only see the negative one.

All these attitudes and beliefs are influenced by the socio-economic context you grew up with, national culture, ethnic group culture, the beliefs of your parents/family/educators, regional culture, and across all those are expectations held about men/women and their role in the family, society and economy, and norms/values a religious belief may bring along. Passion is still the most important and convincing emotion for buyers, investors, staff and other stakeholders. Passion needs to materialize in a commitment to do what is needed to achieve your aims and what you believe in.

"Insight by experience" refers to all the relevant insights you need to acquire to develop a *sustainable start-up*. A lot of that insight will be developed through *doing* something, in particular engaging in market testing. Knowledge gained by reading and research is only a starting point. We differentiate information from knowledge in that information is outside of you personally; it only becomes knowledge when you can integrate it into your personalized insights. Insight thus is a combination of applied knowledge and experience, some tacit knowledge you might have difficulties in putting into words. Knowledge includes business-related knowledge in finance, marketing, sales, operations, people and people management and regulation.

"Skills" refers to all the needed behaviours in the above-named knowledge fields relevant to starting and running a business, and relationship skills. They include financial skills, marketing skills, sales skills, skills in dividing and running operations, communication skills, people management skills, skills in complying with regulation (following the required implementation of) to name some of the most important skills areas.

"Working with others" is such an important area that I listed it as a separate factor. For a *sustainable start-up* you need to realize that even if you are self-employed and working for yourself without staff, you will always have to work with other people to some extent: these are the suppliers, clients and professional service providers such as an accountant or solicitor. Even if you run an online business with no real-time communication with anyone, you will always have to work with people. For that reason, being able to work with different types of people is an important part of life and being in business. Your attitudes towards other people and how work "should" be done influence how you perceive others and react to them. Having worked with many different people is an important basis of being successful in collaborating with others in business, even when self-employed. Co-creation practice depends on you being able to relate to other people.

"Actions" summarizes all activities you carry out that are the more convincing and effective if the appropriate attitudes, guided by your norms and values, are leading them. Passion for what you do is great to have, and it needs to show in your actions. While they do not have to be perfect at all times, they need to be focused on making the difference you want to make, often led by a vision you let other people know about. Integrity and reliable behaviour (delivering on promises in terms of quality of offer and timing) need to guide your actions with all stakeholders alike, including your associates and suppliers.

"Personality traits" indicates that some personality traits are more often found in entrepreneurs, or much more developed in entrepreneurs, than in traditional managers and employees. Typical traits include willingness to take risks (though always calculated ones), and the others discussed in Section 2.4.2 above.

"Self-awareness and management" is a very important area, if not the most important area. At any age you can be aware of who you are and who you would like to be. In business this is most important, as you need to be aware of how people perceive you and if there is a gap between this perception and the self-perception. Similarly, you need to be fully aware of the added value and limitations of your product and be clear about what potential limitations are. Being able to develop insights about business and yourself requires a good level of self-awareness.

If an attitude you took on while growing up is getting in the way of starting a business, then you need to be able to review that attitude and make a decision if you are willing to change it to be able to succeed or change the kind of business you are aiming to start. Activity 2.2 provides an example.

 Activity 2.2 What advice would you give Cliff?

Cliff, a start-up I know, has the attitude that nothing comes between him and his weekend. His weekend starts at 5pm on a Friday and finishes at midnight on Sunday. He does not want to work but focus on his hobby and area of interest – football. He plays in a local league in the midfield and trains one evening per week and is at games and training camps most Saturdays and Sundays. Cliff lives on his own and has a girl-friend, who is a football fan and happy with the weekend arrangements. Cliff's business start-up is a marketing consultancy, mainly working online, and with rare meetings with clients. As clients increasingly come to him now, he has to make a choice: work over the weekend and reduce his football commitment, or employ a staff member or use subcontractors. Cliff has been trading for eight months and is just about covering his costs. Not taking on more work is not good, he does not yet feel confident to increase his prices, he is not yet earning enough to be able to employ someone and a subcontractor would need training or supervision to provide the quality and style Cliff has developed.

What would you suggest Cliff does?

Typical aspects that need consideration include attitudes to:

- Hard work;
- Flexible working times;
- Working at weekends/evenings;
- What is unethical business practice you will not tolerate;
- What is the ethical business practice you expect from clients/associates;
- Pro-bono work – working for free to get some good feedback for good work to use for advertising, or to support local charities.

There are thousands of tests promising to give you an insight about your skills, knowledge needed and some limited self-awareness, yet less so on attitudes and beliefs.

Figure 2.3 shows a star with seven lines; each one has a scale from zero to seven, where zero means no knowledge/skills/experience/etc. and ten means having a great amount of the same. The second time the star is shown illustrates what to do in order to gain some

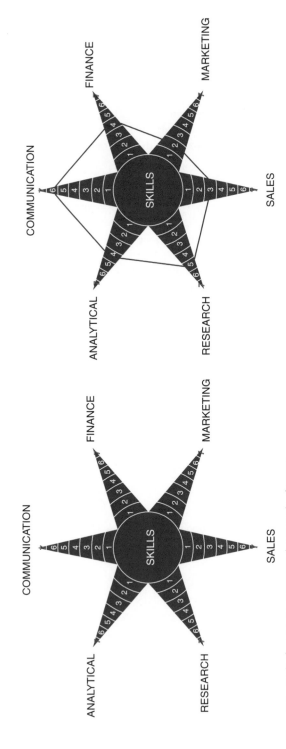

Figure 2.3 Scales for assessing WAASSIP, the example of SKILLS

insight on how you are doing: simply connect the various numbers to indicate your quick self-assessment.

 Activity 2.3   Self-assessment in WAASSIP

Make a cross on each scale for each of the seven areas to indicate where you feel you are right now. Copy the outcomes star in Figure 2.2 or download it from the companion website to this book (www.palgrave.com/companion/hill-start-up). Then ask people who know you and have a positive attitude towards you to fill in the same stars indicating where they feel you are on those scales. Then compare the results. Where there are differences between your and their assessment, ask some questions about why they think this is the case.

Include the results in your start up diary with the dates. Then repeat the self-assessment in six months' time.

Box 2.3 lists a number of websites you can use to assess where you are in your development towards start-up. A note of caution about all tests and their results: they only showcase those traits the test developers regarded as useful. Ideally, you carry out at least three different tests on the same aspect of an entrepreneur and compare the results, and then take from the test results what appears convincing to you.

Box 2.3   Websites with useful tests to carry out a self-assessment

All of these tests show the results immediately and give a short explanation of what they mean.

General test

www.get2test.net – a general enterprise test that attempts to assess entrepreneurial traits, developed and fine-tuned since 1987 (free of charge).

Personality

http://www.entrepreneur.com/personalityquiz – a number of tests that support you in assessing a variety of traits and skills.

Creativity

www.Testmycreativity.com
http://www.mindtools.com/pages/article/creativity-quiz.htm

Social enterprise

www.palgrave.com/companion/hill-start-up

The next question I am asked very often by those preparing to get into business is: when am I ready? There is not an absolute answer to this question that applies to everyone. If you look at the failure rates and reasons for failure outlined in Section 2.1.3, some basic financial skills are important even if you will have an accountant or bookkeeper doing the accounts for you. When comparing your test results and the overall self-assessment in WAASSIP with the most important reasons for failure, which are also discussed in more depth in Chapter Thirteen, you should be able to identify where your development needs lie. Practically speaking, it will help to have some research done on market and industry, and the change to customer experiences that are needed and some practical things in place such as a bank account. Chapters Fifteen and Sixteen discuss getting ready and up and running in more detail.

There are many risks if you just jump into a new venture start-up without knowing enough about yourself and your strengths, weaknesses and opportunities for skills and knowledge development:

▶ You might lack an essential skill or knowledge to at least be able to analyse and monitor what suppliers/partners are doing for you; if you cannot do that, you cannot be on top of your venture, and become rather dependent on others that they at all times have your best interest at heart.
▶ You might not be aware of your most important strengths, and working towards those can save you a lot of time and money; the risk is that you do things that are not meeting your way of thinking and doing things.
▶ You might not bring in a skills set that you lack via partners or mentors so that an important area essential for your venture success is addressed.

There is plenty of training and education for those wanting to become entrepreneurs or simply gain business skills they are lacking, and there are plenty of mentoring support offers. The next section outlines these possibilities and offers. The reason I discuss them in a chapter early on in the book is to indicate that whatever the test results, if you really want to start your own business at some point in your life, there is support available to address some of the gaps identified. For your *sustainable start-up* journey, it is very important to find out early on if you need a particular skill or knowledge, so that you can develop that while exploring if a business idea is an opportunity that can make money. Checking out the need for support and learning early on addresses the practice of sustainability – you need to find out early on if this potential venture is actually one you can and want to carry out. While you can always buy in skills through staff, will you have the money to do so?

2.6　Business skills development and business support

2.6.1　Business support using mentoring and coaching

Mentoring is a conversational approach that offers guidance and supports one person in a semi-structured way. The mentor supports the mentees in reflecting on what they do, what they think and feel about themselves, assists them in developing confidence in themselves and in their business skills. The mentor acts mainly as a sounding board and as someone who encourages the mentees to do what they do better.

A mentor is a person with more experience in business, or simply in life, who can help entrepreneurs hone their abilities and advise them on navigating new challenges, acting as a guide. A mentor can be a boon to an entrepreneur in a broad range of scenarios, whether they provide pointers on business strategy, bolster your networking efforts or act as confidantes when your work life balance needs adjusting. Mentors share their experiences gained in the same sector or transferable experiences to shorten the learning process of the mentee.

Experience has shown that the ideal mentor has industry sector expertise, either work experience and/or sector knowledge to advise on the actual market entry and market positioning in the most optimal way. Most of the time, this sector experience cannot be found, so that mentoring focuses on the personal development and the general business issues, and specialist mentors with sector expertise are asked to add the sector knowledge to the process.

What do you look for in a mentor? There are infinite possibilities, but some core competencies include:

▶ Genuinely interested in helping someone else succeed;
▶ Reliable, honest, trustworthy to keep conversations confidential;
▶ Able to apply active listening;
▶ Willing to empower;
▶ Willing to share knowledge and learning and expertise in an encouraging and non-patronizing way.

The impact of business mentoring is often highly rated by mentees of all ages starting new ventures (Kyrgidou and Petridou, 2013, NESTA, 2014). Typical effects known for face-to-face and online mentoring include:

▶ A higher survival rate;
▶ Knowledge exchange and creation;
▶ Skills development for both mentor and mentee (management, marketing and financial skills in particular);
▶ Increased turnover and growth;
▶ Increased self-confidence of the mentee;
▶ Higher ability to find and execute strategic direction for the company or own business activities;
▶ Higher capability to innovate;
▶ Flexibility;
▶ Increased speed to set and achieve business objectives;
▶ Access to wider networks.

Box 2.4 lists a selection of mentoring networks in the UK, US, Australia and New Zealand that are fully supported by volunteers.

Box 2.4   Mentoring networks for start-ups and SMEs

http://www.business.govt.nz/support-and-advice/advice-mentoring/mentoring-services – New Zealand-based mentoring

https://www.sbms.org.au/ – for Australia

www.micromentor.org – US based

http://www.sba.gov/content/mentor-protege-program – for the US

http://www.mentorsme.co.uk/ – UK based, aiming to be a gateway for business mentoring; many mentoring organizations are listed

"Ethnic coach for ethnic minority entrepreneurs" in Denmark across the country (see OECD, 2013, http://www.keepeek.com/Digital-Asset-Management/oecd/indus-try-and-services/the-missing-entrepreneurs/denmark-ethnic-coach-for-ethnic-minori-ty-entrepreneurs_9789264188167-18-en#page3)

AntrES Women's School of Entrepreneurship in Romania, http://www.antres.ro

The downside of this type of peer mentoring is that:

▶ No formal mentoring training takes place.
▶ No quality check happens to ensure that only those with appropriate knowledge and/or experience give advice.
▶ As a mentee you do not know if the advice given has sufficient quality, as start-ups cannot check the quality themselves; how do you know what you do not know how to ask about?
▶ No protection of intellectual property rights is carried out, as often start-ups are not aware of how to protect their idea, and good ideas are copied/imitated by others.

Keep in mind that it may be beneficial to have more than one mentor, as the support you need might be in diverse areas, and often one person is not able to provide that support so that several mentors are needed. It also means you are not taking too much of one mentor's time.

For social enterprises in the UK there is a mentoring programme run by Inspire2 enterprise, a social enterprise founded by Northampton University and Exemplas, a for-profit company. The service is free of charge, yet is carried out by business support professionals. Thus, this programme counteracts the last three points made above. Box 2.5 gives some further details on the programme.

Box 2.5   Inspire2enterprise.org

Founded in late 2012 as a joint venture between Northampton University and Exemplas, a business development consultancy, the community interest company (CIC) Inspire2enterprise offers free advice, information, coaching and mentoring support to (1) individuals thinking of starting up a social enterprise, (2) established social enterprises and (3) the public sector in activities to outsource services and start social enterprises. The service is predominantly phone-based, but also increasingly offers face-to-face support by regional service delivery partners.

Their three key objectives highlight the national role they intend to take on as a "one-stop shop" aiming to increase sustainability, growth and social impact of organizations. Similarly, they aim to support stakeholders aiming to deliver outsourced services by the public sector or services delivering social change. They wish to work in partnership with other organizations to support enterprise development and success, including market breakthrough of a strategic nature. Funding ends at the end of 2015.

Mentoring is often set against coaching, a support service that is much narrower in approach and does not allow the coach to make suggestions, even if s/he first asks the coached individual for permission. While mentoring and coaching share a number of goals – to empower and encourage the participating individuals – the coaching outcome is much more action-oriented towards clearly defined goals and objectives, related to particular skills or performance areas. The coaching relationship is usually limited to a set number of meetings, while the mentoring relationship can continue over months or years. Most often, coaching is a paid-for service, where more often mentoring is done by volunteers.

In practice, both approaches are often mixed, and business advisers use coaching and mentoring where appropriate.

The practical arrangements of mentoring can vary widely in terms of time period covered (between six weeks and two years), frequency of meetings (weekly to monthly or quarterly), and location of meetings (online, online with webcam, phone, face-to-face, via email) and a mixture of all these varieties.

2.6.2 Business support – focus on business strategy and development

In the UK, there has been no formal government-funded face-to-face business advice since 2010, when Business Link closed, apart from specialised services for manufacturing businesses; it was replaced with online information and some telephone advice from central locations, and not regionally localized staff. Some local authorities in the UK offer some form of business support through their business development departments or externally funded projects followed by regional growth hubs and/or local economic partnerships.

Business support is a mixture of

▶ Providing information;
▶ Signposting to other forms of support and sources of information;
▶ Checking on and supporting writing business plans, funding bids or applications for finance;
▶ Some mentoring/coaching, based on the abilities of the staff member, to discuss potential ways to create a value proposition and operate the business and any other necessary support.

Box 2.6 shows an example of a charity focusing on building enterprise capacity within communities in remote rural areas in Scotland, Growbiz. The approach used is an intensive workshop programme combined with one-to-one support provided by two very experienced enterprise professionals (Figure 2.4).

Box 2.6   Growbiz, a community-based business support programme

Growbiz is a community-based enterprise support service covering Eastern and Highland Perthshire, Scotland, since 2007. It has the legal form of a charity. A small team of two very experienced business support professionals and one administrative staff supports the region with start-up support free of charge; many professional volunteers support the team and the start-ups from the region. Training and one-to-one mentoring are the most important services. The website describes the roots of their approach to community development:

It draws on the principles of Ernesto Sirolli, who believes that the growth that comes from within the community is the best and most sustainable type to have, helping to create vibrant thriving communities in areas which may otherwise struggle.

Over 100 organizations with over 200 jobs had been created by the middle of 2014 (www.growbiz.co.uk, accessed October 2014).

2.6.3 Training

What training is needed and what is on offer? In Section 2.5 you were invited to carry out some tests on your skills, knowledge and experience with business-related tasks, as well as testing your creativity.

Figure 2.4   Growbiz logo
www.growbiz.co.uk

This should have given you a good idea of where your development needs lie. Some skills or knowledge gaps can be addressed with training. There is not currently, and never will be, an overview of business skills related training in the UK, or any other country, as so much changes so quickly.

If you are not currently studying business or are not a student at this point in time, but would like to gain some general management and leadership skills for business start-up, you could do a foundation degree part-time and run at weekends such as by Kyra Ltd (http://www.kyrabirmingham.org.uk), do a part-time degree at a university or attend one of many training courses your local college offers. If you do not study business, a number of universities offer summer courses full- or part-time running over a couple of weeks.

Additionally, you can contact your local council in the UK and find out if it runs any business start-up courses. In the UK, the Business Link helpline mentioned in Section 2.6.2 might be able to help. In most regions in the UK, there are offers for start-up training to get some of the basic skills, such as those offered by NBV Enterprise Solutions Ltd (http://www.nbv.co.uk/).

You could also access some free online training courses via Alison.com or paid online courses in small bites via Learndirect.com.

Essential knowledge and skills to get right to start a business include financial skills, marketing skills including social media for business, and communication skills. The latter are best learned in a group environment.

The next section briefly outlines features of support increasingly offered alongside funding. Funding for start-ups is discussed in Chapter Nine, which focuses on finance.

2.6.4 Funding associated with support

Chapter Nine has a subsection on funding for start-ups with a focus on those that offer a combination of grants or loans with mentoring and training. If you want to inform yourself about those opportunities now, go to Section 9.4.1.

Funding, training and mentoring programmes usually run for a limited period of time such as a year or two years, as funding is rarely given out for longer periods of time. For that reason only examples can be discussed briefly in this book, as the landscape in the UK and other countries changes very quickly due to the limited funds available.

There are a few established organizations in many countries, often in the form of charities or government-backed support, that offer enterprise support for a longer on-going period of time. One example of good practice is the Prince's Trust in the UK, which focuses on young people aged between 18 and 30 (http://www.princes-trust.org.uk/need_help/enterprise_programme.aspx). The enterprise offer by the Prince's Trust in the UK is a combination of a week-long training in business planning and idea development, support in developing the business plan from staff with the Prince's Trust, a small loan of up to £5,000 and mentoring support using volunteer mentors for at least two years. The mentors come from all areas in society, including many retired business people.

The following case study box summarizes the kind of support our student and graduate start-ups actively sought: you can see that they use a variety of sources of support at different stages of the venture creation process, in particular during the pre-start-up phase. Frinter founders Shivam and Muhammad are based in an incubator with permanent office space (see the next section), Ben Smith only ever used the free hot-desking, and Alison and Kathryn benefited from the Prince's Trust. Kathryn also sought other support to develop her niche enterprise, combining mentoring with a small grant through the School for Social

Entrepreneurs; Alexandru Damian gained his most important pre-start-up support during his Master's dissertation at Aston University, where I was his supervisor, and from his family.

 Case study Business support some of the case study start-ups actively sought

HumAnima CIC, Kathryn Kimbley, Wolverhampton (animal assisted therapy)

Kathryn started on her pre-start-up journey with a local business support organization, Access2Business, a social enterprise. She attended their workshops and received one-to-one support while having successfully been accepted onto the Prince's Trust Enterprise programme. After the initial training on business planning, Kathryn applied for and received a loan of £2,000 and a mentor she worked with for nearly two years. In 2013 she then gained a place on a unique programme run by the School for Social Entrepreneurs, a UK-based social enterprise that offers a year-long support programme with a small grant of under £5,000. This programme consists of workshops lasting a day, placement in action learning sets of eight participants, a mentor from the private sector, Lloyds Banking Programme and the small grant previously mentioned. In her second year in business, she decided to engage a private sector coach. For Kathryn, the support by the Prince's Trust and the School for Social Enterprise were the most important support elements from pre- to start-up phrase, and now it is the private sector provider.

Kathryn's situation is unique in the sense that there was no existing market, as animal assisted therapy was not established in the UK at the time of her start-up (see Chapter Nine for more detail on how she financed her start-up). For that reason she sees the main function of the support in the emotional and conceptual re-confirmation of the approaches she is developing to gain customers, and the confirmation on what a long and lonely journey it is to have to create a market for her services.

Frumtious Ltd; Ben Smith successfully gained access to a variety of grants and business support programmes:

At his home university Aston he gained a place on the BSEEN programme, a local start-up support programme funded by Birmingham City Council for students of the three local universities (Birmingham, Aston and Birmingham City University). This gave him access to a small grant of under £5,000, training and a mentor from his sector (the food industry), and access to a business address and hot-desking in an incubator. He then won the 2013 Aston graduate entrepreneur competition (gaining publicity and a small prize of under £300) and a further grant by Santander (for more about his access to funding see Chapter Nine). Ben regards the support from the mentor with experience in the food industry as most beneficial, followed by the easy access to other start-ups in the incubator environment on Birmingham Innovation Campus.

AMD Nobel Pharmaceuticals SRL, Alexandru Damian

Alexandru decided to do his Master's dissertation on the idea to import eye-care products and technical equipment from the UK to Romania (check out his short profile in Section 1.9). He took a module on business start-up as part of his postgrad-uate course, but the main support came during the nine months of his dissertation through his supervisor, which I had the pleasure to be. His most important learning point from the university support was in how to research and to find secondary sources that are already published. Secondly, the ability to develop information sources through existing networks where no information is officially available was an invaluable learning experience for his industry research more so than his market research. During the pre-start-up phase after graduation he worked closely with the associate business partner he met during his extensive research for his dissertation, his parents and their existing networks. He did not seek any external business support in Romania.

Frinter Ltd, Muhammad Ali and Shivam Tandon

The co-founders of Frinter were accepted onto the E4F programme (Entrepreneurs for the Future, an incubator based at Innovation Campus Birmingham, http://e4f. co.uk/). The core service of their business is to offer free printing and photocopying to users in convenient locations. They cover the cost of printing by placing ads with discount vouchers on the back of the printouts. Ad-free printing starts to cost the customer more, but is still less than traditional copy shops or universities charge. The programme by E4F is focused on start-ups in Birmingham that use technology in innovative ways to launch, develop and grow their businesses; they do not have to be alumni of any of the universities. They offer a 12-month programme, with access to an entrepreneur in residence, access to shared hot-desking, and individual office space at a fee, advice on accessing finance, start-up resources, signposting to opportunities and investment. When requested, they also help in finding a business mentor. Shivam and Muhammad experienced the easy access to other start-ups and the mentor as the most valuable support they got, in combination with finance.

2.6.5 Incubators

Many universities and colleges across Europe and the US offer extra-curricular support for learners wanting to start businesses, either while studying or after graduation. In some cases they offer both types of support. Across the UK, organizations and universities are still learning while running incubators what works best for them in their region; the US has a longer experience in running incubators within and outside of education. The term "incubator" is used for small units that offer nurturing support to start-ups (similar to the incubator used to support babies in case of need, such as premature birth).

The sole purpose of provision of those facilities is to provide a nurturing environment for start-ups and in particular find and/or create high growth start-ups (in the research literature called "gazelles", Culking, 2013). The facilities offered can include "hot-desking" where a number of desks with Internet access are available: you can either turn up to use one or can book one on an hourly basis. Other facilities are meeting rooms available to hire on an hourly basis, or permanent shared office space, consisting of a desk access, with telephone and Internet access. Often, in the same facilities, individual rooms can be hired as office space on a contractual basis for six months or a year, exclusively for the start-up. Sometimes, start-ups are happy to have only a business address and occasionally use the hot-desking facilities, with access to broadband Internet. Start-ups can form networks with other start-ups, mentors, business professionals and investors, to name the most important stakeholders in the networks.

Associated services often include:

▶ Reception services (where visitors register and wait to meet the start-up);
▶ Phone answering services, when the start-up is out of the office;
▶ Access to business angels and investors facilitated by the management of the incubator;
▶ Workshops and training in key business skills relevant for start-ups;
▶ Provision of a mentor;
▶ Networking events for incubator tenants;
▶ Access to high-tech meeting rooms for conference calls, using the latest technology in meetings.

Incubators can focus on a particular industry sector, such as creative industries or digital media. Ohio University, Athens has a digital media incubator within its Innovation Centre (see http://www.ohio.edu/research/innovation/digital-media-incubator.cfm, accessed 10 November 2014).

Others operate virtually. With the help of technology, a national virtual incubator (NVI), run by CISCO with support from the UK government, has offered online support since 2011 in the UK. The NVI connects incubation centres, research facilities, science parks and academic institutes through its growing number of national incubator bases (check out the website for further information and which universities have so far joined the network of hubs or nodes, http://nvinetwork.com/). In order to access the facilities, you have to go to one of the connected incubators.

Some universities share facilities, for example in Birmingham in Faraday Wharf, the Birmingham Innovation campus (see http://www.innovationbham.com/contact-us/, accessed 10 November 2014). Birmingham University, Aston University and Birmingham City University run the innovation campus together, and offer a variety of facilities for start-ups. Here is where Ben Smith started his venture. The added value students and graduates gain includes easy access to other start-ups to bounce ideas with, training, networks and business mentors as entrepreneurs in residence.

2.6.6 Accelerators – how are they different to incubators?

Business accelerators are fundamentally different to incubators: an accelerator selects businesses, which have started to form and have developed at least a prototype or done some test trading. The very first seed accelerator was opened in the US, the Y Combinator (see Box 2.7 below). In the UK, accelerator programmes really took off in the late 2000s, one milestone could be the first accelerator programme offered by Seedcamp in London in 2007, modelled on the Y Combinator from the US. Sometimes, successful serial entrepreneurs want to improve the business environment for high growth start-ups and invest into an accelerator programme; few universities have run an accelerator programme. Programmes in the UK only exist in small numbers in 2014, as Box 2.7 illustrates. Investments into start-ups vary between £15,000 and £50,000. As in the US, most accelerators work with cohorts of start-ups. Box 2.7 (Page 66) lists a number of accelerator programmes in selected European countries and the US. Very often, the focus of accelerators is on digital and/or technology start-ups.

The difference between an incubator and an accelerator is comparable to the life stages of childhood and adolescence. While incubators nurture those with a business idea, and support them also to identify growth businesses, comparable to the childhood phase in human beings, accelerators focus on selecting those growing start-ups that will definitely, or rather hopefully, grow quickly into million-making businesses (dollars or pounds), the ones in the adolescent phase of life.

Other differences are:

- The duration of accelerator programmes is often much shorter, such as nine weeks or up to a maximum of six months in most cases.
- Most accelerator programmes take a share in the start-up company (between 5% and 12% most often) in return for the "free" support and start-up investment given.

While accelerators operate slightly differently across the globe, the following criteria have been identified (Christiansen, 2014b):

- Only teams are taken on (with very few exceptions).
- Small cohorts of start-up teams of between five and 15 are taken on at the same time.
- Support is limited in time (between three and six months, rarely longer).
- The application process is open to all, yet few are accepted.
- Investment is provided in return for equity.

While there is not yet clear evidence what criteria the start-up needs to meet in order to be ready for an accelerator, across accelerators the criteria they mention include:

a) A team of founders with equal shares in the new venture;
b) An ability to talk clearly and convincingly about the problem your service/product is addressing and who the market is;
c) Evidence from market testing and research that shows the potential of the product (often called validation of the idea);
d) Evidence of your commitment and passion;
e) Readiness to focus solely on the business and eagerness to take any feedback that can improve the business and act on it;
f) Readiness to grow the business; founders are eager to scale the business activities and receive investment to do so.

What can confuse is the fact that some incubators run accelerator programmes in their facilities for a small selected number of businesses. As the name indicates, there is evidence that start-ups who manage to get onto an accelerator programme grow much faster than others not on the programme (up to 12 times faster) and attract more investment. Overall, access to investment, increase in reputation through having been accepted on the programme and access to mentoring are the most important features "graduates" of accelerators reported (Christiansen, 2014a).

 Case study

Lillie Ranney, one of the case studies in our book, benefited greatly from the Innovation Engine Accelerator for media and digital start-ups offered by Ohio University in 2013 (see Section 1.9 for information on her background). Once she had worked for about a year with her former module lecturer at university on developing the idea, developed a business plan and designed some rough online demos, she applied to the university accelerator programme focusing on digital start-ups and was accepted. As with most start-ups on the programme, she received $20,000 in return for a 5% share in the company to the accelerator, and access to hot-desking, free training, access to resources, information, professional advice (including legal advice), contacts to investors and mentor support, for four months. She came to use the accelerator facilities several days during the week; however, she went back home after graduation to live in Columbus, Ohio. As part of the programme, she regularly had to pitch to potential investors and learned a lot about what investors are looking for and the questions they ask. The exposure to other businesses on the programme, the free support by professionals in IT, legal issues and business mentors combined with the skills training and support were great experiences she did not want to miss.

Box 2.7   Selected business accelerator programmes in Europe and the US

Business accelerators in the UK

- Oxygen – based in the West Midlands, operating Europe-wide
- Seedcamp – based in London
- Wayra UK – for technology start-ups, in London
- Wayra UnLtd – a partnership with the social enterprise UnLtd, supporting digital start-ups that improve society
- Techstars accelerator – in London and Manchester, Barclays Accelerator.

Business accelerators in the Netherlands, Norway, Finland, Denmark and Sweden

- Rockstart Accelerator (the Netherlands) – mobile and web start-ups, smart energy start-ups
- betaFACTORY (Norway) – no specific sectors
- SICS Start-up Accelerator (Sweden) – technology focus
- SE Outreach Accelerator Program (Sweden) – social enterprise accelerator in Stockholm
- Startup Sauna (Finland) – no specific sectors
- Startupbootcamp mobility (Denmark) – mobile devices and related technologies.

Business accelerators in the US

- Y Combinator – focus on digital and mobile-focused start-ups
- Techstars – $118,000 seed funding
- DreamIt Health – for healthtech start-ups, $50,000 seed funding
- Launchpad LA – for California, between $25,000 and $100,000 investment
- Betaspring – up to $20,000 investment as seed funding for technology and design entrepreneurs.

2.6.7 Impact of pre- and start-up support

There are only very limited findings on the impact the various types of support have on the journey from idea to actual start-up. It can be said that existing formal support by professionals is under-utilized across Europe and the US.

The impact of working within professional support varies; it includes:

▸ The increase in numbers of pre-start-ups that actually start trading (Delanoe, 2013);
▸ Increase in speed of venture development, and thus a shorter period of time till firm birth or registration;
▸ Increase in skills that allow for more effective start-up and venture management;
▸ Increase in confidence that leads to increase in skills acquisition, speed in getting to market, higher earnings etc.;
▸ Increase in growth aspirations, and actual time to high growth reduced;
▸ Increase in investment gained and amount of investment secured.

2.7 Concluding remarks and application of new insights

This chapter introduced you to a variety of information about who starts businesses, and pointed out that the likelihood many young people will at some point be self-employed during their career is increasing. The most important motivations for starting a new venture were discussed for for-profit ventures and social ventures. The fast-moving changes in technology mean that many companies in the near and longer future will be employing fewer people overall, and will change their staff, so that many of us will have times of self-employment followed by times of employment; it is important to identify early on the many different flexible ways of doing business today.

The brief introduction to entrepreneurial traits, skills and knowledge needed to be successful in business led to the reflection on your skills and attitudes, using the WAASSIP model. For those who found out where their gaps in skills, knowledge and behaviour might lie, the business support overview helped to develop the confidence that every potential gap can be bridged with appropriate training, mentoring and knowledge development. Throughout Chapter Two and with the help of some of the revision questions further diary entries were developed for the pre-start-up journey.

Revision questions and application of new insights

1 What are the main reasons that business fail in the first years?
2 Define motivation.
3 Explain the difference between push and pull factors in motivation. List some examples.
4 What three contexts does *Start Up* see as factors in motivation?
5 What do you understand by the term "portfolio career"?
6 What has changed in the way of doing business and working?
7 List some common traits of entrepreneurs. Do you have any of these traits?
8 What traits would you look for in a mentor?
9 What would motivate you to start a business? Have you got a skill/talent/hobby you are passionate about? Make notes in your pre-start-up journey diary.
10 Do you know what support for starting a business is available in your town and region? Go and find out and include it in your pre-start-up journey diary.
11 Select some of the tests mentioned in this chapter and carry them out; take note of your results and include them in your pre-start-up journey diary with the date you took them. In six months' time, do the same tests again and see if your answers and results have changed.

WHICH IDEA IS A BUSINESS OPPORTUNITY FOR YOU?

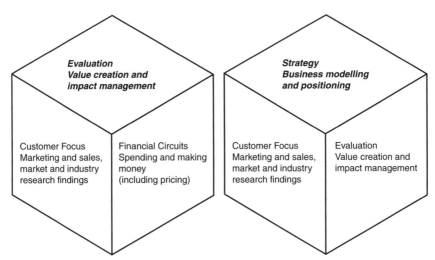

Figure 3.1   The Cube Evaluation and the Cube Strategy
Source: © Hill, 2012.

Summary

The chapter starts by exploring creative problem solving and idea generation techniques, based on recent findings on creativity and problem solving. We outline a possible journey from idea to business opportunity and illustrate briefly some journey experiences. This chapter introduces three key concepts: the business idea (idea generation and discovery), business opportunity and feasibility.

We create a framework for understanding the need to explore if there is a way to make money with an indea and outline the aims of the next seven chapters, which address the feasibility study. We then link to Chapter Eleven, where the conclusions to the explorations of Chapter Three to Ten are drawn. We identify ways to establish if a business opportunity is appropriate for a particular individual or team and finish by discussing business sectors that are expected to need innovations the most and are expected to grow in the next decade. These explorations implement Evaluation and Strategy of the business model cube Figure 3.1)

CONTENTS

3.1 Discovering ideas for starting a venture

3.1.1 Creativity and ideas, logic and "outside the box"

So many people say to me that they cannot start a business because they are not creative at all or not creative enough; after all, you have to be creative to come up with a business idea. Really? What they mean by "creative" and I mean by creative is different.

Problem spotting and problem solving are key skills in business, agreed. But creativity with the meaning of "coming up with something new that has not been thought about or invented before or drawn with brush or pencil" is *not* a requirement. I hope you are relieved now! Remember, Richard Branson made millions without having invented anything completely new, and so did many others.

Creativity is a skill that can be developed. Children are more creative than adults, naturally, and look at, for example, tangible objects in a different way, as they have not been conditioned to think in certain ways. Children, for example, can quickly turn a table with four legs into a ship, by just turning it upside down and using a tablecloth to create a sail. At school, college and university we are often taught to conform in our thinking and behaviour to be successful, and give up some of the creative skills we had as children.

If you always do what you always did, you will always get what you always got.

If you reflect on that statement for a moment, it illustrates that we usually do things in a certain way and rarely vary how we go about our activities. This means that a new *use* of an existing product or service is a good idea, leading to new results or outcomes, and may possibly lead to an opportunity of making some money. But I will talk more about the making-money side of creativity later on in this chapter. For now, follow the invitation for some creative practice: Activity 3.1 invites you to carry out a number of exercises in thinking creatively.

 Activity 3.1 Some creativity exercises

1) Picture 3.1 shows a paper clip. List all the potential activities you could use a paper clip for. You should come up with at least 10 different ways of using it.
(Tip: You can create a simple straight piece of wire out of the metal paper clip!)

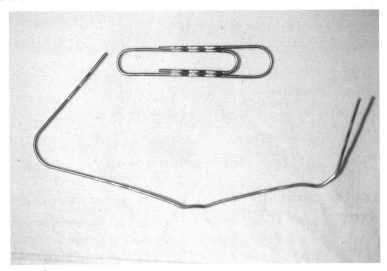

Picture 3.1 Paper clips

2) The next image Picture 3.2 shows two different sponges. Look at the sponges from a number of perspectives, using the following list as a starting point. What could the sponges be used for, in the daily work in that profession or phase of life? Make a list. Add as many as you can think of.

a) Primary school teacher
b) Artist who paints
c) Child carer
d) Elder care worker
e) Car repair shop
f) Two-year-old child

Picture 3.2 Bathroom and kitchen sponges

People often refer to something called "thinking outside the box". "What box?" is the first question. Did you know that most people have about 80% of the same thoughts every single day? The thought loops we carry out, often only half consciously, do not change a lot unless we make a real effort.

Or in other words, once you start looking at something – an event, an object – from different perspectives, you can train yourself to do it more regularly. In one sense, our brain skills or thinking can be developed. In coaching, there is an exercise of re-framing an event, which tries to achieve a similar change of perspective: if you were your best friend X (for X substitute for your friend's name), how would s/he look at the same situation? What would they say? Or if this same event would be in a Western, or comedy, what would the characters have to do to fit into the context?

Similarly, some people think that they are only logical and not creative. Let us unpack that statement. Logic is reasoning conducted according to strict principles of validity. One of the Ancient Greek philosophers (Aristotle) is known to have referred to a particular system using the principles of proof and inference. However, the principles vary in different cultures and professions, and so does logic. There is no single logic system or set of principles that applies in all contexts and is used by all people. Having qualified logic, its link to creativity is simple: apply different sets of reasoning and making conclusions, based on different principles to the same situation, and you will see different elements gain higher or lower priority and new meaning. Is that too theoretical?

 Activity 3.2 A creativity task

Let us take the second exercise in Activity 3.1: a sponge is a sponge you might say? Yes, and no. What materials could be used by the professions listed above to be able to do the tasks you listed in exercise 2? What could they do instead of using a sponge?

And think of a tribe in a remote corner of the rainforest that has no concept of what a "sponge" is. But it has a concept for a leaf with an absorbing material that fulfils some of the absorbing functions we associate with our use of a sponge. Break down the assumed only function or use(s) of the sponge and find other ways of using it. Go beyond the principle that a sponge has only absorbing and cleaning functions and apply principles of having fun.

Applying creativity to come up with business ideas is only one possible application. Edward de Bono, one of the leading experts on creative thinking, developed the term "lateral thinking": a conscious systematic process that leads to innovative thinking (de Bono, 2009). De Bono's techniques leading to innovative thinking include:

▶ Alternatives/concept extracting – finding the common principles and steps in existing common or shared processes that work, and discovering ways to apply them to other processes;
▶ Focus – focusing all attention on seemingly minor and unimportant aspects of daily routines at work, what can you find out about these processes?
▶ Random connections – while exploring an idea, coming up with a random addition, such as a word/picture/image, and then finding out what these two – the idea and the randomly chosen element – might have in common (surprising results are possible).

Box 3.1 offers some background information on creative thinking and creativity, with further information on Edward de Bono. I find it is helpful to explore creativity further and gain experience in thinking creatively.

Box 3.1 Creativity and creative thinking

Edward de Bono is originally from Malta and is a British citizen. He holds degrees in medicine, psychology and design. He held faculty appointments in UK and US (Oxford, Harvard, Arizona) universities, has published over 50 books and trained business people as well as government advisers in being more innovative. His easy-to-read books include:

- *Lateral Thinking* (1977)
- *The Six Thinking Hats* (1985, rev. 1999)
- *Simplicity* (1998)
- *How to Have a Beautiful Mind* (2004)
- *Think! Before it is Too Late* (2009).

The six thinking hats technique invites a team of people or you as an individual to focus on various aspects of a situation (de Bono, 2009, latest edition). These aspects include

- Facts and information needed;
- Potential difficulties and ways something might not work;
- Emotions, hunches, gut instinct;
- Possibilities, alternatives, solutions, new ideas;
- Values and benefits and reasons why something might work;
- Process management of thinking, including focus, next steps and planning ahead.

Where do business ideas come from then? You could apply the six techniques listed above in Box 3.1 to student life or a particular sports activity. There is a long list of starting points for business ideas I could give you; here are some of the most common ones (see also Figure 3.2):

- Many happen by accident, singing (or no singing) in the shower, or while carrying out routine tasks and getting very annoyed with a barrier or something else in tasks that take too much time or resources.
- Post-it notes were a result of a glue-development process gone wrong, as a pot of the new super sticky glue fell down and the notes fell with it, and onto the pot with glue; the technician working on that glue jumped to get the paper off the pot and noticed that it was sticky, yet not permanently sticking to the glue. That was the starting point for Post-it notes and glue types that do not permanently stick two parts together.
- Others come from a need in industrial production processes, where for example the speed of the process needs increasing or waste needs to go down or a raw material is too expensive and needs replacing to enable lowering prices, etc.
- Customers and their complaints and feedback can give pointers for further development or coming up with a new product or service.
- Wish or longing for something to be very different, for example a car with doors that open upwards rather than to the side.
- Change in government regulation or new a law coming into force.

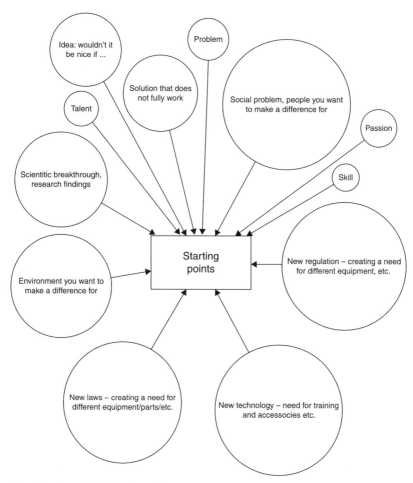

Figure 3.2 Starting points for business ideas

As a summary, there are plenty of sources for ideas for a new service or product, and everybody who wants to be can be trained to find an idea for a potential new start-up. However, if you have not got the patience and/or belief that you can come up with ideas, there are others who are happy for you to take theirs, as outlined in Section 3.1.2, and others who, for a fee, will give you an already proven business model and way of making money – their way – through franchising (Section 3.1.4).

3.1.2 Ideas others have had and published

The world is full of ideas – that is not the problem. It is making them work and turning them into a service or product that can make sufficient money for a long(ish) period of time that is the big challenge. In this section I continue showing you some sources of ideas without evaluating them as yet.

Box 3.2 offers some web links, where others publish trends and developments they regard as in need of new ideas or business ideas.

Box 3.2 Ideas others publish and trends for new businesses

Some online articles and websites include:

Catherine Clifford's article "Hunting for Business Ideas? Consider Looking at These 8 Hot Industries", Entrepreneur.com website (http://www.entrepreneur.com/article/225693, accessed 25 August 2014)

Entrepreneur Press and Cheryl Kimball's "Need a Business Idea? Here are 55", an excerpt from the book 55 Surefire Home Based Businesses You Can Start for Under $5,000 (2009) (see http://www.entrepreneur.com/article/201588)

The Startups Team's article "What Business to Start in 2013: Lean Start-ups" (http://startups.co.uk/what-business-to-start-in-2013-lean-start-ups/)

An online place where people share ideas, Ideaswatch.com (http://www.ideaswatch.com/#)

Richard Branson's article "Top 10 Back Of An Envelope Start-up Ideas" on Virgin.com (http://www.virgin.com/richard-branson/top-10-back-of-an-envelope-start-up-ideas)

A special issue of the NY Times online magazine featuring innovations by their readers "The Innovation Whiteboard" (http://www.nytimes.com/interactive/magazine/innovation-whiteboard.html?module=Search&mabReward=relbias%3Ar)

The above web sources are only a starting point, as there are many other ideas published by others.

3.1.3 Sources for social enterprise ideas

Many ideas for social enterprises also come from daily lives, for example:

The grandchild who regularly visits her grandmother and finds out that the food she gets via meals on wheels is of low quality and not very tasty is inspired to set up her own enterprise, The Gourmet CIC, a social enterprise (http://www.dudleymealsonwheels.co.uk/).

A neighbourhood identifies the need for getting the older people out and about and forms a social enterprise to meet this need.

 Other ideas come from government initiatives, such as the right for individuals, staff or communities to ask to deliver services themselves via a particular form of social enterprise. Here are some typical examples of why individuals and groups of people have formed social enterprises:

- Individuals with an interest in health form a group and then a social enterprise and ask to deliver children's services themselves.
- Council staff who have been made redundant due to cuts in spending find ways to deliver the service, which was previously part of their jobs, and offer other services.
- A need of people with a specific health problem, such as sight loss, is not met; they need specially equipped flats and houses to live independently.
- Young people are unemployed for too long and take the initiative to form a social enterprise that employs young people.

Increasingly, ideas for social enterprise arise where for-profit businesses have had to close down and find different yet still profitable ways of creating the same products and/or services, yet with less resources and smaller profits.

Other starting points for finding ideas, or rather for co-creating ideas that can be opportunities for social enterprises, include:

a) Research on customer satisfaction for a particular product or service and/or the whole company offering it;
b) Problems in the service delivery, often identified as the service gap – the difference between customer perception of a service and company perception;
c) The market introduction of a new tangible product that changes the set-up of the related services;
d) The application of new technology in a sector, which leads to a reconfiguration of existing services;
e) The impact a new regulation or law coming into force will have, training and knowledge and internal systems needed to comply with that change.

The most difficult challenge is to find a way to generate sufficient income that allows for the delivery of the community or social benefit. We discuss this later in Chapter Seven under business modelling.

For those interested in starting a social enterprise, finding the one motivating social mission is important.

The next section outlines a good way into a first start-up for some people: using an existing system, brand and product that works in other places, called franchising.

3.1.4 Starting someone else's developed idea and business format – franchising

Franchising has been around for such a long time, in early forms since the 18th century, some say even earlier. In the 19th century the origins of what we would call franchising today were developed. There is a big difference between just granting a license and format franchising as explained below.

Format franchising refers to the formal act where someone who has had a successful business concept and established their brand, the franchisor, grants permission to another individual or a team, the franchisee(s), to pay for a license and trade under the brand of the franchisor, for a fixed period of time. A contractual agreement regulates in detail what is included and what fees have to be paid to the franchisor. The franchisor remains in control over the way the products are marketed and sold, the brand, the standards of operation and product quality.

There were just under 1000 franchisors in the UK in 2013, that is, a business with a proven concept that has been successfully trading for at least 12 months, ranging from the business-to-business (B2B) and business-to-consumer (B2C) fields to home-run, office-run and van-based enterprises. The franchisor is the company that sells the business concept and system on to a franchisee.

Dependent on the franchisor, the franchise package can include:

▶ Training – fixed amount of days and content;
▶ Assistance through one-to-one support for a fixed period of time;
▶ The brand name and product variety;

> Marketing material;
> Right to sell the franchise on to a third party;
> Support in site selection;
> Support in purchasing materials;
> Quality certification and vendor certification.

The person or organization ultimately benefiting is the franchisor. They sell the concept, marketing, branding, quality standards, etc. that are put into practice by someone else, and often gain a regular income share from the franchisee, or a fixed fee, the management service fee.

Box 3.3 lists some useful websites on franchising that also offer a list of available franchises in the UK, the US, the Netherlands and Scandinavian countries.

While taking a downfall in franchises purchased in the year immediately after the recession, since 2009 there has been a continuing increase year-on-year in the UK in the number of franchises bought. While in general start-up failures are high (see Chapter One), those for franchises are particularly low in comparison, and fewer than 10% of them fail.

In 2013 over 560,000 employees worked for about 39,000 franchise units in the UK, of which the majority held a part-time job; the sector contributes 1% to the GDP (NatWest/ BFA, 2014). Women represent less than 25% of all franchisees.

Box 3.3 Selected national franchise organizations

A book store franchise: http://service.bruna.nl/over-bruna/een-eigen-bruna-winkel-beginnen, NL

The British franchise organization: http://www.thebfa.org

The Dutch franchise organization: http://www.nfv.nl/

A one-stop entry point for franchises in Scandinavia: http://www.franchisearkitekt.com/

The Swedish franchise association: http://www.franchise.se/

A one-stop entry point for franchisors operating across Europe, this link is for Denmark in particular: http://www.franchiseeurope.com/internationalfranchises/denmark/56/

The Finnish franchise organization: http://www.franchising.fi/

Franchises in the US: http://www.entrepreneur.com/lowcostbusinesses/

What are the features adding value and limitations of franchising? That depends on whose viewpoint you are taking, that of the franchisor or the franchisee. For now, we focus on the viewpoint of the franchisee. The most significant limitation is the potential high investment cost for buying the franchise license and the whole package. Where a bad or no credit history exists, that can be a great barrier. While banks may be more open to lending money to a start-up investing into an established franchise system, the loan still has to be gained and then repaid with interest, and this is on top of any monthly fee payable to the franchisor, which all has an effect on the cash flow in the business. Table 3.1 shows, with the

Table 3.1 Added value and limitations of starting a business using a franchise

Added value	Limitations
Much lower failure rate of franchises, therefore less risky for a first start-up.	Initial investment cost (can be several millions), yet no success guarantee.
Higher profitable rate when compared to other small enterprises (for the UK 91% in 2013), higher return on initial investment.	Franchisor retains control over the way in which products and services are marketed and sold, controls the quality and standards of the business.
Opportunity to build personal capital quicker than with individual start-up.	Royalty fee to pay on a monthly basis.
Easier to access bank finance, as major banks more positive towards established franchise systems for start-ups.	Responsibility of following a given system, not much diverting possible.
Less uncertainty when using an established system and quality procedures; less complexity.	Low or no scope for innovation in product and ways to run the business.
Benefits offered through the package bought, including mentoring, training and management support.	Low autonomy in some decisions.
Access to low-cost materials (food ingredients where appropriate) and buying in bulk through franchise system.	No influence on quality of products/ingredients.
Using an established marketing and branding system that works.	
A possibility to gain experience in running a business that can be used for later individually owned start-ups.	
On-going support when up and running that saves money and time.	

longer list of added value features than limitations, that for those happy with less freedom and autonomy for business decisions, franchising can have many positive points. The table, however, does not offer a weighting of the points listed.

Research has identified some of the features listed as adding value as motivations why some individuals start a business using a franchising approach (Mendez et al., 2014):

- Access to a known trademark;
- Assistance pre- and post-opening;
- Higher profitability and faster business development;
- Lower operating cost;
- A possibility to gain experience;
- Higher job satisfaction.

Personal characteristics have not been linked to the motivations listed above in the research cited, which could add value to weight the importance of the motivational factors listed. In their own research, Mendez et al. found that there is a positive link of choice of franchise for individuals with a lower tendency to taking risks, low tolerance of ambiguity and being extrovert (Mendez et al., 2014).

In practice, many franchisees own more than one outlet of the same franchise (called multi-unit franchisees); this has been found for example for McDonald's franchise owners in the US (Lafontaine, 2014). Franchisors gain advantages in giving such a master franchisee control over several units, providing they are good and well established. The new unit benefits from the local knowledge and know-how already developed in the area, and ultimately leads to more profits for the franchisor. Franchising is an established strategy for growth for the established franchisor that is well documented in the academic literature (Lafontaine, 2014, Mendez et al, 2014).

A last thought in regarding franchises is to ask if starting and running a franchise is thought of as an entrepreneurial activity? Our answer is yes, certainly, even though there is some academic debate about how entrepreneurial it is to use an existing proven system of doing business with a given service or product that works elsewhere (Ketchen et al., 2011). As we will point out later in the book, not every business works, in the meaning of is profitable in every location, and for that reason alone finding an appropriate location that allows the franchisee to make money is a key part of an entrepreneurial selection and management process.

 Activity 3.3   Analysing a franchisor

Use the link in Box 3.3 for the UK list of franchisors that are members of the British Franchise Association and select one franchisor. Then answer the following questions:

How much does your franchise opportunity cost?

What does this price include?

What capital costs will be incurred in addition to this price?

What fees will be charged? Do they take any commission on supplies of goods or materials to a franchisee?

Do you have to purchase all or just scheduled items from them?

Does this also apply to equipment?

On what basis do they choose franchisees – how selective are they?

The next section looks at a special hybrid form of franchising, social franchising.

3.1.5 Social franchising

There are also a number of social enterprises that have gone down the franchising route. The history of this type of business model is much shorter, and much less well researched for developed countries (Tracey and Jarvis, 2007, Zafeiropoulou and Koufopoulos, 2013). But do the same principles and goals apply here? Some do, others do not. The journey to finding a suitable business idea that matches your values and market possibilities might be addressed with this business approach. More detail on these kind of considerations are offered in the next sections in this chapter.

From a practical viewpoint, the social franchise is often set up to enable people to work together and share ideas, information and services/products, and to provide employment for the disadvantaged. The founders and franchisors are usually driven by a social goal, such as the employment of the unemployed, the democratization of the economy or tackling climate issues, or addressing poverty and healthcare issues. The social franchise has predominantly a social purpose, and it is often owned by its social franchise members; but it is also a business that makes profits, however, it uses the profits as a vehicle to achieve social impact, making a difference to the lives of selected groups of people.

From an organizational research viewpoint, social franchising can have the two functions of organizational growth (as for business format franchises), while using the commercial objectives and profits to address a social issue and make a social impact (see Zafeiropoulou and Koufopoulos, 2013, for a detailed comparison of social franchising to business format franchising, Volery and Hackl, 2012).

It is acknowledged in the movement around social enterprise franchising that local ownership is important to create dynamic, entrepreneurial organizations that are responsive to local needs. A social franchise often combines both local ownership and the creation of economies of scale that enable more effective enterprises to be developed to satisfy local needs and demands.

Social franchises operate in many different ways; some have a very clearly defined business format that is replicated, while for others the business format is less important. Many social franchises are owned cooperatively by the social franchisees. And usually the social franchisees pay the social franchisor a fee for their support, but neither is a defining feature. For example, for members of the European Social Franchising Network both franchisor and franchisee have to be social enterprises. However, a franchisor always enters into an agreement with the franchisee that regulates rights and obligations (Sivakumar and Schoormans, 2011). Box 3.4 shows some examples of international social franchises from the Netherlands, Italy, the UK and Sweden, and provides the web address of the European Franchise organization; Box 3.3 above also lists the national franchise organizations in those countries.

Box 3.4   Social franchising examples from across the EU

Care for the elderly, ASSIXTO Franchise, Italy (http://franchising.assixto.it/en/)

Open cinema network of film clubs, UK (http://opencinema.net/)

Family planning services for women worldwide, Marie Stopes International (http://mariestopes.org/news/social-franchising)

Supporting young people in creativity, The Mighty Creatives (TMC), UK (http://www.themightycreatives.com/)

Reuse and recycling, handcraft and design, Macken, Sweden (http://www.macken.coop/)

Distributing food sponsored by local people to local families and individuals in need, for emergency situations, Foodbank Network, UK – not a format franchise, but using an established business model (http://www.trusselltrust.org/foodbank-projects)

The social franchise organization for Europe (http://www.socialfranchising.coop/)

In 2014, in the UK there were about 100 social franchisors. What is interesting as a business idea is to adapt business models of business format (for-profit) franchises – there

are over 900 in the UK – and add social benefit features: for example, ground maintenance companies, and as social benefit employ disadvantaged people or people with a
disability.

For the remaining sections in this chapter we discuss the elements that need
analysing to decide if an idea is actually a business opportunity. Chapters Four to Nine
offer guidance on how to find answers to the questions raised for exploring feasiblity.
Chapter Eleven comes back to the opportunity-related questions raised here and tries to
bring them to a concluding answer: is there just a nice business idea or truly a business
opportunity.

There is no best possible sequence how you have to go about reading the next chapters.
One way might be to start with Chapter Seven on business modelling, but in order to
understand that you need to know a bit about researching industry and market (Chapters
Four and Five) and operations processes (Chapter Six). Finding and using money is also
important, and that is discussed in Chapters Nine and Ten.

The next section of this chapter explains in more detail ways to develop ideas and find
out if they are business opportunities, applying the co-creation principle and practice.

3.2   Opportunity development from a *sustainable start-up* viewpoint

3.2.1 Problem spotting and solving as co-creation skills for the start-up

"Be happy and smile" is the motto – isn't that true? There is an attitude amongst some
people that problems do not exist, as you "have to go with the flow" and "let things
happen" and evolve.

A problem, technically speaking, is a perceived gap between the existing condition
of a tangible product or a situation and the desired condition. Does that sound simple?
Problem solving is then a mental process that involves discovering, analysing and solving –
bridging the gap. The ultimate goal of problem solving is to overcome obstacles and find a
solution that best resolves the issue at hand.

And how do you find a challenge or problem?

As a student, think about your daily life, as a professional think about working from your
home. Are there any situations where you feel time and again: if only I had or I could do this
differently, quicker, easier etc. This is the starting point. How do you find a solution? The
steps below try to map out a path for getting you to one.

Seven steps in problem solving:

1 Define the problem.

What is the current situation? What does it feel like? Look like?

*(It would be great if chocolate bars do not melt when left in the car in the sunshine or in a
pocket. Currently, melting chocolate can create a mess in a bag, when the melting chocolate
and fat affect the bag or car seat or leave a stain in the pocket; the taste of the chocolate
changes as well.)*

2) Write an effective problem statement that contains:

▸ A "how" question
▸ Identification of a responsible party to do the task
▸ Action verb, representing a positive course of action
▸ A targeted or desired outcome.

(How could this melting process be prevented? The chocolate manufacturers should use wrapping paper that does not allow the chocolate to melt; I would like to be able to carry a chocolate bar in my jeans pocket without having to worry about it melting, changing in taste and leaving a stain.)

3) Restate the problem so as to uncover the real problem and talking to another audience.

(Chocolate bars should not melt due to heat and should retain their taste and shape.)

4) What is the source of the problem?

(A component in chocolate – fat – changes texture under certain temperatures. Packaging currently allows the temperature change in the external environment to reach the chocolate bar.)

5) Come up with several solutions, even if they may sound silly. At this step anything goes. Consider:

▸ Quantity of ideas over quality;
▸ Capture every idea;
▸ Piggyback on ideas and create new combinations and modifications.

(Thicker wrapping paper of different materials, a metal box with similar materials that protects frozen food in particular bags, frozen liquid in the packaging that melts much slower than chocolate, etc.)

6) Identify the pros and cons for potential solutions.

7) Get feedback from others for these solutions.

8) Evaluate solutions:

There are a number of criteria that play a critical role in solution identification:

Explicit: time limits, cost of the solution, budgets, constraints

Implicit: considerations of personal and team influences such as intuition, team culture, preferences, prejudices, etc.

As a next step, it is important checking early on if that idea or opportunity is right for you, which I call personal-ability. This check realizes the practice of "sustainability", as outlined in Chapter One. The associated steps are explored in the next section.

3.2.2   What is personal-ability of the business idea?

A personal-ability study looks at the viability of an idea with an emphasis on identifying potential problems and strategic fit with the life phase you as the potential start-up are in and your values in order to answer one main question: Will the idea fit into the founder(s) life/lives and values and life stage?

What we call personal-ability is a conscious approach to evaluating your idea and the associated potential market opportunity and its timeliness in the phase of your life you are in or are about to enter. If the latter does not match the opportunity, a start-up would become a personal liability and lead even more likely to a failure.

Is this new? The concept of feasibility has been around for a while, and one approach has considered the team's capabilities and aspirations. What is different is the focus on linking personal life considerations with the business opportunity on the one hand and find out if there is a strategic fit between the opportunity and the personal values and norms on the other hand before business planning even starts. And if at first sight there is no match, then re-evaluate the values needed for realizing the business opportunity and match them to your personal values and norms through adjusting the business model and operational realization strategy.

The process towards the *sustainable start-up* is a dynamic customer-focused approach that evaluates at each stage if the founder(s)' values and the market opportunities can be matched and finds different ways to realize the match. And if a match cannot be realized, then this potential business opportunity is no business opportunity for you and/or your team at this point in time. The reasons can include values, personal norms, skills, financial resources available at the time and phase in life (single parent or carer for an older relative, unemployed etc.). This situation is illustrated by one of our case studies, Lewis Barnes.

 Case study

Lewis Barnes had to realize that the potential business opportunity he had seen for his first start-up was actually not "his" to exploit. These are his words:

> There was a road safety device, a travel device, an American company had it, and I was in talks of getting it over here to be able to distribute it exclusively. Fantastic idea, fantastic product, but the issue was me. I was biting off more than I could chew. It was an opportunity but then I wasn't ready at the time to execute it. The timing wasn't right and where I was with my knowledge and skillset was nowhere near adequate to fulfil the potential of the opportunity.

What kind of values are we talking about? This is briefly discussed in the next section.

3.2.3 Values for personal-ability

 If you think that values are just for older people, then think again. You have values that guide you in what you do. Here is an example: As a student, you do not tell the lecturer that a classmate has copied your work and then just rewritten it. There are values in there – being a mate first, norms related to that you are always supporting your class-mates, never telling the lecturer when a student does not do the work they should.

Values exist in everybody's life, whether you recognize them or not. Life can be much easier when you acknowledge your values – and when you make plans and decisions that make them happen.

Your values are the things that you believe are important in the way you live and work. They determine your priorities, and, deep down, they are probably the measures you use to tell if your life is turning out the way you want it to.

When the things that you do and the way you behave match your values, life is usually good – you are satisfied and content and even happy. But when these do not align with your values, that is when things feel … wrong. This can be a real source of unhappiness. This is the main reason why making a conscious effort to identify your values is so important. Here is an example of a potential mismatch:

If you value family, but you have to work 70-hour weeks in your job, you will not have much leisure time. Will you feel internal stress and conflict? And if you do not value competition, and you work in a highly competitive sales environment, are you likely to be satisfied with your job? Activity 3.4 invites you to consider your personal values.

 Activity 3.4   What are your values?

Here is a list with a variety of values, sorted into categories. If there are values not listed, just add them at the end of the given list under "other". Some values might fit into more than one category, such as "reliable" – it can be in the psychological as well as behavioural category.

Have a look and make a list of the ten most important values for yourself when working. Then try and reduce this list to five. Record the findings in your start-up diary. Carry this exercise out again in six months.

Physical values:
Accurate, clean, organized, orderly, punctual, high quality of output and outcomes, responsive, speedy, effective and efficient.

Other:

Organizational values:
Customer-oriented, committed to continuous improvement, loyal, people-centred, cooperative, team-oriented, communicator, accountable, disciplined, productive.

Other:

Psychological values:
Creative, decisive, innovative, resourceful, loyal, autonomous, with a will to succeed, committed, passionate and having integrity.

Other:

Behavioural values:
Honest, reliable, trustworthy, friendly, approachable, team-oriented, open-minded, responsible, dependable, supportive, sensitive, respectful.

Other:

Value creation in business was mentioned in previous chapters. What does that mean then? It has different meanings for different people. One easy definition is actions that increase the worth of goods or services or even the whole organization.

Many business managers now focus on value creation both in the context of creating better value for customers purchasing their products, as well as for shareholders in the business who want to see their stake increase in value.

A simple example: Customers increasingly value positive corporate social responsibility (CSR) activities carried out by the manufacturer of products they buy, and retailers they use. Increasing CSR activities may be a meaningful way customers appreciate that costs money, but also retains customers and can even bring in more and new customers. It has been confirmed that firms with customers who already have a high awareness of what the firm does realized through intense advertising activities can benefit from appropriate CSR activities that are aligned with the firm's values (Servaes and Tamayo, 2013).

Additional value creation opportunities are discussed in the next section.

3.2.4 Co-creating a business opportunity and start-up

A business opportunity is a proven possibility to sell a product and service in the market to identified target customers for a price that covers the cost and allows you to make a profit that meets your personal and social goals.

The suggested processes are based on my 12 years of business support experience and my own successful service start-ups. Not many start-ups have a plan or steps they go about, and not all advisers follow a structured approach on how to support what their mentees or clients do. For that reason, in 2011, I pinned down on paper the outline and the steps that are the basis of this book, and I validated them through the business support experience I had the pleasure to be involved with.

As outlined in Chapter One, co-creation is a principle and a practice for a *sustainable start-up*, that is, a start-up that does not fail in year one as about one-third does, and neither in year two, just in case you wonder. The essential areas we identified in Chapter One that guide this book and fit around a Cube are:

1 Business Processes: operations and process management
2 Financial Circuits: spending and making money (including pricing)
3 Frameworks: internal frameworks (governance) and legal issues
4 Customer Focus (and Environment): marketing, sales, market and industry research
5 Strategy: business modelling and positioning
6 Evaluation: value creation and impact management.

In previous sections I already mentioned using customer complaints and feedback as the starting point for idea and customer development and outlined the principles and associated practices. For the *sustainable start-up* the following steps are implementing the principle and practice of co-creation for opportunity development.

The processes focus on *creating a change in customers' experiences*, a change that has sufficient benefits so that customers are willing to pay money for gaining these different experiences. And, possibly needless to say, these experiences need to make your product/ service stand out from the others, give it a uniqueness that creates an advantage over other offers in the market, in business terms often called competitive edge.

These processes apply the *theory of change*, a simple but powerful process that focuses on the pathway of changes towards the desired final outcome of the intervention (which may be the result of several smaller changes). An intervention can happen through applying a service or product that creates a change in a user's experience, be that through using a product, a website, eating chocolate or receiving services (including for example a haircut). The outcome you are looking to achieve is to come up with a sufficiently big experience of change so that someone buys the product (or service) and that you are willing and capable of creating this change.

In all start-ups I have met or worked with, including my own, at the bottom of why they are creating the business is that they want to create a change in someone's life, including their own. Box 3.5 lists one example of a possible journey with all the processes from starting points for ideas to start-up that this book explores with you. Just to make it clear, just like the dice falls, the sequence in the steps will be different for many start-ups, dependent on money available, sector and product type; however, at some point they will go through most of these "steps" in some way.

Box 3.5   Processes with 18 steps leading to a *sustainable start-up*

0 Starting points (see Figure 3.2).

1 Idea about a customer *problem* and ambition to *make a change* to customers' lives or work.

2 Offer a *solution* to a situation or a gap/problem, with potential to make money focused on making a difference to the customer's life or work. Develop the first version of theory of change stating what customer experiences are essential to change.

3 Create a *change statement* summarizing the benefits your solution can bring to the customer.

4 *Research* Part I: Conduct secondary industry research, including competitor research, research on competing products/services, suppliers for potential solutions to be produced. Conduct secondary market research, on population, customers, their profiles and behaviours. Within that process develop ideas on who has the problem, develop target customers, look at several possible groups, remain open that group membership/structure can change. Gather information on how this change can be brought about (early considerations on the production of change).

5 *Ask the customer*: Explore the problem or need: how long has it existed? How did it come about? Is the solution you plan to offer different from what is out there, and can it make a difference? If not – adapt the solution.

6 *Refine* the change statement and develop the next version (2) of the theory of change. What experience needs to change so that customers actually want to pay for those most important benefits (one or two or more) and associated features that make a difference to their experience?

7 Research Part II: *Reality check*.

   a) Develop a mini-product or model of your product, a test product, based on the findings so far. Research customer views on solutions they really need and want to pay for, what the most important change is they are seeking; research the scope of a price they are willing to pay for various degrees of change and which features can achieve that in the best way, and the level of sophistication/depth of that feature. Can you narrow down the target customers to one or two groups?
   Aim to find out the answer to *less is more*.

   b) Research industry experts and their views.

8 Refine the test product after the research phase: Check if something has to change in the theory of change and what features are essential, which are nice to have; try some *test-selling* of services/products where possible.

9 Research Part III: Check if you have to *refine the offer* through even more customer research through offering the trial version or model; gain scope of price customers are willing to pay for various degrees of change experience.

10 *Refine the change statement* (3), focusing on the clearly most important change(s) a customer group is seeking, with the features that are required.

11 Start *business modelling* in all areas: how can these features be added/produced that can make the most important change customers are seeking? Look at operations and cost in detail and decide on a legal form and governance structures. Create the *customer persona* – a detailed profile of the persons who will buy the product straight away.

Have you got all the information you need to establish how you can generate customer value and make money? If not, do some further research, go back to 6) and go through the steps 6 to 10 again.

12 *Financial planning and forecasting* in business modelling – those considerations can be seen as part of step 11.

Check: can you produce at the cost you need to be able to so that you can sell at the price customers are willing pay? If not, what cost can you change?

Decide even if there is no scaleable business opportunity that can make millions, potentially, if you are interested in going ahead with it.

13 Pretend a storm destroyed all your notes and findings – go through steps 3 to 11 again.

14 Finalize the conclusion you can draw towards identifying that you have a feasible business opportunity; if that is not the case, repeat steps 3 to 11, and if that does not help, go back to the very beginning, step 0.

15 Start *business planning of the actual start-up* (addressed from Chapter Twelve onwards).

16 Decide *what kind of outcome* you need and who for, an informal document and lots of flip charts/online whiteboard files or a formal written business plan.

17 Work with your stakeholders on the planning and at the same time *prepare the actual official start of trading.*

18 Write two versions (at least) of a *business plan* – for internal use and for marketing PR purposes/investors/banks, etc.

START UP

As this is only Chapter Three, do not worry if you do not understand all the processes listed in Box 3.5. The book guides you through the process in the following chapters.

Part of that longer process is to find out first if a business idea you are interested in is in fact a possible business opportunity. The following eight steps focus on the process of identifying if an idea is a business opportunity, and offer a shortened version of the first 14 steps in Box 3.5. This opportunity exploration process is often called feasibility study, and ends with step 14 in Box 3.5.

Step 1

a) Have you got an idea? Does this idea solve a problem, address a customer problem or add true value to a customer experience? If not, engage in customer checking – do they share your belief that there is a problem, a need for change?

b) You do not have an idea? What area in life are you passionate about/interested in/care about?

Read customer reviews, customer complaints, talk to those working with users of solutions in that area.

Once you have identified something that can make a change to customers' experiences, these considerations get the dice (Cube) rolling, onto one side; ideally you are looking now at the "market and industry research" side.

Step 2

You have identified there is a problem/need customers have; explore this problem or need. How long has it existed? How did it come about?

Do your research and go to Chapter Five on industry. Consider, what other solutions exist, which other companies and trends in that industry? Follow the guidance in Chapter Four – who has the problem, can you divide them into groups based on the problem? These processes of industry and market research can happen simultaneously.

Are there any legal issues/ethical challenges why this problem should/could not be solved?

Step 3

What do customers say the solution could be? Go and ask them, and find out what they have published already on social media and discussion groups.

Step 4

What is needed to make the solution happen? Look at the operations chapter and find out which activities need carrying out to achieve the change and what input in terms of resources are needed (Chapter Six), and find out what a business model is (Chapter Seven). What can you change?

Step 5

Can you and others afford it (production cost and selling price)? And what money can be made with it? (Chapter Nine)

Step 6

Create a solution prototype and then test it; what works/does not work? Can you adapt what does not work? Do you need to know more? Go back to Step 2. If it is a service, offer the service for free to one of the target customers, what do they say? Gain their feedback and adjust the service where appropriate. What you are looking for, something that makes enough of a difference and does not cost too much to make, is often called a "minimal marketable product".

Step 7

After another carrying out another version of Step 2, review the cost and operations – adjust the business model Step 4, repeat Step 6, check personal-ability.

If this idea is still not an opportunity, repeat Steps 2, 4 and 6.

Step 8

You can draw the conclusion that this idea is an opportunity. Start business planning and preparing the business launch, the actual start-up.

As you need a lot more insight and research findings, the next chapters support you in developing these insights. When I use "insight" I refer to conclusions you have drawn based on reading and research, not just the intake of knowledge, in other words, personalized knowledge. Chapters Four to Ten support you in carrying out the suggested Steps 1 to 7. Section 3.3 explains in more detail and business language what is involved in this exploration process of discovering if an idea is a business opportunity.

3.3 Aspects of business feasibility – an overview

A feasibility study answers the following question: will a proposed business idea work in the marketplace? Meaning, can it make sufficient money for the founder(s)?

"Feasible" is often used as a technical term and means it is possible (and practical) to do something under a set number of conditions. That is why we talk about business feasibility, that it is practical and possible, suitable, within the context of fit between the person, the external environment and the business type and sector to start a proposed new venture.

The question you might have now is: why should I carry out a feasibility study? "I *know* this will work", is something I have often heard when talking to enthusiastic young and not-so-young adults who have a great idea. But *how* do you know it will work?

The *feasibility study* explores various scenarios, for example, on how a business could work; and then one is selected as the most feasible. In contrast, the *business plan* shows the one selected way of how the business will work in great detail. There are great risks if you do not carry out a feasibility study. You might spend money and time on a product or service that does not offer an adequate solution to a customer problem. You might spend all your savings (or those of others) and create a financially difficult situation for yourself. You might find out too late, in a few months' time, that there are not enough customers out there willing to pay the price you need to get. Chapters Four to Eleven assist you in finding out if there is a viable opportunity for you.

Figure 3.3 shows an overview of the areas for opportunity identification. I call them "fit" in order to visualize that it is like matching pieces of a jigsaw together. All areas need to be concluded with: "yes, this area is feasible" in order to be able to come to an overall conclusion that a business idea can be turned into a business that can make money in line with the personal goals of the founder(s).

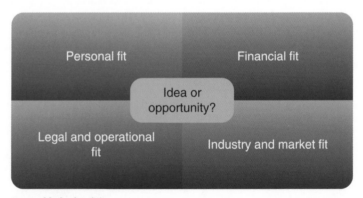

Figure 3.3 Areas of fit for feasibility

Technical, legal and operational feasibility are represented by *legal and operational fit*. What does that include? Here is a list of the most important aspects of feasibility (see, for example, Mullins, 2012), which the next chapters explore:

1) Technical feasibility

Technical feasibility is an assessment of what the technology is that is needed, if any, and what it might cost. This includes evaluating what machines you might need and what their productivity can be, and what other equipment you need. Consider having to take payments electronically and that not everybody will use PayPal. Does the selected site for production meet the requirements of the technology, and vice versa?

Can you outsource production and save money? Or reduce risks?

2) Legal

What licenses are needed? What permissions do you need to obtain to trade legally?

For example, in the UK to sell alcohol to the public from business premises, a number of licenses and permission are needed, including a formal qualification/accreditation that allows you to sell to the public. You also need to have a permission to store alcohol safely and securely. Can you do that with the selected premises? Or can you store it in a location where the premises manager already has all those licenses in place?

What laws affect your trading activity? Health and safety regulations and employment law are the most important ones for most businesses, and environmental laws as well for others.

3) Operational, including management, feasibility

This section aims to establish the optimal way of trading. This needs to establish if you will trade fully or partially online, if you need office premises and/or warehouse premises. The study needs to explore the best value for money in the location of premises. You need to find the best suppliers and their cost, establish the skills needed to run all your operations and identify which ones you might outsource. The latter means that part of the business functions, such as payroll or manufacturing itself, could be carried out by an external party on a contract basis.

Management feasibility. You need to discuss the requirements for the management of the venture, the skills and knowledge needed. Give evidence that the required skills and knowledge are met by the suggested individual/team or that a particular function is covered by a subcontractor, such as a finance specialist who works for only a limited number of days for the company.

4) Financial feasibility

Financial feasibility is represented by financial fit. What does that mean? The main purpose of the financial feasibility study is to indicate the venture's potential to generate income and profit. For that reason it should address, for example, the amount of start-up cost, running cost and the time it takes until your income is larger than the cost, on a regular basis. You need to establish where you can get money from, as your personal savings might not be sufficient to cover the start-up cost and the working capital for the first months or even the year.

5) Market and industry feasibility

Market and industry feasibility are represented by industry and market fit. The purpose of the *industry analysis* is to establish the driving factors in the industry: is it technology (in the subsector of smartphones), limited natural resources (as in the oil industry) or skills of people (as in engineering for aerospace products)? It usually is a combination of at least two of the above. You need to establish how competitive the industry is and whether it is growing or declining (the CD industry sector is in decline). The next chapter discusses these aspects in more detail.

The purpose of the *market feasibility* is to establish what the current and potential size of the market is and establish patterns and trends in demand for this product or service. The study needs to establish what price customers are willing to pay for your suggested product(s), and where these customers shop, for example.

Before you write a business plan, you should be able to outline a feasibility report. This can be done as a mindmap or poster as this is mainly a report for internal use and your internal stakeholders. However, investors and banks might ask for a summary of your feasibility research, and then the headings in Box 3.6 give you the required outline.

For banks, or grant bodies, or even investors, you might have to create a report summary, providing the results of this process and that you have identified an opportunity. Box 3.6 suggests some headings; however, they need to be adjusted to your particular business. Some of the headings might sound unclear, after all this is only Chapter Three. Chapters Four to Ten guide you with more detail in achieving this report. Chapter Eleven offers help in bringing all insights to a conclusion on feasibility of the business idea.

Box 3.6   Possible structure and headings for a feasibility study

Title page

Contents

List of figures, tables, pictures, graphs

Executive summary (about two pages, offering the conclusion that there is/is not an opportunity for a business)

Introduction

    Study objective – to explore if there is an opportunity

    Scope of the study

    Justification for the study – why is it needed?

Industry feasibility

Market feasibility

Technical feasibility

Legal feasibility

Operational feasibility

Financial feasibility

Business model

Personal feasibility

Risks and limitations (with timelines and scheduling)

Conclusion

  (This includes the recommendation to pursue this business idea and in what way.)

References

Appendices

The last section in this chapter briefly outlines what innovation is – discussed in the media and on the Internet too often in a misleading way. The *Start Up* viewpoint is that innovation means the successful launch of a (new) product or service in the marketplace. This means selling it at an appropriate price to target customers successfully. However, you can only sell something if you know your idea is a business opportunity. So why is it in this chapter you might ask? Again, we can unpack the myth that an idea has to be totally unique; innovations can be simply introducing an existing product to a new customer group or new region. Thus, the next section explores what newness for an idea or product really means through exploring the concept of innovation.

3.4 Innovation processes

3.4.1 Is innovation the same as a new idea?

Many people seem to believe that idea and innovation are the same, yet nothing is further apart. An idea is a thought that something would be nice to do or have, such as a car that can also be turned into a plane on pressing a button.

  An innovation is a proven ability of a new product or service to generate sufficient income through selling in at least one market; sufficient means that the sales price not only covers the cost but also meets the personal financial goals of the would-be entrepreneur(s), that is, the amount of profit they want to make.

  And what does "new" then mean? Something that did not exist before, ever? No, newness has to be seen in the context it is put into: new for a customer group who has never used a skincare product before, or new for the region – a product has not been sold in that region before. These are only two examples of how "new" in this context can look.

  The other term used often in this context is "opportunity": that is the possibility to sell a product/service in the marketplace. It does not have to be a totally new product/service. One example: if the idea of having wrapping paper for chocolate that prevents it from melting costs so much to produce that the price of a chocolate bar has to go up to £2, you have a problem. Nobody wants to pay £2 for a chocolate bar if it is the packaging that has increased the price to that amount. Conclusion: there is no business opportunity.

  The suggested steps in Section 3.3 support the related research findings on the importance of spending time and effort on exploring whether the business idea is actually a business opportunity in order to reduce the high start-up failure rates. These activities need to be carried out for their own sake, going beyond establishing some evidence in order to access funding from grant bodies or banks (see for example Yusuf, 2012).

The next section explores ways to differentiate innovation, looking at the focus of what is different, product, environment and business processes.

3.4.2 Types of innovation

Innovation can be differentiated in many ways. One way is product focused (based on Schumpeter, 1982):

1) A new product or substantial change in an existing product, including services. Examples for a new product include the smartphone or the energy drink Red Bull. An example of a substantial change in an existing product is a car that can turn into a boat to be driven in water as well as on the road.

Explore what our case study companies did:

Kathryn Kimbley from HumAnima CIC has a new service for the UK – animal assisted therapy. Frinter's services offered by Shivam Tandon and Muhammad Ali are new – free printing for students with advertising on the back of each copy or print-out, new for the West Midlands at least. Lillie Ranney came up with a truly new offer with online portfolios for her first business; Richard Rodman, Crowdentials, offers a new service in a new market that is still developing, crowdfunding platforms. His offer is a combined service of legal and IT advice with its software implementation.

2) A new process, be that in production, marketing, customer service etc.

Can you use different delivery channels or create a different customer experience? Can you change the customer service? For example, training that is delivered only online and not face-to-face.

Explore what one of our case study companies did:

Lillie Ranney created an online portfolio platform to showcase achievements with Foleeo (see Section 1.8.8).

3) A new market (for an existing product).

This could be a geographical market – selling to a new country or another area in a different part of the same country; or a new demographic – selling to a new customer group, such as selling a product to men that was previously sold to women only. Nivea developed a whole product range for men in the early 1980s. Similarly, introducing those aged over 65 to using PCs and the Internet a decade ago was a market innovation; the existing products were sold to another population group differentiated by age and the lack of experience with the use of the Internet for personal use.

This is what our case study Alexandru Damian did: he imports existing eye-care products into Romania from the UK.

4) New sources of supply.

Examples include using plastic instead of natural materials such as wood, for example, for small tables or flowers.

This is what one of our case study companies did:

Ben Smith, Frumtious, produced fruit jelly. Fruit jelly as a product is not new at all. What was new were the ingredients, all natural in origin, and based fully on fruit juice, without any additives.

5) Changes in industrial organization.

One example can be a change in the supply chain (see below), for example the ability to cut out a step in a manufacturing process, or the wholesaler. A student start-up, Kyu-Kyu, uses her language ability in speaking and writing Mandarin to import gift products directly from manufacturers and wholesalers in China. She then sells them via her eBay shop. She cuts out the UK wholesaler or importer and can for that reason sell the gifts at lower prices, yet still make a significant profit.

This is what one of our case study companies did:

Richard Rodman, Crowdentials, is offering a fully online service combining legal, IT and financial advice in one service offer for crowdfunding platforms. This cuts out those who simply give advice on legal issues, traditional solicitors, as he offers the advice *and* the implementation.

Supply chain is another technical term that summarizes the network of companies and all steps in a process from raw materials to producing and distributing that lead to a final product, such as a pair of jeans. The chain starts with the producers of cotton, then via the handlers of cotton wool and the spinners to those creating fabric, adding colour to the fabric, sewing the jeans, bringing them to the UK and selling them in high street stores.

Since the development of this model by Schumpeter, other types of innovation have been discussed. These include business model innovation: in one viewpoint this includes changing the way a product is delivered and the place of business. There is a great increase in mobile services, where services are delivered at the workplace or home, often in vans. Pet grooming services, for example, have been mobilized and there are a now a number of franchises that offer pet services at home, parking a van equipped to carry out all pet grooming services on the street or in the customer's drive way (e.g. Dial-a-dog-wash, www.dialadogwash.com, or Barking-Mad-Grooming, www.barkingmad.com, accessed 10 December 2014). Mobile veterinary services are also offered (see for example The Mobile Vet www.mobilevetsurgery.co.uk) and similar innovations exist for replacing car windscreens (www.nationalwindscreents.co.uk) and buying car tyres (www.blackcircles.com). Online retail and service businesses innovate similarly, through changing the place of business from face-to-face in real time to online and in a time frame chosen by the customer, the most well-known example being Amazon.

There are numerous ways to differentiate innovation. Another differentiation focuses on how big the difference is in the customer experience through using the new product or service:

Disruptive innovation

A disruptive innovation can be a simple easy-to-use product intended for the masses at a much lower cost. That innovation can be achieved most easily through simplifying the product and/or user experience, lowering the cost and selling price and reducing the complexity through reducing the number of features. This concept of disruptive innovation goes back to Clayton Christensen. One example is the iPod shuffle. The difference was that through a very tiny device the user could ask the device to randomly choose songs to play. The difference in size and weight allowed for the device to be carried around everywhere the user chooses, including at the gym and when jogging, without the awkwardness of having to strap on a weighty device.

Radical or breakthrough innovation

This type of innovation most often signifies a large, discrete step change in performance, technology and/or value provided to end-users. This can take a while and needs lots of research and market testing and research and adaptations and market testing ... One example is the development of the smartphone, a significant step up from the mobile phone functions that existed before.

Incremental or sustaining innovation

A continuous improvement to a product developing generations of the product such as iPhone 2, 3, 4, 5 – until the product reaches the end of its life cycle – you get the idea? Ways to go about these innovations include:

▶ New features and some challenges or bugs have been fixed; iPhone or Samsung smartphones are examples;
▶ Product line expansion or variations, more sizes, colours, different materials, etc.

And some products simply cross over all types above: the iPhone when it came out for the first time was a disruptive and radical innovation in the mobile phone segment.

What can we take from that differentiation? Again, innovation does not have to be something brand new; it can just be doing something for the first time in a geographical market or organization that has not been done there before in the same way.

Some authors focus their start-up advice only on so-called innovative or entrepreneurial start-ups that create unique products and services, and call those who enter a market with a slightly changed service or product or just with the same product or services "me-too" start-ups. Another marketing agency or photography studio are examples where the differentiation to existing competitors is subtle. *Start Up* focuses on all possible start-up journeys, and does value the new ventures started in existing market segments with a slightly changed offer. Realistically, the large majority of start-ups offer something that is already existing in the marketplace in some form. For a large number of self-employed people and partnerships across the world, this is a way of earning a living for an individual and even a whole family and deserves adequate attention and support.

We do not discuss the process of innovation in detail here, as this is outlined in detail elsewhere (see the Further Reading section on the companion website).

3.5   Concluding remarks and application of new insights

This chapter outlined where you can possibly get an idea from if you have no idea yet for starting a business. Franchising was discussed as a way to implement someone else's business idea and use an established business format and marketing. We then discussed several starting points for the pre-start-up journey: a passion and interest, a particular talent or skill, a problem you seek a solution for, something truly fun to do, an insight along the lines of "wouldn't it be great if we could ...". From there we outlined the journey stages from discovering this idea to finding out if it can be an actual business opportunity, a way simply to earn a living for an individual, to make a fortune or to solve a social problem in a profitable way. Most importantly, we differentiated a business idea from a business opportunity.

Part of this journey is to establish early on what your most important values are, and to what extent these values can be addressed with the business idea you have. We then explored briefly a seven-step process of co-creating an opportunity the *sustainable start-up* way this book offers. The technical term for this business exploration was discussed in the subsection on feasibility, and the various aspects of feasibility were briefly introduced (personal legal, operational, financial, market and industry fit).

The chapter finished with a discussion of basic types of innovation, unpacking the myth that an innovation has to be bringing a complete new, never-seen-before product, process or service to market.

Revision questions and application of new insights to your business idea

1 Write down your understanding of the term "creative".
2 List some sources for ideas.
3 What is franchising?
4 Define a business opportunity.
5 Why are values important in business?
6 What types of innovation are there? What is your most favourite recent innovation?
7 What business ideas are appealing to you right now? Start with the "What if *x* existed, my life would be so much easier/I would have so much more time/it would be so much more fun" scenarios. Note them down in your start-up diary.
8 Go into a supermarket and look around and talk to people there. Ask "What could be better for you?" When they have products in their basket, ask why they bought this particular brand. Note the answers in your start-up diary. Have you got some new ideas? Which of those appeal to you? For asking these kind of questions to more than a couple of people you might need permission from the shop manager.
9 Go into a shopping centre and look at what people do outside of shops. What is missing for them? Ask them. What could be done better in their view? And in your view? Have you got some new ideas? Again, note them in your start-up diary.

The next chapter introduces industry analysis, including the analysis of competitors.

4

SCANNING THE ENVIRONMENT – RESEARCHING THE INDUSTRY

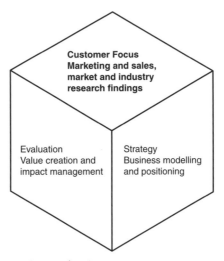

Customer Focus
Marketing and sales,
market and industry
research findings

Evaluation
Value creation and
impact management

Strategy
Business modelling
and positioning

Figure 4.1   The Cube Customer Focus and environment
Source: © Hill, 2012.

Summary

Chapter Four discusses the need for analysing the industry and offers practical ways to go about the analysis, find data and draw conclusions. This research is illustrating how to use the Cube areas "Customer Focus (and environment)" (see Figure 4.1). The practical suggestions shed light on how the feasibility of an industry for a *sustainable start-up* can be established. In the process, suggestions for evaluating the industry opportunity are offered. This chapter introduces a number of frameworks and models that support this process and illustrates ways to apply them to research on a business idea. It discusses PESTLE, Five Forces, supply and value chain, and industry life cycle while providing information sources that can be used to carry out this research successfully.

CONTENTS

4.1   Reasons for investigating the environment and times for research

4.1.1 Why carrying out research is essential for the *Start Up* approach

One of the most important reasons why many businesses fail is that the founder(s) investigated neither the end-users and/or buyers nor the industry sufficiently before start-up and while running the business. Too often, carrying out research is regarded as a waste of time. Agreed, it does take a lot of time, yet it is always worth the effort! For that reason it is worth finding out, what is research? Simply put, in our start-up journey **research is a purposeful search for information and insights** that supports the map creation process.

The two main sources of information for research are (1) already published information and studies you can analyse yourself for your own purposes, called *secondary data*, and (2) information you gather yourself directly, for example through interviews, questionnaires and focus groups, called *primary data*.

Here are the main reasons why research is essential and what it can tell you:

 Having a fantastic product or service is not by itself a guarantee of success. You have to know whom you will offer it to and at what price and what possible substitute products are out there. Conducting thorough research on the environment, sometimes described as "environmental scanning", is one of the success factors for the sustainable business start-up. Learning about what competitors are doing or have done can save you money and time in developing your own product – why reinvent the wheel? There might be reasons that a product or service is not being offered, perhaps others tried it and it did not generate sufficient money to make the production and sales of it sustainable. Similarly, knowing what others found out about the market and the customers' behaviour can save you money and time in selecting the most appropriate first customer.

Research on the business environment is essential because it offers insight into the industry (1) and the market(s) (2).

1) *Industry* is often defined as a group of businesses that either produce the same or similar products (always here including services) and/or are contributing to producing a more complex product such as a car. The companies in the supply chain that leads to the end

product car and competing producers such as BMW and Tata are all part of the same industry. They often use similar or the same raw materials, ways to refine them, technology, etc.

2) *Market*. There are many definitions of "market": one is a group of customers that are buying a type of product. Another one focuses on the exchange and talks about the place where buyers and sellers meet to exchange goods for other goods or money. The customer group can be defined loosely or very precisely, with a lot of detail. Market insight is discussed in Chapter Five.

If you do not carry out any research, and just rely on your "gut instinct" or personal impression and that of others who seem to know (or at least claim they do), you expose yourself to a number of risks. These include:

▶ Not targeting the best possible customer group, and thus you not selling as much as possible;
▶ Offering the product/service in the wrong way – not focusing on solving your customer group's pain;
▶ Spending money on marketing materials for these customers, using language that does not "speak to" them;
▶ Not being to able to sell to anyone beyond your friends, family and their friends;
▶ Losing the money invested, as you do not sell beyond those circles;
▶ Entering an industry that is in decline and other businesses are leaving, and thus wasting money on customers who are about to move to a different distribution channel or product altogether (e.g. CDs and DVDs have to some extent now been replaced by downloading music and films).

The purpose of the industry analysis is to *establish the driving factors* in the industry: is it technology (in the training subsector – online learning), limited natural resources (as in the jewellery industry for luxury items – gem stones), or skills of people (for example, in medical research)? It usually is a combination of at least two of them.

But when should you do research? And how?

4.1.2 When research is necessary

When? The question should really be *how often* should you do it during the pre-start-up journey and while running the business. Once you have an idea and think it is unique and never done before, well, then is the first time you should do some research. Carrying out research is like having regular check-ups with a doctor – it helps you to find out if you are still up-to-date with the demands of the industry and market and if you are still fit to deliver.

The next time you should carry out some research is when establishing what the trends and patterns in the industry are, in particular what technology might affect your product and service, now and in the next three to ten years.

And in order to understand what your potential customers currently like/do/buy/prefer you have to carry out secondary research, establishing what others have found out already, as well as doing your own research. The latter is essential when you have a location for a brick-and-mortar business in mind in retail or in hospitality, such as a restaurant, or a service such as hairdressing or mobile pet services. You have to establish to what extent the general market research findings carried out by others in different locations actually apply to customers in your target area. Or the target area you select for your business to start with.

Finding out who is selling similar services/products in your chosen area is a must, you need to find out who the competitors are – this also applies when starting an online business. You can learn from competitors how big the potential group of customers is that are willing to spend money on your product/service and why they currently buy from existing businesses.

All this kind of research needs to be carried out as early as possible to identify if your idea can be turned into a profitable business opportunity.

A business opportunity is an *evidenced possibility* to sell a product/service in the marketplace to *identified customers* successfully at a price that allows you to cover your cost and make the profit you deem sufficient. This is an important differentiation – an idea is just that, nothing tangible as yet.

Does this apply to social enterprises?

All the considerations discussed so far in Section 4.1 and the remaining parts of this chapter also apply to social enterprises. Additionally, it is worth identifying other social enterprises in the area you intend to start up in, your micro-environment, in order not only to establish who is competition, but also to locate potential partners for collaborative bidding, resource sharing and development. This is addressed further in the following chapters. Nationally, finding a similar social enterprise might serve as a model to learn from and provide you with ideas of how to shape your own social venture. There are a number of databases that list social enterprises that can be searched by location, region or postcode. They are briefly outlined in Section 4.3.

Those women and men who make a second start-up or find out that business is not coming in as expected identify very quickly how important research is, sometimes rather too late, when they have already spent a lot of money on marketing and products that do not bring the profit they were hoping for.

Three of our case studies, Lewis Barnes, Alexandru Damian and Lillie Ranney identified early on how important research was for their success or failure (see Chapter One, Section 1.9 for further details on them and their ventures), and they operate in three different countries.

 Case study

Alexandru Damian points out that learning how to research is the most important skill he learned during his Master's, in particular during his dissertation:

> The highest benefit I consider to be from learning [at university] is how to learn, and learning how to research. This is the one thing that has changed me entirely. Learning how to research. It changes everything because before … and I have friends who feel incapable to get the information you need because [they] don't know how to. Learning how to research, learning how to get the information you need, where to search, that's what made the difference [in my business].
>
> I know how to find people that have that information and how to ask them for that information. I know how to take an interview – I've learned how to do that

during my university studies. And even [if] it may seem a formal thing, knowing how to put the right words at the right time in the right place makes the whole difference when trying to find the information from someone. So [learning] the way of showing respect to your profession has taught me how to get what I need.

Lewis admits that for his first venture he did not do sufficient research before he invested money into it. The research was too basic, and only focused on what was going on in a five-mile radius around him.

Nowadays I will do a hell of a lot of research before a decision is made to try and make it as calculated as possible ... As opposed to a gamble.

In Lillie's interview, she also points out how much time she spends on research. As CEO of Foleeo LLC (providing an online portfolio platform), knowing what her customers want, feel and aim for is essential to her business success: "To be honest, I sit at my computer and research all day about what people want and need in this type of online service. It has consumed my days."

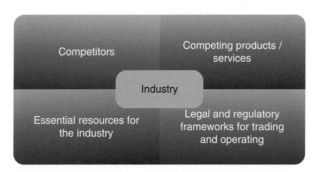

Figure 4.2 Areas for industry analysis

4.1.3 Introduction to industry analysis

The definition for industry is a group of businesses that either produce the same or similar products while targeting similar customers or buyers and/or are contributing to the supply chain for that product. They use similar resources and technology and have a shared way of doing business.

As outlined above, the purpose of the industry analysis is to establish the driving factors in the industry. You need to establish how competitive the industry is, if it is growing or declining. It is also essential to establish what the resources are in the industry that are most important for creating the product(s), and what will happen if there is a scarcity of these resources. Similarly, the regulations and laws affecting the industry are very important to identify. Figure 4.2 gives an overview of some of the important areas for industry analysis, and we will look at others.

The next section introduces you to ways to research the industry and suggests frameworks and models that help you to sort and analyse the information you find. It finishes with guidance on how to draw conclusions and adjust the business idea based on your findings.

4.2   Finding out about similar products

I often hear from those in the early pre-start-up phase that they have come up with something that does not exist and is totally unique. This sounds great, but is it really true? A simple search on an Internet search engine such as Google or Yahoo might change your mind very quickly about the uniqueness of your product.

Similarly, look for patents if your idea is a tangible product. Often in my business advice practice, just using Google and then looking up the list of patents answers the question of how unique something is very quickly. Try the following exercises in Activity 4.1 to find out about similar products to a simple product such as a bottle opener and a more complex technology product like a smartphone.

 Activity 4.1   Activity to find similar products and patents

Use both the UK and US versions of search engines, google.com and google.co.uk to start with.

Use the website of the US Patent and Trademark Office (http://www.uspto.gov/patents/process/search/) to find out the following:

▶ Smartphone – how many patents are listed?
▶ Bottle opener – last time I looked, it was less than 1000 – what do you find?
▶ When was the patent for "Self-cleaning convection oven" filed in the US?

Use the European Patent Office website to search for the same items (http://www.epo.org/searching/free/espacenet.html), selecting the United Kingdom or another member state:

▶ Smartphone – how many patents are listed?
▶ Bottle opener – how many do you find?
▶ What is the first result you get for "Self-cleaning convection oven" on this database? In what year and country was this patent filed?

 Activity 4.2   Task for reflection and analysis

Within the industry, you need to find out what other businesses, your competitors, are doing (see Section 4.3), and what factors – industry trends and patterns – influence how you can do business (see Section 4.4).

What solutions do the products sold by your competitors offer – and for how many can you find listed patents? What customer or user problem(s) do they solve? The product analysis needs to answer these questions. The findings are essential for you to be able to fine-tune your product/service further. Table 4.1 illustrates the beginnings of a competitor analysis for our case study photographer Alison Barton. Two competitors are analysed.

Use the simple Table 4.2 below to reflect on and note findings on similar products, their features and solutions they offer and what possible customer problems they address for your business idea.

Table 4.1   Analysing competing products – photographers

Competitor/ product/ service	Main important features	Solutions they offer	Customer problem they address	Price
Photographer A: Wedding specialist with 20 years of experience; it has two staff members.	Wedding photography; industrial photography; no photography of children and animals; photo studio on high street in suburb	For weddings: various packages ranging between Bronze and Gold – packages differ in terms of hours of attendance and output of photographs, number of viewing sessions, such as a leather bound album with 120 pages and two viewing sessions to select photos for the album – Gold features; key selling points are to take out the hassle, gain peace of mind to capture all the special moments, theirs and those of the guests forever in the best possible way; quality and uniqueness are highlighted; industrial photography – not relevant.	Fear wedding couple misses to capture important moments they have and those of the guests; urge to capture the unique special moments of the wedding as an everlasting memory.	Gold – £2,000; Silver – £2,300; Bronze – £1,800; Standard – £1,400.
Photographer B: General photographer working with associates	Wedding photography; animal photography; family photography with kids; no commercial photography; photographer goes wherever the customer is or wants to meet.	Low cost and price solutions to wedding photography; hours can be flexible as to when a photographer attends; only online communication and phone before event to keep cost down; personalized service; no prints solution is possible to keep cost low; online photobooks offered; high resolution prints can be printed in own time when the money is available at a later stage.	Small budgets of young people and those with little money who still want to have the unique moments captured, but do not have the money to pay out a lot at once; saves money; gives peace of mine; allows for time plan of spending on photos.	Pay is by the hour of the photographer; team of two or three photographers is possible; three photographers reduces the hourly rate.

Table 4.2   Competitor analysis framework

Competitor/ product/ service	Main important features	Solutions they offer	Customer problem they address	Price

4.3 Competitor analysis and the usefulness of competition

4.3.1 Introduction to competitor analysis

Competitors (other businesses that target their products/services offering a similar solution to the same customer group(s)) are often differentiated as *direct* and *indirect* competitors. *Direct* competitors offer the same or very similar products (and services) to the same target market addressing the same specific need: for example, a directly competing product to Coca-Cola is Pepsi. The need that is addressed is a caffeinated fizzy drink with a specific taste: cola. *Indirect* competitors offer products that meet the same need and can replace yours but are different in nature. An indirectly competing product to Coca-Cola would be orange juice. That is a simple example; however, you can also regard any product that quenches your thirst as indirect competition, including other fizzy drinks that are not a Coke.

Here is an example for a service: a spa provider has all other spa providers in a location as direct competitors. All leisure centres and gyms and other service offers that help a person to relax constitute the spa's indirect competitors, even going for a walk in the forest. These possible substitutes constitute alternatives to paying money for a spa use.

When researching competitors it is important to consider both types, direct and indirect, and identify them as widely as possible. Once you have done that, it is essential to research how your competitors do business and market themselves. That includes investigating their

a) Products and services (range, quality, product variations);
b) Prices;
c) Marketing strategies and activities, public relations;
d) Financial performance.

4.3.2 Information sources

Information on the above will allow you to see what they are doing and what might therefore be suitable for the markets they are operating in, and possibly what works for them also financially. It is essential to know a lot about all of these aspects before start-up to position yourself and develop your strategies. This information will help you to save time and therefore money. For example, you do not need to invent from scratch what marketing can work and how to go about it. Shaping the pricing strategy and your offers can be learned from other companies, your competitors.

 Activity 4.3   Activity to research competitors

Practice researching competitors by focusing on a hospitality business in your town:

Look for all pizza take-away restaurants within a 10-mile radius of your address.

What information sources will you use?

In the UK, Yell.com allows you to search with a chosen radius, whereas ThomsonLocal.com does not include the radius in their search function, although it does show you the radius in the results.

Keep in mind that not all businesses are listed in these directories, as larger entries cost money. Search local newspaper advertisements, in particular local free or paid-for newspapers as well.

Other websites such as Ratedpeople.com only advertise those tradespeople who pay for it. This means there is only a limited selection of local tradespeople listed.

Going for a walk and/or driving around the area gives you the best picture of competitors for a brick-and-mortar business (that is a business with an actual physical presence). You can see who is competing already and their visible marketing and pricing.

While it is relatively easy to find out about a competitor's products and services, and their marketing activities via their websites, social media and marketing materials, it is more difficult to find out about prices and financial performance. Box 4.1 lists information sources for competitors. There are a large number of online directories available that differentiate business by sector and subsector, as well as if they trade with businesses only and/or with consumers.

Trade associations often offer a free member listing as part of their membership benefits and are worth checking out. What is a trade? A trade or profession often requires training in a particular skill or craft, often with accreditation or an exam in order to be carried out and/or specializes in a particular material and/or resources; one example is the jewellery-making trade.

Box 4.1   Information sources on competitors

- Business directories (local, regional, nationally) often online – for example Google My Business.
- Business directories for sectors such as business-to-business (B2B, companies that only sell to other businesses and not the consumer), examples include http://www.searchme4.co.uk/ and http://www.uksmallbusinessdirectory.co.uk/.
- *Yellow Pages* print directory or online at Yell.com.
- *Thomson Local* print directory and Thomsonlocal.co.uk – similar to *Yellow Pages*.
- Business pages in British Telecom's *The Phone Book* and on Thephonebook.bt.com.
- British Chambers of Commerce, regional and local branches. Listed on their website (http://www.britishchambers.org.uk/find-your-chamber/).
- Specific trade organizations such as the Association of Plumbing and Heating Contractors, the Hairdressing Council or the Advertising Association in the UK (see www.competentpersonsscheme.co.uk, www.haircouncil.org.uk and www.adassoc.org.uk, respectively).
- A list of trade associations for the UK can be found here: http://www.taforum.org/Members.

Information-gathering on competitors' activities and products can be done in a number of ways:
For online businesses selling to consumers, check their social media presence and website carefully, and check if they advertise in specialized magazines.

For businesses selling to other businesses, the website and social media will give you an idea of their offer, but not much else. Lists of tangible products such as promotional items – pens, hats, coasters with a company logo – are often listed on the website, in particular if you can buy them online directly from them. Box 4.2 lists specific directories for social enterprises and their product offerings.

Box 4.2   Directories for social enterprises

Finding other social enterprises offering similar or the same products and services

As pointed out above, there are a number of directories listing social enterprises that can be searched by location and sector. These include:

(1) http://www.socialenterprise.org.uk/membership/our-members/members-directory – the directory of members of the UK social enterprise umbrella body (this only includes paying members of the organization)
(2) http://www.seb2b.co.uk – a directory of social enterprises that trade with businesses.

There are also many regional online directories, and below are two examples:

(3) http://www.socialenterprisescotland.org.uk/our-story/directory/ – a directory of social enterprises in Scotland
(4) http://www.socialenterpriseworks.org/directory – a directory for the West of England.

While competing like other enterprises, social enterprises often collaborate when they have shared goals, objectives and missions; these ways of cooperation are very different to the business alliances competitors in the for-profit sector.

4.3.3 Finding out about prices your competitors charge

It is important to find out about prices other competitors charge in order to identify the price ranges customers currently pay and the value in terms of products and services they get for the money in exchange. This information helps you in developing your product/ service offer and the price you can charge when selecting a pricing strategy.

Prices for tangible products (those you can touch and sense) are often listed with unit prices, either on the website or in a catalogue that may be sent on enquiry.

Prices for some services in particular are more difficult to obtain, as very often they are not listed on a website and are tailored to a client's specific needs. Consultancy, marketing and financial services and insurance are examples of services where the fee may be quoted after receiving a description of the work being requested. For other services, such as beauty and hair styling, the prices may be standardized for a particular common request and set in advance and can be obtained from a website, a leaflet or social media quite easily.

Mystery shopping research is one solution here. In mystery shopping, you pretend to be a real customer and outline the problem you have and ask for a quote for a solution. Mystery shopping is used in a number of industries, including retail and hospitality, to assess the quality of service provided by franchises and/or company owned outlets of shops or food providers and for checking on employees.

However, there are ethical issues to consider: mystery shopping requires you to hide the truth and not be fully honest about who you are and what you do. Does that go along with your principles of doing business? Ethical issues will be discussed later on. The trade organization for mystery shopping providers, MSPA, has a code of professional standards and ethics agreement. Standards for mystery shopping are also published by ESOMAR market research organization, the Market Research Society (MRS), UK and the Marketing Research Association (MRA), US.

4.3.4 Marketing strategies and activities, and public relations (PR)

Identifying how competitors are communicating with their and possibly your target customers is very important – this research and its analysis might save you a lot of time in planning and executing your own marketing.

For that reason, create a matrix and briefly outline what marketing activities your competitors engage in. As marketing strategy is discussed in later chapters, this is just a pointer on what to research. To start with, social media (in particular Facebook and YouTube), websites, advertising in newspapers, trade journals, TV, radio and any printed materials will be helpful to get hold of. On the companion website to this book there is a sample matrix for collecting information (www.palgrave.com/companion/hill-start-up).

Similarly, it is essential to find out if there are regular *press releases* or news features online and in print media (that is all printed/online newspapers and magazines) about competitors. A press release is a published short article by the company itself reporting on a start-up or a new product launch.

Free public relations (PR) is always a good sign of a company with popular products/services. Analyse what is said about them, and add it to your matrix. The analysis of that material will give you ample insight into what marketing works for what services/products for your competitors.

4.3.5 Finding out about financial performance

Most small businesses do not publish annual reports online, only large corporate businesses do. It is essential for your industry analysis to find out about the financial health of companies in your potential sector. How healthy are they? To start with, turnover (money they make through sales of goods/services and other income), profit or profit margins give you a good insight into the company's performance (see Box 4.3).

Box 4.3   Definitions of financial indicators for looking at company performance

Financial indicators showing a company's financial performance:

▶ Turnover – total revenues or income
▶ Profit – what is left after deducting expenses, costs and taxes from turnover
▶ Net profit margin – net income divided by revenue, which indicates how much of every dollar received in sales a company actually keeps, most often expressed as a percentage.

A higher net profit margin indicates a company manages its costs better. If most companies in an industry have low profit margins, that indicates that the industry might not be very profitable.

In the UK, if a business is a company limited by shares (that applies to many small businesses) and limited by guarantee (that applies to many social enterprises), it has to submit accounts to Companies House, where it obtained a company registration number and registered the business name (www.companieshouse.gov.uk). Larger companies might have annual reports on their website, in which they report on their financial and other performance.

There are databases that offer financial information on larger businesses, such as the Financial Analysis Made Easy database (FAME); most universities and colleges have subscribed to this database. FAME offers financial information for up to ten years on private and public companies in the UK and Ireland of public and private nature.

 Activity 4.4   Carry out financial research on John Lewis

Go to your university or college library catalogue available online and find out if they offer FAME.

Then find out about the performance of John Lewis Partnership plc, UK.

Search for when it was registered, and how to access accounts.

Finding out about financial performance of a charity and social enterprise

In the UK, charities are well regulated by the Charity Commission. On their website, you can find out about the financial performance of any registered charity in the UK, with some data even shown visually (http://apps.charitycommission.gov.uk/showcharity/register ofcharities/RegisterHomePage.aspx, accessed 5 April 2015).

Dependent on the legal form of the social enterprise, information is also available via Companies House for companies limited by guarantee and Community Interest Companies limited by shares and guarantee. If a company limited by guarantee is also a charity, the financial information can be gained from the Charity Commission website. Some social enterprises, even smaller ones, publish some information on their performance on their website in a report format. Legal forms are discussed in Chapter Eight.

Competitors are important for other reasons, they challenge you to implement the practices of alertness and interconnectedness (see Chapter One). While the initial failure rate of start-ups in crowded industries is higher than in ones with fewer companies, for those who do survive in crowded markets the survival rate into year three of trading was higher than for industries with little competition (Burke and Hussels, 2013). Of two million companies analysed in the UK that had tough industry and competitive rivalry in year 1 over 70% survived, whereas of those who had easy conditions in year 1 and tough ones in year 2 only 58% survived.

4.4 Trends and patterns in the industry – research and analysis

4.4.1 Identifying the industry sector and researching it

It is essential to understand the industry you plan to enter with your venture, and in particular to identify the most important factors that influence how you can do business – industry trends and patterns.

The atmosphere in an industry can be compared to joining a club, a tennis club or golf club or motorbike club. The members will have their own special way of behaving towards each other, ways of running the club (opening hours, bar services, competitions), established ways of communication, etiquette on how to interact with each other and the resources they use. Often, the products and services they offer vary only slightly, such as prices for the membership, yet benefits offered vary more often.

What does an industry consist of? There are many subsectors and industry classifications: a subsector of the car industry is the car industry for cabriolets. Each country classifies industries in their own ways.

The UK government has identified 99 industry classifications, called UK SIC 2007 (see Section 1.4.2 for more detail).

Often students say that there is nothing on the opportunity they are investigating, as they have not yet identified the wider sector it is located in, for example:

▶ Offering cardio-tennis is a very specialized service. As this kind of fitness is also very new in the UK, it needs to be located in the wider subsector of fitness group training and exercise.
▶ Offering a new mattress type that reacts to body weight and stops an alarm from ringing when the body weight is lifted from the mattress is a great idea. The sector it belongs to is bedroom furniture and associated products.

4.4.2 The PESTLE framework and Five Forces model

A framework does not support you in drawing conclusions, but it offers headings that help you to sort the information you have gathered. You still have to do the analysis and decide which conclusions to draw.

To start with, it helps to identify the most important factors in the industry using a framework often called PESTLE (or STEPLE or SLEEPT). This framework helps you to sort the information on the *external factors* in an industry. P stands for political aspects of the environment, E for economic issues, S for social (and cultural) trends and issues, T for technological developments and issues, L for legal issues and E for environmental challenges and impact. Regard these six areas like large boxes into which you put information relating to each topic.

Other frameworks include additional factors such as PESTLIED. This adds D for demographic issues, often included under "social", and I for international challenges – that could also be addressed under all the six PESTLE factors.

Table 4.3 is aimed at simplifying the search for information in offering some pointers for each of the six PESTLE aspects. Not all pointers will apply to your business idea.

Table 4.3   PESTLE framework and selected important indicators to collect information on

PESTLE	
Political What is the tax rate/VAT?; If you import, what duty has to be paid? Which trading policies are relevant?; Regulations or government policies?; Political trends; (International) pressure groups, such as for the environment, women; Local authority rules/regulations.	**Legal** Health and Safety law; environmental law; Licenses required; Permissions needed at local authority/municipality level for events, etc.; Employment Law; Data protection law; Laws about minors, such as selling alcohol to minors, child labour; Consumer protection law; Industry specific regulations; Intellectual property rights.
Economic Number and nature of competitors; Unemployment rate; Spending power in the local area/nationally; Income of residents where applicable; Market and trade cycles (Xmas, summer); Exchange rates, tax rates, interest rates; Distribution trends (downloading music/films is an example); Access to broadband for businesses.	**Social/sociological and cultural** Population in the area, age range, gender; Religious orientation in the area/nationally; Ethnic origin/ethnicity; Social trends; Fashion trends; Consumer behaviour/buying patterns; Lifestyle; Education levels; Leisure activities and trends.
Technological What technology is needed to a) Run the service/manufacture the product? b) Take payments from customers, process orders, deliver to customers/get supplies etc.? c) Use your product/service by customers?	**Environmental/ecological** What happens to the waste produced by your business? Does it need special treatment? Are your supplies protected, as they are rare (natural sponges)? How do you transport your goods/services? Do you recycle anything?

Why this is important

It is essential to identify future trends, particularly regarding technology. Imagine, you would have been able to predict when downloading of music overtook the sale of CDs.

CDs are still being sold, yet ten years ago most people could not have predicted the rapid decline of that market. In 2013, just 51.4% of sales in the media industry is of physical media, and not downloads (IFPI, 2014).

In order for your new venture to survive you need to identify what factors in the external environment may possibly support or hinder its start-up and growth. These factors could include:

- Those players offering the materials, products and services needed to create the business and maintain it (suppliers);
- Competitors in the industry and the level of rivalry between them;
- How easy or difficult it is for other companies to join the industry and try to get a share of the market, that is, to sell to the same target customers?
- What other products/services are already on offer that are similar to your own planned services/products and might replace them?

▶ How many buyers there are?
▶ How profitable is the industry overall?
▶ How to take advantage of what is on offer, including the restrictions that may apply in the industry;
▶ How easy it is for buyers to switch to another company that offers similar services to yours.

Michael Porter developed a model called Five Forces (1980, 2008) to analyse the above listed indicators for an industry that helps in finding the answers to two fundamental questions:

a) How profitable is an industry?
b) How intense is the rivalry between competitors?

The aim is to gain insight into how to position (or re-position) a company in the industry to gain competitive advantage and compete more effectively.

This model was updated by him in 2008 (Porter, 2008), and he clarified what had been misunderstood in its application to an industry: the analysis should also evaluate other factors, such as regulation, tax issues and legal threats. Collective strength of forces determines profitability/potential profit in industry (Porter, 2008).

▶ Understand strategic implications for individual firms in their industry through application of Five Forces (FF);
▶ Gain strategic insight into how to compete more effectively within its industry.

Useful templates were developed that list for each threat six to eight indicators that can constitute a threat to industry profits, and invite you to identify the driving factor for each force (Dobbs, 2014); similarly, the threats and opportunities for each force need summarizing. I highly recommend using the indicators developed. The impact of rivalry, for example, is differentiated into price cuts, new product development, service and product improvements depending on intensity and what companies are competing in.

A conclusion that can be drawn is how attractive the industry is, its growth in turnover and profits in a given time period.

The Five Forces are

1) Level of competitive rivalry between competitors;
2) Threat of substitution by other products;
3) Threat of new entrants into the industry;
4) Power of suppliers;
5) Power of buyers.

Each of those Five Forces can be analysed with collecting industry data. It helps for the external environment analysis to come to a conclusion for each force: is it high/medium/low, and finally come to an overall conclusion on the level of rivalry and the potential for profits in an industry you consider entering. There are a number of indicators that can be used for each force (see for example, Dobbs, 2014). They could be measured on a scale from low to high, using a six- or seven-point scale.

(1) *Competitive rivalry.* How many competitors are there? Are they competing for a growing market or a decreasing market? Are they competing on price? Is the number of large firms going down or up? What is the amount of start-ups and failures in the industry and

in your subsector? How many different yet similar products are offered? What are the exit barriers for companies wanting to leave the industry? How many new products come into the market each year?

(2) *Threat of substitutes.* How many other products are there, that at first sight are identical or very similar and could be bought instead of yours? How do these products compare in price? What indirectly competing products are there? How do they meet the customer needs you aim to meet? What is their quality?

(3) *Threat of new entrants.* What are the start-up costs and regulation for this industry? Is a lot of investment, into machinery for example, needed in order to get up and running? Is there a lot of regulation to comply with? If you can say Yes to both questions, then the threat of new entrants is low. If entrance is easy, cheap and nearly regulation free, then the threat of new entrants is high.

(4) *Power of suppliers.* How many suppliers are there? Is the raw material needed easy to get access to? If there are only few suppliers and limited supply of materials, the supplier power is high, they can drive prices up, and thus increase your cost. If there are plenty of suppliers, and the input they provide in what you produce is easy and cheap to get hold of, their power is very low. How easy is it for you to switch to another supplier? What profits do suppliers make with you?

(5) *Power of buyers.* How easy is it to switch from one supplier to another for buyers? With many suppliers offering very similar products and buyers not bound by long-term contracts, nor particular equipment needs, switching is easy. This means buyer power is high. What can you find out about loyalty of buyers in the subsector in this industry? Can buyers drive prices down? That depends on the number of buyers. As a rule of thumb, if there are only few buyers, they have the power to dictate terms to you. How profitable are the main buyers, and how much price elasticity do they allow for? This means, how much can the price go up until they stop buying, and/or how much, if at all, can they bring the price they buy at down?

Use the Table 4.4 to record the summary of your analysis on the Five Forces, add comments into each box and data.

If more than two forces are high, you need to seriously consider if this industry is attractive; if two forces are high, a lot more research is needed to evaluate the attractiveness of this industry.

Table 4.4 Recording Five Forces analysis results

Five Forces	High	Medium	Low
Competitive rivalry			
Buyer power			
Supplier power			
New entrants threat			
Substitution threat			
Overall conclusions for the industry/ subsector			

4.4.3 Industry life cycle and position in supply chain

It is also essential to be able to identify how this industry has developed and where it is going. The industry life cycle model offers a simplified way to show four (or five) key phases of industry development.

Do you remember a time when smartphones did not exist? The Nokia snake game consisted of a simple black line dealing with "walls" being shown as other simple black lines. And the only activities you could carry out with a mobile phone were making calls, sending text messages or SMSs, having an address book and playing some very simple games. This industry sector had scope for development and growth.

The first life-cycle phase is called introduction, birth or market development: there are few suppliers offering the product and a limited number of buyers. Sales are increasing rapidly.

The second phase is called growth: more suppliers sell the product, there is a growing number of buyers and there is a high number of new industry entrants. Sales are growing exponentially quickly.

The third phase is called maturity: the growth in numbers of suppliers and buyers has gone down. Towards the end of this phase, the sales are declining slightly.

The fourth phase is called decline: competitors are leaving the industry, thus, fewer companies offer the product. Buyer numbers have declined, and so have sales; turnover has declined, but profit could decline a lot more slowly, as all development cost had been repaid by previous profits and thus more profit is made on each product unit sold.

This does not mean that at the end of the fourth phase, no sellers exist any more; it means that demand is slowing down. Other authors add a product development phase before the introduction phase.

Identifying the phase of an industry is essential in order to identify how more profit can possibly be made and how much the volume of turnover for the industry can increase. If the number of businesses offering the service/product has been going down, and so have the figures for turnover and profit, this is a sign that there is not much money to be made with selling this product/service in a similar way as a newcomer, as to start with there are high investment costs for most products and services. Similarly, if the number of businesses entering the market, as new start-up businesses or existing businesses selling the product as newcomers, is growing and they stay in the industry while overall sales are increasing, a growing industry is indicated. The period an industry is starting to grow is a prospective time to enter it.

Position in supply chain – your product/service

Lastly, it is important to identify where your product or service is positioned within the already mentioned value chain. A value chain, put simply, is a string of companies that use products created by others in the chain, in that sense working together to create an end product that meets a market demand.

The key question that needs an answer is:

How do you change business inputs into business outputs in such a way that they have a greater value than the original cost of creating those outputs?

The value added influences the price you can charge. Understanding the position in the value chain allows you to at least estimate how much profit you can make with a particular kind of product or service.

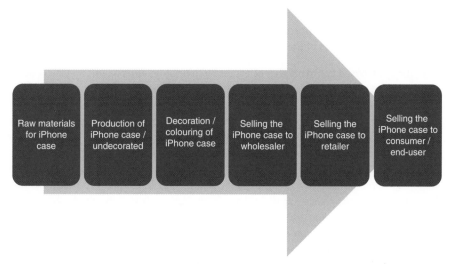

Figure 4.3   The supply chain for an iPhone case

Why do you need to know that for your business idea? If you want to establish how much money you can potentially make, you need to establish where on the way to the end product your contribution is positioned in relation to the end-user. The further towards the end of the chain and closer to the consumer, for some products but not all, the more money can be made when adding value.

The following is an example for a tangible product: iPhone cases. In the current consumer society, the iPhone is a status symbol for stylish and chic consumers, and having a number of different cases supports the consumer's identity statement of being different and standing out from the crowd. From a supply and value chain viewpoint, iPhone cases can be bought already produced very cheaply from China and other countries with low labour costs. If you were selling the cases directly to the end-user, it would mean you are the last element in the chain that runs from the raw material to the iPhone case user (see Figure 4.3).

In the simple chain step 2 and 3 can be one element of the chain (Figure 4.3). How much value are you adding for the end-user? If you make it easy for them to buy something meeting their demand, as briefly outlined below, and your costs are low, then a large profit margin is possible.

For that reason, there are plenty of consumers willing to pay a lot of money for a stylish and even unique iPhone case. The iPhone case for the iPhone user is an accessory yet an essential part of their daily lives.

4.5   Sources of information on industry trends and patterns

At college and university you have access to a well-equipped library. If you are not attending formal education when reading this book, you can rely on your local library, at least in the UK. They can get any book and publication you need via inter-library loans.

For trends on a national, sometimes subnational and regional, and international level, the following established reporting organizations offer a lot of insight (and most college libraries offer at least some of these):

▶ Mintel is a UK-based company that offers research findings and analysis on UK consumer and industrial products and services and European retail intelligence.
▶ Key Note offers market research reports with industry information of nationally and globally most important companies, including company league tables, and an analysis of their performance, sorted by countries and/or products or services. This is an important source for business-to-business and business-to-consumer markets.
▶ Euromonitor International offers research findings for consumer markets and the socio-economic context for many product groups and individual products, including information on market size, market share in the UK, industry trends in each specific industry and information on long-term demographics and how they will shape the markets and industries accordingly.
▶ Global Market Information Database (GMID) offers consumer market research findings on more than 300 products and services. The reports contain similar types of information as those offered by Euromonitor.

The Internet allows you to find out about trade associations and professional associations that keep an eye on industry and market for their members and fellow trade professionals (see Box 4.1 above for a link to help you find them). Check out their websites for reports and statistics on trends in the industry and markets they operate in.

Most libraries offer sector profiles and industry guides from a number of commercial sources. Local libraries also often offer access to COBRA (*The Complete Business Reference Adviser*) profiles for a large number of trades. These profiles offer information on:

▶ Directories;
▶ Market research and statistics;
▶ Small business help;
▶ Trade magazines and newsletters, trade associations;
▶ Internet sources.

On the companion website for *Start Up* you will find a worked example of an industry analysis of the craft environment for a craft start-up business, using the PESTLE framework and Five Forces model (www.palgrave.com/companion/hill-start-up).

In addition to the secondary research sources described above, I would recommend always carrying out primary research, that means in this context semi-structured interviews with industry experts. These can include:

▶ Industry observers;
▶ Suppliers and distributors;
▶ Customers;
▶ Employees of key firms in the industry;
▶ Professionals from service organizations and professional bodies/associations;
▶ Trade shows organizers and exhibitors.

Box 4.3 below offers some key questions to use as a starting point for collecting primary data on the industry.

Box 4.4   Questions to ask about an industry

- ▶ What does the industry look like?
- ▶ Is the industry growing?
- ▶ Where are the opportunities?
- ▶ What is the status of any new technology?
- ▶ How much do industry companies spend on research and development?
- ▶ Who are the opinion leaders in the industry?
- ▶ Are there young, successful firms in the industry? How many?
- ▶ What does the future look like?
- ▶ Are there any threats to the industry?
- ▶ What are the typical margins in the industry?

The next section analyses good practice in a sector and what can be learned from it.

4.6   Good industry practice and best practice as sources of information

Professional and trade organizations often offer good practice advice for carrying out the profession. The term "good practice" indicates an effective business behaviour, often used in the narrow sense of operating practice or working methods, that shows an efficient acquisition and management of resources for achieving an agreed result.

Best practice is a term used to signify business practice that has shown very good results consistently over a longer period of time by different types of businesses in different contexts. These business processes are called "best practice" when they have been accepted and/or appreciated widely. "Good" refers here to results of superior quality and/or quantitative output with given resources.

Box 4.5   An example of best practice for treating gum disease

The quote below is from the introduction to a document for treating elderly patients.

"The aim of this best practice statement is to provide relevant and useful information to guide those active in the clinical area, who are responsible for the management of skin care in an ageing patient population."

(Wounds UK, Best Practice Statement. Care of the Older Person's Skin, p. 3)

The fact that there are many awards and competitions showcasing and selecting good practice show their significance for doing business well. There are many retail industry best practice awards in most countries, to name one industry type. The World Retail Congress Global Series states that they are worldwide the only platform to share best practice. ("Annually the Congress attracts delegates from over 50 countries, from the US to Uganda, India to Italy and China to Canada. Uniquely the Congress also attracts delegates from all major retail sectors, including Grocery, Fashion, Luxury and Health and Beauty. This international, high-level cross market mix creates dynamic discussions and the only platform to share best practice." https://www.worldretailawards.com/world-retail-congress, accessed 16 April 2014.)

 Case study

As another example, the UK daily newspaper *The Guardian* offers the Sustainable Business Awards each year. Prizes are given to businesses showcasing successful application of sustainability principles in business operations. Judges are briefed to look for a holistic effective application of sustainability principles. They seek to reward good practice that pushes the boundaries of current ways businesses approach sustainability.

Knowing what these business practices look like for established and recent industries is vital. If you know what works well this insight helps avoid bad practice and costly ways of doing business. Your research needs to identify the most relevant ones.

4.7   Analysing and selecting suppliers

Section 4.2.3 analysed the role of suppliers. But how do you find out about how good they are and what the quality of their work/products is before buying from them? The CROT framework below allows you collect and sort information on suppliers in a simple way. The example of the craft business is continued for selecting a felt supplier in Table 4.5.

Box 4.6   Analysing suppliers – selecting a felt supplier

Supplier 1

I Want Fabric, a specialist retailer of quality fabrics.
www.amazon.co.uk – search for "I Want Fabric".

Below is a customer review that is verified and from a real customer that paid them: the only review that is on amazon.co.uk

"This cloth's texture and nap has been perfect for using with velcro. I have problems with blu tac and drawing pins because they require so much pressure. A few weeks ago I realised that hanging children's artwork could be done easily by substituting the usual background paper for felt. A winner in my books!" (amazon.co.uk)

Postage and packaging:
Royal Mail tracked 2/3 day service; delivery cost is £3.31 for the first item then 0.60p for every item thereafter; the company sends fabrics folded to comply with Royal Mail dimension guidelines. It can send them rolled but with different cost for delivery as expedited courier option needed; if ordered before 12 a.m. the order will be sent out the same day; express delivery is possible.

Returns policy terms and conditions:
Within 14 days a refund is possible, but buyer pays return postage when the items are simply not wanted; return postage costs refunds shall be capped at the original postage fee unless otherwise stated prior to return.

Conclusion:
A flexible supplier, that can deliver not only felt but also other crafts related necessities quickly in various sizes, colours and formats, at a low cost when compared to competitors.

Supplier 2

Ainsberry on eBay. It has an eBay shop and a retail shop. It is an eBay top-rated seller – that means it consistently receives highest buyer ratings, dispatches quickly and has earned a track record of excellent service. The actual eBay shop is not fully developed; information is missing in a number of places. The customer rating on eBay is 99.8% for the last 12 months, based on 7,348 reviews. Customer reviews are very short, less than one line, and do not provide a lot of information.

Postage and packaging, payment:
From £2.65 upwards, £2.95 for standard Royal Mail first class, and £1.50 or £1.80 for standard delivery for each additional item; it dispatches the same day only if payment has arrived by 3 p.m. that day; it offers a lot of different payment methods including PayPal and credit card payments. Express delivery is possible.

Returns:
Within 14 days refund is possible, but the buyer pays return postage when the items are simply not wanted; return postage costs refunds shall be capped at the original postage fee unless otherwise stated prior to return.

Conclusion:
Not a specialist supplier for felt fabric, it offers only fabric and no associated products; when more than one item is purchased, the delivery cost is higher than for I Want Fabric.

Based on the sample information gathered it can be seen that there is a large number of suppliers available offering felt in all forms, colours, thickness and sizes. Differences seem to be in terms of quality of the fabric, in cost for postage and packaging and who pays when goods are returned. Out of these two suppliers, Supplier 1 is the better choice, as it is a specialist for fabric and associated goods. When ordering more than one item, delivery costs are lower, which reduces the overall cost for raw materials.

4.8   Drawing a conclusion on industry attractiveness for your business idea

Assuming you have applied these frameworks and models to your industry, you now have to come to some conclusion. That sounds easier than it is:

Table 4.5   Researching suppliers CROT

C-R-O-T	C – Compare	R – Research	O – Observe	T – Test
How	Offers, products, services, prices, product range, sourcing of their products and raw materials, delivery time, location and requirement to pay duty if outside of UK; returns and refunds.	Customer views and experiences, expert views where available; quality marks and accreditations such as ISO; use Amazon reviews, eBay reviews, TripAdvisor, user groups, company website user groups; awards they might have won.	What do they publish about themselves? Have they got an up-to-date website? Follow them on social media and via their newsletter; Do they have scandals about faulty products? What do the media say/write? A lot of product returns or faults? What they do – how sustainable are they? Do they protect the environment? Contribute to reduce social disadvantage/ corporate social responsibility activities?	And experience or trial or taste them; use mystery shopping research; ask for samples to try; go to retail outlets where appropriate.
Example: Craft business looking for suppliers of felt to make felt bags For more detailed information and analysis see Box 4.6	See Box 4.6 above	Feedback Rating for "I want Fabric" on amazon.co.uk: 4.8 stars over the past 12 months Based on 1,819 ratings; see customer review below (see Box 4.5).	This information is not available for both sellers.	Order samples or smallest number of felt squares to try out for use/ order free samples if possible; make a bag and test its durability, reaction to water, getting stains out etc. "Sold by the metre with a width of 90 cms – free samples upon request" for "I want Fabric"; no information for Ainsberry on eBay.

How can you predict the future is one often-posed question trying to squash the need to carry out thorough industry research.

Table 4.6 below offers a template for summarizing your findings and making some conclusions. The factors listed in the first column are establishing the conditions that are relevant for a completely new business (and not an additional service/product by an existing large company). The empty row indicates that you might want to add one or

Table 4.6   Conclusions about the industry

Factor	Facts about the past and present (growing, stable, declining)	Future trends as known	Effects: A problem with effect on a) Time b) Money needed increases c) Specific skills and licenses needed	Effects: A positive effect: a) Reduces time needed for entry b) Reduces cost needed for entry
Number of new entrants				
Number of closures/ failures				
Number of specialist companies				
Profits				
Competing products/ services*				
Suppliers				
Supplies/ materials				
Industry good or best practice				
OTHER				

more factors that help you make a decision (the worksheet below can be found online at www.palgrave.com/companion/hill-start-up to download). In particular the competing products need a detailed analysis; this has to include a list of their benefits and potential customer problems/needs they can solve.

The next chapter explores the rationale for market research and ways to go about effective market research before discussing how to apply the findings to shaping the creation of your venture and the product/service offer, called value proposition.

4.9   Concluding remarks and application of new insights

Chapter Four discussed the important area of industry, which was defined as the group of businesses that together create similar types of end products. We established what potentially are the shared resources/technology most firms in an industry share and what the way of doing business in that industry is like. We introduced a number of analytical frameworks and models (PESTLE, Five Forces, industry life cycle, supply chain) that allow us to draw conclusions on how competitive the industry is, if it is growing and profitable.

One other focus was on where to find data on the industry that have already been collected by others, so-called secondary sources. Where these data are not available, we established ways of gathering these data ourselves, using a number of interview techniques, including researching awards for good and best industry practice that run regularly. Finally, we established ways to find and select suppliers for our business idea. The last subsection gave assistance in drawing overall conclusions for the industry analysis. If you have carried out all the activities in this chapter, you should now have a reasonable understanding of the industry you are aiming to enter.

Revision questions and applying the new insights to exploring your business idea

1 What is the difference between a framework and a model?
2 What model helps you to analyse the level of competition in an industry? Why? How?
3 What does PESTLE stand for? Why do you need to find information on legal issues?
4 Where do you find information on the industry you might want to enter?
5 What are the reasons for carrying out research? What can you prevent from happening or reduce through having studied the industry?
7 For your business idea, write the results of all analysis carried out in your start-up diary. Note also what skills you have developed so far in your start-up diary (research skills, analytical skills improved).
8 Apply the Five Forces model to your industry: what is your overall conclusion?
9 Which industry is your business located in? What are the trends in technology over the last five years? Who are the most important competitors?

Further books and academic journal articles on this topic are listed on the companion website at www.palgrave.com/companion/hill-start-up.

5

FINDING OR CREATING A MARKET?

Summary

This chapter develops the market research process needed to develop a customer-centred value proposition for the *sustainable start-up*. It introduces essential definitions around market, market segments and consumers before discussing methods and sources for gathering and analysing secondary and primary research. Customer insight is introduced as the overarching goal of market research that needs to be the basis for shaping the value proposition. It highlights the necessity for the sustainable venture to consider a balanced approach to sustainability that creates value for not only consumers and the owners, but all stakeholders (Figure 5.1).

CONTENTS

5.1   Market(s) and customers

5.1.1 Definitions for market

Every day the media report about "the market" and market trends. But what is actually meant by this term?

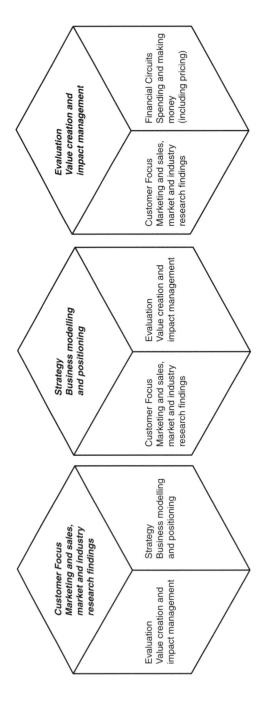

Figure 5.1   The Cube Customer Focus, the Cube Strategy and the Cube Evaluation
Source: © Hill, 2012.

As you will have found out by now, at university or college you need to at least accept ambiguity – there is no consensus on what "market" actually means. It is worth considering a few definitions before deciding what, for our purposes, the meaning and concept of "market" is.

Apart from the physical market space or place, such as a weekly farmer's market, in business we often refer to "market" when alluding to a place either physical or virtual in nature where buyers and sellers meet to purchase and sell goods and services, called commodities. The exchange of commodities for money and commodities for other goods/services are both possible. The "meeting" does not imply any direct contact between buyer and seller.

Another meaning for "market" refers to all buyers of a particular good or service, such as the "market for tablet computers".

The last two definitions are relevant for our discussion and our creation of the *sustainable start-up*. It is essential to know as much as possible about your potential buyers, including their:

▶ available money to spend;
▶ current spending behaviour in your sector on similar goods/services;
▶ customer profiles in terms of socio-demographic features (including gender, age, ethnicity, income, employment, geography, interests) for consumers and business size and sector;
▶ recent trends in spending and buying behaviour.

This insight and information is essential when deciding on how to select buyers from all the possible buyers, called segmentation, and deciding on communications channels and forms as well as prices that meet the ideal buyer's profile(s). This will be discussed in more detail in Section 5.7.

5.1.2 Types of markets – some standard differentiations

There is some established thinking about types of markets worth considering:

▶ mass market;
▶ niche market;
▶ multi-sided market;
▶ geographical markets;
▶ demographical.

A *mass market* refers to a large group of consumers willing to buy a particular product. The group in itself consists of many subgroups with different needs, which can all be met with one and the same product. Marketing, however, has to be different for the various subgroups. A large number of people own a smartphone, however, within smartphone owners, there is a large variety of customers with different profiles for which different benefits of the product need to be highlighted.

A *niche market* is a small highly defined group of customers or segment. Often, this segment is willing to pay a higher price, providing the package of goods and/or services meets their very specific needs. An example is designer bags, which meet the customer's need for high quality and exclusivity.

The *multi-sided market* or market platform exists for a number of products, online and off-line. A "free" newspaper has at least two customer groups: the businesses that advertise in it for a fee, and the readers who get the newspaper for free. Similarly, a free app or game for a phone often has advertising at the bottom of the page and when you open the game.

Geographical markets are differentiated by location type, such as city/urban or rural markets, or by existing administrative regions, such as West Midlands, Texas, the EU or non EU-member countries in Europe.

Demographical markets differentiate between demographic characteristics, such as the age or the gender of the target group. Demographic features are characteristics that divide a population into groups based on the characteristics of the person. These can include:

- Age
- Gender
- Ethnic origin
- Race
- Employment status
- Marital status.
- Education
- Profession
- Income
- Languages spoken
- Dis-/ability

Nivea, a company that predominantly sold products to women, decided in the 1980s to enter a new demographic market and started to develop different products to sell to men.

It is also common to differentiate markets very broadly, by their main customer groups. The most well known are B2B – businesses which sell to other businesses – and B2C – businesses which sell to consumers.

We can also differentiate businesses that sell to government departments and agencies only (B2G), and businesses that sell to so-called third sector organizations (I call them B2T). And we all know C2C marketplaces such as eBay, where consumers sell to consumers; a car boot sale is another example of a C2C marketplace. (Just as a reminder, the third sector is that group of organizations, which are first and foremost creating profit in order to support communities, society and the environment.) Finally, there is a growing marketplace of T2T, third sector organizations (social enterprises and charities) that only sell to other third sector organizations.

New markets can be seen from two viewpoints: a new market from the viewpoint of a business offering its products to geographical or demographical markets not sold to before. And from a user/buyer viewpoint a new market exists if customers can do something that they could not do before. An example is the new market created for portable phones at the time when only landlines existed. Customers/buyers were not able to make phone calls on the go before the portable phone came out. This meant, when the new portable phone was available, not much was yet known about its potential buyers.

5.1.3   Recent thoughts on market differentiation

Steven Blank (2006) differentiates between two mutually exclusive markets, the existing ones and the new markets. In existing markets, there are stable ideas on who the customers and sellers are. Product features and performance predominantly define the unique selling points (USPs). In new markets, there is not yet much knowledge on a customer profile, and a vision of the benefits of a new product has to be sold so that a customer buys the product. This means that market launch and marketing need a lot of investment. It might even be the case that there is not yet a competitor out there and you are the first mover into the market.

An example: imagine a world without tablet computers. Only desktop computers, laptops and netbooks are known. How do you create a market for this new product, where seemingly all aspects of existing users' needs have been addressed? You need to uncover and address all the issues consumers have with the existing products and create a vision of how their life will be with a tablet computer. What changes will occur in their experiences? What stories of change can they tell? That creates a need for a lot of resources, product testing and product samples to get the benefits of owning one across clearly enough.

 Finding the most appropriate customer group in four steps using Blank's customer development model (2006) helps us to put into practice our principles and practices of co-creation and sustainability. The four steps are: customer discovery, customer validation, customer creation and company building. Customer discovery focuses on clearly identifying the customers' problems and needs; customer validation concentrates on developing a replicable sales model; customer creation works on pushing the demand for the product with end-users; company building is ensuring a quick growth of a company with a marketable scaleable product. What is important to note is that this is not a linear process, but an unpredictable one with repetition of the stages individually and of the whole process.

For our purposes, I reinterpret the conceptualization and meaning of customer validation as the validation of *sufficient* numbers of customers to make the product marketable. As with other authors, Blank aims to identify the *scaleable* product, yet the search for the scaleable product does not apply to every start-up, only a small percentage. In other words, not everybody is interested in creating the Next Big Thing – a product that changes the world as tablets did.

5.1.4 Differentiating customer types

It is worth considering at this stage some basic customer types when it comes to selling new products, often discussed with the term "diffusion of innovation". While this is based on technology-related products, it can be applied to other products as well. This is helpful for us, as dividing customers into groups with similar characteristics and buying behaviour creates a focus of marketing and selling activities. Applying the principle and practice of co-creation requires you to partner to some extent with your customers and meet their expectations.

So, there are the enthusiastic customers, also called *innovators*, who try everything new because, well, it is new. These are great customers to keep in focus when wanting to sell something really new, as they are willing to take a risk. They often read extensively and/or use social media a lot, and have a high degree of confidence. However, they only represent a very small group of potential buyers. They may influence a few others, yet by themselves will not ensure a wide spread of the benefits of the new product. Depending on the marketplace, they can constitute as little as 2% of the total customer base.

Then there are the *early adopters* who are happy to do what the enthusiastic innovating customers do, so as to be in with the trendsetters. They draw on the recommendations and experiences of the innovators to make their decision. Once this decision is made, they can be opinion leaders and set trends for a larger group of buyers. Some say they represent about 15% of the buyers.

Then there are the *mass followers*, who buy what others bought and judged as useful and to be part of the crowd. They follow new trends less quickly, look for real yet small improvements and consider carefully who the seller is and what the quality of the product is. They need to know that others have fully embraced the new product, and it has real value to them before they buy. They constitute about 39% of the buyers.

And then there are the *late adopters*, happy to finally do what others tried out so they do not waste money or time in trying something that is not useful or helpful to them. Some of them wait until prices have fallen and the product has been established as a solution to a common problem. They care a lot about price and cost to them, and customer support. They constitute about 38% of the buyers.

The last group are the *laggards*. They wait until the price has truly fallen, the competition is intense and at least several similar products are on offer. By then, often the product has been established as a must-have and essential. They only constitute about 4–5% of buyers.

These types need to be kept in mind when selling an innovative product or service. Ideally, you would like to sell to the "early adopters", as this sale will influence others (opinion leaders).

It is important to spend time and effort identifying who the customer is: the customer determines all the other components of creating the sustainable living sculpture of our new venture we call the *sustainable start-up*:

▶ What the entrepreneur will offer;
▶ What the value proposition is;
▶ How the benefit will be delivered to the customer.

All the terms used above will be explained in context with more detail in this chapter.

5.2 Market research – what is it and what is it for?

5.2.1 Market research – what is it?

Market research has many definitions. The one below is from the European association for qualitative market research, ESOMAR, and serves as the basis of how this book relates to market research. It also touches the important issue of ethics in research, which is discussed in more detail in Section 5.5 below.

> Market research, which includes social and opinion research, is the systematic gathering and interpretation of information about individuals or organisations using the statistical and analytical methods and techniques of the applied sciences to gain insight or support decision making. (http://www.esomar.org/knowledge-and-standards/market-research-explained.php, accessed 10 June 2014)

The definition continues then to point out that the identity of respondents will not be revealed to the user of the information without them explicit consent. More importantly, no sales approach will be made to them as a direct result of their having provided information.

It should be noted that there is a difference between market research and marketing research. In the context of our pre- and start-up research, market research is focused on identifying the attitudes, feelings, consumption and/or usage behaviour of potential buyers of the product under development.

Marketing research often includes research on what marketing competitors carry out, which is discussed here under industry research.

A social enterprise also needs to consider all of the aspects discussed so far in this section. In addition, it is necessary to research the beneficiaries of the social enterprise (who may be different to the customers) and their needs. Beneficiaries are the recipients of the results of the enterprising activities, they may be people with a need that is not currently sufficiently met, or the environment or other organizations in society that need support, such as charities. In order to be able to calculate what should be done to support them, secondary and primary research is needed to identify the most important needs and demands to address. Co-creation, or working *with* beneficiaries, is essential for creating the sustainable living sculpture of an enterprising social enterprise. This will be discussed further in the sections below.

5.2.2 Market research – what for? Identifying the purpose of your investigation

"'Small businesses: the importance of knowing your market' – Entrepreneurs often ignore the need for market research, but knowing that your product is commercially viable is the difference between a successful business and a hobby." So says James Caan, founder and CEO of Hamilton Bradshaw, UK (*The Guardian*, 11 June 2014, http://www.theguardian.com/small-business-network/2014/jun/11/james-caan-market-research).

Before embarking on the journey of asking potential customers questions and finding existing already published market information, the aim of this research needs to be identified.

What exactly are you trying to find out?

We have identified previously that customers or buyers have a problem (sometimes described as pain) that needs addressing or solving. While having a great idea is fantastic, the important point is – does this idea solve an existing problem? If so, what is the shape and texture of this problem in detail? What other solutions do other products offer? The last part of Section 4.2 in the previous chapter helped you to get to grips with the current solutions existing products offer. But do the current solutions solve all the problems customers have?

"Where do you start?", you might ask. One important starting point is customer reviews of products. If you go to the Amazon website in any country, you will find a lot of reviews from customers and their problems. Or when you search online for a particular product and pose a question at the same time, you find lots of people asking similar questions and the solutions well-meaning users offer. These discussions give you a starting point for identifying the problems with existing goods; technology-related problems in particular become visible. Using customer reviews and problems posted on discussion boards can be thought of as part of the co-creation process in designing your product discussed earlier. The sooner you identify the challenges they have, the better you can design your own research into what else they might need solving in a particular situation.

One example: creative solutions are still needed to the problem of having your phone battery run down while on a journey and you forgot your charger. Solar-powered chargers using sun-collectors to generate energy for charging is one of the offered solutions. But what do you do in winter when there is not much direct or indirect sunlight on your journey? Once you have searched customer reviews, you have a reasonable scope of the kind of problems that still need solving. Another good starting point is existing market research. Many trade associations and professional associations do their own research and publish reports. These are available online via their websites (see Chapter Four on industry analysis for a list of trade associations and where to find them). There are large-scale reports published by commercial research consultancies such as Mintel, Key Note, GMID, Euromonitor and Nielsen. These organizations and their reports were already briefly discussed in the industry analysis section; their reports are mainly on market trends and developments, but also have industry analysis sections. Most college and university libraries have at least some of those reports in their library; and most local libraries have at least one of them and can order others in for you.

The next step is putting a few reasonable questions together to identify the most important problem(s) customers have and gain detail on the scope, shape, textures, feel and importance to them of this problem. Draft questions about the current solutions they have put in place or other suppliers are offering. You need to find out what they currently pay and would be willing to pay for the ideal solution. It is also essential to find out who your customers are, their profile. The table below allows you to summarize the purpose of your research of the market. Being aware of customer perceptions and carrying out consumer/buyer research is an important part of the co-creation process of the new venture as a living sculpture. The principles and practices of "alertness" and "co-creation" are applied here.

Activity 5.1, which follows, allows you to apply the list of areas to an example, that of the problem of no phone charger when travelling outlined above.

 Activity 5.1   Activity to identify the purpose of the market research

Practice planning market research for the above problem of no or limited access to a plug for using a phone charger when travelling.

Identify the question topics your research needs to address and draft questions in order to have a focused approach for finding information in secondary sources and to use as a base for the questions you will ask potential buyers directly. To start with, use the available secondary research, that is, already published information and research findings.

Table 5.1   Identifying the purpose of your research

Detail on issue*	Issue/purpose
Who is buying the current product?	Customer profile
What are they paying right now? How much would they be willing to pay?	Price that can be charged
Where are they buying the product?	Channels for communication and buying
What are the problems they have?	Problems your product needs to address
How good a solution are the current products offering?	Shortfalls of current solutions offered by current products
What are the details of the offered solutions to the problem(s)	Scope, shape, feel and texture of problems and the solutions
How often do they buy the product? How many variations do they own?**	Buying behaviour
What can the product be replaced with?	Current main competitors, locally, online as appropriate, and their products

*"product" always includes service in this table.
**Most women own more than one necklace, for example.

How often should you carry out this market research – only once? I am afraid to say that the consumer insight process should be carried out to start with, and just before going into production and/or launching the business, and again eight to ten months into being up and running. Why? The external environment changes constantly, and so do consumer tastes and habits, sometimes rapidly, due to elections and/or catastrophes such as flooding, other new products having entered that affect your value proposition. You need to be in touch with what customers' experiences are on an on-going basis. As pointed out before, many business start-ups fail, as they did not research the market thoroughly enough and/ or did not keep on track with changing customer wishes once up and running. Principles and practices of "alertness" and "co-creation" are the guiding force here.

And what do you do first, industry or market research? While this book has the chapter on industry first, this does not prescribe a sequence of this research. On the contrary, market and industry research starting with customer reviews of products needs to be done both concurrently, that is, at the same time. It helps to understand the competing solutions in the form of products before going deep into the market research, while the other secondary industry research can happen at the same time as the secondary market research. The deeper understanding of both views on why customers buy and use certain products from different companies at particular times is closely connected.

5.3   Planning the research and selecting data gathering and analysis methods

5.3.1   Planning the research and gathering secondary market information

Once you have identified the areas you need to gather information on, as outlined in Section 5.2, it is time to select the methods you will use and decide who you are going to select for the research. The latter is essential for choosing ways to approach research subjects. The process for your market research can be visualized as a circle of a number of actions.

Figure 5.2 identifies nine actions taken in the process of pre-start-up market research. These actions are not just done once, but should be repeated throughout the pre-start-up phase until a suitable product/service has been co-created with all stakeholders. The first step of identifying the research purpose was addressed in Section 5.2. Questions for research were also explored in the previous section (see Table 5.1 above).

The term "research design" describes the combination of methods for data gathering and data analysis. In the analogy of the living sculpture, sculptors have to select the right tools to carve, shape and mould the particular material they will use to create the sculpture. As indicated in the previous chapter on industry and in particular competing product analysis, and in Section 5.2, it is essential to start with analysing customer reviews and their discussions of issues, and including the analysis of social media as an area in the research design.

To start with, it helps to read what other business people and researchers have already found out, called secondary research. Reading these findings will help you to get an overview. You can then compare their findings to what you learn from customer reviews and online discussions.

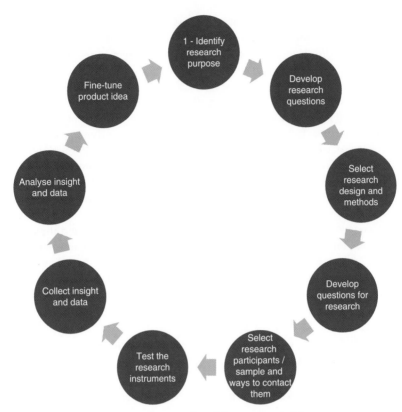

Figure 5.2 Steps in the market research process for gaining customer insight
Source: © Hill, 2013.

In Section 4.5 important sources for industry and market information were identified and briefly explained. Often start-ups come and say that there is no report on their particular product or service. Then it is essential to identify the product groups your product is part of. For example, you might not find anything specifically on bicycle holidays, but you will find a lot of reports on active holidays and tourism and hospitality. A librarian can help you find all the reports their library stocks.

It is essential to research user groups for products and customer reviews. While both do not provide reliable data, gaining customer insight is set wider than just established large-scale market analysis reports.

The limitations of those large-scale reports by Key Note and others are that they are very rarely for a local area. The differentiation of data below country level for the UK is often limited to the larger regions such as Northwest England, South England or Scotland.

Other sources of market information with more local data include:

▶ Local chamber of commerce;
▶ Council or municipality website;
▶ Regional reports by national organizations such as the Federation of Small Businesses, a lobbying and membership organization for small businesses in the UK;

▶ Regional newspapers may publish local surveys – if you cannot search their content online, contact their press office and archive.

Once you have identified your questions and some sources for answers, it is time to put your research design together, a description of both the data collection and analysis methods.

Business research methods books offer plenty of general information on the advantages and disadvantages of particular research methods (see for example Bryman and Bell, 2011, Saunders et al., 2012). The most commonly used methods are questionnaires, focus groups and interviews. Social media are also essential tools, not just to send out links to online surveys and text documents with a survey or interview questions.

5.3.2 The most important methods for primary market research

Research themes and method overview

Asking potential buyers directly is an essential part of what you need to do in order to be able to identify what shape, texture and feel your offer needs to have in order to be bought. In some sense, it needs to be co-created by the buyers to some extent, yet not fully defined by them, as pointed out in Chapter One.

You have to investigate the attitudes of buyers, their current buying behaviour and other related behaviour, their feelings towards a problem and existing solutions, and their market and product knowledge. Table 5.2 outlines the areas your market research needs to address to identify the customer's current situation and aspirations to make a change that may lead to buying your service/product.

There are more than ten methods for directly contacting buyers. The most commonly used for primary research relevant to our context are:

▶ Survey;
▶ Interview (structured and semi-structured);
▶ Focus group;
▶ Observation;
▶ Field trial or product testing.

Market researchers usually use more than one method to gather market insight. In terms of making valid statements about what potential buyers really need, want or are actually willing to do, at least three research methods should be combined, one of which is normally secondary research.

Survey

Survey is a method for gaining systematic insights from a target population. Usually not the whole population can be assessed, so a representative sample or group are questioned and their opinions, answers, views or data are used to draw conclusions about the larger target population. Often the word "survey" is used to refer to questionnaires. The questionnaire is more like a tool that is used to carry out the survey process. Questionnaires exists in many shapes and forms, from the three questions on a card in a hotel or restaurant to a 20-question questionnaire sent to you via email; the basic defining feature of a questionnaire is that it is a series of questions. Research can be carried out in a facilitated

Table 5.2   Themes your market research needs to address

Theme	Sub-themes
END-USER	Is the end-user also the one making the buying decision? If yes, fine. If no, which of the benefits the end-user seeks are supported by the one making the buying decision? Details on their socio-demographic profile: lifestyle, typical behaviour, where in their life/work they use the solution you intend to offer; geographic location; occasions they buy/buying patterns; benefits they seek; current solutions they have or seek; price, where they buy, when, how often, how they buy, satisfaction with current solutions; their motivations for buying the solution, fears, heroes; leisure preferences such as holiday type, socializing at weekends; what makes them unique and identifiable? What are they willing to pay for your solution? What aspects are most important to them?
DECISION-MAKER for purchase	What benefits would they support that the end-users are seeking? What additional benefits might they seek for themselves and/or the end-user?
MARKET: thought leaders in the market segment	Who are the thought leaders in the segment? How can you win them as customers?
MARKET: barriers and enablers	What in the market would support or prevent the adoption of the new product?
MARKET: size	If you were to sell to 100% of the segment, how many buyers would there be?
INDUSTRY RELATED: Partners/ complementary product sellers	If you do not offer the whole solution to the customer problem, who or what would be able to do that? Could you work with them, market together the complete solution?

way – via phone, face-to-face – or self-administered online, via email or on paper. They usually contain a variety of the following question types:

▶ Yes/No questions asking you to indicate if you do something or not or have seen something or not;
▶ Ranking questions that ask you to rank several products or buying options;
▶ Scaling questions that ask you to rate your opinion or perception of a situation or a product against a scale, see Likert scales;
▶ Multiple-choice questions asking you to choose from a limited set of responses the one that best applies to your situation;
▶ Questions where you can tick all or some of the options offered, such as when asked what other product brands you use to brush your teeth;
▶ Open questions that allow you to express your views or perceptions briefly in your own words. These kinds of questions are very rare.

There is a misconception that conducting a survey is an easy option that gathers useful results quickly and cheaply. Surveys need care and effort to create so that they serve an identified research purpose. Many surveys lack this clearly identified purpose, and thus the data gathered does not offer the market insight needed to create a viable product/service.

The following are justifiable reasons to use a survey:

- You have explored customer/buyer needs and wants anecdotally and need to collect quantifiable information on their behaviour.
- You have a clear idea what you want to test and measure.
- You have the time to carry out a survey effectively.
- You have a sufficient number of representative people to survey.

There are many ways to deliver a survey. The most important ones for our context are:

- Self-administered questionnaires, delivered and analysed using online software (see below) or sent via mail or email;
- Telephone survey, asking a set of questions over the phone or via Skype;
- Face-to-face survey, for example interviewing visitors to a shopping centre.

There are a number of online questionnaire tools that help you to create a weblink to send to participants who can then do the questionnaire in their own time. The tools they offer also help to structure questions (see Box 5.1).

Box 5.1   Tools for online questionnaires

Online questionnaire tools often help to structure questions and a questionnaire in the way they ask you to build your questions. There are several free-of-charge ones to use, with some limitations on functionality and, time period it can be used, advertising, level of customization and number of survey participants. There are many paid-for more powerful tools. Check if your college or university has access to one that you can use as part of your studies. They might have software you can use such as Snap Surveys that those outside of these organizations might have to pay for. These online tools often also offer a simple question-by-question response data presentation and offer data to download in Excel.

Selected websites offering some free use:

- SurveyMonkey.com (free for up to 10 questions)
- FreeOnlineSurveys.com
- KwikSurveys.com
- SurveyPlanet.com
- eSurvey Creator (https://www.esurveycreator.com)

Interview

Interviews are a much more personalized way of gathering insight into buyers' views. Interview is a social and business research method that allows respondents plenty of options to express their views and perceptions in their own way using the words that suit them best and in the time they need. The main important types relevant for pre-start-up and start-up research include *semi-structured* and *structured interviews*. Semi-structured interviews use themes and topics and invite the respondent to develop their answer in their own words and time. They can use prompts such as pictures or videos alongside a few words outlining a topic an interviewer intends to gather information on. Structured interviews have a number of carefully worded questions that all respondents are asked in the same way (see Bryman and Bell, 2011, Saunders et al., 2010).

The value for both types includes:

▶ Respondents feel more relaxed, especially when opinions and impressions or experiences are sought.
▶ The interviewer can ask follow-up questions to clarify the meaning of what is being said.

Limitations include:

▶ They are very time-consuming and therefore costly. For that reason, not many can be carried out.
▶ The analysis takes a lot of time, and therefore increases cost.

Interviews are most useful to explore a specific issue more deeply, establishing motives for using existing solutions (exploring *why*) or for gathering perceptions of colour, feel or experiences when using a product.

Focus group

Focus group research involves bringing a group of people together to discuss particular themes. The group may meet physically, in a room or, increasingly, online. This qualitative research method is well used. The discussion is usually guided by a moderator, often the researcher, who aims to encourage participants to discuss amongst themselves and bounce ideas off each other. Focus groups have the same advantages as interviews as well as additional ones, such as the synergy effects that occur if other participants mention an aspect of a topic one participant had not addressed, spurring wider discussion and thus broadening the insights gained by the researcher. For that reason, they are great to explore a theme or a new area of use for an existing or new product or service and are often used before carrying out a survey. However, once the scope of usage of a product has been established via a survey, they can be used to explore in depth the usage. Focus group research is often used in combination with product trials (for food products, technology, etc.) to gather experiences and insights on the use and consumption of a new product or service. It is often also combined with observational research (see below).

Limitations include managing the group dynamics such as one group member talking all the time and over others, and some members not fully taking part, and thus their important contributions risk being lost, which may not have happened in a one-to-one interview. Interviewing and focus groups are done most effectively outside the participants' normal work/home environment if that is possible. Otherwise, interruptions from staff, family or phone calls might interfere with the interview or discussion. Yet, this is time-consuming and might prevent a respondent from taking part.

Recording your interviews or focus group discussions is a quality-improving way of ensuring you capture all the relevant information and insight shared by your interviewees. As a matter of ethical behaviour, you must seek permission to record them from participants in advance and ideally gain a written or emailed confirmation from them indicating they are happy for you to do that. The section on ethical issues below discusses the reasons for that consent in more detail (Section 5.4). If they would rather not be recorded, then take as many notes as suitable and appropriate for an interview situation. You have to keep the interview going and keep the essence of a conversation alive and cannot ask constantly for time for taking notes.

Observation

Observational research is used in order to establish the behaviour of customers in a particular context or setting. The main types are *open observation*, or overt observation, when the buyer knows they are being observed, and *hidden observation*, or covert, when the buyer does not know they are being observed. In both overt and covert observation the behaviour could be watched without any interaction between researcher and buyer. Or observation could be undertaken where there is interaction between them, most often in hidden observational research. Usability testing is a way of observing buyers when trying out a new product or service or when using a prototype, either with or without interaction between researcher and potential buyer. (A "prototype" is an early model or sample of a tangible product that is used to test the market.) Usability testing lets the researcher learn from the reactions of potential users/buyers and investors; these reactions are then used to fine-tune the product further, maybe you decide to do another round of prototype testing before finally producing the new product in larger quantities. Observing shoppers and their behaviour in retail environments is another form of observational research, as is mystery shopping as discussed above.

For this type of qualitative research, the purpose needs to be clearly defined and points of observation clearly identified before starting the observation to make it a valuable contribution to gathering insight on customers' needs.

5.3.3 Effective primary research using the Internet and social media

The term "e-research" is often used to describe a growing trend for research undertaken using the Internet and social media. Email surveys have been used for a number of years; however, using social media for market research is an approach that has grown much more recently.

Virtual online communities have flourished, and hundreds of thousands of people regularly participate in online discussions about almost every imaginable issue (see for example Wright, 2005). One advantage of virtual communities as sites for research is that they offer a tool through which a researcher can gain access to people who share *defined* interests, attitudes, beliefs, behaviours and values regarding an issue or activity. For example, there are many interest groups for specific health issues that communicate openly about their challenges, as the online forum allows them to remain anonymous – they can take on another name or identity so that nobody can recognize them in the physical world, so they can openly share their feelings and experiences without feeling exposed. The Internet enables communication amongst people who may be hesitant to meet face-to-face, for example due to religious beliefs, or may be hindered by physical location or a disability.

The value of e-research includes:

▶ Access to harder-to-reach communities of practice or values or beliefs;
▶ Less time needed to do the research;
▶ More efficient use of time as other tasks can be carried out while online communities discuss amongst themselves without the constant online presence of the researchers as it would be necessary in face-to-face research such as focus groups;
▶ Greater availability and access for participants as answers can be given outside of office hours via e-channels;

▶ Reduced expenses – for travel, room hire, paper, etc., per research phase (compared to one-off cost for online access or software for online research).

Limitations of e-research that are worth noting include the unknown profile of the participants in existing online communities in terms of socio-demographic characteristics such as age, gender, ethnic origin, occupation. This means that parts of the population are not represented in these pre-set communities. Additionally, you need to know roughly how many members are in a community in order to be able to give percentages of how many answered a question in a certain way. That is difficult, as some members communicate more often and regularly than others, so that conclusions on the sample size are more difficult to make (Preece et al., 2004).

Research using social media can take three forms:

▶ Analysing existing comments on social media such as Facebook or LinkedIn by consumers/users or specific online communities, such as iPad owners;
▶ Using social media to send out links to online surveys and word documents with research questions;
▶ Gathering insights and answers through community discussion either within an existing user group or by creating a new user group for research purposes only.

Box 5.2 outlines how a student went about using social media to invite SMEs to take part in her research. This is a good example of using Twitter for getting surveys filled out, but also of how to advertise your business with special offers.

Box 5.2   Using Twitter to win SME participation in research

Monday to Friday every week, from 2 to 4 p.m., there was "business hour" on Twitter. At this time you can sell your product, seek investors or ask for participants in your market research (https://twitter.com/b2bhour, accessed 29 November 2014). One undergraduate student used this business hour successfully to gain over 100 participants in one day for her market research on the use of social media for small businesses.

The last point in the above bullet list addressed the need to attract a wider audience than in pre-existing online communities. How can you go about creating a social media research group for gaining insight into the current issues potential buyers might have? You could go to an existing user group or fan group for a product and invite members to follow you into your purposefully created new Facebook group. The same applies to B2B for business users. If you do that in a number of existing groups for similar products, you will get a reasonable number of participants.

Researchers in commercial market research and marketing agencies have come up with the following success factors for research groups on social media:

▶ You need about 30 contributions of at least half a page.
▶ The group needs to have a clear starting point and end point known to all participants from the start.
▶ You need about four months' time to run the research group and then clearly close it.
▶ You need about 120 to 140 participants in the community to gain these 30 contributions of about half a page.

Robert Kozinets (2002) coined the term "netnography" as an online marketing research technique for providing consumer insight. Netnography is ethnography adapted to the study of online communities. Ethnography is best known for research on indigenous communities, when the researcher lives with a clearly defined community for a while, understanding in depth their practices, routines and values through participating in them. Ethnography uses a combination of research methods including diaries, participant observation, observation, unstructured interviews and focus group research, to name only a few. The above list of methods for traditional ethnography needs to be transferred to netnography and replace face-to-face communication with observation of online partici- pation, collecting information on length of contributions, use of pictures, quotes, etc., to name a few measures that can be used. Applied to pre-start-up research this means that the researcher becomes part of the online community, contributes to discussion threads and creates new ones, invites a few participants to discuss an issue separately and acts for a while as a participant.

5.4 Designing and testing questions for researching potential customers

5.4.1 Designing questions

In the previous chapter, research was differentiated between gathering primary and secondary data. The first one is the result of research you do yourself, often by asking questions directly to potential users or consumers of products. Designing questions needs to follow the KISS principle – keep it short and simple or sharp. All questions need to be easy to understand the first time they are read or heard, as nobody wants to spend time thinking about what a question means or is trying to establish. Box 5.3 offers an example of questions that can be used as a starting point for researching alternatives to the plugged-in phone charger cable when travelling.

Box 5.3 Questions to ask potential customers for a new solution to recharging your phone while travelling

Researching consumers' views on current use of mobile phone chargers

The questions below are only a starting point; they need fine-tuning if they are used for an online survey and for structured interviews.

Have you ever run out of battery for your phone when travelling and being away from any possibility to charge it? *This helps you to identify the possible customers.*

The following questions help to identify the scope of the need of the customer and the value of current solutions being used and/or on offer:

How often does this happen?

What are the main reasons for running out of battery?

How do you feel if that happens?

What do you currently do if that happens?

Have you bought a device that bridges that time?

Which one(s)?

For each, what solution does it offer?

How happy or satisfied are you with the offered solution?

How much did you pay?

What should the ideal solution offer?

What should it look like? Size? Weight? Robustness?

What are the most important features?

How much are you willing to pay?

Box 5.4 below offers ways current providers of solar phone chargers offer the benefits of their products and some of the features. One conclusion is that these solar-powered chargers also work when there is no direct sunshine.

Box 5.4   Example of a benefits-oriented product description for a solar power charger

"Our Solar Chargers are Environmentally Friendly, which means running out of battery mid-conversation or half way through your favourite track on your iPod will become a thing of the past – even if you are kilometres from the nearest power point!

Our Solar Chargers have powerful solar panels, which have been specially designed to soak up the sun's rays, collecting the energy and storing it. So even when the sun is not shining, our energy-saving solar chargers will come to the rescue, charging your powerless portable charger and have you back in business with your conversations, music, games and movies: even if you are in the middle of nowhere!"

http://solarchargers.com.au/product-and-descriptions/iphone.html (accessed 15 April 2014)

Detailed guidance on how to design questions for survey research and structured as well as semi-structured interviews is available in many places, including researching methods books and Internet portals. Further reading on the companion website offers a small selection of research method textbooks and quality online support.

5.4.2 Testing data and insight gathering tools

All quality research first tests the data gathering tools with people similar to their target customers to check if the questions designed actually bring out the findings you are looking for and measure what you need. Piloting the questions is the technical term often used, and the rule of thumb is to test the questions on about 10% of the number of people aimed for in the actual research.

By testing this way you can find out:

▶ If your questions are clear and easy to understand;
▶ If the answers you get are those you need to make business decisions;
▶ If the questions generate reliable results.

Go as far as creating a spreadsheet to review the questionnaire data and look at the structure of the data you get. What can they actually tell you? Is it what you need?

Testing helps you to avoid wasting time and contacts with questions that do not bring the results you need – a problem I have often seen in new venture research by first-time researchers and start-up businesses.

Most researchers will agree that the final questions they use for the research are the fifth or seventh version. There is always something not as clear or effective as you thought when writing and fine-tuning survey and interview questions. Testing questions with respondents that are very similar to the ones you actually would like to interview will allow you to find out that you are asking the right questions in the right way using the most appropriate methods. This is essential, as if you do not do all of those aspects, then you cannot get the results that allow you to decide if this business idea you are researching allows you to make sufficient money. Business decisions based on poorly designed questions can be flawed and lead to losing money.

5.5   Ethical issues and codes of (research) practice

There are a number of ethical principles that need consideration (see for example Bryman and Bell, 2011)

▶ Voluntary participation;
▶ Informed consent;
▶ Avoid risk of harm as result of participation;
▶ Confidentiality;
▶ Anonymity.

The principle of voluntary participation means that the researcher should not force participation in the research. That is particularly relevant for established businesses where managers want their employees to take part and they feel forced to do so as it is the manager asking them. Similarly, informed consent requires the researcher to fully inform participants of the procedures and risks involved in the research and must gain their consent for participation. The researcher has to make every attempt to avoid any harm occurring to the participants resulting from research participation. "Harm" can refer to both physical harm, which is less likely, and psychological harm. In the above-mentioned research situation of staff participation within a company – imagine they are asked to identify flaws in the products they sell and their anonymity is not provided. If the production manager finds out who criticized "his" products and cannot take constructive criticism, he might want to punish or disadvantage individuals, which would constitute harm.

In order to protect the privacy of research participants, their identity should remain hidden to any third party and remain unknown.

In business, there are a number of professional associations and societies that have a code of conduct for carrying out market or social research. A code of conduct sets the principles to follow while carrying out research. The Market Research Society has published a code on their website that is worth checking out: https://www.mrs.org.uk/standards/code_of_conduct/. For the European level, ESOMAR has a published a code and guides for market and social research that can be accessed here: http://www.esomar.org/publications-store/codes-guidelines.php. These codes are much more detailed than the five principles outlined above. Check with your lecturer at your college or university if your institution has an ethical research committee (it most probably does), and if your research has to be approved by it before you are allowed to carry it out. As a rule of thumb, you need to consider gaining permission if you intend to interview minors (people below 18 years of age) or vulnerable adults (people with an intellectual disability or learning difficulty, older people that are in care, people suffering from drug addiction, etc.). If you have any doubts about whether you need approval or not, discuss it with a project supervisor or business mentor.

Once all the above issues have been addressed, it is time to collect your data and gain insight into buyers' lives.

5.6   Collecting insight and the story of change

Collecting data and insights is a great experience for the first time researcher. It is important to keep note of what is done, when, and what challenges arise while carrying out the research. As a rule, challenges always come up in some form. Noticing them early on in the research process is most important, in order to address them and avoid any possible negative impact they might have. The pilot is the first milestone to check for potential problems as outlined in Section 5.4.

Insight is the best term to use to summarize the wide range of information and data you can collect on potential buyers. Sources can include:

▸ Their websites and social media use for B2B buyers;
▸ Facebook profiles of individuals and other social media profiles;
▸ Social media discussions;
▸ YouTube videos;
▸ Newspaper articles;
▸ Online features;
▸ Survey results;
▸ Notes taken during interviews and/or observations;
▸ Transcribed interviews.

   Depending on your product or service, the best idea is to engage with customers using the real product or service, or a "thinned-down" version of it. In manufacturing industries, the prototype is a model of the possible actual product made as much to scale as possible that is used to explore or test the market. It is used to gain an early insight if there is a need for the product and what features are demanded and why.

The *lean approach* (Ries, 2011) to start-up uses a number of different terms, the "minimal viable product" describes a similar concept of a product with minimal cost created and minimal features that is used to learn from customers what they think and what features might be essential or useful and which ones are not. Features that are nice to have but do not make the difference between a customer buying a new product or not could be left out in order to get quickly to market with a marketable product.

Explore what the *story of change* is for customers, and the *theory of change* in your view. This way of thinking is based on the idea of the theory of change and has its origin in the social sciences and development theory; yet it can be applied to the effects new products and services have on buyers' working lives/production processes or personal lives. When customers buy and experience your product/service, something changes for them. That is the benefit they gain. Categorizing the changes in customer experiences from your viewpoint is the theory of change, the actual change they experience through the use of the product or service is the story of change you need to sell to them. It is the story of change they experience that makes them buy the product or service.

Attending a training workshop is a great experience, and the change experienced in addition to knowledge or skills gained is the change in confidence and other emotional experiences. Reading a book that makes you feel better about yourself is a convincing story of change to buy the book, wouldn't you agree? The example in Box 5.4 tells a convincing story.

Your market research has to help you unpack and discover the ideal story of change in customer experiences that they are looking for, and find ways to categorize this change so that you can make it more generally available for other customers of the same type. Your market research has to provide you with the insight on what solutions customers need so much that they really want to buy the product that solves their problem.

Some of you might wonder how long this research can take? Expect it to take at least several weeks or even months, as the first round of questions might not reveal all the information you really need for fine-tuning the product, understanding what features are essential and discovering what price customers are willing to pay. You might need a second round of research with a further fine-tuned product model or service offer, and use that to gain further insight.

Once you have carried out your market research, the point comes to analyse all the information you have gathered and identify the customer group(s) you want to focus your communication and selling activities on.

5.7 Analysing and interpreting insight and data, and market segmentation

5.7.1 Tools for analysing market insight

There is plenty of technical advice and help available for students at college and university on how to analyse questionnaire data using spreadsheeting software such as Excel, Numbers or SPSS. For that reason, I advise you to use the IT support services of your college, university or company, if you are currently a student or employee. In addition, the help function in the software and free online tutorials offer plenty of advice for learning.

For most market research for start-up purposes, results of descriptive statistics such as frequency analysis (how many people answered a question in a certain way) differentiated by consumer socio-demographic criteria such as age, gender, income bracket, location, are easily produced using "cross-tabulation". This is essential information when attempting to segment customers.

For differentiating business customers, data collected on turnover, staff and other business characteristics will be essential to use to differentiate answers and segment all business customers. You might want to differentiate answers to your questions by say, business size, or business sector, or business sector *and* size. For example, someone who wants to sell printing services to small businesses and researches their needs for high quality printing that office printers cannot provide might want to find out what type of businesses in terms of staff number and turnover might be willing to outsource printing services instead of purchasing a machine themselves. It would be interesting to find out as well if small businesses in the catering sector such as large restaurants have the same or similar needs as taxi companies or giftware retailers.

For analysing interviews, having used either the semi-structured or structured interview format or focus groups, all researchers recommend writing down word-for-word what the interviewees said from an audio recording. Recording interviews was briefly outlined when discussing primary research methods in Section 5.3.2. While this is rather time-consuming, it is worthwhile, otherwise a lot of information gets lost. You might think you remember well what they said, but by shortening and summarizing it you are already interpreting what was said. The method for analysis of text in the widest sense is called "content analysis".

There are many ways to go about using content analysis. Most important is to focus on the research purpose and keep it manageable. Identify key themes and words used to express the meaning from the customers' view. Words can be used as the basic unit and words listed that describe a theme, then they can be searched for in the interview transcripts. The short list of steps below is a very simple shortened way to analyse interview content. For more sophisticated ways use any business research methods books, including the two listed at the end of the section.

1) Identify themes based on the defined research purpose and additional ones that might arise while you read the transcripts.

2) Identify words and/or short phrases that relate to the theme; start with a list based on what you know and add others while you go along. You might have to go back to the first transcripts to see if the added words are used in there.

3) Copy the full sentence the words are in to identify the ways potential buyers describe their feelings and experiences.

4) Compare the sentences you have and look for common ways of expressing a problem or concern and the kind of solutions looked for. These words and word sets might be useful for further research and or language to use when marketing the product eventually.

5.7.2 Direction for analysing market information

The research analysis needs to be guided by the defined purpose of your research (see Section 5.2.2) and the research questions developed. Defining the market groups/customer groups/buyer groups you want to sell to is one of the most important outcomes of your research. The most important customer group(s) who you sell to first and foremost is called the target customer group(s).

The list below identifies what you need to decide on, based on the analysis of your information.

▶ Who is most likely to buy your products first and has the money you need to charge now?
▶ Are they one group or several; if it is more than one group, you have to select one group only to start test trading in a small market segment?
▶ Define the profile of that buyer group and what criteria the marketing will address (this might include age, gender, location, income, money to spend, hobbies, professions, car ownership, travel behaviour, etc.).
▶ Where do these buyers gain information on products?
▶ Where do these buyers buy the product and what is the most effective way to offer it?
▶ Where are these customers and how do they communicate, so you can plan your marketing accordingly.
▶ What are the biggest problems they have and what are the most important and urgent solutions they need?
▶ Does your product or service need changing/adapting?
▶ What prices they are paying now (where that applies) or how much they are willing to pay.
▶ If customers pay a lot of money right now, is there a chance for a low-cost player to offer the same product cheaper?
▶ Are there enough customers who want to buy the product at the price you need to at least break even?
▶ Is there a section in the market that would pay more for that product providing more features and a service offer are combined in a value proposition?
▶ Who are the ones that do not buy any of the products the competition offers, and how can you attract them?

The next section outlines what to do with already created customer groups for selling to and how to create customer groups for that purpose, called market segmentation.

5.7.3 Market segmentation the traditional way

Alcohol delivery services or a fusion restaurant are start-up ideas many students have for new venture creation and business plans. When asked for the target customers they say, for the alcohol delivery service: students in halls or house shares who have no easy access to buying alcohol, in particular those without a car. When I ask if they think they sell to *all* students, I get the answer, yes.

There are two things happening here:

1) They are projecting their own needs or wishes onto all other students.
2) They have not established if all students are really interested in that offer.

The effect of those assumptions is that they project astronomical sales figures based on the number of students at colleges in their locations. What is missing is differentiating students, as they are not a homogenous group. This means that just because they share one demographic characteristic (occupation – being a student, see above), it cannot be assumed they all share the same (interest in drinking).

Students registered with a college or university in one city might be living in another, so are not in need of the service. Or they may not drink for personal or religious reasons. Or they may not have the money to buy drinks that will be more expensive than those cheapest at the supermarket. And there are mature students, who rarely join in with the young student drinking behaviour. While students may have the reputation of drinking too much too often, in reality this does not apply to the majority of them.

For restaurants, I often hear as the customer targeted, "Everybody, in particular families and young people". Well, how do you market to both of them at the same time, I wonder? What kind of families and what age are the kids? And what type of young people, the assumed homogenous group of students, or young professionals?

The benefit of creating a clearly defined group of people or organizations is to form a group of like-minded units with similar buying behaviour and background, as the goal is clearly winning them to buy from you. Your market research will help you with that. Do not rely on existing market segments working for you in the same way. Too often segments created by competitors might not be based on sufficient research and might not work for you.

Blank (2006) suggested ways to differentiate existing markets: to create a low-cost market for the same products and to create a high-price market with an appropriate packaged offer.

We all know the *low-cost* market strategy – Ryanair, EasyJet and others created a low-cost market for air travel. The market was already well matured and dominated by a small group of companies offering flights at relatively high cost. Can you do something similar in an existing market? And can you gain new customers who previously could not afford to be part of this market?

The *high-price* niche market can be created when re-segmenting an existing market and creating a group of potential buyers that is willing to pay a much higher price for the product that has better features, uses better quality material and has a service offer as part of a package. Rainbow watches are a particular type of watch that uses high quality materials and offers the additional feature of changing colours when the hands go round. Their price is higher than that of other watches using similar materials.

Traditional market segmentation uses a number of characteristics, as pointed out in Section 5.1 when explaining the various market types, which represent the outcome of applying a number of individual characteristics. Demographic segmentation (characteristics of individuals such as age, gender, ethnicity, income, for example women over 60 years who never worked) and geographical (based on location and residence of a potential buyer, for example customers within the M25 around London) have already been mentioned. Other differentiators look at behaviour and psychographic issues. Behavioural features differentiate individuals by the actions customers perform, such as leisure behaviour (for example the frequency they go on holiday each year, or attend a gym) or occasions they use the product for. Psychographic characteristics look at lifestyle, attitudes, class identity and personality, for example middle class, keen to appear to have achieved something in life, wants to be seen to be able to afford to spend money on a car. Another way of segmenting is to differentiate between needs of customers to identify what position the customer is in now, needs segmentation, and sales segmentation which aims to identify the customer who is most willing to buy the product *now*.

Activity 5.2   Market segmentation

Example

A crafts business start-up that creates bags, jewellery and brooches has arrived at the following target segment: women between the age of 18 and 45, who are mothers of girls under 13, who have little time for shopping in brick-and-mortar stores and are happy and able to shop online out of shopping hours and they tend to carry out online impulse buys for themselves and their daughters.

Activity

For the above craft business, identify the following:

Is this a strong or weak segmentation?

Are there other characteristics that could be used? If yes, which ones and why?

The market segmentation process can contain between five and ten steps, dependent on the author and practitioner. For the *sustainable start-up*, it is essential to go through the steps more than once – better three times – before identifying the one customer group the new venture plans to sell to first.

1) Identify a rough outline of the problems many customers have.
2) Research what kinds of customers have the problem in depth, using secondary and primary research, and what kind of solutions they currently use. Ideally, use a prototype or minimal viable product for this research, so that customers can actually have some experience of the potential product or service.
3) Find ways to differentiate further the problems and solutions.
4) Discuss with customers what solutions they would ideally like.
5) Develop a product that meets as many of those needs as possible while keeping an eye on the production cost; keep your vision of what you want to offer fresh.
6) Test the new product with customers.
7) Identify which customers would pay the price you need and actually would buy it as soon as it is on offer. Identify the innovators and early adopters (see Section 5.1.3).
8) Get as much information about these customer groups as you can.
9) Fine-tune your product offer.

5.7.4 Market segmentation using the *Start Up* Turquoise Lake approach

Background to the Turquoise Lake approach

The Turquoise Lake approach is my own model developed as an adaptation of Blue Ocean strategy. Blue Ocean is a strategy concept developed by Kim and Mauborgne (2005) that abandons the idea of looking at competition as a measure for the own business activity and aiming to increase the own customer base at the cost of the competition, meaning taking customers away from them; this concept was aimed at large corporates and their products and services. Red oceans are all the industries that we know about today with relatively clear markets of buyers. Blue oceans describe markets that can be created with new products, where the size, scope and depth of the market are unclear and in need of exploration, an environment where there are no competitors, as the positioning of the product and/or company is of a kind that gives it a unique edge.

The tools and strategies based on this concept have been researched for hundreds of large companies, and some small companies. For start-ups, the tools need to be applied and adjusted. Yet, the main idea of not focusing too much on the competition (while still acknowledging it) but putting energy and money on creating new markets is still valid. I call the scope, width and depth of the initial market part for selling the marketable product to a very focused customer group, Turquoise Lake. The use of the word lake indicates the smaller size of the initial market while the different colour corresponds to the colour of the sea in shallower areas. Very often the start-up does not have the resources to create a deep blue sea and stays in the shallow waters – that means a smallish clearly defined target market segment. Naturally, the market can possibly be developed into an ocean. The ocean would be made up of a variety of target customers with a variety of slightly or largely differing needs.

The Four Actions framework described in *Blue Ocean Strategy* can be applied to the pre-start-up intending to create a new market via re-segmenting an existing market and adding value. While originally applied to the industry, the questions can be applied to existing markets and create, for example, the low-cost market for an existing high price product, and the high-price niche market for an existing product.

I use the example of acrylic yarn for knitting – that is an alternative to yarn spun from animal products (such as wool, mohair, angora, alpaca, etc.). It consists of 100% synthetic fibre and is produced by machines in a factory.

Q.1 What can be eliminated?

For producers who want to create pullovers, it is more expensive to gain access to woollen yarn, as there are only so many sheep or other producing animals in the world that generate a limited amount of wool, that then has to be processed into yarn before they can buy it. Because demand exceeds supply for raw materials, the price for woollen yarn has been rising. What can be eliminated is the limited supply by creating a yarn that uses different raw material but meets nearly all the same customer needs as natural wool.

Q.2 What can be raised?

What elements can be raised above the level (of quality, time, speed etc.) they are at now? In our example what can be raised is the ease of washing a product made from acrylic yarn. A wider colour range can be created, and a pure colour white is possible. This increases the range for the new yarn and range of customers wanting to buy it.

Q.3 What can be reduced?

The high cost for raw material can be reduced, which reduces the overall cost of production. This can lead to lowering the selling price of acrylic yarn. Similarly, as less natural resources are being depleted because no animals are needed for yarn production. This has a positive impact on the environment.

Q.4 *What can be created?*

In our example a unique material for the low-income knitter can be created that reduces cost for buying yarn. For buying ready-made clothes based on acrylic yarn a range of clothes that are affordable for more customer segments can be created that allow for easy washing and reduce time needed to be spent on household activities.

Once you have answered the four questions in as much detail as possible, the answers provide the basis for creating a unique package or value proposition that puts you ahead or next to the competition – competition can be eliminated as you are offering something they do not provide to a specifically created target customer group.

By now you can say to any contact you talk to exactly who your target customer(s) are and how they can be characterized. The next section explores how to apply the findings on the market to further shape and fine-tune your product.

5.7.5 Positioning your product

What does positioning of a product (or company) actually mean? Some authors talk about creating a specific image of the product in target customers' mind. Note that it is a verb in as much as a noun, the latter indicating the end result after having analysed the market and target customers thoroughly and found the best way to convince the right number to buy the product from you. Note as well that this customer-centric view needs to focus on the benefits the product has to offer. Benefits are discussed below in Section 5.9.

What factors need to be considered for positioning?

- Perception of price of the product;
- Compelling reason to buy;
- Product's placement within a product category (for example cat food);
- Primary competitors offering the same benefit;
- Key difference of the product to others;
- Packaging;
- Product performance;
- References and media recommendations.

At the end of this process you should have a brief statement that explains to the customers how the solution you offer is their answer to the problem they currently have. It will specify who the product is for (target customers), who has a compelling reason to buy it, product placement in a category ("our product is …"), what it provides (the reason to buy it – the key benefit), the most important USP in relation to specified target customers.

The next section explores how to apply the findings on the market to further shape and fine-tune your product offerings.

5.8   Applying the findings to shaping a service/ product further

5.8.1 Is that opportunity for you?

By now you have identified the scope and shape of the market opportunity. The next question you need to answer is: can you exploit this opportunity? Have you got the financial resources, time, skills and people to exploit it? Do you want to pursue this opportunity? Does it match your values and what you want to do right now in your life? If you have not done the exercise in Chapter Three on person-ability (Section 3.2.2) of the business idea, now is the time to do it, and maybe redo it if it is a few months since you reflected on your values.

As an example, I would love to have chocolate bars wrapped in paper that adjusts to the temperature in the environment, and cools down to protect the chocolate from melting. The wrapper would also be biologically degradable. The chocolate bar size I am thinking about is like a Snickers or Mars bar.

It turns out that the raw material for a wrapper like that is based on a rare rubber found in the rainforest. Import is restricted and expensive, but possible.

Production of the wrapper would need specialist machines and trained staff to use them. The investment costs are high for both.

Overall, I would need £600,000 to start production of this chocolate bar wrapping paper.

The selling price needed would mean that a chocolate bar would cost at least £2.20. A Snickers bar typically costs about £0.50–£0.80. At the higher price, this bar is then only of interest to very few people who do not mind spending more money than usual – remember, this is not improving the chocolate quality, it is just a special wrapping paper.

Would you be willing to spend that much on a chocolate bar just to prevent it from melting? Creating a very special chocolate bar is needed as well to match packaging with content to justify an extra price. The luxury market segment is possibly an option to explore – women and men for whom money is no issue.

Well, so while the production is do-able, it is very costly and for that reason for me not interesting. I do not have the skills nor the interest in working in this segment. And I do not want to start a business for which the investment costs are that high.

 In order to identify if an opportunity is for you it is important to be able to answer most of these questions with yes:

- Have I got the necessary skills to run this business?
- If not, can I afford to buy them in?
- Have I got the money to invest to get this business up and running? If not, am I willing to take on an investor in a partnership in return for some share in the business?
- Am I in the right location for this kind of business? If not, am I willing to move my life to the location of this business?
- Have I got the time to invest to do the research and get this business up and running? If not, can I make the time? Or can I afford to pay someone else to do it? Do I want to get someone else into the business?
- Does this opportunity fit into my life right now?

The next section offers some guidance on how to apply the findings of your market research to your business idea.

5.8.2 Shaping a product offer and focusing on a target market

Here is an example about a designer and web designer.

A professional designer with eight years of work experience wanted to start her own business. She wanted to offer the whole package of design services and had started to learn website design. With the industry growing, and so many designers starting each month, a particular target customer group or groups was needed. The designer is of Chinese origin, yet had not considered that an advantage as yet.

As an adviser I asked her if she could use her ethnic origin and language abilities to her advantage. She had not thought about that and was guided to explore the relatively closed community of Chinese businesses in her city. She managed to submit two bids to different organizations within two weeks and was told in meetings that she was the only designer they had come across who is Chinese and how lovely it was to communicate in Mandarin and be able to trust that the organizations' and community's cultural needs would be considered in the designing of a website and flyers for a restaurant.

While the core services remained the same, the package she is able to offer to Chinese-owned businesses provides added value through cultural understanding and skills (for example in the use of colour) and language abilities to write website copy in Mandarin and English.

You have to find the most important solutions one customer group needs that can now afford to buy your product. How you might ask?

Answer these questions to shape your product further to meet the customer needs and still make the money you want.

▶ Who is the first customer group you sell to?
▶ What are their most burning needs?
▶ What solutions can you offer that they are willing to pay for?
▶ What added value can you offer in contrast to the competition?
▶ What twists and shaping or packaging of the offer do you need to make to provide solutions to the burning needs?
▶ What other target group or target groups, who also communicate with the first customer group, have very similar needs so that you can offer your product to them next?

Now that you have identified the key features of your product/service, it is time to work on presenting it by looking at it through the eyes of your buyers, highlighting what they really gain when buying and using your product/service.

5.9 Developing the offer(s) and the benefit-focused value proposition

5.9.1 Benefits, features and USPs – for-profit businesses

We have already identified that you do not have to come up with a unique never-seen-or-heard-of product or service to be able to run a successful business. Having said that, however, you need to be able to point out to potential customers (and possible investors) what is different about your product/service and way of doing business. The latter is part of the package of offers you make to the customer, often called value proposition. Simply put, why should someone buy, for example, food from you and not from any of the many other providers out there?

This unique selling point or points (USP) needs to be presented in a clear, concise and winning way to the customers so that they can see immediately how they benefit from buying from you, and none of the competitors.

Have you ever heard the market stall sellers, to be found at fun fairs or weekly markets, selling large numbers of flowers and plants (or tickets)? They have a great way of packaging the offer with their sales pattern, pointing out what else the customer gets when they buy the package, included for free so-to-say. Here is an example:

> *For £10 you not only get this lovely smelling flowering carnation in a pot and a 1-metre high palm tree, you also get a bunch of ten fresh red roses and a bottle of fast-grow plant soil – it won the prize for best product in its category in 2012 – AND you get a flower pot to go with it. All that for just £10! In flower shops you would pay at least £25 for the plants alone; you save at least £15 or £20. And if you give me a smile I'll even add an extra-long red rose to it. This will last for at least five days if you cut it every day.*

While this might sound exaggerated, to some even sleazy, it illustrates how a package of offers together provides great customer value. Saving money is highlighted as well as gaining quality products. The mentioning of the smile adds the very human touch to it and addresses the short relationship between seller and customer and the exchange of value – a smile for a special red rose.

Added value can be provided in a number of ways, here are some examples:

▶ Additional products of small cost or no cost to you but great value to the customer:
  ▶ Extra sauce for a sandwich or burger provided at no cost to the customer
  ▶ Free-of-charge luxury paper or a card for flowers bought over a certain purchasing value
  ▶ Free delivery over a certain purchasing value for take-aways
▶ 10% or 15% or x% off the next purchase within a given time period
▶ A money-back-guarantee if specified satisfaction rates are not met
▶ A free after-sales service offer such as a review of how you experience the use of the product and free advice on further use.

 Activity 5.3   Activity for value creation for customers

In addition to your product or service, what other value can you offer to your customers?

List at least two added values.

Benefits versus features

Many business founders and staff focus too much on lengthy descriptions of what the service/product does and lose customer interest quickly. From the customer's point of view, the bottom line is: what do we as customers get out of a product or service that makes a difference to our lives? While seemingly buyers are purchasing a tangible (product) or intangible service, what they really ultimately buy is the difference this product/service makes in their lives. What is the story of change? The reason why benefits are highlighted is to provide a compelling reason to buy the product. Activity 5.4 invites you to make a decision on benefits you are seeking.

 Activity 5.4   Activity for deciding on product benefits

Here are two offers – compare them and decide quickly which one you would buy if you had the following problem:

Problem: Nasty cough, with attacks of coughing both at night and during the day; you like fruity tastes and smells but dislike menthol.

Offer 1: Organically grown menthol and herbs are used to create unique tasting sugar-free sweets that calm your throat and reduce coughing, naturally.

Offer 2: Sleep well at night with sugar-free sweets taken an hour before you go to bed. Choose from a number of fruity tastes and herbal options including one with menthol. Each sweet allows you to stay cough free for at least six hours. We only use natural ingredients, including concentrated fruit juice. Which product will you buy?

What you can learn from these examples is that with offer 2 you immediately know that your problems are addressed quickly and hopefully effectively so you get more sleep at night.

Benefits that offer a solution to a customer problem or pain usually address the following core basic human needs and interests:

- Safety
- Security
- Well-being
- Fun
- Relaxation
- Time
- Speed
- Money.

You want to increase, develop, enhance, etc., some of them, or reduce, eliminate, conquer their opposites, such as stress, anxiety, illness, etc.

Features describe the "thing" or its parts/components, what a product can do and its appearance. Benefits, however, contain a value judgement in the eye of the user/buyer – for example, easy to use, saving time. For each feature, get to the outcome/result this feature has in the buyer's life. This insight is essential for the story of change.

You need to know the pain/need/problem of your customers/buyers that your benefits address/solve to start with. This is the starting point we used in Chapter Two – where to get ideas – and in the two research-related Chapters Four and Five.

Table 5.3 on benefits below offers you a starting point, you also find an empty table to download on the companion website (www.palgrave.com/companion/hill-start-up).

5.9.2 USP and value creation for social enterprises

Social enterprises differentiate their service offer in a number of ways. They usually have a beneficiary group or the environment they focus on adding value to. Very often, profits are used to provide free services for those beneficiaries. Thus, their profits make a difference to society, the local community and/or the environment. This is part of their unique selling points and needs to be highlighted.

Table 5.3   Benefits and features of your product

Customer problems and preferences	Benefit – coughing sweets	Feature(s) of your product that deliver(s) it
Severe coughing that interrupts sleep	Less coughing	Herbs and fruit mixed together reduce coughing and do not keep awake
Severe coughing during the day that exhausts and makes sleepy	Less coughing	See above and caffeine keep awake
Fruity tastes and smells but dislike of menthol	Nice fruity taste without sugar	Fruit juice without additives or sugar

Beacon Centre for the Blind is a social enterprise that uses all their profits to provide free services for those with vision problems (www.beacon4blind.co.uk). This is highlighted in their service and product descriptions. For example on their website page about their charity shops, they also highlight in what other ways they create value for the wider community, society and the environment:

> The income generated through our shops is vital to continue our care of blind and partially sighted people, but the shops also offer a valuable service for local people. They recycle and reuse unwanted goods, helping with local waste management and relieving pressure on landfill sites. They also offer people a way of buying goods at low prices. (http://www.beacon4blind.co.uk/services-and-resources/charity-shops/our-shops/, accessed 13 April 2014)

Other social/environmental benefits that other social enterprises offer and are essential to highlight include:

- Job creation for those disadvantaged in the labour market;
- Planting trees or plants for increasing the oxygen output;
- Offering apprenticeships.

The next section discusses value creation for all stakeholders for the business.

5.9.3 Wider value creation for all stakeholders

 For a sustainable healthy business, you need to be aware of how you affect individuals, groups, organizations and the environment around you and how they affect you. These are often called *stakeholders*. Giving value is a principle that sustainable business owners and start-ups address from the start. All business relationships should ideally be regarded as two-way relationships.

So, what other value can you give, and to whom? Figure 5.3 offers a list of the most important stakeholders (yet not all of them):

Here are a few key relationships discussed further below.

Suppliers

Not only do you buy from them, but you can also show your respect and appreciation by paying your bills on time and giving them leads to other potential customers. What else can you come up with? Sustainable business activity is always about taking and giving. The more you give the more you will receive, believe me, I have been there and it happens that way.

Business support providers

You receive valuable information and/or training from them, and can recommend them to others or provide a written testimonial about how great their work is for their marketing. Keep them up-to-date with information on your business activity.

Professional organizations

You refer other contacts to them for membership, spread the word about them, include a link on your website to them and mention them in your social media. In return, you

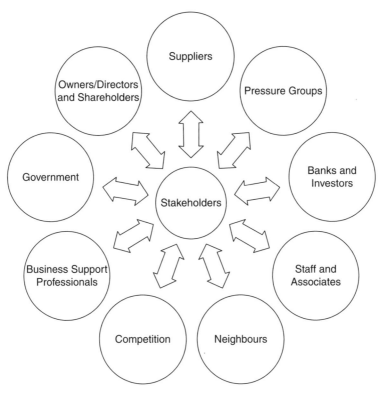

Figure 5.3   Stakeholders to the start-up

may be listed as a case study on their website or contribute comments and opinions that feature your name and business.

 Activity 5.5   Activity for value creation for non-customer stakeholders

Decide which of the stakeholders listed or discussed above are most important to you and your business idea?

Why?

What can you give to them that adds value to their lives?

Here is an example of what one of our case studies does for their most important stakeholders.

Case study

Frinter founders Shivam and Muhammad have the co-creation attitude well rooted in their minds and act on it daily, in supporting their stakeholders. They are keen to give back to their university and come into classes to talk to students learning about new venture creation to act as inspiration and role models. Students are also the beneficiaries of the free printing, you might say, but offering presentations and being available for talks is part of their relationship-building strategy. The stakeholder they have in mind is the lecturer teaching on the modules.

They are also committed to providing placement opportunities for students, with or without business studies or work experience. They support other start-ups in the incubator since they have left the programme and are now paying tenants on innovation campus.

They pay their suppliers on time and provide leads for them to other stakeholders they know. They bring their contacts together when they feel there could be a synergy effect between two or more of their contacts and they could benefit from each other, not only as regards to direct buyer–seller relationships.

Shivam has started to offer his insights on business start-up and became a mentor on the business start-up programme with loans spearheaded by James Caan. (For more details on Frinter, see Section 1.8.4.)

5.9.4 Value proposition – customer centred

After you have identified the benefits of the product you intend to offer, you need to put together a very concise summary in a sentence or two that crystallizes these benefits, the target customers and how they are achieved. Several authors talk about the value proposition: this is a sentence or two (maximum) that nicely summarizes the value you offer using the above-mentioned USP, benefits offered and service/product explanation. It sums up, ideally in one sentence, what benefit you provide, for whom and how you do it uniquely well.

Add a sentence about what changes in the customer experience, the *story of change* for them. This way of thinking is based on the idea of the theory of change and has its origin in the social sciences and development theory; yet, it can be applied to the effects new products and services have on buyers' working lives/production processes or personal lives. When customers buy and experience your product/service, something changes for them, that is the benefit they gain. Categorizing the changes in customer experiences from your viewpoint is the theory of change, the actual change they experience through the use of the product or service is the story of change you need to sell to them. It is the story of change that makes them buy the product or service.

 Here is an example of how the CEO of Harley Davidson describes his business. He does not say "I sell motorbikes". He talks about the experience a city professional will have when he uses his motorbikes – putting on leather gear in black and riding through small towns experiencing (or imagining) that people will be afraid of him. This is the story of change for the customer from the customer's viewpoint.

The theory of change is that city professionals can change roles and temporarily take on another identity (that of the motorbiker, with the associated images of the reputation Hells Angels have had of scaring people through their violent behaviour in some events), and thus have very different experiences while using the motorbike.

Many service providers at start-up point also need to be aware that they are selling themselves, or at least the image they create of themselves. Some professions have to be fully aware of the professional etiquette and professional standards. In particular, accountants and lawyers need to be more careful about how they sell their services and themselves than artists and crafts people.

At this point in time on the pre-start-up journey it is of massive help to focus your mind on what you would like to achieve for the buyer/consumer. The value proposition has to be revised over and over again until start-up, when insight into the market and industry grow, and regularly revised when up and running.

The quote below is from the website for the Beacon Centre for the Blind, a social enterprise.

> The Beacon Centre for the Blind is here to help local people with sight loss live fuller and more independent lives by offering them the finest facilities and support. Our services include a mix of residential, day care and community services, and we continually look for ways to improve what we do. (www.beacon4blind.co.uk/about accessed 26 June 2014)

There is a lot contained in this statement consisting of two sentences – after reading it you know clearly what this organization is about and offering:

- A local focus of beneficiaries – "local people";
- A clear definition of beneficiaries – "local people with sight loss";
- A goal the organization tries to achieve – "live fuller lives, and more independent lives";
- How they achieve this goal – with the services they offer, "a mix of …";
- And the striving for excellence – "and we continually look…".

 Activity 5.6   Writing your value proposition

Based on the market research you have carried out so far, write your value proposition. Remember, a maximum of two sentences. It needs to focus on the *benefits* your solution(s) offers for the client. The features are just the vehicle used to deliver them. What is your theory of change now? What is the story of change?

Note the value proposition in your start-up diary. Once you have looked at finance in more detail, you might have to write it again; once you have some test trading, check if it is still valid – you might have to adjust it several times.

There are plenty of books on business research and market/marketing research that are very comprehensive. Further reading on the Palgrave companion website includes a number of those that are easy to follow.

5.10 Concluding remarks and application of new insights

This chapter took you through the process of market research, using a number of approaches to divide the wide range of market segments and explored the possibility of creating a new unique market segment using the Turquoise Lake approach. To start with, secondary market research was outlined, listing some report sources as well as places to start your research journey. The chapter offered a lot of guidance on what research methods to select, what kind of questions to ask about the end-user, the market, how to identify the person making the purchasing decision and what themes your primary research needs to address. This approach allows you to create a new group of customers who have very similar needs or problems in one area and show very similar buying behaviour and a willingness to pay a particular price. This approach is also called re-segmenting a market.

The chapter then continued to offer assistance in how to apply the findings to your business idea using an example and how to draw conclusions on market feasibility, linking back to the overview presented in Chapter Three. Throughout the chapter, a number of activities allowed you to work further on your business idea and develop a value proposition statement, focusing on the benefits of your product.

Revision questions and applying the new insight to your business idea exploration

1 What are the most important official sources for market information your library offers?
2 Where else can you look for market information?
3 What are the reasons for carrying out market research? What can you prevent from happening or reduce through having studied the market?
4 What does the Turquoise Lake approach require you to do?
5 What is the meaning of re-segmenting a market?
6 What is value creation useful for? Why is it important to consider it at pre-start-up stage?
7 Add all the results from the activities on your business idea into your start-up diary.
8 For the business idea you are currently exploring, describe, as focused and narrowly defined as possible, your first customers as you imagine them based on your secondary research.

6

OPERATIONAL DESIGN AND SET UP

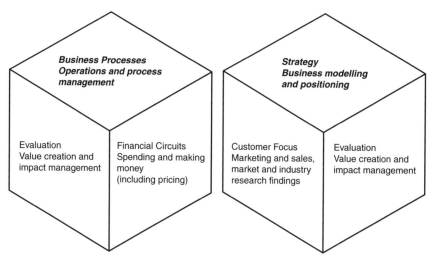

Figure 6.1   The Cube Business Processes and the Cube Strategy
Source: © Hill, 2012.

Summary

Chapter Six reflects on how you *create and deliver* the services or products you want to sell, which is often called "operations" (Figure 6.1). This section is very important for pre-start-up explorations, as the way you set up your operations influences the costs you have. The costs you have in turn influence the prices that you charge your clients. We explore tools that assist you in breaking down operational processes into smaller activities and important steps. We differentiate two main types of business processes: those you have to carry out as the start-up, and those that the customer experiences with you. While these overlap, there are distinct differences between these two sets of processes. We then discuss the operational challenges three major types of businesses face based on their location: operating online, operating from business premises and businesses started from home. I also discuss the challenges faced by service businesses in general.

The decision whether to start by yourself or to start with a team is essential and has also a great impact on your operational set up, costs and credibility for funders. Networks and networking can compensate for not having a business partner only to some extent.

CONTENTS

6.1   Starting with others or by yourself?

6.1.1 Founding team or starting by yourself

The decision to start a venture by yourself or with others, and who to start the venture with, needs careful consideration. More people in the UK and the rest of Europe than ever before are going into self-employment; the UK has one of the highest figures in the EU. Self-employment means that they either lead the business by themselves or in a partnership, for which they are still formally regarded as self-employed (not only in the UK). This professional arrangement covers 4.6 million people in the UK. As we had pointed out previously, the self-employed can have staff, and the staff can be part of the founding team (European Commission, 2014).

 Many ventures, however, are founded by just one person, for practical reasons as much as having decided to do something following a passion and realizing it your way. Many creative industry professionals such as fashion designers or jewellery makers, as well as solicitors, accountants, consultants, IT specialists, software programmers, beauticians, health professionals, home-based cake businesses – just to name a few – start by themselves. It is practical if the home is the office base only and clients are seen on their premises, the clients' homes or in public places, such as hotel lobbies or restaurants.

Here is an outline of what some of our case studies did:

 Case study

Frumtious Ltd founder, **Ben Smith**, started by himself and now works with a number of associates and uses subcontractors, who carry out part of the tasks for business start-up development. This included research on the product ingredients and product testing, marketing and branding.

Alison Barton, photographer, started by herself and does not want to employ anybody else, even after a couple of years in business; to start with she was keen to keep her costs low, and did all the start-up tasks and activities she could herself.

Kathryn Kimbley, HumAnima CIC, has one active director, herself, and two directors who advise but are not actively involved in running the social enterprise. The co-directors act as advisers and mentors, providing their networks and input when required in an informal way.

Lantyx founder **Lewis Barnes** decided to get employees into his venture within a few weeks after start-up, as he did not want to carry out some routine and administrative tasks himself but rather focus his time on the value-adding tasks of bringing clients in and working on business projects.

Co-founders **Muhammad Ali and Shivam Tandon** started as a team from day one, and never regretted it. They bounce ideas of each other, share workloads and responsibilities.

Richard Rodman started his business Crowdentials LLC with a friend, and now has two more founders and business partners with whom he shares the ownership. For him, friendship and professional respect are essential for working with someone as a business partner, and he highly values the possibility to bring other skills and capabilities into the business.

The first two case studies decided consciously to start by themselves as they worked on realizing their vision. Kathryn has two non-active directors that advise and support her. Lewis Barnes brought staff in yet not as business partners, whereas the last two team start-ups were from day one a team of at least two. Richard had learned from his first start-up how important a team is for speedy start-up and quick growth; and the investors for Crowdentials required at least one other team member. Research has shown that ventures founded by teams are more likely to be successful and grow successfully and more quickly, providing the partnership works. (But that is often the tricky part, to make the business partnership work.)

Starting by yourself has some advantages and some risks. The risks of starting by yourself include:

▶ Less money available from private savings and friends and family, as only one set of networks can contribute to the new venture (financial and operational risk);
▶ Fewer assets to bring in or use for the business (financial risk);
▶ Less credibility with funders and banks if only your expertise and experience can be put on the table when applying for funds (financial risk);
▶ Having nobody to bounce ideas with on a regular basis makes a mentor and other business support networks more necessary, which requires more time (operational risks);
▶ All tasks have to be carried out by the person starting, or outsourced to professionals, which costs money (financial and operational risks) and doing it all in-house takes more time (operational risk);
▶ It is a long and lonely journey, and that can lead to delays in making decisions and taking the most appropriate business actions at the right time (operational and people-related risks).

Team-founded ventures are one realization of the co-creation principle guiding the suggested *sustainable start-up*. There are many value-adding features in partnerships that work well, including:

▶ Synergy effects when discussing challenges together and finding solutions, having more ideas and quicker ways to find creative workable solutions;
▶ Sharing workloads;
▶ Adding a partner's skills to your own;
▶ Having access to more private capital to inject into the venture;
▶ More contacts and networks;
▶ Increased speed in getting things done;
▶ No loneliness and a constant partner to bounce ideas against.

The limitations include:

▶ Separation at the end of the business relationship can be costly if the responsibilities and shares are not fixed in a contract;

▸ Personal stress can increase if the working relationship does not work out;
▸ Commitments of team members will vary, and the hours that they can invest into building the venture;
▸ Making decision can take longer if agreement has to be achieved where views differ;
▸ Compromises have to be made;
▸ Financial input may vary between team members, which could create unequal power relations in a founding team or dissatisfaction.

> The biggest risk for founding team members is not having sorted their relationship out before starting the venture. Assumptions everybody makes about what will be done, how the money and shares will be divided, etc., need to be made explicit in order to assess if those assumptions are shared and if all aspects of the collaboration, including financial input, ownership, responsibilities and duties have been sorted out. Chapter Ten illustrates a method for how to sort out the shares for co-founders, which was used by our case study Richard Rodman.

The relationship between co-founders needs to be strong before the venture is started, as otherwise the stress the start-up process puts on it can get it to breaking point and beyond. As a pre-start-up adviser I have seen three out of four venture teams break before the venture was even registered (teams of two to four members). Why? Because the founders had not truly agreed on the venture's goals, its strategic direction, and there was an unequal commitment in terms of time to making the venture work, yet equal financial shares.

6.1.2 Starting with organizational partners

Some ventures can be started with a partner organization instead of an individual. This way of starting up is another way of realizing co-creation. It brings with it a lot of practical advantages, yet also some limitations. The value-adding features lie clearly in bringing the expertise in running a venture and the core skills for the main important business activity, and financial input as well as the existing contacts of the partner organization.

For a very narrowly focused business area or product it makes good business sense to form a new venture as a joint venture. This will combine skills, expertise, finance, market and industry knowledge in a unique way to the benefit of all partners in the new company.

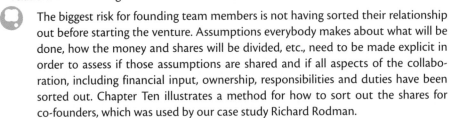

Case study

One example: In Birmingham, UK, a new social enterprise was formed by an individual with the passion and skills for cooking healthy organic food and a charity. Both shared an interest in creating training and employment opportunities for young people who had been offenders to integrate them in a different way into society. A catering services and pop-up restaurant was born that offered different buffet-type food for corporate and private events as well as regular pop-up restaurant events. The charity partner provided premises and social enterprise expertise. Financially, the person with the cooking skills got a salary out of it, and the members own the organization.

Strategic alliances have a number of advantages including – from an operational viewpoint – that either resources are added and/or costs are reduced by resource sharing, often both. Furthermore, marketing can be carried out together to save on printing or radio time cost. Furthermore, the partners can share resources for production, for cakes for example, timing the use of facilities and even staff, the network of suppliers and customers can be extended.

How will you create and deliver your service or product? The next section offers tools and insights into how to identify business processes and the most important activities within them.

6.2   Operational set-up – understanding business processes

6.2.1   Practical essentials for mapping business operations

Why is it important to look in detail at how you create and deliver services and products? The way you go about creating and delivering your product, influences how much time and input is needed, and ultimately what it will cost.

 Talking to many established micro-businesses, they had never been told, taught or supported in understanding the operational process of their own small organizations and had not costed all the process elements. This meant their planned production costs were too low, and the actual profit margin too small or non-existent. The latter can happen if you do not include the cost for all materials and steps you need to carry out, and consequently set your prices too low; this then means that you might not take enough money to cover your costs. As a business adviser I came across more than one situation where the young start-up was wondering why the business was not making enough money to live on and asked for help. In many cases the daily activities had not been planned and researched, and not all costs had been accounted for in the price calculation so that only very little money was taken to cover more than the fixed on-going cost of the start-up.

The easiest way to capture and display the essential activities in the internal operations is with a flow chart. This is a tool to map the steps in a process as well as the associated resources needed to carry out each step: staff time, skill and material input. Figure 6.2 shows a simple flow chart for making a cup of instant soup using hot water.

Some common symbols are used in flow charts, including (see Figure 6.2):

- Diamond shapes for decision points;
- A rectangular box with rounded corners for the start and end of a process;
- A rectangular box with sharp corners for an activity;
- A parallelogram for input/resources needed for a process;
- An arrow with a direction to indicate the next step.

This flow chart shows a number of things. It is surprising how many activities are contained in the simple action of making a cup of soup with hot water! The flow chart also shows, which activities can happen at the same time, while you wait for the water to boil in the kettle you can do other things to prepare for the next steps. The processes in Figure 6.2 show the optimal processes for making a cup of soup. With this chart you can now also start costing the processes, as you know the activities and can add the time needed as well as the input needed.

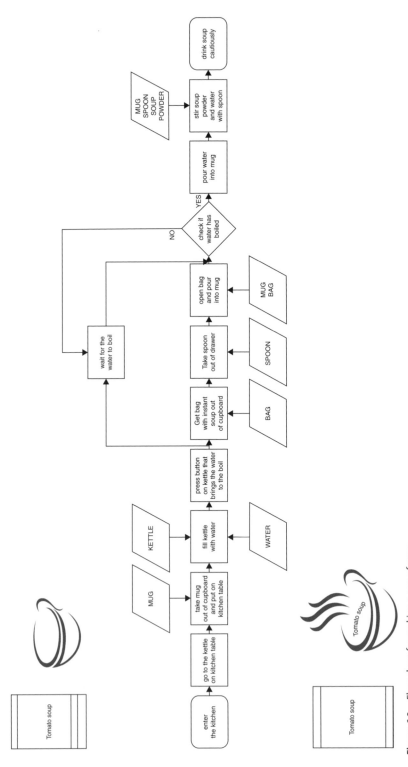

Figure 6.2 Flow chart for making a cup of soup

Here are some pointers that assist you in creating a flow chart:

▶ List all important activities in the sequence they need to be carried out and number them.
▶ List and link all processes that can happen at the same time and all decision points.
▶ List the duration of the activities.
▶ For each activity, list the resources that are needed (staff time, skills, materials, equipment/machinery).
▶ Create the flow chart (or use a Gantt chart).

Gantt chart or a critical path analysis can also be carried out and add value. It is useful to quickly compare the two ways of illustrating the processes, Gantt chart and flow chart; Figure 6.3 shows a Gantt chart illustrating the same steps as the flow chart uses in Figure 6.2. It is also important to highlight the linkages between process steps, which can be done with all three methods. What can be seen easily is that the flow chart illustrates decision points with a diamond, whereas the Gantt chart does not offer that option to show decisions. However, both types of charts show equally well the simultaneity of tasks, that is, activities being carried out or happening at the same time. The duration of each task is demonstrated more clearly in a Gantt chart, as each task is depicted with duration, which can be read from the X-axis. For the flow chart the time needed can be written into the activity box, but the core purpose of the flow chart is to showcase the sequence of steps visually, whereas duration is of secondary importance.

 Activity 6.1   Mapping opening a bottle of apple juice

Create a flow chart of the process of getting a glass of apple juice, from the point of entering the kitchen to get the apple juice bottle to sitting down in the living room on a sofa. Remember to get an empty glass, open the bottle and drink the juice. What are the critical success factors for this process to be effective and use as little time as possible?

At least two types of processes need to be mapped with flow charts for the *sustainable start-up*:

1) Business processes needed to create the product/service, as part of the on-going business activities to keep the business going, not the start-up process;
2) Customer journey processes and interaction.

Activity / Time in minutes	1	2	3	4	5	6	7	8	9	10	11
Enter kitchen	■										
Go to the kettle on the kitchen table		■									
Take mug out of cupboard and put on kitchen table			■								
Fill kettle with water				■							
Press button on kettle that brings water to the boil					■						
Wait for water to boil						■					
Get bag with instant soup out of cupboard							■				
Take spoon out of drawer							■				
Open bag and pour contents into mug								■			
Check if water has boiled								■			
Pour water into mug									■		
Stir soup powder and water with spoon										■	
Drink soup cautiously											■

Figure 6.3   Gantt chart for making a cup of soup

While these processes overlap, it helps to identify all steps needed and their costs, eventually. For now, it is important to identify what needs to be done in order to create the service or product.

6.2.2 Customer journey and operational processes from the business viewpoint

For the co-creation practices it is essential to have well-designed customer journeys to meet customer needs and exceed customer satisfaction. Ideally, these journeys also allow for some form of interaction by the customers on their journeys with your company, even if that is only online. The interaction creates the impression of being a contributor to the buying experience, which will stick much better in customers' minds.

The starting point for the customer journey is usually the first contact with your business, be it through the website, a LinkedIn company page, email, phone call, finding a printed flyer on a car or seeing a sign on a board. For the customers in Figure 6.4 the first contact to this pizza take-away was through a flyer in their letterbox at home, and they decided to try out the pizza take-away. Figure 6.4 shows the customer journey through the eyes of the customers.

You can see that there is a step in Figure 6.4 where the customer sits down and reads a newspaper while waiting for the pizza to be made. The input for the newspaper comes from the business, the take-away. This little extra step offers the customer a good experience to catch up with some local news or gossip from the newspaper offered, a detail the customer will remember.

Again, using flow charts will help to visualize the steps the customers make and the resources needed to make this step happen for them as well as potential challenges this process might face. The aim is to make the customer experience as smooth and positive as possible.

For the *sustainable start-up* this would mean practically to carry out some test trading, offering free product samples or offering free or low-price services in return for some feedback by customers. Even for buying a tangible or physical product online there is a customer journey to be mapped.

There are several important risks you may encounter if you do not break business activities down further:

▸ You overlook steps you have to carry out and do not include the time needed; time is money and you might need additional staff to carry the task out, and that cost needs to go into the cash flow.
▸ You overlook resources or input you need to carry out these tasks; that input will cost money to buy or create, and not considering it will mean that your planned production costs might be too low.
▸ Both of these omissions might mean that you calculate your production cost as lower than it really will be and you might charge a price too low to cover your cost and make a profit. Thus your profit will turn out to be lower than you planned.
▸ Carrying out these process maps and writing activity of listing resources can help you to see early on if you have to consider increasing your selling price or find ways to reduce your costs.

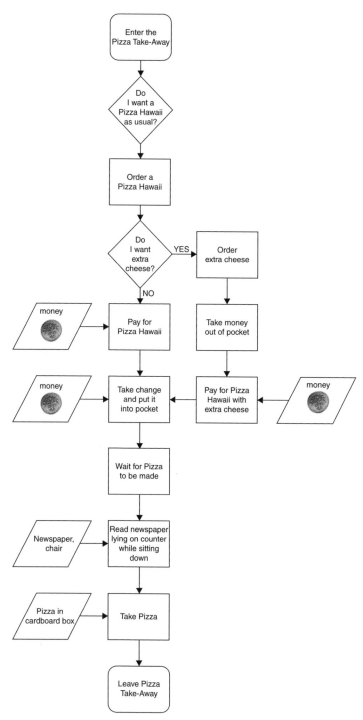

Figure 6.4   Customer journey for buying a takeaway Pizza Hawaii

After having mapped the actual customers' journey, the next step is to create a blueprint, showing what the ideal or optimal journey for the customer should be like, if the least amount of resources are used and the least amount of waiting times are considered; at the same time, the product itself has been decided on (it has the features that make a sufficiently big change to customer experiences so that they want to buy it). These considerations will lead to creating the *most viable business processes for the customer journey* (MVBP-C) for the minimal or most marketable product. This term MVBP-C is new and the associated aspects need clarification.

As a reminder, the minimal marketable product (MMP) was identified as the product with those features that make enough customers buy it, as the product makes a big enough change to customers' experiences (without those features that are only nice-to-have and come at an additional cost). You need to find ways to identify the minimal steps in getting the marketable product created and delivered to the customer for a fee they are willing to pay. The minimal marketable product is the product that can be sold in sufficient numbers to customers. However, if you operate in the luxury market segment and aim to excel in quality you might make a different decision about what the "minimal marketable product" for your customer is and intentionally keep or add features that add value customers appreciate; ideally, this feature does not cost you a lot but creates additional value. These added features can lead to the most marketable product. Your detailed market research is able to give you indications which feature(s) that might be.

When discussing the processes in previous sections, we talked about an optimal process, but the *most viable* process is more precise, as we are interested in the most important activities that use the least resources to get the result we need.

The *sustainable start-up* needs to consider two further process cycles:

1) Business processes needed to create the product/service and to meet a customer order. This is the business view of the customer journey that goes beyond the activities the customers see and experience, abbreviated as MVBP-CB, where CB refers to the business view of the customer journey.

2) Wider business processes including purchasing materials and/or non-production-related costs. This examines the essential activities that keep the business going, with or without a customer order, abbreviated to MVBP-B, where B refers to the business activities.

The two processes described under (1) and (2) benefit from detailed analysis and mapping. As a rule of thumb, try to break each activity down into at least three more steps before saying this is the lowest level you can go to.

Figure 6.5 shows the business process activities for creating a Pizza Hawaii for a waiting customer from the business viewpoint and shows the MVBP-CB for this, and Box 6.1 lists the wider business activities essential for a pizza take-away MVBP-B.

> **Box 6.1   Most important activities for a pizza take-away to keep the business going MVBP-B**
>
> This list is not complete but gives an idea of what is needed.
>
> ▶ Buying ingredients for pizza-making, drinks, and packaging (cardboard boxes, bags, etc.);
> ▶ Making enough dough for the day fresh in the morning;
> ▶ Marketing the business;

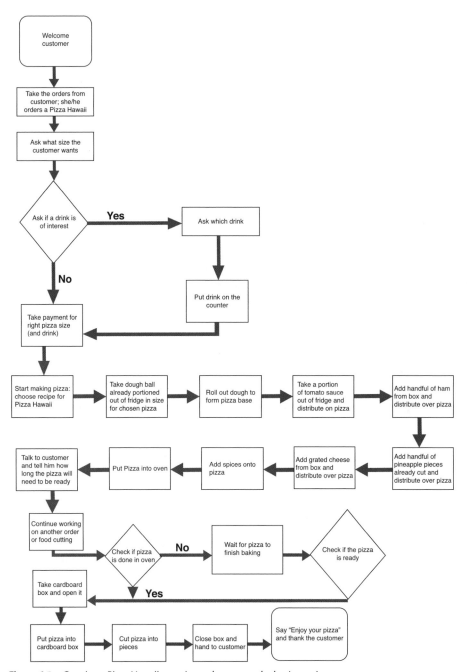

Figure 6.5   Creating a Pizza Hawaii at a pizza take-away – the business view

- Dealing with customer orders on the phone, at the premises and via website;
- Making the pizzas;
- Taking payments from customers;
- Maintaining the website;
- Cleaning the kitchen and premises;
- Improving recipes and designing new pizza flavours;
- After-sales service.

Many of these activities happen at the same time, and if you look for ideal activity combinations, you can come up with optimal processes or MVBP-B, for example while a pizza is baking in the oven, you can take payments. While serving customers, you can come up with new ideas for recipes, talk to them about their likes and preferences and your perceptions. Does this give you an idea?

Now that we have a list of the most important activities, we need to start getting ideas of what they cost. Guessing is not good enough, you must make the best estimate possible, so it helps to do research on prices, for example using the websites of companies that sell all you need. Costing is discussed in more detail in Chapters Nine and Ten.

Activity 6.2 invites you to map your most important business activities and processes, while considering all essential inputs.

 Activity 6.2 Your business processes

1) Where does the customer journey start for your potential start-up? Map the steps a customer has to carry out to reach you and gain the product. Create both the MVB-C and MVBP-CB.

2) What are the most important activities you need to carry out to keep your planned new venture going? Come up with the MVBP-B. Make a list, and then add the input/resources needed to make them happen. Have you included all the activities with a cost you need to establish? All of them? (We talk about that more in Chapter Nine.)

The next section discusses the most important challenges faced by three business types, based on their location – online, home-based or with business premises – and then looks at the particular challenges service businesses face.

6.3 Operational challenges for the most common start-up types

6.3.1 Do you need business premises?

 In Chapter One I outlined that for the *sustainable start-up*, considerations of how and where to operate are very important. Having business premises costs money on a regular basis even if no income is generated (rent is a fixed cost, it has to be paid, whatever happens in the business). Consider carefully what can be done online or in a public space. The principles and practices of alertness, resourceful impact and responsibility are most important when considering business premises.

Retail can be operated online or via temporary stalls at markets, etc. (or craft fairs for creative industries) if the value proposition has not been finalized. Retail premises typically rent on at least six-month leases, more often a year. Do you really need premises or can you work from a hotdesking facility or from home? Can you sustain that commitment? There are increasingly "pop-up" shops across the UK that allow newcomers to trade for a limited time (often up to six months) to see how the product sells.

And do you really need office premises? Can you operate from home? Over 60% of businesses across Europe are started from home (European Commission, 2014). So, can you do that? Can you meet with your team in hired meeting rooms maybe twice or three times per week and the rest of the time everybody works from home or mobile in shared workspaces? This is an increasingly popular way of operating that keeps overheads, that is, fixed costs, low.

There are many shared workspaces where for a small monthly fee you can have access to hot desks with Internet access (a limited number of desks that can be used ad hoc and not booked in advance) and the option to rent meeting rooms by the hour when you need them. There are commercially run buildings and a number of locally organized shared office spaces, in many countries. Below are two examples of internationally operating organizations.

 Case study

An international company like Regus Offices (with more than 200 locations in over 100 countries, www.regus.com) also offers reception services, phone services, letterboxes or just business addresses to give the impression you have business premises. Alternatively, you can meet with clients for business meetings in large hotel lobbies, restaurants or coffee shops. Increasingly, in the UK services stations on motorways offer meeting facilities.

Another alternative is using co-working spaces such as Impact Hub, with over 60 co-working spaces across the world. They originated from a social enterprise and a movement founded by a UK businessman in London in 2005. The aim is to offer an ecosystem for start-ups and small businesses working from home that make an impact on their local communities. Facilities are similar to Regus Offices, but the Hubs are often owned by their members; and each Hub is part of the global association of Impact Hubs, using the same branding, similar to a franchise system. The intellectual property (IP) and brand of ImpactHub is owned by the Impact Hub Association, a collective of all Impact Hubs, which owns the management company Impact Hub GmbH, based in Austria (www.impacthub.net).

At the end of 2014, there were two of these hubs in the Netherlands (Amsterdam and Rotterdam), one in Bucharest in Romania, one in Sweden (Stockholm) and Bergen (Norway) in Northern Europe, five in the UK (including London and Birmingham), thirteen in the US and several in the Czech Republic, Germany, Austria; others are in India, Mexico, African countries and Singapore.

Many cities across the world and many universities offer incubation spaces, with hot desking facilities for start-ups and supported fees for small offices. Check out our discussion of incubation spaces in Chapter Two.

The hospitality industry business predominantly happens face-to-face – but have you thought of trying out selling the new meal or food or ingredients via market stalls? Have you considered delivering it to customers and creating a food delivery service to homes and/or workplaces? Have you considered a pop-up restaurant? This would mean you operate maybe once a month for three days, or every fortnight, and the remaining time offer catering services.

If after these considerations you think you must have business premises early on your journey, then you need to carefully evaluate where to locate them. The next section discusses considerations for location.

6.3.2 "Bricks-and-mortar" retail business

"Bricks-and-mortar" is an expression used for businesses that use physical premises to carry out their business activities, and deal with customers face-to-face.

For retail businesses from selling goods to food or drinks in restaurants, the changing demands and longing for an experience has changed the face of service provision. Some outdoor clothing retailers now offer experience scenarios providing artificial rain in enclosed spaces to experience the outdoor clothing in "real-life" situations. Restaurants offer other services on site including entertainment and beauty to keep the customers there for longer. The scale of services have become so much more complex and expensive in one extreme and at the end of the continuum services have become much more automated for buying so that no staff is seen until the till, or none at all where there is a self-service till.

When you have made the decision to have your own business premises, here are some pointers for choice of location.:

Ask yourself, is my business interested in footfall customers? If yes, then high street or near high street needs to be considered, dependent on the cost. Alternatively, a street leading from/to a train or bus station is another consideration. If the main customers are other businesses, then business centres might be interesting. Similarly, if the product is aimed to be used by children, the parents are most likely to be the actual paying customers. Their attention might be gained around the school gates and the daily duties, including shopping centres, supermarkets or doctor's surgeries.

If your business needs footfall customers such as retail units, hair and beauty salons, restaurants or bars, you need to clarify as much as possible the optimal combination of location features. Using a weighting system to a series of questions, for example between one and three, where one means very important and three means not so important will help when comparing possible locations.

Premises cost and physical positioning

▶ Do I have to be in the city centre? Is a suburban centre sufficient?
▶ Are there businesses complementary to mine that I could locate myself nearby to?
▶ What businesses/workplaces are in the radius of three miles?
▶ Are any of them competitors? What does the SWOT say about these competitors?

SWOT stands for strengths, weaknesses and opportunities and threats a situation or a business represents for your own.

▶ How much is the rent? How much of a deposit do you have to pay up-front?
▶ How long is the lease for? Can you get out of the lease within the first 9 months? If so at what cost and conditions?

- Is there sufficient street lighting?
- Is it a safe environment?
- Are the surrounding properties damaged, graffitied, empty?
- Is it a clean environment?
- Is rent in the wider area affordable for staff?
- Are staff with the right skills available in the area?
- Who is living or working nearby (to the potential business premises)? Can you get access to income rich customers that can actually buy the product now?
- Where is the nearest parking?
- Where is the nearest bus stop/train stop?
- Where is the nearest motorway?
- What/who are the neighbours?
- Who is living or working nearby (referring to nearby to the potential business premises)?
- Is it important for you to know businesses in the area?
- Is it important for you to have parking right in front?
- What distance should it be from your home?

The next section explores the challenges for home-based start-ups.

6.3.3 Home-based business start-ups

Did you know that over 50% of all businesses in the UK in 2013 were home-based and have been for a long while? And 70% of all businesses are started from home, in bedrooms, sheds, garages and kitchens (Department for Business, Innovation and Skills, 2014b).

 Case study

> Have you heard of Levi Roots? He is well known in the UK, as a singer and performer who created hot sauces for accompanying meat and potatoes in his home kitchen with his wife. He then went onto the *Dragon's Den* TV series, where he bid for money from the business angels to produce the sauces on a commercial level and sell them more widely. He gained investment and had to part with 40% of his business shares; and now, a couple of years later, he is a multi-millionaire. The homemade sauces started in his kitchen, and now most supermarkets in the UK stock his Reggae Reggae Sauce (see www.leviroots.com).

What are the value-adding features for a home-based start-up? There are few additional costs if you work from home and use the home only as an office space; this reduces the cost as you do not need to pay out money for rent. You do not need another phone line set up, nor pay for additional utility bills. You have less travel cost as you only need to enter the room in the house you work. The home as the workplace allows you to work flexibly, and have time to pick up family members/friends and work in the evenings. Enabling factors are the technology available to work remotely, share files and screens when communicating, and use Skype for long distance and international calls.

There are also a number of limitations:

▸ Legal issues and regulations (such as conditions on a home rental agreement or mortgage agreement) could prevent you from doing that in your country, check for conditions. Usually, when the home is the office only, and not a place where clients come to, that is possible.

▸ Work–life balance can be endangered, as the need to work can easily take over when deadlines loom and work needs to be done.

▸ Similarly, it is difficult for children to grasp that when mothers or fathers are at home working, that nevertheless they cannot be available to them. Children and family life can provide distractions and interfere with, for example the phone calls on a landline.

Operational challenges of home-based businesses are:

▸ To be able to work effectively in what is usually limited space;

▸ To be able to accommodate meeting clients to ensure legal and financial requirements are obeyed (e.g. household insurance restrictions);

▸ Storage limits may make getting the best prices on purchased goods for sale through business a challenge;

▸ Maintaining technology or systems that may not be shared for non-work use or by family members (e.g. virus protection, file back-ups).

There are even a number of franchises that are home-based and can be run part-time. There is a large number on offer; check out Box. 6.2 for a list of some of them across Europe and the US.

Box 6.2   Home-based and part-time international and UK franchises

Jetts 24 hour Fitness – it originated in Australia and has franchises in the Netherlands, Spain and the UK (part-time).

My World and I – educational business to create customized children's products, focus on books, worldwide (home-based).

Cloudy2Clear – glass replacing services for double-glazed windows, worldwide (home-based).

Raring2go – local magazine and website publishing, UK and Ireland (part-time and home-based).

SmartPA – administrative and PA (personal assistant) support services to businesses, internationally (part-time, home-based).

Many home-based businesses are online retail or service businesses. These are briefly discussed in the next sections.

6.3.4 Internet-based businesses selling tangible and intangible goods

There are many fully online businesses now that have no physical space where the customer meets the seller face-to-face. Examples are Amazon, eBay, Etsy and

Bottica (for designer jewellery from across the world). But the business backyard is still a physical one, as there needs to be an office space from where the business is operated, and storage space for storing goods sold online.

While the shopfront is online, for the place of exchange between buyer and seller, there is still a need for plenty of activity in physical spaces.

Amazon has huge warehouses in many countries and locations, and they need to be managed. And even the second-hand bookseller or tyre seller will need business premises or a space in the flat to sell the items from. Transport needs to be organized for getting goods or parts in and ordered goods need to be taken to the post office or picked up by a delivery company. That costs time and money.

Really understanding the operations of an online business needs flow charts for the customer journey, from online ordering to delivery. It also needs a flow chart for the business in order to establish what activities are carried out to process an order placed online, and the general business maintenance activities that will involve online and offline activities.

There are various types of online businesses: the content-based type charges a fee for accessing information, but does not sell goods nor additional services.

The information-based type offers information for free to users, yet businesses have to pay a fee for being listed.

The transaction business type carries out selling of products or services itself, such as book sales, assessing your CV, online marketing or learning a language. Other types are partially free but, offering podcasts and videos, but can cost a fee when you want to use them for advertising (social media such as Facebook).

There are number of on-going business activities that are the same for all online businesses, selling services and goods:

- Website maintenance;
- Marketing (via social media, blogs, email, at events and conferences);
- Building a community – often via social media, such as through discussion groups;
- Customer relationship management, in particular after-sales service;
- Creating new entries on the website;
- Developing new products or services/buying new products services into the business;
- Stock control – for products only.

The next section analyses the general challenges service businesses face from an operational viewpoint.

6.3.5 Service businesses

Services dominate the economies in most countries in both the developed and less developed world; they constitute over 60% of the GDP (gross domestic product) worldwide (OECD, 2014). Service subsectors that grew over the last decades in particular were financial services, tourism, healthcare, professional and business services and education. And unsurprisingly, most jobs are created in the service sector, and there is no end in sight for the growth of services.

But what are services? They are transactions between human beings, most of the time, either face-to-face or online, that offer benefits to the customer without the customer gaining ownership of something; often customers are renting something, such as a seat on a plane or in a taxi. Rent is rather widely used in services design, as it includes access to facilities, such as a gym, access to shared physical spaces, such as a zoo or an amusement park, rental of expertise such as car repair, marketing services, or access and use of systems or networks as in banking or telecommunications and television. The benefit they gain is an experience and a solution to an issue.

Services can be differentiated in a number of ways, such as business and consumer services:

- Business services, such as research services, marketing services; within that FIRE as the most profitable services: financial services, insurance, real estate services;
- Hospitality services (in restaurants and bars, etc.);
- Education services;
- Delivery services/distribution services;
- Maintenance services;
- Tourist and leisure services;
- Health and care services;
- Personal services;
- Retail services.

It is important to differentiate services directly to people and possessions (Lovelock et al., 2009), which has implications for service design and operational processes for the service provider.

Services can deal with physical objects, people or data. Four different categories of services are identifiable:

1) Services to objects people own on which tangible actions are carried out: possession-processing services. This applies to waste that is disposed of, or pets that are cared for, for example. Customer involvement is limited.

2) Services to possessions that are intangible actions: information processing services. This applies to banking, accounting services, medical diagnosis and law services.

3) Services to people carried out on their body: people processing services. This applies to hair and beauty services, health care, food and drinks in restaurants and transport services.

(4) Service to people that provide mental stimulus. This applies to education, marketing and PR and investment advice, as examples.

Another way of differentiation is based on level of customization and complexity:

- Simple standard service, such as buying a train ticket;
- Complex standard service, such as booking a holiday;
- Simple customized service, such as getting a hair cut;
- Complex customized service, such as marketing services and architectural services for designing your house.

One reason for the continued growth of services is, for example, that household services are more and more being outsourced, when they cannot be done by technology, as in many households both partners or parents work, either by choice or of necessity to earn a living. These types of services are often summarized as personal services. Other reasons are social changes in lifestyles, government policies and privatization, advances in technology and globalization.

There is growth to be expected in services in the non-ownership category such as labour and expertise rental (house cleaning, car repair); place rental (storage spaces, seats in airplanes, suite in office buildings); access rights to physical environments such as toll roads, theme parks or trade shows; rented goods services for hiring boats or equipment for construction; and services that allow to access to systems and networks, such as utilities online, telecommunications and banking. Often these types of services occur together in one activity, such as hiring a taxi where you pay for the use of the car and the driver driving you somewhere, as transportation services.

 Operational challenges have their causes in the amount of customization of those services and managing the balance between providing a service as tailored to the customer needs as possible on the one hand and as standardized as possible on the other hand to save costs.

For service mapping, and flow charting and ultimately costing and developing the service offers, this means creating three scenarios, the most customized one, the most standardized one and the medium customized one. This means that for a service such as "a stall on a trade show" for example, the three types of scenarios that need to be flow-charted could be:

a) A very customized service with multiple stalls and access to facilities and security personnel;
b) A standard service for a standard size stall, no extras, no security;
c) A standard service for a standard size stall with extras for lighting, electricity, etc., yet only in one location and no security personnel.

This only covers the business processes from the viewpoint of the business itself, and the MVBP-CB have to be established for each of them. For each of those processes, then the customer journey as viewed by the customer has to be mapped as well, in order to develop the most viable processes for creating the minimal marketable service.

These activities and resources including time can be mapped and the cost can be calculated ("costed").

All services will lie in between and can for that reason be costed based on those three calculations using percentages below or above the calculated values if a service is less or more customized. This simplifies the process of getting an understanding of costs for the purpose of the feasibility study (that is the exploration aimed at finding out if enough money can be made). For the actual business plan the costs would need to be fine-tuned much more detailed.

6.3.6 Hospitality and leisure industry

This term "hospitality industry" addresses a wide range of services, from food and beverage suppliers (restaurants and bars) to accommodation (hotels and private rooms) to leisure industry offers (theme parks, such as Disneyland or Walt Disney World), cruise lines, and events such as music events and sports events (mega events such as the Olympic Games, football games and competitions and tennis tournaments). It is part of the service industry, and a subsector with a distinct profile.

Part of this distinct profile is that the face-to-face contact is part of the attraction of the services, combined with the need for physical premises. While some services can be automated, such as ordering food in a restaurant online before you come to the premises using a mobile device for example, and online booking and reservation and ticket purchasing, there is and will remain a large part that needs personal contact and exchange between staff and customers.

 Working in this sector can be hard, requiring long hours on the feet, at a fast pace, yet the growth prospects are positive. From an operational viewpoint, designing smooth and rewarding customer services and processes are at the core what makes a start-up successful and sustainable. However, too few people truly understand and can implement these essential customer processes. Mapping the actual physical journey of the customer through the premises is very important, as the MVBP-C and MVBP-CB provide the insights needed to plan the use of space and associated cost

Manufacturing is not addressed in this chapter, as this has much more complex challenges and is so much less frequently set up than other business types by graduates and students outside of engineering faculties. The further reading on the companion website to this book lists some titles that specialize in technology-related and manufacturing start-ups.

6.3.7 Social enterprises – is anything different in their business processes?

Social enterprises operate in many ways like for-profit businesses. As indicated in Chapter One, there are some differences. In operational issues, one important difference is managing volunteers. Managing volunteers from the idea development phase onwards can mean having to manage a larger group of people who might only be willing to put in the odd hour here and there, and who sometimes have a lower level of commitment to investing their time and/or money than co-founders who want to earn a living with the new venture. This can slow the start-up process and can make it more unpredictable. Volunteers drop out of the process more easily when their personal and job circumstances change. Many meetings need to be held in order to create a consensus of goals, directions, and roles. This is discussed in more detail in Chapters Fifteen and Sixteen, where other differences are explored, including finance, marketing, governance and staff management.

6.4 Organizational structures for start-ups

When you build your *sustainable start-up* and employ staff, you need to be clear on what type of organization you want to build as this influences your style of management from the first employee. You may be setting the tone for all further employees to arrive after that.

Which structure you choose also has cost implications and for a three-year plan that is worth considering. Legal challenges and duties when employing staff are discussed in Chapter Twelve.

For the self-employed and partnerships the topic is not relevant at the set-up stage, unless they employ staff straight away. For micro-businesses with less than ten employees the most common form is an entrepreneurial one, where all staff report directly to the owner/manager or director(s).

Other structures are:

▶ Pyramid hierarchical structure – where there are one or two people at the top of the organization, and at each level of the pyramid there is a slightly higher level manager to the one below them;
▶ Flat structures – where there is one senior manager, the owner or director(s), and then a larger level of middle managers, below which is only the level of frontline staff;
▶ Matrix structure – this type of organizational structure groups employees by function and product, which is more applicable to larger organizations than start-ups. In practice, teams of employees work together to accomplish projects.

With the large number of teams working in different locations and less travelling, structures have become less hierarchical and much more flexible in many small and large organizations.

Case study

Lewis Barnes, one of our case studies, points out how important the "big family" of team members is to him. At the time of the interview he had four full-time and two part-time staff. He experienced a lot of that close community feeling at the tennis academy he went to. Yet, he makes it clear that he always makes the final decision, this illustrates the entrepreneurial structure where everybody reports to him while all staff are equal and part of the decision-making process to some extent.

For the *sustainable start-up* it is essential to be fully clear from the start on what the business activities consist of. For social enterprises, these organizational structures can be the same. The formal governance is often different dependent on the legal form; this will be discussed in Chapter Eight.

The next section outlines the purpose and some ways of using networks. Networks and networking are essential for realizing a *sustainable start-up*, implementing the principles and practices of alertness, resourceful impact and co-creation. Networks provide access to all resources, from staff and funders to clients and information. While the section largely addresses the benefits of networking from the seeker's point of view, the *sustainable start-up* needs to give what it seeks.

6.5   Networks for start-ups and newly established businesses

6.5.1   Networking – purpose, timing, ways and value

Networking is essential for all individuals starting and growing a business or freelance activity. The simplest reason for this is that people still buy from people, not companies. Richard Branson still appears in his own adverts, even though he is a multibillionaire. Why? Because he created a brand around his personal values and his person.

So what is networking? Put simply it is making connections to the "right" people. What does that mean? You need to make links to potential customers and those who have your potential customers in their networks. How do you know that they have your potential customers in their networks? If you have done your market research, defined your market positioning, you know who your target market is to start with, who the businesses or individuals are.

What networking is NOT:

▶ A list of business cards or contacts you met somewhere at some point;
▶ A direct lead to sales;
▶ Something you can clearly measure return on investment on.

What networking IS:

▶ Building relationships with other business professionals you share interests with, such as on social media;

- Exchanging information on conferences/networking events/books/news for the sector/ in specialist areas;
- Sharing your expertise, sometimes for free in newsletters and/or blogs or white papers – free reports to download that are short and to the point and can be shared easily via link or email;
- Building ambassadors in your network, making contacts knowledgeable about what you do and the services/products you offer.

The most important aim of networking is to develop professional relationships with people. It is less important to get your name and your products/services known to the right people; that happens anyway if you have the relationships. That means you need to link with either those potential customers directly and with those people who have the "right" customers in their networks. You need to build trust and show that you mean business, in essence that you are reliable: deliver on your promises, listen to customer demands, show some flexibility and deliver the quality you promise.

Secondly, in the spirit of reciprocal relationships from which two people gain (you can call it win-win), in order to create a sustainable business you need to have the attitude of asking yourself what you can give to a contact, instead of wondering what you can gain from them (meaning sales). And would it not be great to have some fun talking to the right people? Like-minds enjoy the same things.

Networking done appropriately can save you a lot of money. This can be the case when you have a suitable network and work it appropriately. How to work the network is discussed below. Networking can be a very valuable tool to generate sales. The reason was outlined above: people buy from people and rely increasingly on recommendations from others.

If you look at some LinkedIn profiles and see the number of contacts individuals have you may wonder if they have actually met these 500 or more people. Just because someone has 500-plus contacts does not mean that they are actually good at what they do. They might just know lots of people.

Networking is something that you will do at several key points in the start-up process, and it is on-going once you are up and running. For the pre-start-up process that means:

1) Following on from what was said in Chapter One and subsequent chapters, in order to identify what customers want or complain about regarding existing services/product, you have to network and carry out market research.

2) When you fine-tune your offer, you need to check with potential customers what they think; they might have useful ideas and suggestions for developing the business model and operational set-up. You can do that formally via market research and informally through chatting with several people at informal events or formal networking events.

3) If you think you have got your offer and value proposition as well as your operational set-up all sorted out, check again with your hopefully by then already built networks of selected stakeholders that you really understood what they needed and on their willingness to buy the offer.

Once up and running, ensure you inform them regularly about business changes, updates successes.

Many business owners or business managers go to lots of networking events, where they mainly collect business cards and have a chat, yet do not develop their network. *Working your network* is essential, so instead of collecting more business cards, work the network you have on a regular basis. Working the network is simple: on top of sending a newsletter and update via LinkedIn, phone and/or meet or Skype with them. Box 6.3 explains two ways of working the network.

Box 6.3   Working your network

Use the contacts you have listed on a database or in your LinkedIn contacts. If you have just met someone at a networking event or conference, email him or her to ask if they are happy for you to give them a ring. If you do not get a "no", ring them and find a suitable time to talk further. Often if you ring at the right time, it can happen straight away. If that is not possible, agree another date/time, and then you call them back. Ask them questions about how the event you met at went for them, any useful outcomes, and if you get talking, ask how their business is doing. Only then it is time to ask if they mind if you tell them a bit more about what you do and who you are. It is a simple rule, once you have listened and asked questions that show a genuine interest, they will be more open to listening to what you have to offer. And even if they do not need your services/products, they might know someone who does. Always close by thanking them for time spent talking together, and have an offer ready of information for them, to send to them in the future. That gives you permission to get in touch again in a few weeks/months, and they will remember you for that piece of information. After that call send them information on your products electronically or paper-based, and thank them again for an interesting chat. Do not make this first chat too long, sometimes 10 minutes is all that is needed. I have a 12-minute rule: it is good for 12 minutes, it can get stale after that. You will get a feel after about 8 minutes if that is the case, and then stop the conversation early enough. It works! Carry on re-connecting about every four to six months.

In this section, we have discussed various channels for networking: phone, Skype, face-to-face, email. Naturally, there are other channels, not to forget social media. I mentioned LinkedIn already, and there are many others you will have heard about such as Facebook, Google+, Pinterest, just to name a few. The limitation of social media sites is that it is rarely two-way communication, you send out updates to all the contacts in your network, and that is not very personal. While you can send personal messages, they then rarely differ from email messages. Social media will be discussed in more detail under personalized marketing in Chapter Thirteen.

The next section briefly discusses types of formal networks you can use.

6.5.2   Networks for start-ups and established businesses

There are thousands of established networks for business start-ups and on-going businesses and the self-employed. Some networks run a formal events programme with external speakers and require a fee (that often includes a meal), others are informal and exist solely for members to meet and exchange contact details. Meeting times vary between weekly, fortnightly and monthly. Networking in some of those regular formal networks follows a pattern or system.

For example, Business Network Initiative (BNI, see www.bni.com for the US or www.bni.co.uk for the UK) is an American approach, in which membership is regulated so that in each local chapter or group only one member of one profession can attend a meeting. Attendance at weekly breakfast meetings is expected regularly. Members have to get up and do a 60-second pitch about an aspect of their business and what kind of business leads they would like to gain. The membership fee includes training materials and face-to-face training in these types of pitches. After the 60-second pitch every member does at each meeting, one or two members have the chance to do a 10-minute presentation at the weekly meeting. Once this part is over, breakfast starts or continues followed by a discussion of any chapter issues that need talking over.

One key element of BNI meetings is to provide leads for other members and hand them over to them. There is a "champion" per year or quarter, who is selected based on having provided the most leads; a lead is written on a printed form with two copies and handed during the meeting to the chapter member in question; the chair of the chapter gets a copy and the person making the lead gets a copy as well. After about 90 minutes the meeting is over and informal networking takes place. Members are encouraged to meet one-to-one with other chapter members to learn more about each other's businesses.

BNI chapters exist in most of our case study countries, including Romania, UK, US and many Northern European countries such as Sweden, Norway, Finland, Denmark and the Netherlands.

This is one of the most structured networking approaches, which is clearly business-lead focused. There are many similar yet less rigorously structured meetings, examples for the UK are the British Referral network or Business over Breakfast clubs (BoB, see www.brxnet.co.uk and www.bobclubs.com). What these types of networks have in common is a chance of limited membership so that only one or two of the same trade or profession are members of the same local group and the possibility to talk to the whole group about your own business activity and ask for leads.

 Case study

Our case study Alison Barton, photographer, gained good business leads and actual paying work from her local BoB club and still attends the meetings regularly. BoB clubs exist in the UK, the US and seven other countries where English is the official language. Check out http://www.bobclubs.com (accessed April, 5, 2015).

What all these networks discussed so far have in common is that members have to pay a membership fee and attend meetings regularly. Benefits may vary and may include reduced cost for business insurance, free or reduced training for members or business resources for better business practice, such as marketing and sales. Other business networking meetings are held on a local or regional level by professional bodies, such as for architects, SME lobby organizations such as the Federation of Small Businesses in the UK, and even some local councils organize business networks. In Chapter Two we discussed networks for business support.

There are also many women-only network meetings in every country. In the UK, examples are Women in Business, the Athena Network (focused on referrals), Everywoman, the Association of Scottish Businesswomen, Women in Business Network (referral focused with many local groups), Women in Rural Enterprise (WiRE) and regional and local business women networks. Some business networks exist only online such as Mumpreneurs, a network for mothers starting and running businesses – this is one network our case study **Alison Barton** gets many referrals from.

In Canada and Ireland there are the Women's Executive Network WXN, and for Canada Company of Women. There are a number of international networks such as the European Professional Women's Network (with national networks in many countries including Romania, the Netherlands, Sweden, Denmark and Norway), WEConnect Europe, and the International Federation of Business and Professional Women.

6.5.3 Networks and networking for social enterprises

Do social enterprises network in the same places you might ask? As so many are so young, in the UK and elsewhere that is difficult to answer quickly and with a "yes" or "no". From a practical viewpoint, social enterprises need to network more with traditional for-profit businesses, and some most certainly do. Some also network in social enterprise/non-profit-only networks, and a number of them only network there. Box 6.4 lists a number of networks particularly for social enterprises in European countries and the US (this is only a selection and not meant to be a representative list).

Box 6.4   Social enterprise networks

International

The Global Social Enterprise Network (GSEN, http://gsen.unltd.org.uk/) is a recent network founded by a UK social enterprise to bring together networks and social enterprises across the world; it is supported by the UK government.

Social Innovation Exchange (SIX) is a network of social innovators across the world, based in the UK.

On Meetups.com there is a social entrepreneurs group with over 90,000 members in over 45 countries, they hold local face-to-face meetings.

Ashoka Innovators for the Public holds local meetings and training for its fellows.

US

Social Enterprise Alliance

UK

Social Enterprise UK

There are many local and regional UK networks, such as SEN for the Merseyside city area

Romania

The Romanian Social Business Development Consortium (RSBDC) is a collaboration of networks to support social entrepreneurs in Romania, founded in 2011.

Sweden

Forum for Social Innovation Sweden

The Netherlands

Willemijn Verloop (SocialEnterpriseNL)

There is a great variety in the quality and quantity of social enterprise networks across Europe and the US. One reason is that the UK has been active in and with community enterprises and social enterprises for decades, more so than many other countries, in particular in Eastern Europe.

Chapter Eight explores possible legal forms, licenses for trading and requirements to comply with the law and formal decision-making and ownership issues. Chapter Seven discusses business modelling to find an optimal mix of all elements for value capturing and creation.

6.6 Concluding remarks and application of new insights

Starting a business by yourself has many advantages, including that you can do things your way and do not have to rely on others to make decisions. However, it is also a lonely process, and you have to rely solely on your own contacts and networks as well as your credit history to gain access to external funding, if the latter is of interest to you. Team start-ups can be more successful and grow more quickly, provided the team works well together; the additional skills, contacts and work input a partner or team brings can add enormous value. Yet, teams have their challenges in how to share ownership and to work smoothly together, making decisions quickly and effectively. Unfortunately, too many team start-ups do not survive the first year.

Thinking ahead how your potential *sustainable start-up* will operate is very important; for that reason we discussed ways to establish what the most important steps are and what input is needed for each of them to be successful. The aim is to develop the minimal viable processes to create the minimal or most marketable product. We differentiated clearly between the MVBP-C, the customer journey as experienced and seen by the customer, and the customer journey as seen by the start-up, MVBP-CB. The activities achieving this aim were identified. We identified the most important reason for breaking operational processes into small steps as all inputs and activities have an effect on cost: more steps need more staff time and effort out; more input means more money needs to be spent to buy the materials or resources. To start with, making lists of these steps and the input needed will open up insights into all activities and their resource needs. In order to ensure that you do not forget an important step or input, we discussed ways to break these steps further down into three more steps each as a rule of thumb. Gantt chart and flow chart are two methods illustrated to show the steps, their dependencies and, in the case of the Gantt chart, duration.

Networking is one of the most important start-up activities with many positive effects on the business. We discussed ways to network and channels (online, face-to-face, through social media). Networking can help in the phase of research, finding business partners and staff, gaining leads for business and simply building a brand. Several formal networks and associations were introduced for the case study countries.

For social enterprises operational processes are not very different. One of the main important differences discussed is the recruitment and management of volunteers, members and boards.

Revision questions and applying the new insights to your *sustainable start-up*

1 What are the advantages of starting a new venture by yourself?
2 What are the advantages and disadvantages of starting with at least one other person?
3 Explain what a Gantt chart can offer for showing business process.
4 Why is it important to map business processes in the pre-start-up phase?
5 What are the advantages of using a flow chart?
6 What is business networking about? Why do you need to do it?
7 Create a list of at least ten local, regional and national networks in your country.
8 Imagine you are an online retailer of smartphone cases: Create a list of the important steps in processing a customer order from you receiving it to the services/good arriving with the customer.
9 Consider your own venture: Will you start by yourself or with someone? If you start by yourself, have you done the skills assessment from Chapter Three? How will you address your weaknesses? Write the answers into your start-up diary!
10 Where does the customer journey start for your start-up? Map the steps a customer would have to carry out to reach you. You were asked in Activity 6.2 to carry out this mapping – write briefly in your start-up journey diary about the experience. Was it easy or difficult? Did you finish it quickly? Did you check it out with customers in a trial?
11 What are the essential/most important activities you need to carry out to keep your planned new venture going? Make a list, and then add the input/resources needed to make them happen. Have you costed all of them? Are they in the list of costs? Note the results of this activity and any thoughts that occurred to you while carrying it out.

7

BUSINESS MODELLING THAT FITS

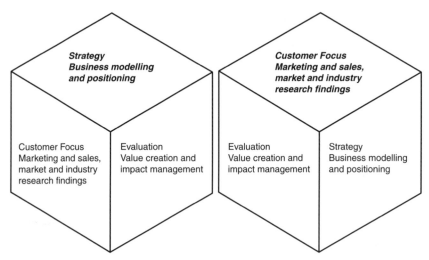

Figure 7.1   The Cube Customer Focus and the Cube Strategy
Source: © Hill, 2012.

Summary

This chapter focuses on business modelling, an on-going practice for the *sustainable start-up* approach. We introduce business modelling approaches and tools to provide help in developing a model that shows how your potential start-up will capture value while creating the change in the customer experience needed for a customer to buy what you offer. This is summarized more technically in meeting the requirements of the marketplace and/or the industry, and includes the necessary operations and resources as well as the skills, interests and values of the founder(s) (Figure 7.1). For social enterprises the business modelling process needs to be led by the social mission it aims to fulfil and find ways to balance the needs of generating commercial income and fulfilling these social objectives. The chapter finishes by linking these reflections and actions to adjusting the value proposition where appropriate.

CONTENTS

7.1 What is a business model?

This chapter discusses the important Cube area of "Strategy", the aspect of business modelling. It is one of the most important processes of the sustainable pre-start-up processes that impacts on all other areas. Its position as Chapter Seven is helpful as you need to understand a number of important business processes before you can gain value from bringing your insights together and engaging in business modelling.

Business models are increasingly discussed yet are the least understood aspect of creating or running a business, and even less understood by the large majority of start-ups. For *Start Up* we talk about business modelling to indicate the on-going process of developing the way of doing business. In other words, the development and change in the way the potential start-up can generate, capture and give out value to all stakeholders. (Just a reminder, stakeholders are all the people and organizations affected by and affecting your start-up (see Chapter Five).) It has to be an on-going process of doing, evaluating and fine-tuning (or even redesigning where appropriate), as outlined in the bootstrapping start-up approach in order to remain sustainable in the markets and industries the start-up operates in, or simply to survive and make money. This applies to social enterprises in the same way.

The business model is the system of how a company does business, the way it captures, generates and distributes value to meet the perceived market need. It refers to the interactions between the various resources (people with skills, financial resources, materials and intellectual resources), their activities and the dependencies that exist between them.

In business practice and planning, a business model is a strategic tool that guides strategy development and implementation, simply defined as resource acquisition and distribution, from start-ups to established businesses.

There are plenty of definitions around of what a "business model" is and what it means, yet the practice is often very different. Box 7.1 lists a few recent academic definitions and provides an insight into the history of the term. What these definitions have in common is that a business model is a tool that captures value for the founder(s) and the organization and explains the skeleton or framework of how the business operates, and, importantly, how a company makes money, and the way an organization competes and structures relationships, allocates resources and interacts with stakeholders.

The principles and associated practices introduced in Chapter One for the *sustainable start-up* that are realized with business modelling are alertness, interconnectedness, resourceful impact and co-creation.

Chapter Six discussed operations and Chapter One discounted some inappropriate assumptions or myths, for example the often falsely assumed need to have permanent physical office space, and offered various ways to start-up in a much more flexible way.

Answering the questions then what a business model should address creates similar problems, as there is no agreement on the components. Dependent on author, they vary between three and 42 factors (Amit and Zott, 2012, Shafer et al., 2005). Osterwalder and Pigneur (2010) identified nine elements (they call them building blocks) of a business model that describe from the outside what the business does; they called it the "business model canvas". While they did not add anything new, the visual combination of the four areas and nine components offers a business snap shot at a specific point in time. This descriptive business model is explained in Section 7.3.2. The elements most authors agree on include the customer, the value proposition or offer, the ways of distribution and making money.

Box 7.1   Definitions of a business model

The history of the term "business model" is short as it only entered formal academic writing in 1950 (Baden-Fuller et al., 2010). Many definitions exist, yet there is no agreement on one, neither on its meaning nor its conceptualization – is it a framework, an approach, a tool, a value capture system or the architecture? According to the following sources, a business model (is):

A method for generating values; it is a company's blueprint and explains the current and future state of a company. (Bowman and MacInnes, 2006)

An abstract representation of an organisation, be it conceptual, textual, and/ or graphical, of all core interrelated architectural, cooperational, and financial arrangements designed and developed by an organisation presently and in the future as well as all core products and/or services the organisation offers or will offer based on these arrangements that are needed to achieve its strategic goals and objectives. (Al-Debei et al., 2008)

[It] articulates the logic, the data and evidence that support a value proposition for the customers and viable structure of revenues and costs for the enterprise delivering that value. (Teece, 2010)

A set of capabilities that is configured to enable value creation consistent with either economic or social strategic objectives. (Seelos and Mair, 2007)

A conceptual tool, a description and delivering this value and relationship capital, to generate profitable and sustainable revenue streams. ... The rational of how an organization creates, delivers and captures values. (Osterwalder and Pigneur, 2010)

The next section discusses reasons for considering business modelling and when to engage in business modelling in the start-up process.

7.2   Why business modelling and when to do it

7.2.1   Why business modelling is important for the pre-start-up and start-up processes

Practitioners and researchers alike identify the need to have a strategic fit between an organization and the market(s) it operates in, and I add for the *sustainable start-up* the strategic fit with values, life stage and capabilities. While easily said, it is more challenging to suggest how to ensure that this fit is happening. Mullins (2012) points out the importance of a business model as essential to create a *sustainable start-up* as well: "if your business model doesn't add up, your business won't last" (p. 125).

There is a business case for ensuring this strategic fit is there at all times, in order for a start-up to achieve optimal business performance, with focus on effective and efficient production and sales, to make a profit (and for social enterprises as well, not instead, to give best possible value through free or reduced services to those who need them). Some research goes as far as to point out that a business model can be used to predict business performance (provided there is little change in the external environment); that is rather ambitious as so many conditions are constantly changing, which we mentioned in Section 1.3.

Before engaging in actual start-up, that is, launching the venture in the market-place, it needs to be clear that the business idea is feasible or viable, which means it can create the amount of money the founder(s) wants to generate. We have discussed the four areas of fit for which feasibility needs to be researched. This research implements the practice of sustainability. These four related areas are:

▶ Finance (Chapters Nine and Ten);
▶ Operations (Chapter Six; legal issues, governance and management will be addressed in Chapter Eight);
▶ Market (Chapter Five) and industry (Chapter Four);
▶ Person-ability of the business idea in relation to life stage and personal values (Chapter Three).

There are plenty of examples to show that some businesses nearly failed or did have to close down as they did not re-consider their business model, and in particular technology and customer channels. A survey carried out with CEOs and senior managers of large organizations pointed out that the majority of them prefer to innovate by developing a new business model than developing new products/services to achieve or improve competitive advantage (Amit and Zott, 2012).

Borders, the US-based bookstore giant, is an example of a business failure to react in time to important changes in the external business environment and customer behaviour, and adapt the business model accordingly; this example is outlined in Box 7.2.

Box 7.2   Business failure due to neglecting to revisit a business model in a timely manner

Borders opened its first bookstore in the US in the 1960s, offering a traditional model of a physical brick-and-mortar bookstore. Customers could enter to search or browse for books, buy books over the counter or order them in. By 2011 it had over 650 stores worldwide. When customer behaviour changed and online buying of books increased, Borders outsourced online buying to Amazon.com in 2001, so that a link was on its website that directed customers wanting to buy online to the competitor. This had a detrimental effect on branding and customer loyalty. What Borders realized too late was the increasing importance of e-books and e-book readers. It did not invest into e-reading timely, did not develop its own e-reader early enough and only opened an e-book store in 2008, after ending the relationship with Amazon.com. The marketing of their e-books that could be used on existing e-readers was too slow and not effective in establishing the company as an e-book seller. The number of bookstores had to go down due to the changes in customer buying behaviour, and the book buying experience in stores had to change, something else which Borders did not react to early enough. Competitors such as Barnes & Noble in the US did identify the drivers for change early enough; they came up with their own e-reader, the Nook.

Businesses must be aware of existing business methods, ways of doing business, and possible patents for them before putting innovations out to use in the marketplace; at the same time, they need to protect their way of doing business if it is sufficiently unique. Increasingly, business methods have been patented, although only in some countries. (That patent laws vary across countries is briefly discussed in Chapter Eight, "Legal Issues and Governance".)

In the future, ways of doing business will become an increasingly contested ground in business. All start-ups are well advised to think about their business model carefully and research what has been patented before you implement a different or new way of doing business.

7.2.2 When to engage in business modelling

Based on the previous two sections it is not surprising that the *sustainable start-up* approach is to start on business modelling *early*, in order to express how value could be realized in the best possible way for all stakeholders after having identified one or two core business ideas to consider.

 Building on the need to create a *sustainable start-up*, re-considering a number of times how the various elements of a business model can contribute to value creation is needed during the pre-start-up phase. The points in time for business modelling in the pre-start-up process include:

1) Once you have identified a business idea, done some industry and market research, clarified your most profitable customer segments that are willing to pay money for experiencing a big enough change in their customer experience and identified channels to get the product to them;
2) Once the operational projections have been carried out for the first time;
3) Once the financial research and ways to cover costs have been addressed;
4) Once the legal research has identified how and at what cost the enterprise will comply with regulations and the law;
5) After market testing has been carried out and any further customer insight has been gained that might require adjustments to the business model;
6) When the feasibility study is being done, when various business scenarios are suggested, and one is selected as the most suitable;
7) On an on-going regular basis, when changes in the external environment, customer behaviours, internal changes have been carried out.

There is no sequence prescribed with the above list of one to seven. Rather, whenever this exploration has been carried out, the business model needs to be re-considered and possibly re-adjusted.

The next section explores a small selection of business models we can base the business modelling process for a *sustainable start-up* upon.

7.3 Business modelling for the *sustainable start-up*

7.3.1 Modelling how to create the kind of change customers experience

Once you have identified the change you intend to create with and for the customers, the one that makes them buy the product, you need to clarify the process the customer will experience when using the new product or service and the impact it will have on their lives and create the *story of change*. This was discussed already in Chapters Three and Five. By now you should have developed a change and benefit statement based on your research.

The very simple business model used in Chapter One (see Section 1.4) identified typical changes, with the focus on what happens to the materials put into the change process, such as assembling parts into a finished product, packaging finished goods and selling them on, or changing raw materials through processing into ready-to-use products.

An example to illustrate the idea of the theory and story of change is Apple and their introduction of iPad tablet computers.

Remember when there were only desk PCs, laptops and netbooks (small laptops)? They all had in common that you have to press a button and wait for the machine to start, which takes time. Their battery life was limited, which meant you had to recharge quite often, dependent on the machine. You had to use a mouse, or touchpad, to access information. This could be clumsy, particularly when travelling. Someone must have thought, "It would be so nice to just click a button and have the computer ready to use the Internet (the phone screen is so small)" or "I'd like to be able to use my fingers, no mouse". This is a call to save time, use less steps and do things more easily. The theory of change has to be developed, looking for the nature of the problem and what the desired activity/condition looks like. Then steps to get there need to be looked at. Again, it is the processes to get there and the experience of the changed state that are guiding the production design.

The *sustainable start-up* approach provides a guide through the six areas of business start-up highlighted in the Cube that was described with the six principles and practices outlined in Chapter One.

This Cube image works well guiding our business modelling for the *sustainable start-up*. The six areas of the Cube represent:

1) Business Processes: operations and process management;
2) Financial Circuits: spending and making money (including pricing);
3) Frameworks: internal frameworks (governance) and legal issues;
4) Customer Focus (and environment): marketing, sales, market and industry research;
5) Strategy: business modelling and positioning;
6) Evaluation: value creation and impact management.

You should ideally by now have most of the information and insights available for business processes (1), customer focus and environment (4) having continuously applied evaluation during the journey so far (6), following the considerations of the principle and practice of resourceful impact. Through the discussions, research and insight developed in the exercises in previous chapters and then having tested your product or service in the market, you will have adjusted it further, and refined the change and benefits statement. Now you have identified the most viable processes to create the minimal marketable product.

Or you might not have managed to arrive at such an outcome. In either case, I suggest carrying out the modelling activities below. If you have found the most viable business processes to create the minimal marketable product, check that the outcome actually sufficiently addresses the problem the customers most need solving to buy the product at the appropriate price. In case you have not found that price or marketable product as yet, this process might help you to identify some issues you need to address.

1) Define the customers' most important problem(s) that need solving and define the customer as you have developed the profile so far. What happens in the current situation? What does it feel like? What does it look like from the customers' point of view?

2) Write an effective problem statement that contains:
- A "how" question;
- Action verbs, representing a positive course of action;
- A desired outcome.

3) Restate the problem so as to uncover the real problem as if talking to another audience.

4) Name the source(s) of the problem customers have.

5) Summarize the most important essential change(s) the customers need to experience in order to buy the product, and outline the benefits that this change brings them.

6) Identify the pros and cons for potential solutions and changes you can offer. You should know the minimal marketable product, that is, the product that creates the smallest viable number of changes that makes customers want to buy the product.

7) Get feedback from stakeholders for each solution: you need ideas about costs, ways to finance the solution creation process, resources to create the solution, partners you might need. What are the most effective ways to do that?

Steps six and seven are the core business modelling process steps. While you have developed potential solutions, you still need to identify ways to make them happen. The next steps need to be planned practically – what tools are out there that you can use that help to structure this process? And practically, how do you apply the Cube as a tool to gather the necessary information together? If you have not read the finance chapter, it may be helpful to work your way through the financial considerations described in Chapters Nine and Ten and then come back to this section.

 Let us start with the last point. Practically, for business modelling, flip charts with lots of flow charts, drawings and lists are a useful tool to remind all stakeholders involved in the process what happened. Pictures of each of the six areas can easily be shared online with all the stakeholders; and they can, at any time in any place, make contributions to develop any area. Figure 7.2 gives you a flattened Cube to transfer to a flip chart or onto a whiteboard to bring information together.

The Cube image reminds us that all areas are connected, like the six areas of a Cube. One is always directly linked to four others and through them indirectly to the sixth one. And it does not matter which one(s) are you are focusing on at any point in time. Should you make changes to one of the six areas, ensure you make the associated changes to the other five areas.

Use flip charts to work collaboratively and answer the following questions for each area: *why* something should be done; *how* it should be done; *with what* staff, tools or materials; *when* it should be done, including a time line and duration of each activity (using a Gantt chart for example); *where* it should be done, include meeting places or online meetings;

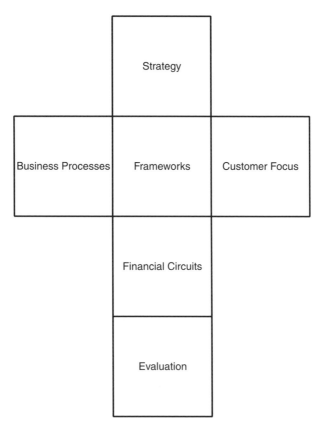

Figure 7.2   The practical application of the Cube for sorting information

who should be involved, staff and stakeholders, including external stakeholders; what *risks* are involved carrying out an activity and not carrying it out; and the mid- and long-term *impact* each activity will have. Online whiteboards can be used in a similar way to flip charts, where all participants in a team can see each other's ideas, comments and changes at all times.

Action plans can be physically or "virtually" pinned to each of the six areas, with enough copies for each staff member, volunteer or stakeholder to take down and away when they are pinned to a wall. Electronically, action plans can be shared as easily accessible text documents for a limited circle of stakeholders.

You also need a tool that allows you to understand better how the various aspects of doing business fit together; I suggest that this tool can be the business model canvas (Osterwalder and Pigneur, 2010). The next section outlines what the canvas can offer. Box 7.3 outlines my critique of the limitations of the canvas model. However, it can add value and is a practical addition to guiding you on your start-up journey. There are a number of business models in circulation that address similar aspects, such as the lean canvas attempting to address missing aspects. In my view, this canvas version by Osterwalder is the most straightforward one and the missing areas are addressed with this Cube nicely. Alongside that very general canvas, for online business I suggest to explore a particular model adding value.

7.3.2   Business model canvas

Osterwalder and Pigneur (2010) identified nine critical factors, they call them *building blocks*, and called it the *business model canvas* (see Figure 7.3). This is a descriptive business model that summarizes at face value how the business captures value. These four areas and nine elements are shown below. Their terminology is displayed surrounded by quote marks. As the business model canvas uses some specific language that is different to established business terminology, I add other simple phrases or words:

▶ The customer area – "customer segments" (or target customers), "customer relationships" and "channels";
▶ The offer area – "value proposition", the packaged offer made to the buyer(s);
▶ The infrastructure area – the "key activities" and "key resources" needed to run the business, and "key partners", in our words the most important stakeholders (Section 5.9.3);
▶ The finance area – "cost structure" and "revenue streams."

The following paragraphs are based on Osterwalder and Pigneur, 2010.

Customer

"Customer segments" refers to the target customers or customer groups an enterprise is aiming to sell to. Focus should be on carefully assessing these customers' needs before putting a value proposition together. As discussed in Chapter Five, customers need to be created and developed, and potentially segmented to create the best fit between meeting the most important needs of profitable buying customer and the possible product features. Go back to Chapter Five for checking on identifying the first customer segment.

"Customer channels" addresses the ways an enterprise communicates with and delivers the value proposition to customer segments to meet their needs, also called distribution

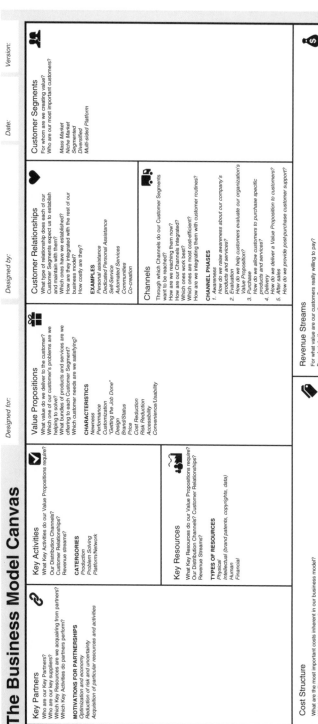

Figure 7.3 Business model canvas
Source: Osterwalder and Pigneur, 2010. Strategyzer.com.

channels. The known phases that need channels are raising awareness, evaluating the offer, purchase, delivery and after-sales. For those familiar with the seven Ps in marketing, channels overlaps with "place".

"Customer relationships" attempts to summarize all types of relationships with potential, current and past customers in existing segments. The steps that are addressed include customer acquisition, customer retention and customer extension or upselling. For those familiar with the seven Ps in marketing, customer relationships partially overlaps with "promotion". It also addresses types of customer relationships. These types are differentiated by the amount and quality of personal customer service and range from tailored individual service (as offered by dress designers and tailors) to fully automated service (offered by online stores).

Value proposition

"Value proposition" refers to the package of services and tangible products offered to selected target customers, also called the market offer. The focus is on the benefits and value delivered to customers, going beyond a possible clearly defined product or service. This includes aspects such as customer service and experience, product design and packaging, price, service and delivery speed, additional products/services provided free of charge. For those familiar with the seven Ps in marketing, value proposition is related to the "product". We have so far talked about the benefits and change statement, and the product features that can bring about that change. Key features that need addressing in the value proposition include performance of a product (for example speed, quality of output or storage), the degree of tailoring a product to the needs of the customer segment, convenience, cost saving, increase in accessibility and usability, lower price while offering similar value.

Infrastructure

We discussed in Chapter Six important business processes, and started to identify the input needed for them to work smoothly and effectively. The Cube face Business Processes addresses the more conceptual approach to resources. "Key resources" takes a snapshot of the input and summarizes the key input needed to create and deliver the value proposition to the customer and make the business work. Resources include financial (money), human (staff), physical (for example brick-and-mortar shop, IT infrastructure or warehouse) and intellectual elements (intellectual property rights such as a patent or copyright). We discussed these processes that are important in their dynamic way and broke them down into particular activities and steps in Chapter Six. "Key activities" in the model summarizes all activities that make the business model work.

"Key partnerships" sheds light on the external stakeholders that make the business model work. They are often overlooked and underestimated in their significance, until something goes wrong. They include payment processors, such as banks, credit card companies, suppliers of goods and other services, trade unions and employer organizations (providing membership is in place). We discussed stakeholders in a number of previous chapters and highlighted through applying the principles of responsibility and impact the dynamic nature of the processes, which the *sustainable start-up* needs to engage in.

Finance

"Cost structure" summarizes the approach to costs and the kind of costs generated for creating the value proposition and delivering it. The approach to costs can be simplified into two approaches: high value approach or value driven and low cost or cost driven approach. While the latter focuses on keeping cost as low as possible, the high value approach focuses on offering a premium value to customers. All cost types should be gathered and figures added up, before a decision for the cost approach is made. This consideration links to the market positioning discussion for every product/service, where the price decision is added in order to find the best fit for market positioning. In reality, most business models fall in between these two approaches.

Cost driven business models minimize all costs everywhere possible; this is often realized through low price value propositions that maximize automated non-personalized customer relationships and often outsource extensively in order to reduce cost. Amazon is one example for a cost driven approach, low-cost airlines are another.

Value driven business models focus on offering the highest possible value, often combined with premium prices in a premium value proposition. This value proposition is often realized with highly personalized services and products, such as one butler serving one hotel room and where bathrobes also bear the name of the guest stitched onto them.

In practice, although often both approaches are combined, in most businesses one approach dominates.

The "cost structure" area also summarizes all costs incurred to make the business model work. These costs can be added up once business processes and input have been defined and developed, as we started to do in Chapter Six through differentiating between customer process, business view of managing the customer order and the business processes used to maintain on-going business activities; we continue that in Chapters Nine and Ten on "Financial Circuits" (one of our Cube faces).

"Revenue streams" is the income generated through the customers purchasing the value offer and all other income streams, such as interest on capital, rent on buildings owned, and pricing strategies. Focus is on developing more than one cash generator in the long run. Other income streams possible include advertising (on the website or packaging or emails or printed materials), merchandise (such as what football and ice-hockey clubs sell: mugs, T-shirts, hats, etc.), license fees, sale of associated services to products (after-sales service that is paid for; insurance services for products purchased such as expensive TVs or computers) or products to services sold (hairdressers selling haircare products), memberships and/or subscription services (paid monthly and giving additional benefits only members gain), in-app purchases to get more quickly to a higher level in a game and similar products.

How all the elements or building blocks are connected to each other needs further explanation and illustration, and this is where the value of the *sustainable start-up* approach lies. Changes to one factor often mean a change to at least another one.

The advantage of using the canvas for learning about start-up as a process is that more aspects of a business venture are linked together than traditional models offer to do. Having used it with many young learners and adult start-ups, the approach offered by the business model canvas has to be supported with other information. The Cube this book applies with the six main process areas offers the needed additional information.

For the pre-start-up process it is helpful to apply a SWOT analysis to each of the nine building blocks/factors in order to establish the limitations as well as potential of each factor and gain insights into the sustainability of the start-up.

Finding similarities between combinations of key activities and resources, or customer channels and value propositions etc., could mean that they follow a business model pattern. These business models also share some business behaviours or ways of doing business and characteristics (Osterwalder and Pigneur, 2010). I suggest reading more about those patterns once you have looked at various ways to combine resources to create the minimal or most viable product.

Table 7.1 shows an example of a business model canvas for one of our start-up case studies, **Alison Barton.** What you can see is a simple summary of her way of doing business: her target customers are consumers and small businesses, and the relevant value proposition for each customer group. The approach to costing is mixed, as she has developed her own minimal viable businesses processes for creating the minimal marketable product. In her work with clients, she offers highest quality within the resources and budget given.

What needs to happen to be able to tell the story of change for the customer is more than the content in Table 7.1 offers. In Alison's case it is easy as I have seen her working as a photographer for a group I was part of and know her story, even before I asked her for the research interview.

 Case study

Alison is working in a competitive market of photographers, where most newcomers differentiate themselves through offering their services and products cheaper than the established small and medium-sized businesses. And at first glance it looks like Alison is just offering what others do, photographs for individuals and families, wedding photography and small business pictures to use for marketing materials. Neither of the benefits I listed in the box for each target customer group truly paints the picture of Alison's unique selling point nor would the list of service features.

So, what is the story of change then? Customers will experience a very personalized service through a young woman who focuses totally on them (or the product/business) when she takes pictures. The customer experience of change is feeling more valued and appreciated after sessions with Alison, and having fun during the sessions. They feel they gain insight into a different side of themselves (or the product for businesses) through the picture taking process, as well as the physical results they gain. True value is added to their lives/businesses, which they will not forget. It is this story of change for customers that convinces them to buy your product you need to find and write for your start-up.

7.3.3 Particular considerations for online businesses

Online services and online retail have expanded significantly over the last decade and are still growing. In particular, profits for apps that are bought at small fees and those for in-app purchases have risen exponentially. While the amount of people willing to pay upfront for an app is still small (25% in 2013), the number is growing steadily (OECD, 2013b). Similarly, in 2013 there was an exponential growth in turnover from in-app purchases, indicating the trend that this will continue to increase for the next years. This trend is further evidenced by a US mobile apps survey in 2011 in which nearly three-quarters of the 650 respondents pointed out that they would replace existing channels with mobile apps if they were able to (Clickfox in Weill and Woerner, 2013). These data reflect the trends we have all experienced

Table 7.1   Business model canvas for case study Alison Barton, photography

Key partners / stakeholders	Key activities	Value propositions	Customer relationships	Target customers
Local SMEs who link to her website and recommend her services; suppliers (for example, for maintaining the car, buying photo supplies); customers; banks; business networks and their members; social media (Facebook, LinkedIn, etc.); managers of business directories.	Updating her customers via social media and the newsletter; marketing; networking at events; taking photos and creating memorable tangible memories; printing photos; sending digital photos; buying supplies.	**Consumers:** • Problem: wish to capture moments with a high quality medium and share them with friends and not the skill nor time to do it to a high standard; • Timeless images which capture memories and moments. • Having fun in sessions with her through dedicated personal service. **Small businesses:** Problem – need to get a clear visual message about the business offer across and not the skills in-house to do that at a high quality. Perfect first impressions of the business for clients that convey the individuality and quality of the business and lead to enquiries and sales.	Entry in business directories; newsletters; social media updates; personal meetings at networking events; tailored services meeting specialist needs for consumers and small businesses. **Customer channels** Updates via social media, email newsletter; phone calls; word-of-mouth and face-to-face meetings; website updates; word-of-mouth through contacts; Entry in business directories.	Consumers; small businesses.
	Key resources Cameras; equipment for shooting photos; car; website/Internet; social media; phone; equipment for printing photos and creating albums; materials for creating merchandise; intellectual property (logo, branding, networks); financial resources to do all of the above.			

Cost structure: Cost driven in business processes; value driven in client work.

Main important costs include:
Internet/website/hosting, transport cost to see clients and suppliers; her salary; cost of supplies; utilities' bills, marketing costs; equipment; printer and printing supplies.

Revenue streams
Selling photos self-created; selling photos with photo albums; merchandise with photos such as mugs, key rings, etc.
(At start-up personal savings; a small start-up loan.)

caused by the increasing digitization of customer experiences and relationships, the growing number of people who have grown up with online experiences and services from a young age, generation Y, and the increasing significance of the customer voice via social media and rating sites (for example TripAdvisor LLC for leisure activities).

 Case study

Our two American case studies, **Richard Rodman** and **Lillie Ranney**, and **Vivek George**, in Hong Kong, illustrate the trend to take business processes fully online: services to comply with the changing financial and legal requirements for crowdfunding (which in itself is an online service) by Richard and his team; portfolio collation and services for landlords by Lillie Ranney; marketing services across the world by Vivek George.

Box 7.4 outlines a model adding insight on features particular only to online businesses. It is worth considering the unique features online services require in order to fine-tune the value proposition.

One business model for digital businesses focuses on content, experience and platform (Weill and Woerner, 2013). In their view, the business does not have to excel in all three to have a competitive advantage.

Box 7.4   A digital business model for the changing demand for online buying

Content

This is the label for all information including product information offered on the website, including price, product features and reviews or ratings from other customers and actual digital products, such as presentations, movies, audios, e-books or software that can be used online.

Experience

This label summarizes the whole experience of what it feels like on the customer journey using the platform, buying physical or tangible products such as books and electronics or obtaining a service, such as online learning. Important features include:

▸ Usability, ease of use, speed in finding what a user is looking for;
▸ Payment options on offer;
▸ Colour schemes;
▸ Use of Flash or other tools that might not work on a table computer or smartphone;
▸ Messaging options such as via text or email;
▸ What searches can be carried out, if searches are remembered and stored or not;
▸ If a shopping list or a gift list can be created;
▸ Personalized recommendations for the customer, etc.

The way customer-centred content such as reviews and ratings can be accessed and created are all part of the customer experience.

Platform

This label summarizes all internal and external business processes, data and infrastructure features that are digital. Internal systems include all business processes and data that the customer does not see and/or experience, such as customer analyses carried out on the search and purchase history (the way Amazon does it, for example); external systems or platforms address the interface between the company and the buyer/consumer (PC, laptop, tablet, smartphone), the telecommunications network, the interface between the company and delivery partners –like UPS or Royal Mail in the case of Amazon – and those companies that generate text messages and emails.

Source: Weill and Woerner, 2013

According to Weill and Woerner (2013) the competitive advantage the optimal digital business model can offer is either excelling in one of these or, better, in two of them; very few companies excel in all three. They recommend focusing on digital content if the strategic goal is to generate income first and foremost, as their findings across a number of industries show that content focus is most effective in gaining or maintaining competitive advantage across all industries. However, focus should be on customer experience when trying to maximize income per customer.

The limitation of that kind or research is that it is based on large companies such as Apple and Google, which have large resources they can invest. For start-ups this means that digital content and customer experience can be the two most important areas, and while the focus at start-up can be on the customer experience, the content side should be constantly improved.

 Case study

For their first businesses, our case studies **Lillie Ranney** and **Richard Rodman** offered the first minimal viable products with a focus on platform and content for their first ventures, and improved and developed the customer experience and content with on-going interaction with clients. This illustrates the co-creation process, which is at the heart of a pre-start-up journey discussed here.

As pointed out in the discussion of minimal marketable product, when you start selling not all product features need to be there. As long as the features make a sufficiently big change in the customer experience, applying the theory of change, to make customers buy the product, you are on the right track. Additional features can be added later if necessary. Once you know the minimal marketable product features, you need to think about in more detail how you can go about creating those features that make the biggest and necessary change to the customer experience. Service design and product design are well-documented processes; while the starting point is not always the customer development and focus, they offer valuable tools and approaches that I highly recommend studying. We can only briefly touch on them here. The further reading on the companion website outlines useful books that explain the service design process in detail.

7.3.4 Insights from new product/new service design processes for business modelling

In Chapter Three we discussed starting points for finding a new product and various types of innovation. While the value proposition in most business models showcases the end product of a development process, the business model discussion has not yet linked sufficiently new product development (NPD) or new service development (NSD) with the value proposition nor addressed any of the processes on how to get to the package of product(s) and/or services organized.

The business case for optimizing the product and service development process for start-ups is simple: the less time spent on development, the earlier the product/service can be launched in the marketplace and the quicker you can start making money. The more efficient the process is, the less time is spent.

Based on working with hundreds of start-ups developing their service(s) offer or product/service combination, I know that many feel lost during the process. For many products in the B2C market, there is some service element included in the customer journey with the company, so that the service logic can be applied first to designing the customer journey as part of the business modelling, should you not have carried that out as part of the operational considerations discussed in Chapter Six.

Chapter One briefly outlines selected growth areas for new products and services, and gave an indication of the turnover some business sectors have in the UK economy. Chapter Three then outlines sources of ideas for new services as well as indicating the economic significance of the service sector for all economies.

What is a service then? The following features have been identified as essential: inseparable, perishable, variable, intangible, simultaneous (Lovelock et al., 2009).

To be effective and meet customer needs, a service needs to be carefully designed. Chapter Six already outlines the importance of mapping and optimizing the customer journey. The discussion does not yet detail how this might be achieved. Box 7.5 offers a useful definition of service design by Ghosh et al. (2004) from a strategy perspective. The term "design" is usually used in the narrow focus of putting a service and its parts together; for our purposes we need to identify the starting point and the end point when launching the service successfully in the marketplace.

Box 7.5 Definition for service design

Service design here refers to the design of facilities, servers, equipment, and other resources needed to produce services. It includes blue print of service system, specifications, procedures and policies. (Ghosh et al., 2004)

There is no agreement on how many steps there should be in an optimal NSD process as there is not yet much evidence of best practice, and suggested processes have a variety of steps between seven and fifteen (see for example Curedale, 2013, Stickdorn and Schneider, 2014). As these suggestions are based on existing, often large businesses with numbers of staff, they can only serve as guidance. We focus on the kind of steps that need addressing. There is no agreement either on the best way of modelling service development, as a circular or linear process. For new business development practice, there are some steps that ideally are carried out sequentially, yet they go back to core points/milestones that have to be done several times, so a circular sequence can be seen as well.

7.3.5 Bringing it all together

The six Cube areas offer a framework that is helpful to use alongside the business model canvas when considering ways to go about establishing how to create the changes in customer experiences that are needed. Using them as a process guidance tool to work your way through the pre-start-up processes is a good idea to gather the needed insight on what needs considering when exploring what is needed to get the business up and running, and considering if the business is feasible, that is, if sufficient money can be made.

> The six Cube themes address the areas that start-ups seem to struggle with when only applying the business model canvas: the strategy and tactics needed in creating their own business processes. While ingredients for business processes are addressed through the infrastructure area, these building blocks only provide a snapshot of the input required yet do not provide help in how these ingredients are linked. Customer focus and external environment bring together not only the customer-related findings, but also the results of the analysis of the environment that impact massively on the way the customer focus can be realized in the value proposition. We suggest adding to the value proposition the story and theory of change statements.

Practically speaking, I suggest using the Cube areas to sort the information and insight needed, as we did so far, and then create a business model canvas next to it, transferring part of the information needed to the canvas. As indicated above, financial circuits have not been addressed here so far, and legal forms need addressing as well. This is done in the next three chapters.

The next section explains three business models for social enterprises balancing in different ways the focus on realizing a social mission and meeting social objectives and generating money and surplus to do so.

7.4   Guidance for selecting social enterprise business models

The business model canvas can only be applied to some extent to social enterprises. The areas of infrastructure, key partners and resources and activities only vary slightly, similarly to cost structure, whereas revenue streams, change and benefit statement and target customers vary more widely. And most importantly the story of change is closely linked to the social mission, which is at the core of the purpose of the organization.

The following paragraphs provide an overview of three descriptive business models, differentiating social enterprises by the impact the way of trading can have and how it is related to financial returns (based on Venturesome, 2008). The three descriptive business models below help social enterprise founders to select an appropriate form that balances commercial income generation and fulfilling the social mission in different ways. This differentiation is useful for social enterprise start-ups, as it focuses their attention on the sixth Cube area "Evaluation – Value creation and impact management" in a differentiated way and "Strategy". It is a particular application of the principle and practice of "resourceful impact" for social enterprises, introduced in Chapter One.

In the academic view, social enterprises are called hybrid models of business, as the ways of combining generating income and using the profits differs so much from for-profit approaches and balances financial returns with social impact in different ways. The effect is that strategy decisions vary sometimes significantly from those made by commercially oriented enterprises. This way of doing business is called hybrid organizing in several recent academic journal articles that attempt to pin down the core business model and ways of organizing trading, the commercial activity, with "doing good" (Battilana and Lee, 2014, from an organizational study viewpoint). Consequently, social enterprises are often called "hybrid organizations". Box 7.6 outlines a summary of some of those findings.

For the process of forming new social enterprise start-ups, *sustainable social enterprise start-ups*, only very few practical insights can yet be gained from this kind of research, that is grappling with the partially innovative and flexible ways of doing business and creating income while serving a social purpose so many social enterprise engage with. The various differences between them and for-profit businesses were outlined in Chapter One and continuously addressed in other chapters.

 Case study

In Chapter One we already discussed the "social business" propagated by Muhammad Yunus: a commercially oriented business formed with a social mission and objective in mind, such as providing low price yoghurt to the very poor people in Bangladesh. It can be reconceptualized as a business model for social mission-driven organizations. As this is a very recent organizational form, it is still being developed in shape, and different realizations exist in different parts of the world. Kurt Reitz, CEO one of the European Grameen labs, explained in a personal conversation with me in autumn 2014 that existing legal forms for commercial businesses are suggested for social business founders, while clarifying that investments will be repaid but no return on investment will be given. All profits should remain inside of the social business and be used for fulfilling the social mission further. This creates another possible balance between profit making and fulfilling a social mission.

Box 7.6   Academic insights on social enterprise business models

As pointed out before, social enterprise is a label used for organizations that have charitable activities and business (trading) activities, and where there is no clear priority of one of them to the outsider. The difficulty many outsiders to the social enterprise networks have is the different use of language and meaning of words: for example, profits are usually reworded as surplus that is used for different purposes than personal gain of shareholders. Resource allocation within the organization will always need to be rebalanced between using it for commercial activities and those that provide services to the beneficiaries.

Battilana and Lee (2014, Battilana and Dorado, 2010) discuss social enterprises as the "ideal type of hybrid organisation", combining organizational forms of business and charity. Their conclusions are based on an analysis of social enterprises studied in 95 academic journal publications and book chapters. Social enterprises are seen as ideal in the way they make sense of a variety of organizational forms and combine them in practice. Battilana and Lee rightly point out that theory development is catching up with practical developments, as practitioners have for a while built institutional structures, including new legal forms such as the Community Interest Company (CIC) in the UK to manage the tension better and improve the chances for impact investment and thus make social enterprises with some legal forms more attractive to investors.

By creating a dichotomy, an either/or of "business and charity" instead of regarding these organizational forms as shapes on a continuum, they continue the assumption in practical and theoretical terms of a more legitimate organizational and legal form the business has in some ways, and charities have in others. The practical consequences of choice of legal form, and often the organizational form that follows then, can be the limited legitimacy of some legal forms for social enterprises for investors and funders such as banks, simply by having a legal form that is not well known by funders so that they might attract less funding. Similarly, groups within the more established charity sector see more legitimacy for social enterprises as a threat to their position and ability to attract funding and gain contracts and even opposed it. Their dimensions of hybrid organizing (culture, organizational design, workforce composition, organizational activities, inter-organizational relationships) have been addressed throughout the book, and I added features that differentiate social enterprise currently from solely commercial businesses.

Similarly, Doherty et al. (2013), identified hybridity as a defining characteristic of social enterprises, based on the analysis of published journal articles, such as Battilana and Lee's contribution. Other authors describe them as being situated between "market and mission" (see also Hockerts, 2010). They define the pursuit of the two missions of financial sustainability and social purpose as hybrid behaviour and focus in their analysis on the impact of hybridity on management of the social mission, gathering financial resources and human resources.

Many long-term established social enterprises have a simple and effective business model: one side of the business generates profit through trading, sometimes called "profit genera-tor model", type one. Making profits or rather a monetary surplus is a condition for being able to create social impact, and the main purpose of the trading activity is to generate a surplus. The profits are then used to provide services free-of-charge or at a reduced price to beneficiaries who are people in need who cannot pay for services they essentially need. Or the environment is supported, for example though planting trees or protecting a particular type of animal. This model also applies to CSR activities as much as trading arms of charities, such as Oxfam, which create a profit and then pass it on to the charity to use for charitable projects. Beacon Centre for the Blind generates some of its profits with a similar approach.

Beacon Centre for the Blind is a social enterprise specializing in services for blind people and those with vision difficulties. It has a number of service offers that generate income and create a surplus (a) that enables it to offer free services to those with vision difficulties (b). It also holds contracts for local authorities in the area to deliver services on their behalf to those with vision difficulties (c). Box 7.7 explains the details of services offered to people with sight problems and ways to generate income.

Box 7.7 Services offered by Beacon Centre for the Blind

The income-generating services (listed on the website under Beacon4business) include:

▸ Charity shops (6) selling second-hand goods (clothing, books, crockery, games, furniture, etc.);Conference services – offering state-of-the-art conference facilities with all the equipment needed for data projection, etc. that can be hired for busi-ness and individual parties;
▸ Sight awareness training for employers, carers and public authority staff;
▸ Hair and beauty services.

The services they offer for those with vision problems include (services and resources section on the website):

▶ A specialized IT suite;
▶ Social groups for those with sight loss/limits and their partners;
▶ Equipment and advice services – sales of equipment to support independent living and advice on what is useful for what type of sight issues;
▶ Employment support for those seeking work;
▶ Active eyes – support from volunteers to engage in activities otherwise not possible;
▶ Activity centre – Monday to Friday from 10 a.m. to 3 p.m. offering activities by staff trained in working with those with limited or no sight, from crafts to IT, sports and indoor bowls;
▶ Children's services – one day a week for children between 5 and 18 with transport from home to the facility and back;
▶ Community talks – for the wider community on sight loss and the work of Beacon Centre for the Blind.

Services delivered on behalf of social services or for paying clients include:

▶ Respite care for those people with sight issues so that the carer can go on holiday;
▶ Sheltered housing at Beacon Court – for older blind and partially sighted people (two-bedroom apartments built to support moving around with limited or no sight);
▶ Beacon extra care – home care services through staff trained in supporting those with sight difficulties.

Source: www.Beacon4blind.co.uk, accessed 31/5/2015.

A second known model capturing value creation with social enterprises is when the trading activity itself makes a direct social impact, sometimes called trade-off model, and a balance has to be found between making financial surplus and having social impact. If financial surplus is reduced, at the same time more social impact can be achieved, and vice versa – through reducing social impact a higher financial surplus can be generated. This can be realized through offering the same service or tangible product that is sold to those who can afford to pay for it, yet it is offered free of charge or at lower fees to those who cannot afford to pay for it. Beacon Centre for the Blind's home care service is an example of this: those who can afford it have to pay for the specialized home care service, those who cannot might get it paid for via social services or, in special circumstances, free of charge.

Another example includes businesses only buying supplies from fair trade suppliers and trading in ethical ways only, so-called fair trade businesses.

Social firms – companies that employ those disadvantaged in the labour market – make a direct social impact, as they enable individuals to get off unemployment benefits or social benefits, and offer them employment, providing them with skills and an employment record. The trading activities of social firms vary widely, from consultancy, training to catering, to name a few sectors they operate in. There are two types of social enterprises in this category:

▶ Social firm – market-led social enterprise set up to create good quality jobs for those disadvantaged in the labour market;
▶ Work integration social enterprise – an enterprise focusing on improving employment prospects through offering a variety of work-based opportunities, often to enable those furthest from the labour market to become employment ready.

Social Firms UK is the British national membership and support body for these kinds of organizations (www.socialfirmsuk.co.uk). For the European level there is a body called Social Firms Europe. Box 7.8 shows examples of social firms. As indicated in Chapter One, the term "social firm" might be translated only badly into other languages; in many countries organizations exist that specialize in this type of business activity, including Sweden, Italy and Australia.

Box 7.8   Examples of social firms and associations of social firms

Fountain House in Denmark

Vates Foundation in Finland

Asociatia Europa pentra Dezvoltare Umana (AEDU) in Romania

SC HR Specisalists SRL in Romania

Rysseviken AB in Sweden

Daisies Café in the UK

Ink**lusive** CIC – in the UK

A third model focuses on trading to generate profits. Organizations using this model are often member-owned and oriented such as cooperatives and credit unions. However, the possible financial returns can be below the commercially attractive level. Social impact increases or decreases parallel to the financial return made. Members and the annual meetings of all members decide on the direction of the organization. Members predominantly buy the products and services offered, for example, in cooperative shops they earn points towards gaining a reduction in price for other shopping. And they gain a share of the profits that are distributed in relation to the money they spent on buying food or other products sold by cooperatives. Examples in the UK include Co-operatives UK and regional cooperatives and credit unions.

A credit union is a financial institution that offers loans and saving possibilities for its members only at a local or regional level; there are also profession-based credit unions (for example, transport credit union) or workplace ones (for example the NHS credit union). Some credit unions offer bank accounts, pre-paid cards and in few cases mortgages. In 2013, there were 375 across the UK with over 1 million members. Worldwide in 2013, there were 57,000 credit unions in 103 countries, including in several of the countries we have looked at in *Start Up*: Hong Kong has 44 credit unions, Romania has 20 and the United States 6,681 (World Council of Credit Unions, 2014).

In practice, larger social enterprises use models one and two or even all three models combined, through charities that are incorporated having trading arms, that is, several legally independent companies that are owned by the charity and transfer all profits to the charity.

 Case study

What does this mean in practice? How does a social enterprise start-up choose one of those models? Our case study **Kathryn Kimberley**, HumAnima CIC, sheds some light on the decision and selection process (for details on Kathryn see Chapter One, Section 1.8.5).

Kathryn has a number of income streams that create direct social impact (following business model two, trading that has social impact). She works with grants (money she does not have to pay back) with which she has to generate outputs and outcomes as agreed in the successful funding bid, one example is a grant from the Big Lottery Fund, UK. Once the money has been used she has to stop operating that service. She also works directly for clients who pay her personally for her services, for as long as they wish to get them. All these services have a direct social impact.

Kathryn also sells training services in animal assisted therapy to other counsellors. This is the biggest profit maker, and she uses the surplus generated to provide low-cost or even free services to those named beneficiaries, residents in Wolverhampton with mental health issues, who would benefit the most from animal assisted therapy. This part of her revenue model would qualify as the first business model, trading for profits. The surplus gained through offering specialist continuous professional development training to professional counsellors assists her in making an impact through using the profits for low-cost or free services to beneficiaries. The more training workshops she runs, the more social impact she can make, a trade-off.

For those starting a social enterprise, you need to find your way of balancing the need for commercial income for covering costs and your salary with the need to fulfil the core purpose of the organization, the social mission. The above described business models can provide direction on which way to go, but ultimately the way to generate income has to be decided by the individual founder(s) and the most important stakeholders.

 Figure 7.2 shows the flattened business Cube with the area of Evaluation and Impact at the very bottom. For social enterprises this might be the starting point for a discussion with stakeholders: there is a need to clarify again the social mission and the most important differences they want to make and for whose lives or for what aspect of the environment. Similarly, the weight of financial independence and sustainability will influence potentially to select the "trading for profits" model as the core business activity. The selection of business and financial model will influence the resource distribution and ways to organize operations, and how to finance it.

Developing and selecting a business model for a social enterprise is an exciting and fascinating process. Having been part of the formation process of a local community-based social enterprise I know how lengthy that process is and how much time is needed for discussion and clarification of goals and core social mission. A lot of circular processes are needed from deciding on a revenue-generating model and one of the above business models to exploring possible operational processes and finding the most viable business processes and going back to financial circuits of costing the potential solutions. The example below of an eventually failed development of a shared workspace highlights the challenges this decision process can face.

 Case study

The potential community venture I was part of explored the creation of a shared workspace, led by a passionate community leader. Her vision was guiding many of the volunteers and co-founders. After gathering information on legal forms a decision was made and realized, which took over one year. It was towards the end of year two of the development process that pop-up shared workspaces were created, using an empty commercial building on the local high street.

The biggest challenge that eventually was not mastered was the decision on how to generate the money to lease or buy one of the empty buildings in the area; and as not enough money could be raised, the potential venture did not take off. What had never happened was the consideration of the most viable business process that can allow the shared workspace idea to flourish within in the local context. While an emerging model for a co-working space was used that worked in many other countries, the local community structures were not open or financially generous enough to facilitate the development of this workspace.

7.5   Concluding remarks and application of new insights

Chapter Seven introduced the very important process of business modelling: from a practical viewpoint, when exploring if a business idea is a business opportunity fit for you (and your team), this is a step in the pre-start-up phase that needs to be carried out a number of times until you are able to say you have a business opportunity. The feasibility of an idea can be evidenced with a detailed business model – a way to summarize how an organization brings in resources, manages and distributes them and gives value to customers and other stakeholders.

Business modelling is a very important process as part of strategy and realizes all five principles and associated practices from alertness, responsibility and resourceful impact to interconnectedness and co-creation. We discussed the places in the pre-start-up and start-up processes when business modelling should be done and reviewed.

One useful tool to bring various aspects of exploration we carried out so far together is the business model canvas as introduced by Osterwalder et al. (2010); we extended the identified four areas and translated the language of the canvas to the language we use for creating the *sustainable start-up*. For social enterprises the business modelling process needs to be led by the social mission it aims to fulfil and ways to balance the needs of commercial income generation and fulfilling these social objectives.

Revision questions and application of new insights to your own potential start-up

1 What is a business model? Write a definition.
2 When would you use a business model?
3 List the six elements of the business modelling Cube.
4 List some starting points for new service development (NSD).
5 Take a small business you know, ideally a recent start-up, and apply the business model canvas to summarize their way of doing business. How long does it take you?
6 Use the Cube in Figure 7.2 and bring together the information you have collected on your venture so far. Write down the change and benefits statements and the story of change in customer experience. Include these notes in your start-up diary.
7 Apply that learning to your business idea: using the business model canvas, write down what you have found out so far in the boxes. Include the filled-in canvas in your start-up diary. What else do you need to do to be able to fill it in fully? Take note of that as well.

8

LEGAL ISSUES AND GOVERNANCE

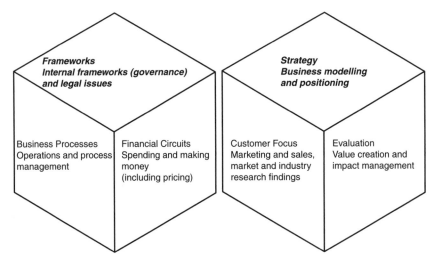

Figure 8.1   The Cube Frameworks and the Cube Strategy
Source: © Hill, 2012.

Summary

Chapter Eight introduces you to legal forms for trading (Figure 8.1). While the focus of the explanation of legal forms is on the UK, there are plenty of links to websites in the US, Hong Kong, Romania, Netherlands and Scandinavian countries. Licenses for trading are essential and need to be explored during your considerations if a great business idea could be a business opportunity, as you have to comply with them and might need additional training or staff with certain accreditations or training to be able to do so.

Protecting your idea and associated business processes is an important aspect for the idea explorations, as intangible assets such as trademarks or copyright form an essential part of the value of the start-up. Managing a start-up can take various forms, and bringing in additional skills and expertise can be realized through advisory and steering groups. Dividing shares in start-ups with more than one founder is a challenging issue, and we discuss a simple approach how to go about attributing value to the various contributions founders make. The information presented here is brief and focuses on the

UK context with examples from other countries; they should not be regarded as legal advice. My aim is to outline some of the issues the *sustainable start-up* needs to consider, signpost to any areas in which challenges might be met, and indicate resources for further information. It is important that, if necessary, advice is sought on the particular details for your situation.

CONTENTS

8.1   Choosing a legal form

8.1.1   Legal structures for for-profit start-ups

This section focuses mainly on the UK, as legal structures for each country are very different and need a lot of local knowledge. Box 8.1 offers links for other countries discussed in this book as a starting point for finding out about the most important and common legal structures. However, the process of choosing a legal form is similar in whatever country you start up, so reading on will be helpful for readers in all countries – the explanation of the process and the reasons for considering the most appropriate legal form on several occasions during the pre-start-up process is essential. In a nutshell, the legal form has implications for the personal liability of founders and owners and financial effects in terms of tax liabilities, legitimacy as an enterprise and access to funding.

Table 8.1 lists the most common legal forms for start-ups and explains each briefly in the second column. Sole trader and company limited by shares are the most frequently used forms.

The table outlines the key advantages and disadvantages in terms of cost, personal liability and amount of administration for each legal form. It then discusses some practical implications of the legal forms and gives examples with links to the companies accompanied by the link to find further information.

Most creative professionals working for themselves choose sole trader, as the example of our case study Alison Barton shows. Consumers as customers do not care about the legal form and often do not know about it.

 Perception of legitimacy as a business is another considerations when choosing a legal form. If you plan to supply to other businesses, or local authorities, then the company limited by shares is better in the long run. Still today, many large corporates prefer to work with companies, and not individuals trading as sole traders or

Table 8.1 Most important legal forms for for-profit start-ups in the UK

Legal form/ set up	Key features	Advantages	Disadvantages	Examples	Further up-to-date information
Sole trader	• One person is responsible for tax and all business responsibilities; • Staff can be employed.	• Free to register (no fees); • Easy and quick to do (online/ phone) in a day; • You can employ staff; • Easy manage as simple structure; • Limited potential to raise finance with traditional finance institutions.	• Full = unlimited personal responsibility in case of loss/damages to third parties with all personal belongings (= assets)*; • Profits are taxed as income**; • Lacks credibility in some cases: Large companies/public sector prefer incorporated organisations = registered.	Most are in service sectors: photography, hairdressing, construction and business-related services; to start with maintenance businesses and many skills related businesses; www.alisonbarton photography.co.uk.	http://www.hmrc. gov.uk/working/ intro/selfemployed. htm
Partnership	• Two or more individuals are responsible for the business at the same time; • Staff can be employed; • Partnership agreement should (but does not have to) how to split profits, ownership, liabilities, what happens when a partner leaves, etc.; • Each partner has to be registered as self-employed; • Each partner has to file his own tax return as self-employed; • Each partner has to pay Class 4 National Insurance contributions (NIC) and Class 2 NIC.	• Shared responsibility and liability between partners; • Can do own tax return to HMRC; • Less administration and "red tape"; • Limited potential to raise finance with traditional finance institutions.	• Full = unlimited responsibility for the whole business for each partner • Large companies/ public sector prefer incorporated organisations = registered.	This legal form is rarely published with a company, so no example here.	https://www.gov. uk/set-up-business- partnership

| Limited partnership | • One or more general partners that can be human beings or legal bodies (such as a company limited by shares), liable for all debts and obligations of the company individually;
• AND;
• One or more limited partners, can be persons or legal bodies, who contribute money or physical assets (such as property);
• Limited partner only liable to the value they invested into the business;
• Limited partners should not be involved in running the business;
• It has to be registered with Companies House. | • Low cost: fee of £20 or £100 for same day filing with Companies House
• Quick acceptance, usually within 24 hours
• Limited liability for partners not involved in running the organization
• Full = unlimited responsibility and decision power for those running the organization
• No shares are given away to financial sponsors
• More administration and "red tape" than partnerships, yet less than limited company by shares
• Low accountancy fees compared to limited company. | General partners who are individuals are still personally liable with all they own if the company becomes insolvent. | This legal form is rarely published with a company, so no example here. | http://www.companieshouse.gov.uk/about/gbhtml/gpo2.shtml |
| Limited Liability Partnership | • Legal business entity with limited liability for the members = partners; liability is limited to the amount they invested into the business;
• At least two parties are needed – one human being and a legal body or company; at least two members must be "designated members" for appointing auditors and signing accounts. | • Limited potential to raise finance with traditional finance institutions, but better than the last two forms above;
• Limited liability restricted to money invested;
• Organisational flexibility of a partnership while limited liability;
• Low cost for registration: £ 13,- or £ 30,- for same day filing and registration in 2014 online; paper based is more expensive; | • More bureaucracy:
• Each member has to register as self-employed and do their own self-assessment return to the HMRC;
• The LLP itself has to carry out a self-assessment as well; AND
• LLP must register and file accounts with Companies House; | http://barkerbrettell.co.uk/ | http://www.companieshouse.gov.uk/about/gbhtml/gpllp2.shtml;
http://www.companieshouse.gov.uk/about/gbhtml/gpllp1.shtml |

(continued)

Table 8.1 Continued

Legal form/ set-up	Key features	Advantages	Disadvantages	Examples	Further up-to-date information
		• Low cost for registration: £13,- or £30.- for same day filing and registration in 2014 online; paper based is more expensive; • More freedom than companies for decision making and distribution of profits to members.			
Company limited by shares	• Registered with Companies House; • Unlimited number of shares can be given out; • Shares often held by a sole director or two directors only with start-ups; • Share value can be as low as £ 1. ; • Two types of constitutional documents required: Memorandum, Articles of Association – setting legally binding rules for shareholders.	• Limited liability – limited to value of shares; • Face-value/nominal value of shares is all they can be held responsible for in a normal case; • Incorporated entity that large companies and many public sector bodies like working with for subcontracting; • NO personal liability of share holders or directors; • Low cost for registration: £ 15,- in 2014 – online or on paper £ 100.- directly with Companies House in the UK; • More credibility with corporate clients and the public sector.	• Higher accountancy fees for filing tax return; • More administration and accountability with accounts with Companies House; • Need to pay corporation tax; • Need to make monthly PAYE payments to all employees including directors; • Annual accounts, abbreviated, are put in the public domain (can be accessed by everyone).	Frinter Ltd. http:// www.frinter.co.uk with two directors	https://ewf. companieshouse. gov.uk//runpage? page=welcome

Note: * that includes a house, the car, valuable computers/equipment, etc.

** more important when you earn above the threshold to be taxed at 40 % income tax, £ 41,866 to 150,000 in 2014/2015 tax year.

sole proprietors. Similarly, dependent on what sector your start-up is in, some local authorities prefer the same.

Investors also look for particular legal forms for the start-up before they invest. Richard Rodman was asked by investors to choose the US limited liability company (LLC), as otherwise they would not have invested in the start-up.

Tax liabilities are different for sole traders and companies. Sole traders or sole proprietors are taxed personally, for all the income that is generated. Companies pay the director(s) a salary, and some profits can be taken as dividends in the UK, which are taxed at a lower rate than the income tax charged on the salary in 2015.

When choosing a legal form it is vital to consider personal liability issues, in particular when you deal with more dangerous substances and processes such as gas or engineering-related professions where there is danger for human beings. Liabilities for debts and damage are also different for sole traders and companies. Sole traders, by themselves or in a legal partnership, are personally liable for all the debts the partnership might incur, and each partner is liable for the whole debt, not just for 50% in case of two partners. This liability extends to all they own, from houses to cars and other objects of value, shares and money. Directors of companies, on the other hand, are only liable up to the value of their share in most cases, and not with their personal belongings. While business insurance can offer cover for some damages and legal fees, if say in case of an accident that was not sufficient, then as a sole trader you would still be personally liable.

8.1.2 Legal structures for non-profits

Introduction to legal forms for non-profits

Most people have heard of charities in the UK, and can name a few such as Oxfam or the Prince's Trust. What is less known is that both of them have a number of formal legal forms they operate with. Table 8.1 lists selected for-profit legal forms with some advantages, limitations and examples, whereas Table 8.2 lists the most common non-profit forms in a similar way.

Making a decision on a legal form is not easy. For social enterprises in the UK this decision is even more important, as some banks and corporate sponsors seem to believe that the community interest company (CIC) is the most convincing legal structure. When a community group starts a social enterprise, many goals and agenda have to be brought together to ensure every member is content with the limitations and added value the proposed legal form brings.

When to choose the legal form

While the final decision is only needed when you prepare for official trading, making the final decision is a long process that can be delayed until you know how you will operate (online only, with brick-and-mortar premises, both) and everything else is sorted. Yet, it helps to start the decision-making process early on.

Table 8.2 shows the most commonly used legal forms for social enterprises in the UK. Confusing language might arise when reading incorporated charity.

In the UK charities have to be registered with the Charity Commission. Being a registered charity is a legal form many people know in the UK for so-called non-profit organizations. We mentioned earlier the examples of Oxfam and the Prince's Trust. I have supported organizations in getting registered; it is a long process that often also needs legal support. At

Table 8.2 The most common forms of legal structure for social enterprise start-ups in the UK

Legal form/set-up	Key features	Advantages	Disadvantages	Examples and further up-to-date information
Registered charity	• Needs to register with the Charity Commission; • Objectives need to be covered by the set pre-defined charitable areas recognised by the Charity Commission; • Charities may benefit from some tax exemptions or tax reliefs for income and profits.	• Tax exemptions and reliefs; • Easy to gain donations from large and small companies which can gain tax reduction for donating; • It can own property and other assets.	• The trustees are personally liable for what it does; • A charity will not be able to enter into contracts or control some investments in its own name; • Two or more trustees, a corporate custodian trustee or the charities' land holding service will have to 'hold' any land on a charity's behalf; dependent on income; • Need to pay corporation tax and do tax return with HMRC; • More bureaucracy than unincorporated organisation; restrictions on trading activities.	Princes Trust, www.princes-trust.org.uk Oxfam www.oxfamorg.uk; Further up-to-date information www.charitycommission.gov.uk
Unincorporated forms – for example charitable trusts	• Often the main task is grant giving; • Not many staff can be employed; this applies to most voluntary and community organisations in the UK; • Assets need to exist to start with; • Organisation can hold property; • Most voluntary organisations are not incorporated.	• Easy to manage and set up; • No formal regulation by regulatory body; • Simple governing tools, often a constitution or association rules.	• Personal liability of members and/or management committee members; • It may have to pay corporation tax and file tax return dependent on income.	

CIO – Charitable incorporated organisation (foundation CIO, association CIO)	• An incorporated form of a charity, which is not a company; it has to register with the Charity Commission only; • It can enter into contracts in its own right and • Owning freehold or leasehold land or other property is possible. • Assets are locked = can only be used for charitable purposes.	• It can enter into contracts in its own right and • its trustees will normally have limited or no liability for the debts of the CIO; • Owning freehold or leasehold land or other property.	• It has more bureaucracy to deal with, new documents to create when changing to this legal form. • Not really disadvantages: • Foundation CIO: This form is best for existing organisations with no voting membership, strong governing trustees and existing trust deed or conveyance. • Association CIO: This form is best for existing charities that have a wide membership with voting rights on important organisational decisions and have a clearly set out constitution.	https://www.gov.uk/government/organisations/charity-commission
Company limited by guarantee	• Governing body is a board of directors; • Limited by guarantee means that each member's liability is limited to the membership fee that can be £ 1.-; • It has a separate legal entity independent of members.	• A legal personality separate from members and directors; • It can enter into contracts and own property and other assets; • Directors can gain a salary.	• Increasingly perceived by investors into impact as not sufficiently community or society benefit focused, which may limit raising grant aid; • More bureaucracy: has to file accounts and annual return with Companies House and the HMRC; • Change in directors and registered office have to be filed with government bodies.	https://www.gov.uk/limited-company-formation https://www.gov.uk/government/organisations/companies-house

(continued)

Table 8.2 Continued

Legal form/set-up	Key features	Advantages	Disadvantages	Examples and further up-to-date information
CIC community interest company – limited by shares	• It must satisfy a community interest test and is regulated by the CIC regulator; • Assets are protected – they cannot be sold for the profit of the directors; • It cannot fall under control of non-members; • It can pay dividend to members when resolution is filed; • It can pay dividend to private shareholders, which will be capped.	• It can use a number of models for operating; • Directors can be paid; • Legal identity is separate from members; • It can enter contract as a separate body independent of members; • It can own property; • It can attract investors that can gain some dividend.	• More bureaucracy as it is regulated by Companies House and the CIC regulator; • Additional obligations: in addition to annual return and tax return an additional return to the CIC regulator; • Limited attraction to some investors as there is a cap on the dividend that can be taken out.	Bristol together http://www.bristoltogether.co.uk/ My time http://www.mytime.org.uk/ (for and by menal health affected citizens) https://www.gov.uk/government/organisations/office-of-the-regulator-of-community-interest-companies, Office of the Regulator of Community Interest Companies http://www.cicassociation.org.uk/ – association of CICs
CIC community interest company – limited by guarantee	• It must satisfy a community interest test and is regulated by the CIC regulator; • Its assets are protected – they cannot be sold for the profit of the directors; • It cannot fall under control of non-members; • No dividend can be paid.	• It can enter contract as a separate body independent of members; • It can own property; • It combines various business models (as discussed in Chapter Six).	• More bureaucracy as regulated by Companies House and the CIC regulator; • Directors and investors cannot get a share of the profits; • Additional obligations: in addition to annual return and tax return an additional return to the CIC regulator. • Not so attractive to investors as no dividend can be paid.	CommunityEnergy Solutions http://ces-cic.org/ Women like us – helping women into work, also around family commitments http://www.womenlikeus.org.uk/ https://www.gov.uk/government/organisations/office-of-the-regulator-of-community-interest-companies, Office of the Regulator of Community Interest Companies; http://www.cicassociation.org.uk/ – association of CICs

Registered societies (former Industrial and provident societies) either as community benefit or co-operative society	• Organisations run and owned by members; • They may operate for benefit of the wider community; • They can own property, enter into contracts as a separate legal entity independent of its members; • They can issue shares and take out loans; • They are regulated by the Financial Conduct Authority; • Most recent Act is the Co-operative and Community Benefit Societies Act 2014; • Some can carry out financial services business and have access to the Financial Ombudsman Service.	• Democratic ownership and control through co-operative organisational structures; • It can own property and enter contracts separately from members; • Limits liability of members to their share.	• Not so ideal for organisations that have hierarchical structures; • Additional bureaucracy for gaining permission to conduct financial services; • Additional regulation by the FCA.	http://www.fca.org.uk/firms/firm-types/mutual-societies/industrial - link to the Financial Conduct Authority as the regulator; The Wine Society: owned by its Members; exists exclusively for their Benefit to introduce members to the best wines at a fair price. www.thewinesociety.com; The Co-operative Group: various retail companies, including food and supermarkets, and services; owned by its members www.theco-operative.coop http://www.fca.org.uk/firms/firm-types/mutual-societies/industrial http://www.uk.coop/about/co-operativesuk

the core of the process is that only certain activities are regarded as "charitable". Checking that the activities of the enterprise seeking registered charity status meet the requirements is regulated by the Charity Commission on behalf of the UK government (see https://www.gov.uk/government/organisations/charity-commission/services-information, accessed 2 August 2014).

 What is often not known widely is that many charities are also registered as companies limited by guarantee, thus are *incorporated*. Incorporation means that a legal entity is created that limits the liability of the individuals that usually sit on the management committee or board of a charity that has no independent legal entity – the trustees on the board in a way "loan" their legal personalities to the charity to carry out business activities, including signing contracts with other organizations. That also means that trustees are personally liable, can be sued and can hold a title of property (together all trustees can own property on behalf of the charity). Until 2005 the company limited by guarantee was the easiest and most commonly used form of incorporation. In 2005 the UK government then introduced the community interest company (CIC) as a new legal form. A CIC is a limited company, with features created for citizens who intend to conduct a business activity for community benefit (including environmental issues).

Since 2013, the charitable incorporated organization (CIO) has been available to non-profit organizations. This form aims to address the limitations of a charity by creating a legal body itself that can enter contracts, and therefore the legal liability rests with the organization and not the trustees.

For all social enterprise start-ups the choice of legal form is much more important as it has impact on the perception of legitimacy as an organization for community benefits and the possibility of investment: CIC is regarded as the most suitable form by many investors. The quickest way to start a social enterprise is to register a company limited by guarantee. This legal form can be changed later to a CIC if and when that is regarded as more suitable.

Considerations when choosing your legal form

1) What is the main purpose of your start-up/organization? Raising funds to service a disadvantaged/under-serviced group of citizens? Giving grants to others?

2) Will profits be raised that are significant and need distributing to members? Registered societies as well as CIC limited by shares can address that.

3) Will there be investors interested in shares and access to shares in the profit? The easiest way to address that situation is with a CIC limited by shares.

4) Do you want to raise donations and gain corporate donations? Then a charity that is also incorporated is the best option.

5) Do you want to gain investment in the context of impact investment? Then the CIC is the best option.

Box 8.1 offers web links for the Netherlands, Northern European countries, Hong Kong and the US for finding out about national legal structures. The most important insight when comparing legal forms across countries is that each country offers a legal form for the sole trader or sole proprietor who is personally liable, a quick way to start a business. Similarly, all countries offer a legal structure that allows small companies to trade with limited liability of the owners. In terms of legal structures for non-profits, in 2014 the UK has the most sophisticated offer of legal forms.

Box 8.1   Information on legal forms for countries other than the UK

All web addresses were correct at time of writing (last accessed March 2015)

USA, U.S. Small Business Administration, https://www.sba.gov/category/navigation-structure/starting-managing-business/starting-business/choose-your-business-stru

Hong Kong, Invest Hong Kong (for foreign investment), http://www.investhk.gov.hk/setting-up-your-business/register-a-business-in-hong-kong.html

Sweden, Business Sweden, http://www.business-sweden.se/en/Invest/Establishment-Guides/Starting-a-business/Starting-a-private-limited-liability-company/

Norway, Altinn Business Information Service, https://www.altinn.no/en/Start-and-Run-a-Business/Before-start-up/Choosing-an-organisational-structure-/

Netherlands, Answers for Business, http://www.answersforbusiness.nl/regulation/legal-form

Romania, Infiintari Firme Noi, http://www.infiintarifirmenoi.ro/formajuridica.html (in Romanian) or the National Trade Register Office, http://www.onrc.ro/index.php/ro/, a government department, providing all the information on legal forms, business registration and business start-up

8.2   Licenses for starting and running businesses and regulatory requirements

8.2.1   When to consider licenses and legal and regulatory issues in the start-up process

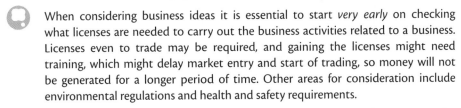

When considering business ideas it is essential to start *very early* on checking what licenses are needed to carry out the business activities related to a business. Licenses even to trade may be required, and gaining the licenses might need training, which might delay market entry and start of trading, so money will not be generated for a longer period of time. Other areas for consideration include environmental regulations and health and safety requirements.

Timelines and the cost need to be considered when forecasting cash flow in particular and estimating the time needed until trading and trading profitably. It might also mean that additional funds for training and/or getting the license might need to be raised.

8.2.2   Licenses needed for starting and running business activities

There are a number of business activities that need licenses in order to operate legally and comply with existing regulations and the law if you want to start a business in the UK. For example, you need a license to play music others have produced, including radio and TV, on commercial premises. In the past it was rather difficult to find out what these regulations and licenses were without professional help. There is now an online search engine on the government website, which has made it much easier for start-ups to find out (https://www.gov.uk/licence-finder, accessed 7 December 2014).

There are a number of business areas that have to deal with a lot of regulation: two examples are selling or distributing alcohol and food businesses. In the case of alcohol, the law regarding selling to minors and dealing with drunk people in pubs needs to be understood for which a personal license is needed; then a premises license is also needed for selling and storing alcohol.

Activity 8.1   Licenses for food business in the UK

Follow this link and list the licenses needed to open and register a food business in the UK: https://www.gov.uk/food-business-registration.

In Europe, in many countries, apart from the UK, the registration of the business with the local Chamber of Commerce is a legal requirement; this applies to Romania in as much as the Netherlands, for example. Box 8.2 lists links for finding out about licenses in the Netherlands, Northern European countries, Hong Kong and the US. Most EU countries have set up one-stop online entry points to assist foreign companies and citizens to find out about starting a business.

The next section addresses the highly important area of intellectual property. It explains copyright, trademarks, patents and design rights, based on research findings and recent reports by the UK Intellectual Property Office, with some short further explanation of European and worldwide patent and trademark issues.

Box 8.2   Finding out about licenses in the Netherlands, Northern European countries, Hong Kong and the US

US, U.S. Small Business Administration, https://www.sba.gov/category/navigation-structure/starting-managing-business/starting-business/obtain-business-licenses-

Hong Kong, Invest Hong Kong (for foreign investment), http://www.gov.hk/en/business/supportenterprises/businesstopics/licensing.htm

Norway, Altinn Business Information Service, https://www.altinn.no/en/Start-and-Run-a-Business/Before-start-up/Planning/Do-you-have-to-ask-permission/ (English version)

Netherlands, Answers for Business, http://www.answersforbusiness.nl/subject/licences-permits-qualifications. For information on registering the business with a chamber of commerce and being entered into the Trade Register of the Netherlands, see http://www.answersforbusiness.nl/regulation/trade-register-and-tax-administration

Sweden, Verksamt.se website, https://www.verksamt.se/en/web/international/alla-e-tjanster/find-permits (in English)

Romania, the National Trade Register Office, a government department, provides information on legal forms, business registration and business start-up, http://www.onrc.ro/index.php/ro/

8.3   Intellectual property

8.3.1   Why and when to protect your creation from being copied or imitated

The importance of intellectual property and intangible assets is increasing worldwide, particularly as the value of a brand or trademarks constitute an important factor in maintaining a competitive advantage. Most authors agree that the value of a company this century consists of at least 70% of its intangible assets. Research findings on the effects of effective intellectual property strategies suggest that SMEs protecting their intangible assets early on perform better than those who do not or only at a later stage (Rassenfosse, 2012). For these reasons, as a start-up it is valuable to begin considerations on how to protect the results of your creative activities as early as possible, as ownership of IP combined with founder(s)' education can ensure long-lasting impact on firm performance and growth (Wang, 2014). This behaviour is an implementation of the principles of sustainability and resourceful impact (see Chapter One, Section 1.3.1).

This means that it is very important for start-ups and even before actual start of trading to be careful when sharing information freely on potentially money-making innovations. Naturally, early on you do not know how important an idea could become. But once you are closer to turning it into a new venture, it helps to protect the intellectual property of the result of your creative actions – through for example using a non-disclosure agreement or confidentiality agreement when talking to advisers or suppliers, this is discussed briefly in Section 8.3.6. The *sustainable start-up* acts responsibly towards its own creations and creativity and ensures that a brand or tangible product cannot be copied. For that reason, your *sustainable start-up* protects its competitive advantage; it also regularly evaluates how different the idea or its execution is.

I highly recommend starting to look at protecting your intellectual property (IP) early on in the new venture creation process. The reasons include that if you are developing something really unique, you want to keep it that way and prevent advisers and other stakeholders from imitating it. And that happens more often than you might imagine.

All applications to protect intellectual property in the UK are made to the Intellectual Property Office (https://www.gov.uk/government/organisations/intellectual-property-office). There is online training available as well. Protection is available through:

▶ Copyright (an automatic right that does not need registering for);
▶ Trademarks;
▶ Patents;
▶ Registered design rights.

The next sections explain each type of intellectual property in more detail, and illustrates for the UK what needs to be done. Section 8.3.7 then briefly discusses the need for more than national protection of intellectual property, in the EU and worldwide. Explanations follow the guidance given by the UK Intellectual Property Office on their website in early 2015.

8.3.2 Patents

Patents protect the features and processes of how things work in products and business methods and must be applied for. If a patent is granted, you can take legal action to make someone stop using, importing or selling your patented and thus protected invention without your written permission. The challenge is that legal costs for those court cases are high.

In order to gain a patent your product or business method has to be new, it needs to have an inventive step that convinces experts in the field it is new and not just a modification to something already in circulation and use, and it should be able to be produced or used in at least one industry. You cannot patent ideas, schemes or the way information is presented. The rules for business method patents are very complicated and vary across different countries (see the discussion on Amazon in Section 8.3.6 below).

Once you have applied for a patent, you are first in the queue and can mark your invention as "patent applied for": that means if after your patent application another person comes up with the same invention, your patent will still be granted, as you were there first. The patent allows you to sell the intellectual property rights and license the invention to someone else but keep the intellectual property rights. You have to renew the patent on the fourth anniversary of filing the application for it; after that, you have to renew it annually. Patents can last for 20 years from the date you applied. Patents granted by a national organization in a country only protect the IP in this particular country. We discuss where to go to learn more about protecting your IP internationally later on in this section. (For further information check out the website of the UK Office for Intellectual Property https://www.gov.uk/renew-patent).

Well-known UK patents are the umbrella frame (1852), mechanical television in 1924 by John L. Baird and iris scanning and recognition by James Daugman in 1992. Research findings indicate that for technology start-ups the existence of a patent application and an actual patent increase credibility with potential investors and the estimate of the start-up firm value in the eyes of potential investors (Haeussler et al., 2009).

8.3.3 Trademarks

Have you seen ® next to product or company names? Coca-Cola has that in place; this means that the name of this fizzy drink cannot be used by anybody else. A trademark distinguishes your product or company name from others. It is the legal protection for a brand. Just registering a company name with Companies House and registering a domain name does not protect the name. You need to apply to register a trademark. Once your trademarks are registered, you can take legal action against people who use them without your permission, use the ® symbol and sell or license the brand to someone else.

A trademark can be a word or several words, a logo, colours or a combination of these. They have to be distinctive and recognizable as signs that make your product or service stand out. WHSmith is a trademark, for example. You cannot register offensive words or images, or just describe the object it relates to (see example below, fence could not be trademarked for a fencing company). It also needs to be truthful and cannot be a simple common statement (https://www.gov.uk/intellectual-property/trade-marks, see the UK Intellectual property office for further information). What do you think of the following, Whixon Fence, can that be registered as a trademark?

While everybody has heard the word "fence", the word "whixon" is an invented word. The two together can be registered as a trademark.

You have to apply for protection in each product category your business covers, such as training, coaching and research services. After an initial fee, for each category of products or services you want to protect the name for an additional fee has to be paid (valid for the UK in 2014). Trademarks last for ten years and can then be renewed. (For further information go to https://www.gov.uk/register-a-trademark, last accessed 30 December 2014).

8.3.4 Design – registered design

Any object you design automatically has a "design right" for 15 years after you created the design, or for ten years after the design is first sold, dependent on which event was earlier. Designs of 2-dimensional objects (like wallpaper or graphics) need to be registered to be protected. A registered design protects the way a tangible object looks: visual appeal, shape, texture, materials of the product as long as they influence how it looks, how the various elements of the design are assembled. This can, for example, apply to packaging. For example, a stylist's logo can be protected with design rights. In order for you to register a design, the design must be new and individual in character – that is, individual in appearance. The measure for "new" is that no similar design has been published in the EU or the UK. For example, some Alessi products have registered designs. You cannot register designs that are offensive or include flags or protected symbols such as the Royal Crown.

Once you have a registered design, you gain exclusive usage rights for up to 25 years and can take legal action to protect it, or you can license or sell the design to someone else. (For further information go to https://www.gov.uk/register-a-design.)

8.3.5 Copyright

Any original work that you create is automatically protected by copyright. This includes original writing, music, paintings, photography, illustrations, website content, film, TV, music recordings and broadcasts and also applies to the way the work is set out (the layout). You do not need to register or use the copyright symbol ©, but using the symbol can help to remind other people that your copyright exists. If your country has signed the Berne Convention, your copyright will also be protected in other countries who have also signed. Copyright lasts for different amounts of time depending on the type of work, but for written or artistic work it is usually 50 years, and 25 years at least for photographs.

To use someone else's copyrighted material, you need to ask permission from the copyright holder. In some areas, such as music recordings, or photocopying printed material, artistic work, film, artistic characters, this is organized collectively by so-called collecting societies. They are authorized to agree with users licenses and will collect fees and/or distribute royalties (payments made to the copyright holder). This is essential to consider if you want to run music or radio in the background in commercial ventures such as a bistro or shop. You need to pay for a license to be allowed to do that. Otherwise, you can be fined. (For further information, go to the UK IPO office website, https://www.gov.uk/copyright).

8.3.6 Other protection – even for your business idea

The legal protections discussed so far do not cover all of the potential business areas. What about plants? Or databases?

If you create a new variety of a seed or plant, in the UK you need to contact the Plant Variety Rights Office and Seeds Division at the Department for Environment Food and Rural Affairs (DEFRA) (for further details see https://www.gov.uk/plant-breeders-rights).

A database is regarded as a collection of data or other material that allows for items to be accessed individually. Often, collections or databases are literary works, such as poems or songs. For copyright to apply, there has to be originality in the way the content is selected and arranged and significant investment in making it happen. Database right then applies automatically and cannot be registered for; it lasts for 15 years starting from whatever is earlier, the date of publication or the date it was made.

Although ideas are not officially thought of as IP, they are still worth protecting. When you discuss your business idea with others, and it is potentially worth a lot of money, ensure you do not trust blindly everyone. Many professionals in as much as private individuals you talk to do not have to keep the idea confidential. Once talked about, or made public, anyone can run with it and put it into practice, even before you, if they have the time and money. Few professionals have the legal obligation to keep that idea confidential, such as IP law professionals and business advisers.

For that reason, to protect your idea early on, use a non-disclosure or confidentiality agreement before you share your idea with someone else. There are many samples and guidance available, one very reliable one can be found here, valid not only for the UK: http://www.ipo.gov.uk/nda.pdf (accessed 4 August 2014).

8.3.7 Protection in the EU and worldwide

Some IP rights are automatically protected in other countries that have signed up to the Berne Convention. This applies mainly to copyright.

As discussed in the research section, trademarks and patents need to be applied for in many countries to be protected in them. Amazon's "1-click/One-click" online buying option is debated to be worthy of a business method patent. The feature describes the possibility for registered customers who have also saved their credit card details online with Amazon to pay for a selected product with just one click. It saves them time (and many clicks) because they no longer have to go to the basket, checkout, enter address details or enter their credit card information.

Amazon's One-click shopping method has been granted a patent in the US, and more recently in Canada, yet the patent was denied for the EU in 2013, as the business method is not sufficiently unique, they judged.

While there is no agreement on what constitutes a patentable business method, the patent has to be able to explain a unique way of doing business. For that to be patented, it has to be original, useful and not obvious. These examples support the business case made earlier for spending time on business modelling.

The conclusion from that different treatment of the same business method is that uniqueness and even the judgement of innovation are very much culturally influenced.

Box 8.3 lists some links to websites for intellectual property protection in the EU and the US and ways to protect your intangible assets, another name for intellectual property.

The next section discusses various forms of boards and their influence on decision-making in the start-up.

Box 8.3 Protecting your intellectual property outside of national boundaries

Information on what is happening in the EU, http://ec.europa.eu/internal_market/intellectual-property/index_en.htm

The European Patent Office, www.epo.org

Office for Harmonization in the Internal Market (trademarks and designs) in the EU, https://oami.europa.eu/ohimportal/en/

Worldwide database with patents, http://worldwide.espacenet.com/

Worldwide intellectual property organizations (WIPO) with a portal for intellectual property services, http://www.wipo.int/portal/en/index.html

US government tools and resources on intellectual property rights, http://www.stopfakes.gov/business-tools

8.4   Governance and dividing shares in start-ups with two or more founders

8.4.1 Creating and managing a start-up board – profit and non-profit

Corporate governance is a term that summarizes all rules and practices, decisions and processes by which a board of directors ensures accountability and transparency in a company's relationship with its stakeholders, both internal (staff, community) and external (customers, government, etc.). Dependent on the legal form, governance can be very time-consuming and require a lot of skills going beyond what business schools call management and governance skills.

There are various ways that this board can be constituted and what power it can have. For a start-up board you can create an advisory board, and gather skills and expertise your founding team or founders do not have. This is explained in further detail below. Some boards are constituted of shareholders of the company, and include the director/founder(s). Other boards own the shares, but employ someone to run the company for them, even in start-up cases. If there is an investor who is also a shareholder but not involved in running the company, this can provide the basis for interesting discussions. Some start-up boards consist of the founders only.

Board meetings and important decisions are recorded and attached to the company information. In particular, directors leaving and joining are significant, and who has the right to sign cheques. Boards can meet monthly or bi-monthly.

There are two types of directors on boards: executive directors, who are involved in running a company, and non-executive directors. The board chair is always a non-executive director.

The board's main duties include:

▶ Ensuring continuity for the organization by setting up and maintaining a corporation or legal existence;
▶ Selecting and appointing a chief executive to whom responsibility for the administration of the organization is delegated, offering guidance as well as reviewing his/her performance;
▶ Governing the organization by broad policies and objectives, formulated and agreed upon by the chief executive and employees, including assigning priorities and ensuring the organization's capacity to carry out products/services/programs by continually reviewing its work;
▶ Acquiring adequate and sufficient resources for the organization to be able to operate and to finance the products/services/programs adequately;
▶ Accounting to shareholders including providing fiscal accountability, budget approval and formulating policies related to contracts from public or private resources.

8.4.2 Governance and strategic management of charities and social enterprises

Dependent on the legal form, governance can be very time-consuming. Membership organizations require the consent of members for certain type of decisions affecting the whole organization, and they need to be informed and guided differently. Meetings need to be held, information sent out in a different way.

  Most social enterprises have at least a management committee and/or a board of directors. Directors can be residents in an area or beneficiaries, and for that reason information needs to be presented and managed so that it can be easily

understood without commercial knowledge and experience. Non-excecutive director roles are unpaid in most cases.

Many social enterprises engage their stakeholders from all aspects of society and
community in decision-making processes, which require various forms of consultation.
These take time, cost money and require different skills.

Dependent on the governance requirements, many operational decisions might also
need board approval. Regular monthly board meetings and subcommittee meetings will
require commitment from non-executive directors as well as the CEO to meeting outside
of working hours to match different schedules. All those tasks require more time, different
skills and additional cost.

Usually, the CEO has approval to make expenses only to a certain financial amount that
varies from organization to organization: I have seen limits between £500 and £2000.

8.4.3 Advisory boards and steering groups

 Advisory and steering boards or groups are the least formal and influential boards
for an organization, yet have a number of advantages for the founder(s). Board
members can be appointed by the chair of the board and/or the CEO; for social
enterprises they can also be elected by the members. The added value includes:

▶ Access to a wide range of professionals with expertise free of charge;
▶ No formal need to follow the advice;
▶ A possible occasional pair of hands for emergencies or small tasks free of charge;
▶ Access to a wider range of contacts and networks through the advisory board members.

Dependent on the organization, sitting on an advisory board can be of great marketing
advantage and attract attention:

▶ It can increase the adviser's own status as an expert and influencer.
▶ It provides access to a wider range of contacts and networks of the organization and
   other advisory board members.
▶ Advisory board members have no liability for anything the organization does.
▶ It can give better access to information about developments and events in the sector.

The loose arrangement of advisory boards allows both sides to finish the engagement at relative short notice and without much paperwork. Overall, these advisory boards can be a good
experience for all involved, as they are useful for relationship building and network extension.

 Steering groups are slightly different in nature, dependent on the reason they
were put together. They are often consisting of staff and possibly a few external
members. This power arrangement means that they can have more influence on
what is happening for a project. For externally funded projects that have included
the steering group in a funding application, their decisions must be recorded and
reported to the funder, thus can have the same influence as a formal board as
discussed in Section 8.4.2.

8.4.4 Dividing shares in start-ups of more than one person

Our case study **Richard Rodman** was introduced with Crowdentials, an online service
provider with IT and legal compliance solutions in Section 1.8.9. His story on dividing

shares is interesting to learn about one useful method of dividing shares in a start-up, based on the significance of the contributions and not just by the number of persons founding the venture.

 Case study

Crowdentials is a "C corporation", incorporated in the state of Delaware, US. Many companies are incorporated there, as it offers very advantageous investment and tax conditions for business. Crowdentials now has four partners and shareholders, and the group of investors held 12% as of late 2014. Richard holds the largest amount of shares; the other co-founder, the programmer who wrote the software and designed the platform, holds the second highest amount. Then there are two others, the legal professional and a security expert; the legal professional only joined in 2014.

Richard and his co-founder used the Founders' Pie Calculator by Frank Demmler to divide the shares in the company. They identified five key tasks significant for the business and rated each other's contributions to divide up the 88% remaining shares (investors held 12%). These five areas according to Demmler are:

a) Business idea;
b) Business plan preparation;
c) Domain expertise;
d) Commitment and risk;
e) Responsibilities.

The idea is to weight the contributions of each founder towards these five elements and show the founder's contribution on a scale of 1–10. You then multiply the weighting by the founder's contribution for each factor, and then add up the five sums to an overall score for each founder. Then you add the scores for each founder up to get to the overall points. Finally, you calculate the percentage for each founder based on the sum across all factors.

Founders may decide to select another five elements, as in Richard's case where they chose (a) fundraising, (b) business development, (c) legal issues, (d) marketing and (e) sales. If all shareholders feel they have come short of the share they wanted, that keeps the commitment to the company goals going just that little bit further, to the advantage of all involved, Richard believes.

Chapters Nine and Ten discuss all aspects of finance, helping you to see where the money is or might be found.

8.5 Concluding remarks and application of new insights

Chapter Eight discussed the variety of legal forms available for start-ups, for social enterprises as much as for other start-ups. It outlined the features and implications for personal liability, tax and perception of legitimacy as a business. The essential role of licenses for trading was explored as an essential part of complying with the law that have to be considered in the feasibility exploration process. There can be effects on the time needed before trading is possible if accreditations or even qualifications are needed and particular licenses have to be obtained; and training and licenses might cost money, which will affect the finance needs.

Protecting your idea and developing intellectual assets was discussed as an important part of the pre-start-up journey that has to be considered early on. The various forms of protection in the UK and internationally were discussed. Finally, we explored the forms of formal and informal governance from board to advisory groups and ways to divide shares between members of a start-up team.

Revision questions and applying the new insight to your potential venture

1 What aspects should you consider when choosing a legal form?
2 Why is it important to start considering licenses early on in the business start-up process?
3 Why should the *sustainable start-up* consider its intellectual property?
4 List some of the ways you can protect your intellectual property.
5 How can you divide your shares based on importance of contributions to the business?
6 Start to consider your legal form or structure and include your considerations in your start-up diary. What is most important to you? Tax liability or personal liability, and/ or owning the whole company and being able to take away a large chunk of profits made? Or is your first interest to attract investors?
7 What parts or elements of what you do is worth protecting from copying by others? Even if you think right now it is not, at what point in time do you consider it might be important? Note your answers in your start-up diary.
8 What form of decision-making will you choose? That does depend on your legal form or structure. Consider the dis/advantages of at least two legal forms and possible ways to make decisions, with two founders or more in each case.
9 If you start by yourself, what legal form is the most suitable for yourself? Note reasons and the considerations in your start-up diary.

9

WHERE IS THE MONEY?

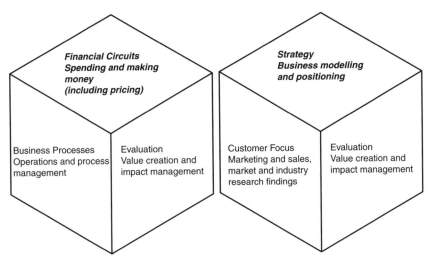

Figure 9.1   The Cube Financial Circuits and the Cube Strategy
Source: © Hill, 2012.

Summary

This chapter introduces you to some financial basics and the sources of finance for start-ups. Personal financial planning is introduced for those who have never budgeted in their own lives and simple bank accounts and challenges with developing a credit history. One section discusses in detail the large variety of sources of finance available, with a focus on recent developments in crowdfunding and peer-to-peer lending. These discussions apply principle and practice of resourcefulness and illustrate the Financial Circuits – the dynamic nature of the flows of money (Figure 9.1). Then we give some help in how to select funding sources, while the last section discusses resource leverage that goes much beyond asking for money and integrates an element of support-in-kind in exchange for money.

CONTENTS

9.1 Finance essentials

This section explains the most basic financial tools, concepts and terms. These terms include types of bank accounts relevant to running a business, interest, credit ratings, personal survival budgets, simple debt and overdrafts and what a loan is. If you are familiar with them, skip this section and go to Section 9.2 on personal budgeting or to Section 9.3 on essential business costs.

To start a business, you need at least a personal bank account (for working as a sole trader), as many of you might have, although some might not. While there is no legal minimum age needed for opening a bank account, when you are under 18 you cannot be made responsible for debts incurred for money used for anything going beyond daily living expenses. This is often the main reason why applications to open a bank account below the age of 18 might be rejected without a guarantor in place. To run a company limited by shares or guarantee, you have to open a business bank account.

Social enterprises need a bank account as well, whatever legal form they choose. This is often a requirement either in order to be eligible for grant funding, or to be given the money once a grant has been allocated. It is also essential for community projects that want to access grants or loans to deliver their work. In many cases, accounts for social enterprises often need two (or three) independent individuals signing for cheques, of which the two signing may not be related to each other. This ensures that the social purpose and the requirements of no personal gain from business activities are monitored on a regular basis.

There are a number of bank account types in the UK. A standard current account is the most common one with easy direct access to your deposited money and usually the lowest interest rate, offering a cheque-book, cash and debit cards, possibility for overdraft arrangements, bank statements and Internet and telephone banking. Savings accounts usually give a better interest on your money but may be restricted in the way you can access the money.

When you deposit money into an account, the bank pays you interest as a reward for keeping money in it. Yet, in a current account this interest is always very low, in the UK in 2014 under 1%.

Normally, you are not allowed to withdraw more money than you have deposited in the account. However, dependent on how much money regularly comes into your account, you might be allowed to take more out than you have put in for a limited period of time, which is called an overdraft. Dependent on the personal account you have, you pay either an agreed interest rate or none for a small amount of overdraft such as £200–£500. If you withdraw (or try to spend electronically) more money than is in your account, this is called an "unarranged overdraft". Often banks charge a high fee – often more than £2– when this happens.

If you owe money to the bank (called debt) and do not repay it as you agreed to, this can be recorded on your credit report. Keeping your credit rating positive is essential for getting credit (borrow money) if you need it. So what is it? How does credit rating work, for example in the UK?

For the UK, companies like Experian, Callcredit or Equifax hold records on your financial behaviour. Every time you open a new form of credit, this activity will leave an electronic footprint on your record. Most countries in the world use credit scoring, and you are advised to check regularly what information is held on you; you can check the records held for a small fee. When opening a personal account or getting a credit card, as well as when opening a business bank account, this record is consulted by banks to check on your money management history and make a judgement (often based on a "score") of your future trustworthiness in dealing with money: credit records contain information on the number of credit cards and major store cards held, your paying back behaviour, mortgage(s), loans held and not yet paid back, how effectively past debts have been paid. The four main sources banks search are:

- Court records judgments – on bankruptcy or defaulted payments;
- Electoral roll information – it is publicly available;
- Account data;
- Address and linked data – results from previous searches on you are available, data associated with your address and other finance providers can be accessed – such as store cards, for example from department stores like John Lewis or Debenhams.

In addition, so-called "payday loans" data are made available via the credit rating agencies as well.

Young people often suffer from a low credit rating, not always because they have been bad financial managers, sometimes because they have a short or non-existing credit history. If you plan to set up a business it is worth checking your current credit score and then follow the available reliable guidance on how to build a positive credit history. Consumer advice agencies in most countries and several websites offer reliable guidance; in the UK, for example, this is the Citizens Advice Bureau (and a number of websites, such as Thisismoney.com or Moneysavingexpert.com). Citizens Advice offer a valuable programme for financial skills for life that offers valuable information on all financial skills and training (http://www.citizensadvice.org.uk/index/partnerships/financialskillsforlife.htm, accessed 4 August 2014).

In order to identify how much money the business needs to make if its purpose is to generate an income for you that you can live on, you need to identify the most important expenses you have for daily living. This list of money needed is often called a personal survival budget.

9.2 Personal financial planning – how do you cover the daily expenses?

We all need to survive financially, that means have the money to spend on essential things for daily survival. What is regarded as essential is debated a lot. In 2014, the UK shopping basket contains 700 items for a household, and their price increase is used to measure inflation in the UK (Gooding, 2014). Minimum income standards aiming to define "adequate" income calculate that a single working-age adult living on their own needs an income of £200 per week, whereas a lone parent with one child needs £285 per week (in April 2013, Padley et al., 2015). When you are living with your parents, this weekly amount will be less; when living in student halls or assisted housing, the amount might be less as well.

What expenses should the personal survival budget contain? There are essential ones that are absolute necessary for you to live and survive, such as money for food and drink, housing costs (rent or mortgage) and clothing. And there are other expenses that are regarded as part of the living cost, yet which are not needed for survival, these include for example expenses for personal training, gym memberships or entertainment costs, such as going to the cinema, buying DVDs. Table 9.1 lists the most important expenses. Write the expenses you have in the second column. The Palgrave companion website offers a downloadable version of this table (see www.palgrave.com/companion/hill-start-up) and an expense list that is aimed at those with family. The list of expenses below does not include expenses for children.

If you do not know what you actually spend on a monthly basis, start collecting receipts now and create a diary for living expenses. The link following allows you to put this into practice (www.palgrave.com/companion/hill-start-up).

The next section discusses the business costs you will have even if you do not sell one single product or service, or "fixed costs", and the unit cost per good/service.

9.3 Essential business costs and how to calculate them

9.3.1 Fixed costs

There are essentially two types of cost: (1) those that do not change with the amount of output, that means even if no income is created or no goods or services are sold, called fixed cost; and (2) those costs that vary dependent on the amount of units produced or sold respectively, called output dependent or variable.

Examples for fixed costs include:

- Rental costs of buildings, or simply rent;
- Costs of leasing or purchasing machinery, technically called capital equipment;
- Annual business rates for business premises charged by local authorities;
- Wages for full- or part-time contracted salaried staff;
- Costs of meeting interest payments on loans, overdrafts, and credit card bills;
- Depreciation of fixed capital – this can be machines or company cars bought by the business;
- Costs of business insurance;
- Phone rental with fixed amounts of minutes each month.

Sometimes, the term "overheads" can be found. This term summarizes expenses that are necessary to the continued operations of the business so it can function successfully, but are not output related.

Overhead expenses can be fixed, meaning they are the same from month to month, or variable, meaning they increase or decrease depending on the business's activity level. They can also be semi-variable, meaning that some portion of the expense will be incurred no matter what, and some portion depends on the level of business activity. Overheads

Table 9.1   Personal survival budget expenses

Expense	Amount you need in £ each month
Housing	
Rent/mortgage	
Gas	
Electricity	
Water	
Council tax/business rates/service charges	
Total – Housing	
Transport	
Car insurance	
Petrol	
Car maintenance/car leasing/registration	
Fees for road/congestion charges	
Use of public transport (buses, trains)	
Taxis	
Total – Transport	
Daily living	
Groceries, household cleaning products, etc.	
Clothing and shoes	
Haircuts and personal care	
Leisure/entertainment (cinema, clubs)	
Hobbies and sports (including gym membership)	
Games, books, apps, TV service subscriptions	
Take-aways and meals out	
Total – Daily living	
Education and training	
Course fees – community college, university	
Books, journals	
Online training resources	
Total – Education and training	
Communication	
Mobile phone bill	
Landline bill	
Internet use/broadband or combination package	
Total – Communication	

(continued)

Table 9.1 Continued

Expense	Amount you need in £ each month
Other	
Insurances	
Debt repayments	
Presents for family/friends, donations	
Savings	
Other:	
Total – Other	
TOTAL of all expenses on a monthly basis	

can also be general, meaning that they apply to the company's operations as a whole, or applied, meaning that it can be allocated to a specific project or department.

Finding sources that give you at least an estimate for the cost you need to consider is not always easy. The following paragraphs give you a guideline on where to start your search, you can then look for further sources using the given ones as a starting platform. The examples used apply to the UK.

Wages and related costs

Have you ever wondered why some employees get paid so much more than others in very similar jobs, yet in different sectors? In the public sector and the education sector certain job roles are more formally associated with certain salary ranges. If you want to attract and keep good staff, you have to follow those standards and salaries.

While there are no clear guidelines about how much you have to pay someone in a senior manager position, the sky is the limit; there are common minimum standard rates for pay in certain jobs and legal guidelines for the minimum wage that must be followed.

What is clearly set are minimum wages by hour for young people and those over 18 in many countries. At time of writing, the national minimum hourly rates for the UK were £3.79 for those of at least school leaving age but under 18, £5.13 for 18–20 year olds and £6.50 for those 21 and over (https://www.gov.uk/national-minimum-wage-rates, accessed March 2015, these rates change so you should check for updates), and a monthly average pay of £1093.73 (in force since 1 October 2013). Check for your country and updates regularly (http://www.fedee.com/pay-job-evaluation/minimum-wage-rates/ for European data for minimum monthly income).

Do you remember the amount adults need to pay for their daily living expenses? That was about £200 per week for an individual. There is a discussion in most countries, that the minimum wage does not actually cover the expenses for a working person, and when you multiply 40 hours by the hourly rate you get a picture of how long it may take this person to save for large expenses, for example to buy a replacement washing machine or heater, to name two essential items. As costs for essentials have risen significantly – for the UK by over 28% since 2008 – salaries have not risen at the same rate (Plunkett et al., 2014).

A "living wage" is another figure put forward to reflect that insight. This is an hourly rate that is set independently and updated annually. For the UK, it is calculated according to the basic living costs for locations outside of London. Employers can choose to pay that rate instead of the minimum wage in the UK. An independent study examining the business benefits of implementing a living wage policy in London found that more than 80% of employers believe that the living wage had enhanced the quality of the work of their staff. Other benefits include a reduction in absenteeism (being absent from work), reduction in staff turnover and positive perception of the employer as an ethical employer (Plunkett et al., 2014, Wills and Linneker, 2013). Not all EU countries have government-set minimum wages as the UK has: Sweden, Denmark, Finland and Germany do not.

For that reason, when you put down figures for salaries they need to be convincing and related to real wages paid in the sector of your chosen business opportunity. Professional organizations or associations often publish reports on average salaries paid. Box 9.1 lists some organizations and their websites for further information on these hourly wages for the UK.

Box 9.1   Information sources on living wage and minimum wage, UK and EU

Minimum wage UK

https://www.gov.uk/national-minimum-wage-rates for the UK.

Plunkett, J., Hurrell, A. and D'Arcy, C. (2014). (http://www.resolutionfoundation.org/publications/more-minimum-review-minimum-wage-final-report/).

Living wage

http://www.livingwage.org.uk for the UK.

http://www.lboro.ac.uk/research/crsp/mis/ – minimum income standard.

Minimum wage EU

http://www.fedee.com/pay-job-evaluation/minimum-wage-rates/ – European data for minimum monthly income data.

Minimum wages across the EU – Eurostat, statistical agency of the European Commission.

Salary on-costs

As an employer in the UK, you have to pay a share of the National Insurance contributions to the government, including pension contributions. The term "salary on-costs" summarizes these additional costs, which you have to consider as an expense on top of the actual salary paid to the employee. In the UK, to make the cost calculation easier, HM Revenue and Customs (HMRC) has created tables that you can use to look up the on-cost for a particular salary paid by your business.

As an employer, you pay National Insurance contributions (NICs) on the earnings you provide to or for the benefit of employees earning above a certain threshold. NICs are calculated and deducted through the PAYE (Pay As You Earn) system; when you operate your payroll you must record the payments on the Full Payment Submission (FPS) and pay the NICs to HMRC. There are also a number of online calculators that can be used by commercial providers. Ensure that you include the on-cost with the salary in your list of expenses in order to avoid underestimating the cost or amount of the operating expenses. The best solution to all those costs is to create a percentage that you add to a salary you pay out to a staff member, in order to estimate closely the additional cost you need to consider yet save time when calculating the actual cost to the business.

Pensions: Since the Pensions Act 2012 came into force in 2012, UK employers with at least one staff member have to offer a workplace pension scheme for all staff between 22 and pension age. The large majority has to engage in a staged process to finish by 2017. For further information check out the Pensions Regulator (http://www.pensionsregulator.gov.uk).

National Insurance: The employer has to pay National Insurance contributions for the company's employees directly to the government as outlined above. For a salary below the threshold of £153 per week (for 2014–2015 tax year), no national insurance contributions have to be made. In the UK, this threshold increases annually; check it regularly by going to the HMRC website.

Depreciation

If you buy machinery or equipment (e.g. computers, cars, office furniture) for the business, the amount is only rarely put down as an expense in full in the year of purchase. As the value of the equipment decreases for a few years the accountant will put down an amount as an expense every year. Usually, in the first year the largest amount is registered as an expense. Capital allowance varies for financial statements.

You might have heard from car owners that the moment a brand new car leaves the forecourt of the car dealer, it loses a few thousand pounds of its value. This alludes to the fact that its value decreases rapidly when the car's status changes from a brand new car to a used car with a new owner.

9.3.2 Tax

VAT

As a UK business, beyond a particular threshold turnover you have to pay value-added tax, shortened to VAT. Similar systems of taxation exist in other countries, sometimes under the name goods and services tax (GST); check the local taxation rules. A threshold sum is fixed every year and normally is increased slightly annually. In the UK, for tax year 2014–15 it was £81,000. This means, if you are in business, you must register for VAT if your VAT taxable turnover for the previous 12 months is more than £81,000. Below this figure, businesses can register for VAT voluntarily (http://www.hmrc.gov.uk/vat/start/register/when-to-register.htm, accessed 4 August 2014).

There are benefits in carrying out an early VAT registration. As a start-up, if you have not yet sold anything or do not sell anything during a VAT accounting period, you may still be able to claim VAT back on your purchases. If you have a lot of capital expenses for buying machinery, etc. it might be worth considering registering for VAT, as all VAT you pay for purchases can be put against the VAT you take and add to invoices raised by you towards your clients.

Sometimes, small businesses register for VAT for what could be described as "psychological" reasons. They want to indicate that they are a larger business as regards to turnover than they actually are. Another reason is that for businesses they are selling to, VAT is not an additional cost for them, but in effect reduces the cost of the product for them when they themselves are registered for VAT. There is a balance to be struck between the implications of being registered for VAT and the related administration time and cost.

If you are registered for VAT, you have to do a VAT return to HMRC, on a quarterly basis. If you cannot do it yourself, an accountant will charge you for that, which is another expense for the business. For up-to-date information check the HMRC website regularly (http://www.hmrc.gov.uk/vat/).

Corporation tax

The legal form of the business also defines what type of tax an organization has to pay. People who are self-employed or in a simple business partnership are taxed individually. Where the company pays a particular tax, corporation tax, the director of a company pays tax privately as an individual on his salary, and he is taxed on any dividends received from the company. The tax rate on dividends is less than that on personal income once the 40% tax rate income threshold has been reached (in the UK for tax year 2014–15); for that reason, directors tend to take less of a salary and take more dividend instead. Dividend is taxed at 20 %.

Companies limited by shares, and many legal forms of social enterprises, including community interest companies as well as companies limited by guarantee, have to pay business tax, called corporation tax. In 2014, the rate in the UK was 20%.

While corporation tax only has to be paid about 18 months after the start of trading, it is advisable to put a fixed amount of money aside on a regular basis, so that when it is due, you can pay it immediately. For that reason it helps to put it down as an expense on a quarterly basis, even if practically speaking you can then put it into a savings account and gain interest on it until it has to be paid.

Income tax is what the business owner pays on the salary they pay themselves. Sole traders pay income tax on all profits the business makes.

For up-to-date figures for the UK check the website of the HMRC www.hmrevenue.gov.uk or the respective government website for your country.

9.3.3 Variable and semi-variable costs

Variable costs vary with output. Generally speaking, variable costs increase at a constant rate relative to labour. Variable costs may include some wages of contract staff or fees for consultants only brought in when there is work for them, as well as cost of materials used in production, etc.

Semi-variable costs consist of a mix of fixed and variable cost. This means costs are set for a set level of production, and become variable when production activity goes beyond a certain level. Overtime pay in a factory or service business such as a restaurant can become variable, while regular wage costs are fixed cost.

The next section illustrates the most important types of funding for financing a venture, with some examples from the UK.

9.4 Sources of finance for pre-start-up and start-up

9.4.1 Pre-start-up and start-up funding sources for all start-ups

Access to appropriate finance has been identified as one of the main reasons why some people do not start a new venture (GEM, 2014b). Research on the impact of pre-start-up and start-up external funding is very limited. Most research has been carried out on start-up funding and it has neglected the time before actual start-up. The existing research on start-up and growth funding is predominantly based on survey research. Unfortunately, there is no consensus on what impact the choice of funding and limited choices have on new venture start-up success and sustainability.

Some authors found that the trade-off between debt and equity finance has a negative impact on venture growth and sustainability, while others point out that difficulties in accessing sufficient appropriate finance constrain survival and growth options.

Researchers and practitioners differentiate between various types of funding.

▶ Informal personal finance, using savings and family money;
▶ Bootstrap finance, defined as informal financing funded from non-formal sources including personal loans for the venture yet excluding personal funds;
▶ Debt finance, all finance that creates a formal debt with a third party, most often banks;
▶ Equity finance, where an investor gives money in return for part-ownership of the organization and/or a significant interest on the investment.

Funds may also be differentiated by the time period they are taken for, such as short-term (overdraft, credit card funding), mid-term (bank loans, loans from alternative loan providers such as re-investment funds, crowdfunding) or long-term (financed by mortgages, for example).

 However, these differentiations do not capture the full picture and range of funding available. I suggest differentiating funding sources in the following way:

1) Direct personal financial sources;
2) Bootstrap finance;
3) Debt finance;
4) Equity and investment;
5) Grants;
6) Crowdfunding or crowd finance;
7) Invoice financing;
8) Asset finance;
9) Credit given by suppliers.

The following sections briefly outline the sources of finance and their added values and limitations. Section 9.5 then gives some guidance on how to select funding sources and what might limit the choice of funding sources.

Direct personal financial sources

This type is a technical term for any finances founders invest or equipment they bring into the business including their personal savings, cash generated through selling assets (including a car, house, computer or music equipment, sports equipment) and money or assets gained through inheritance. This type of finance is unsurprisingly the most common one you can find start-ups use across the world.

Bootstrap financing

This type includes loans from friends, family members and significant others (including partners, husbands/wives). Characteristic for this type of funding is that often no interest has to be paid and that the deadline for repayment is negotiable depending on venture performance.

If you lend someone money or borrow some, I highly recommend that you create a short statement summarizing when you gave/received that money and that it is in effect only a loan, and not a donation or sponsorship. There are too many cases known, where misunderstandings about possible repayment and timelines have occurred, when friendships and family relationships deteriorated, which led to business start-ups collapsing.

Debt finance

Debt finance offers added value, including retaining full control of the business. Limitations include higher risk of bankruptcy in case of inability to pay back the money borrowed or loss of personal securities such as houses. There are many types of debt financing. The most common ones include:

a) Overdraft arranged with the bank holding your account;
b) Credit card financing;
c) Loans from third parties;
d) Mezzanine – a hybrid of debt and equity finance.

Overdraft

An overdraft is a credit facility you agree with your bank. It allows you to temporarily spend more money than you have in your account to cover short-term financing needs. It should not be used as a long-term source of finance – if an overdraft is used persistently your bank may question whether you are in financial difficulty.

You will need to agree your overdraft limit with your bank. The bank usually charges interest on any money you use, and you may also have to pay a fee. This is a very common short-term source of finance, yet costly due to high interest rates or fees if the overdraft goes beyond an arranged limit.

Added value includes:

▶ It is flexible – you only borrow what you need at the time, making it cheaper than a loan.
▶ It is quick to arrange.
▶ You normally will not be charged for paying off your overdraft earlier than expected.

Limitations include:

▶ There will usually be a charge if you want to extend your overdraft.
▶ You could be charged a higher interest rate and a penalty, which make the overdraft very expensive.
▶ The bank can ask for the money back at any time.
▶ You can only get an overdraft from the bank that you hold your business current account with.

Credit card

Credit card financing is more costly, as the interest rates charged can be rather high, dependent on your paying back behaviour in the recent past, particularly if you only pay back the minimum amount each month and spend until the limit is reached. Unfortunately, many start-ups use this type of short-term finance a lot via their personal credit card, in particular when they do not get access to bank loans. Not paying back credit card loans can have a negative impact on the credit history.

Loans from third parties

The third party may include:

▶ Banks – they are very unlikely to grant a loan to young people with no track record in managing finance, and very unlikely to lend for start-ups in general; often banks ask for a guarantor (who agrees to pay back the loan to the bank in case you do not) or securing a loan with a house (which means that if you do not repay the loan the bank can sell your house and use the sale proceeds to repay the loan).

▶ Community development finance institutions (CDFIs), some of which only lend money to a SME or start-up once they have evidence that their loan application to banks has been rejected. The institutions themselves are social enterprises and charge interest rates similar to banks, yet enable an organization to get finance to start with. There are over 50 CDFIs in the UK. Some only lend to local organizations, others lend to those with a particular business area. Box 9.2 lists some examples that operate locally in the UK.

▶ Particular programmes run by private sector companies or government departments; in the UK there is a programme called Start-up Loan, which gives out loans to start-ups from 18 years onwards, providing a mentor has been working with the applicant, promises the start-up mentoring for another two years and supports the loan application.

Box 9.2   Selected examples of CDFIs in the UK

Big Issue Invest, for social enterprises only across the UK (www.bigissueinvest.com)

BCRS Business Loans for organizations based in the Black Country region, West Midlands (www.bcrs.org.uk)

Co-operative & Community Finance, solely for co-operative and social enterprises across the UK (www.coopfinance.coop)

Enterprise Answers, for Cumbria, North Lancashire and Northumbria, for local organizations and small businesses (www.enterpriseanswers.co.uk)

Mezzanine

This type of finance is a hybrid of debt and equity finance. It is a loan for small amounts invested by venture capitalists on an agreed return within a fixed period of time. Should the money not be paid on time and in full at the agreed date, then the money will be turned into shares in the business.

Peer-to-peer lending (P2P)

This innovative and growing form of finance is a loan to a business via Internet platforms. It is much quicker than a bank loan and can be run at better interest rates. The lenders make offers at rates that they find suitable, and even small amounts are possible (www.p2pfa.info).

Microcredit or group lending programmes

Microcredit is a term based on a very successful programme that ran in Bangladesh for groups of women starting business who could not gain credit, called Grameen Banking. Across the world microlending approaches have been developed.

Group lending refers to a situation when a group of up to six or seven individuals forms a lending circle. The first in that group gains a loan to start a new venture. The remaining members of the group support this individual in developing the start-up so that the first group member can pay back the loan as soon as possible. Then the second person in the group gets the loan paid out, and again the whole group supports this individual in getting the new venture up and running to ensure money is coming in to pay the loan back to the funder. This process is repeated until all group members had the loan paid out to them individually and have been able to pay it back.

This type of funding works well for a number of reasons:

▸ The funder never runs out of money, as it is a loan that has to be paid back.
▸ Every start-up has close peer support to ensure the money is used well.
▸ All start-ups learn from the experience of those already using the money so that they do not make similar mistakes, should these be made in the early days.
▸ The start-up is not isolated but has the support of a number of people when needed at short notice.

Equity and investment

Investment finance (also known as equity finance) involves selling part of your business ("shares") to an investor. The investor will take a share of any profits or losses that the company makes. Before agreeing any kind of investment and giving away equity, contact a mentor or a financial adviser. Most people have a fear of letting go of part of their business, even if investors will only take a minority share. This was different for our case study Crowdentials, funded by Richard Rodman, who has had long-term investors backing him and his team since they started, Frinter founders Muhammad Ali and Shivam Tandon, and Foleeo founder Lillie Ranney. Box 9.3 shows some details of their situation.

Box 9.3   Equity finance used by case study companies Foleeo, Crowdentials and Frinter

Foleeo, US: Lillie Ranney gained a place in the Ohio University accelerator and access to $10,000 in return for a 5% share in the company.

Crowdentials, US: Richard Rodman gained for his second start-up a place in the accelerator and gained investment from a group of investors acting as one voice; they hold 12% of the shares.

Frinter Ltd, UK: Shivam Tandon and Muhammad Ali gained £50,000 investment in return for a 40% share in their start-up.

There are two types of equity finance: business angels and venture capitalists. *Business angels* are well known through the television series *Dragon's Den* in the UK; they are individuals with a lot of business experience in creating and leading very successful ventures, knowledge and cash to invest into a growth business or start-up in return for a share in the business. Business angels are willing to back high-risk opportunities, as they offer high returns. Some invest by themselves, others through a syndicate or association, which is the current trend in the UK.

Added value includes:

▶ Investors can bring new skills and opportunities to the business, e.g. marketing or exporting overseas.
▶ You will not have to pay any interest, or repay a loan (even though that can be part of the package as well at later development stages).
▶ You share the risks of the business with your investors.

Limitations include:

▶ It can be a demanding, expensive and time-consuming process.
▶ You will own a smaller share of your business (although your share could eventually be worth more money if your business succeeds).
▶ You may have to consult your investors before making certain management decisions.
▶ Only limited companies can sell shares, so you cannot raise money in this way if you are a sole trader or in a partnership.

Venture capitalists (VCs) usually invest in a portfolio of businesses, where a large number of businesses might fail, so that those who succeed have to compensate for the losses. For that reason, they rarely invest into start-ups. In contrast to business angels, VCs are very unlikely to get involved in the day-to-day running of the business but will often help focus the business strategy. Working with VCs needs a lot of time, and thus has a cost.

Box 9.4 lists selected associations for business angels and venture capitalists in the UK and internationally.

Box 9.4   Business angels and venture capitalists

In the UK

UK Business Angels Association (www.ukbusinessangelsassociation.org.uk)

British Venture Capitalist Association (www.bvca.co.uk)

Information about venture capital investment (www.venturecentral.co.uk)

In the US and Hong Kong

Hong Kong Business Angel Network (www.khban.org)

Angel Capital Association, US (www.angelcapitalassociation.org)

In other European countries

European Trade Association for Business Angels, Seed Funds and Early Stage Market Players

Business Angels Netwerken Nederland (www.bannederland.nl)

Corporate venture capital is another potential source of start-up funding. However, even more rarely is a start-up funded, unless it is a high growth potential privately held technology or manufacturing start-up. The support offered can come in three forms: financial investment in return for equity share; debt financing for an agreed return; and non-financial support such as access to distribution channels for an agreed financial return. Often, there is a combination of financial support, mentoring and advice offered.

Grants for start-ups

Grants are not repayable, and often start-ups have to follow certain guidelines to be successful.

Grants are available in the UK from councils, charitable trusts and short-term programmes with European funding. Some grants are for specific sectors, such as creative industries or the health sector.

For students in the West Midlands in the UK, the European-funded programme SPEED+ offered until spring 2015 small grants combined with training and mentoring. Some universities have their own grant funding schemes to which students can apply. All grants are very competitive, and rejection rates vary.

Crowdfunding or crowd finance

This type of finance involves a couple to a large number of people who each invest (in exchange for equity, profit or revenue sharing), lend (for repayment with interest) or contribute (as donations and sponsorship) a small amount of money to the seeker's project or business idea, the last type not expecting a financial return but perhaps a privilege such as options to buy products at a large discount or getting a product for free or free tickets to a related event. The mainly online platforms offer a quick way of getting finance. Check out the crowdcube.com, the first platform that was accredited by the Financial Services Authority for the UK (the body in the UK that regulates the finance sector institutions). There are two types of crowdfunding:

a) You have to raise all the money you ask for within the time frame you set; if you do not reach that goal, you do not get any money, and the funders get their investment back;
b) You get all the money you raise, independent of the amount you said you needed.

Some crowdfunding platforms are equity based, meaning that investors can gain some shares in the company they invest in, yet these shares often only amount to 10 or 20%; others are debt based, offer revenue sharing, free products for a limited period of time or lifetime membership. Platforms have varied audiences: some platforms focus on start-ups only, others do not support start-ups at all and others again only focus on a particular sector.

Added value of crowdfunding includes:

▶ It provides an alternative to funding from conventional means, e.g. bank loan.
▶ You can raise finance relatively quickly, often without upfront fees.
▶ It can raise awareness of your new business, which is free PR for the business.

Limitations of crowdfunding include:

▶ Your idea could be copied once it is out in the public domain if you have not protected your intellectual property rights.

▶ Any money you raise could be returned to investors or contributors if you do not reach your funding target.
▶ Crowdfunding is mostly unregulated (but from 1 April 2014, loan-based and investment-based crowdfunding has been regulated by the Financial Conduct Authority).

This area of financing start-ups, and business growth, is rising quickly, and in 2014 about 50 platforms existed in the UK alone, with the numbers rising; there are hundreds worldwide, with the majority being in the US. Box 9.5 lists some crowdfunding websites.

Box 9.5   Selected crowdfunding platforms in the UK and internationally

UK

Trillion Fund

Seedrs

Hubbub

QuidCycle

Abundance

Crowdcube

Buzzbnk

Other countries

Netherlands: Symbid The Funding Network, Geldvoorelkarr.nl

Australia: The AppVillage

Sweden: Crowdme.com, Fundedbyme.com (focus on all Scandinavian countries including Norway plus Germany and Spain, focus on start-ups and small businesses)

Finland: Ianinaaja.fi (focus on small businesses)

Denmark: Myc4.com

Germany: Companisto

International focus

Kickstarter, based in the US, focuses on creative projects (films, books, games etc.)

Indigogo, for a wider audience, for any kind of projects

Invoice financing

Invoice financing describes the situation when a company either buys or manages your unpaid invoices for a fee. Invoice financiers can be independent or part of a bank or financial institution.

There are two types of invoice financing in the UK: factoring and invoice discounting. Both kinds of invoice financing can provide a large and quick boost to your cash flow.

Factoring

Factoring usually involves an invoice financier who manages your invoice payments and collects money owed by your customers on your behalf. Your customers know you are using factoring. This is how factoring works:

1) When you raise an invoice, the factoring company buys the amount owed to you.
2) The company gives you a lump sum of the invoice amount (usually around 85%) upfront.
3) The company collects the full amount directly from your customer.
4) Once the customer has paid them the invoice amount, the company transfers the remaining balance to you minus a fee they charge and interest on the money paid out to you in advance of having received the customer payment.

Example: A customer owes you £20,000 for over three months. In order to ensure that your cash flow remains positive, and you are able to pay your bills and suppliers, you sell the invoice to an invoice financier for £17,000 (that is equivalent to 85% of the value, a typical rate). The company collects £20,000 from your customer and pays you the remaining amount minus interest and a fee, which will be less than £ 3,000.

Added value of factoring includes:

▶ The invoice financier looks after your invoice payments, increasing your time to manage your business.
▶ The factoring company credit checks potential customers – so that you are likely to trade with customers that pay on time.
▶ The company can help you to negotiate better terms with your suppliers, thus saving you money.

Limitations of using factoring include:

▶ Your customers may prefer to deal with you directly.
▶ Your reputation might be affected if the company you use does not meet your standards in customer relationship management.

Invoice discounting

With invoice discounting, the external company, or often called "invoice financier" lends money against your unpaid invoices – this is usually an agreed percentage of their total value. And you will have to pay the financier a fee.

When your customers pay their invoices, the money goes to the invoice financier. This customer payment reduces the amount you owe, which means you can then borrow more money on invoices from new sales up to the percentage you originally agreed. You will still be responsible for collecting debts if you use invoice discounting, but it can be arranged confidentially so your customers will not find out.

Benefits of invoice discounting include:

▶ ID can be arranged confidentially; your customers do not need to know that you are borrowing against their invoices.
▶ invoice discounting allows you maintain closer relationships with your customers than in the case of factoring, because you are still managing relationships and communication with them.

Limitations of invoice financing are that:

▸ You lose profit from orders or services that you provide.
▸ Invoice financiers will usually only buy invoices raised with business customers – check if this financing method might work for you when you sell to the public.
▸ Using it may affect your ability to get other funding, as you do not have "book debts" available as security.

This type of finance is more suited to those who already have clients and contracts lined up.

Leasing and asset finance

Leasing or renting assets (e.g. machinery or office equipment) can save you the initial costs of buying them outright. Leasing is best known to consumers for car leasing from car dealers.

Added value includes:

▸ You will have access to a high standard of equipment that you might not have been able to afford otherwise.
▸ Interest rates on monthly instalments are usually fixed.
▸ It is a less risky alternative than a secured bank loan – if you cannot make payments you will lose the asset but not, for example, your home.
▸ The leasing company carries the risks if the equipment breaks down.
▸ As long as you make regular repayments for the period of the lease, the agreement cannot be cancelled.
▸ It is widely available.
▸ Leasing is an allowable expense for tax purposes, so reduces any taxable profit.
▸ The impact on your cash flow is much smaller than when having to pay out a large sum upfront.

Limitations include:

▸ You cannot claim capital allowances on a leased asset if the lease period is less than five years (or seven years in some cases); this means you have less expenses.
▸ It can be more expensive than buying the asset outright.
▸ Some long-term contracts can be difficult to cancel early.
▸ You may have to pay a deposit or make some payments in advance, which impacts on the cash flow.

Credit given by suppliers

There are many formal and informal arrangements possible between suppliers and a start-up. One of them is discussed in Section 9.6.4 under resource leverage (see case study): a supplier allowed the start-up to pay an invoice for business cards in six months' time, with some special conditions attached. There are ways to negotiate later payments; as a consequence of the recession many small companies are supportive of each other as long as there is an arrangement in place that ensures that within payment period of time payment is made.

The next section briefly discusses some programmes that offer grant funding to social enterprise start-ups.

9.4.2 Pre-start-up funding for social enterprises only

The current policy climate and belief in social enterprises making the difference to the way business is done as well as addressing the growing need for social services to reach hard-to-reach groups has generated a number of funding sources solely for social enterprises in the UK. The situation is similar in other countries, not only in the EU, but US, Canada, Australia and New Zealand, to name a few.

The times when predominantly community groups or charities were founding new social enterprises have long gone. Women and young people as much as experienced professionals looking for a step change in the way they work are an important force of individuals and small groups forming social enterprises (Social Enterprise UK, 2014).

While there are many local programmes, some partially funded by European programmes with local match funding, there are also a limited number of nationwide funding programmes in the UK. Three are highlighted in more detail in Box 9.6 to illustrate the type of funding available nationally. There are many grant-giving bodies, often in the legal form of a charity, that provide local and/or regional funding, and some local authorities offer start-up and/or development funding, such as Birmingham Council does through a partially European Structural Development Fund supported programme.

Box 9.6   UK funding for starting a social enterprise – three examples

The British National Lottery was only founded a few years ago in 2004, as a merger of two pre-existing organizations. The **Big Lottery Fund** distributes some funds raised by the National Lottery and also distributes non-Lottery funding on behalf of public bodies such as the Department for Education and the Office for Civil Society. It has a particular type of funding for community projects that could lead to the formation of a social enterprise or be used by a social enterprise. *Awards for All* offers funding of up to £10,000 for specific projects, not organizations, in England that benefit the community (see http://www.biglotteryfund.org.uk). This funding can be used as seed funding for the formation of a social enterprise, testing a service to see if the appropriate people are in place and the service is taken up by the intended beneficiaries.

UnLtd is a social enterprise operating across the UK offering three types of grants combined with mentoring and informal training. There is a small grant programme for individuals or community groups with an idea for a social venture, encouraging the path towards start-up (Do-it-Award); for organizations established for at least one year there is support in helping them to grow and gain some funding for the living expenses as well. The third programme supports fast growth, including social franchising.

The **School for Social Entrepreneurs** is a year-long programme offering up to £5000 grant funding combined with a mixture of structured training, action learning and mentoring. Founded by Michael Young (Lord Young of Dartington), who also founded the Open University, it offers a structured support programme with small grants running over one year for individuals once candidates have gone through a three-stage selection process. There are groups in several parts of England, with focus on London and the West Midlands. It is only one person that can attend the programme, not a community group. The funding is often provided in partnership with a national bank.

What can be concluded from these examples is that rarely in the second decade of this millennium grants are given out without further support attached. Rather, a support package is combined with funding to ensure that money is wisely invested and sustainable organizations are built.

Box 9.7 illustrates a good practice example of a local authority co-funded programme, with match funding via European Structural Development Fund (ERDF) offering phased funding with compulsory hours of pre-start-up business support for social enterprise start-ups and for-profit start-ups in economically deprived areas in Birmingham. The programme is of great benefit for participants, as it ensures that support is taken up by programme participants and they have to work with experienced advisers to fine optimal ways of business development. Many local authorities have similar funding programmes, not only in the UK.

Box 9.7   Enterprise Catalyst programme, Birmingham, West Midlands

Residents in defined economically deprived areas in Birmingham, UK, gain up to 12 hours of one-to-one mentoring and business support and access to training for starting with self-employment, starting a company limited by shares or a social enterprise. Once they have presented their business proposal to a panel, these supported residents can gain a grant of £250. They have to have worked for 12 hours with an adviser before they can gain access to the grant. Another ten hours of support have to be taken and successful trading activities need to be evidenced before they can apply for another small grant of £1000. Once they have been trading successfully for two years, or companies or sole traders already trading for two years without having been on the programme, they can gain access to another grant of £2500. Enterprises that have been successfully trading already for a number of years and are in a position to grow the business can get access to up to £50,000, provided the business can match this grant with the same amount out of its own pocket. One-to-one support is available for those businesses (up to ten hours) with an experienced business adviser (www.enterprise-catalyst.com accessed 4 August 2014).

9.4.3   Start-up competitions

Some start-ups gain a lot of free PR and funding through taking part in start-up competitions. There are hundreds of competitions, some on a regional or national basis, some international ones and some just in the area of a local authority or municipality. Many universities in the UK, Europe and the US run their own start-up competitions.

There are some limitations for those with unique and commercially sensitive business ideas that have not been legally protected. Once an idea is in the public domain and published on a website as a runner-up or winner, anybody can try to imitate it and run with it. For that reason, participation in a competition might only be useful once this intellectual property protection has been put in place.

Box 9.8 illustrates how three of our case study start-ups gained money and free PR by taking part in local (Richard Rodman), regional (Kathryn Kimbley, Richard Rodman and Ben Smith) and national start-up competitions (Ben Smith). Their motivations were identical: to gain free PR and the prize money to spend on the business, while getting some advice from experienced business people and advisers from the panels. Box 9.8 lists some UK and worldwide start-up competitions. The majority of national and international start-up competitions are run by large corporates.

Box 9.8 Start-up competitions

Richard Rodman won four local and regional start-up competitions in Ohio, US: Athens (Ohio) Start-up Weekend, Ohio University Idea Pitch, both in 2012, and first places for start-ups in Cleveland by Cleveland.com and The Plain Dealer.

Kathryn Kimbley won first prize in 2012 for the most innovative social enterprise by Social Enterprise West Midlands, and was a finalist for the same prize in 2014.

Ben Smith won Ernst & Young Aston Entrepreneur at Aston University, an award from Santander Bank, was finalist for The Pitch start-up competition for the ten start-ups to watch, and won Shell LiveWIRE monthly competition.

Selected start-up competitions in the UK

- Shell LiveWIRE – monthly winners of £1000 and one winner of £10,000 per year (two awards for sustainability and innovation).
- National Association of College and University Entrepreneurs Varsity Pitch competition for students in the UK – one in each of the seven industry categories.
- Join the Core – a start-up competition by Ben & Jerry's ice cream for sustainable business ideas.
- Stelios Award for Disabled Entrepreneurs – run in collaboration between the charity Leonard Cheshire Disability and the EasyJet founder Sir Stelios Haji-Ioannou.

Start-up competitions, international and in the EU

- CleanTech Challenge – organized by two UK universities for students from across the world.
- China UK Challenge – for new business ventures for business between China and the UK.
- Intel Business Challenge Europe – run by the company Intel for innovative products, smart technologies and interactive web and mobile applications in the areas of healthcare and medical devices, energy and cleantech, people and society, ICT, biotechnology and nanotechnology.
- Elance Big Idea start-up competition.

Competitions solely for social enterprises

- Dell Social Innovation Challenge, VerbU.
- Hult Prize – for social enterprises emerging from the world's universities.

Activity 9.1 invites you to research what start-up competitions and grants might exist in your area.

Activity 9.1   Grants, support programmes and start-up competitions in your local area and region

Carry out some research on start-up competitions and possible local and regional grants. Use the Internet, local newspapers, local library, government and local authority websites to find out more. Is there a central agency in your country that offers business support and advice? Contact them as well.

The next section offers guidance on how to select finance sources.

9.5   Selecting financial funding sources

How do you select funding sources? Personal values, cultural values, norms and personal criteria as well as the financial context in your country influence which of these financial sources are actually available to you and which of those are personally viable for you. Your choice of legal form and whether you run a social enterprise or for-profit business can limit the funds you can access, as some funds in the UK and the EU are solely for social enterprises, whereas others are for all types of start-ups.

For example, Saeed is a traditional believing Muslim and does not want to take out a bank loan from a high street bank. For his venture – a take-away with Indian food – he needs £89,000 to start up. He wants to rely only on money he can borrow from his family and friends and does not want external influence on his venture. At the point in time he wants to start, he cannot start up as he can only get £55,000 together. For that reason he decides to delay his start-up until he has the amount of money together he needs.

Many people do not like to create debts at all when starting a business. As banks often require some security when they lend money, they like to have even small amounts for a start-up loan secured by the personal property of the start-up founder(s), even if the house is not part of the business. For those people who do not want to risk the "roof over their heads" and have nothing else to provide as security, getting a bank loan will be difficult.

Box 9.9 describes how our case study **Frumtious** funded his early development, without giving away equity, by listing the development of the small fruit jelly manufacturing company and the grant funding received (see Section 1.8.3 for more detail on Frumtious and founder Ben Smith). Ben's goal was clear: he did not want to give away any equity while developing the business at an early stage and wanted to take his time to find the right products and ways to develop his dream venture. For that reason, taking on investors was not on his list of possible funding options. This aspect of personal-ability was decided by Ben early on in the venture development process.

Case study

Kathryn Kimbley, our social enterprise start-up, used a number of funding sources only available to social enterprises in the UK. Kathryn had little money of her own to invest to finance her start-up, as she had just finished her Master's at Keele University when she started. We discussed her choice and access of business support in Chapter Two, and outlined her start-up motivation in Chapter One, Section 1.8.5.

Box 9.9   Funding timelines for Frumtious Ltd and HumAnima CIC Ltd

Frumtious Ltd, Ben Smith

– Beginning of January 2013: Concept testing and product development in home kitchen, development of three tastes pineapple, blueberry, raspberry. Under £50,000.

– March 2013: Ernst & Young Aston Enterprise competition win. £500 plus free market research by external provider.

– April 2013: Accepted onto BSeen start-up incubator. £1000 grant, office space, mentor.

– June 2013: Product development funded through an ERDF-funded Biomarker project.

– September 2013: Erasmus for Entrepreneurs, working with a food and beverage company in Italy to help with Frumtious development for a month.

– January 2014: Shell LiveWIRE Winner. £1000, which enabled purchase of first batch of pots and labels.

– February 2014: Santander Award. £1000 used to finance branding and marketing work carried out by a design consultancy.

– On-going: Relationship being built with Birmingham-based manufacturer.

HumAnima CIC, Kathryn Kimberley

Own money	£0
Prince's Trust Enterprise Programme and loan	£1900
UnLtd start-up grant	£2400
School of Social Entrepreneurs programme and grant	£4000

Kathryn spent the start-up funding on overheads (insurance, professional membership fees), travel costs, conference and event attendance, training and coaching for learning about marketing and identifying the ideal customer profile, and personal development balancing the values of the counsellor with those of the businesswoman. For her, this initial funding had two functions: to enable her to start up and develop the enterprise activities and to gain support that increased her confidence that she was doing the right steps in the right way. As outlined in Chapter Two, when discussing business support, the combination of money and business support are the ideal way to develop skills and confidence while investing the money wisely.

What both examples have in common is that they gathered a number of small grants, always associated with some forms of support, including mentoring. These examples show how funding and business support work together successfully.

The most important factors to keep in mind when selecting funding sources to save time and increase application success are:

1) Do you formally qualify for this funding source? Is your chosen legal form eligible? Is your sector included in the funded start-ups? Should you be trading for at least six months

or not have started trading at all? Is the source for individual or team start-ups only? Are you living in the appropriate postcode area?

2) Are you funding or investment ready?

3) How realistic is it to gain funding from this source you are considering?

For banks, go to the website and explore their lending conditions, and contact an adviser to have a meeting. Check what information they need and at what stage of development they would even consider a loan. Often, you need a well-written business plan with financial forecasts and sufficient market research carried out.

4) Have you got the documents/plans developed they ask for?

5) Have you made a list of what you expect from a funding and development intervention? If not, make this list.

6) Are you willing to give equity to a third party? Are you willing to engage someone else in the business and give them influence on what you can and cannot do?

7) Do you want to grow the business quickly and then exit to start something different? Or do you plan to do this business for a while, as you are really passionate about it?

In Section 9.7.1 you will find an activity to apply the learning to your own *sustainable start-up*.

9.6   Non-monetary ways to fund a *sustainable start-up* using co-creation

9.6.1   Introduction

 In addition to financial or monetary support to fund the business, there are other creative ways of developing resources and gaining capacity to build the business and deliver services using a co-creation approach. This strategic approach is indicated in the Cube by the "Strategy" area; and as the Cube shows a clear link between "Financial Circuits" and "Strategy", strategic considerations on how to bring needed input or resources into the *sustainable start-up* to replace having to use cash or investment are essential to consider.

This section gives a short overview of practical ways to go beyond financial limitations and find ways to bring other needed input to the *sustainable start-up*, using time to build and develop networks.

a) Exchange of services and products/bartering;

b) Offering volunteering opportunities;

c) Leveraging networks and contacts – to gain free supplies for yourself and develop clients.

Network theory is the theoretical background in entrepreneurship research (Leyden et al., 2013), which identified the essential nature of network building and using for successful entrepreneurship. "Social embeddedness" and "social capital" are two other related concepts that are worth mentioning in this context. Box 9.10 identifies some of the findings that can be valuable for the *sustainable start-up* to take note of.

> **Box 9.10   Insights from entrepreneurship research on building and using networks**
>
> Social embeddedness points to the significance of social and cultural factors in economic relations, based on a sociologist's research findings (Granovetter, 1985, McKeever, 2014), which entrepreneurship research applied to the start-up context. Membership of social groups, such as local communities or ethnic minorities, professional communities, wider family networks and groups of interest on the one hand can facilitate and enable building and using networks, and on the other hand can limit start-up success, if those networks are not supportive or open to the new business activity.

9.6.2 Exchange of services and products/bartering

Particularly amongst start-ups, the practice of exchanging goods and services is well used and successful. Often, the time needed to carry out an activity is used as a measure to indicate the cost of a service or making of a product. Here is an example: If an accountant needs some marketing services, he can arrange with a marketing start-up to carry out the bookkeeping and tax return preparation. In return, the marketing start-up agrees to provide a set of marketing activities, limited to a fixed amount of hours or set of activities. As long as this is fixed in writing, with times, dates, hours, this can create a win-win situation for getting the support both partners need at that point in time. Similarly, there is a combination of activities possible that combines payment of small amounts of money, used for materials and resources that have to be paid for, with time.

Being part of a number of networks for start-ups will facilitate this exchange amongst peers, whereas established businesses are often much more reluctant to engage in this kind of exchange.

This arrangement can work very well as long as from the start there is a clear agreement on what quality and level of exchange and time is expected. Informal agreements might work, but as the point in time of delivery in the chosen example of accounting services is rather towards the end of the year, whereas marketing is needed at start-up, a more formal written agreement might be helpful.

9.6.3 Offering volunteering opportunities

Start-ups after official launch can offer volunteering opportunities, to students and young retired citizens, for example, who want to gain skills or remain actively involved. As long as you are clear on what needs to be done and have carried out your detailed process maps of the activities that need to be carried out, how long they take and what resources are needed, then you can develop small job descriptions for tasks. Chapter Six on operations discusses the need for breaking down all business activities into smaller steps and either creating flow charts and/or using Gantt charts to ensure all necessary activities are costed for and considered.

In Chapter Fifteen we explain in detail how the case study entrepreneurs, Frinter Ltd founders Shivam Tandon and Muhammad Ali, brought in student volunteers to share their insights and passion for start-up and gain additional pairs of hands to get the marketing and awareness raising for their services done in a cost-effective way. They offered some incentives in kind including mini iPads and free copying and printing to volunteers.

9.6.4 Leveraging networks and contacts – to gain free supplies for yourself and develop clients

Personal contacts and networks are often referred to technically as "social capital". The use of the word "capital" indicates that it is of similar value to money. In my early business support practice I came across an amazing young IT trainer start-up who told me how he managed to get his luxury business cards. His story illustrates one way social contacts can be used to add resources to the business, here to finance the best possible business cards he decided he needed. This type of gaining of resources is typical of the co-creation approach.

 Case Study A case study illustrating the co-creation principle and practice to resource leverage

With the co-creation approach in mind, here is an interesting practice an IT consultant used to make the pound go much further; he is one of the many start-ups in London I worked with from disadvantaged backgrounds who had to combine resources creatively and had managed to start a business on a shoestring, an expression for starting a business with very little money.

John had very little money and was living in Hackney, North London. He had identified that high quality business cards were important for him to get to the decision-makers, who selected IT training for their staff. John was also very well networked; he could not tell me how many people he actually knew, hundreds he pointed out, some better, some less well. In his network was a printer, a contact of a friend of his, who produced the high quality full-colour business cards on thick glossy paper the way he wanted them. When he asked his contact for a quote the price shook him, it was nearly £200. He went away and came up with a solution: he offered the printer the following deal. He would sign a contract that he would pay the requested price in full in six months' time if he had not managed to bring in ten clients to the printer who would order printing for at least for the amount John had to pay for his business cards. The printer thought about it for a moment, then agreed and signed the piece of paper John had produced. He took the order for the business cards that day and had them ready in two days' time. John had his high quality business cards. The printer had nothing to lose, as he would get paid anyway whatever happened, possibly just six months later.

After four and a half months, twelve of John's contacts had ordered from the printer. Next time John saw the printer, he tore the contract to pieces with a big smile, and said, "Great to do business with you, John. What else do you need to have printed?"

 Can you borrow any of the resources you need from contacts? And pay them back in kind, with free services or something one of your contacts can offer free-of-charge to them? Or can you get a reduction of the fee for something they want to do, such as spend a day in a leisure park, or hire a car?

What conclusion can we draw from this approach? This is a truly co-creation example for value creation between a start-up and a supplier that goes both ways, for the original giver and recipient. John used his network consisting of his own contacts and their contacts as a resource to create value for himself and a supplier, social capital is a term used for contacts and relationships. Activity 9.2 invites you to develop some potential social capital of your own.

Activity 9.2   What non-monetary capital can you develop for your start-up?

Make a list of your contacts, and their contacts if you can, and find out who runs a business or has a skill that could be useful to you. If you do not know their contacts, you could meet up with your contacts over the next couple of weeks over a coffee/tea and ask them informally who they know and who is in their networks.

As a next step, list them with their name and skill or product. What could you offer in return that might be of value to them? If that is too daunting to start with, go back to your notes, and find the lists with your skills and strengths, and then match the potential value for them with your needs for non-monetary resources.

The last step is to start working down your list and meeting up or talking to those contacts via social media, if no face-to-face meeting is possible.

And there are other ways to reduce start-up costs, renting equipment and cars or vans and buying them second-hand. Under asset leasing we explored the use of leasing, and it can be helpful for smaller tools and equipment as well. Equipment can be hired on a short-term basis when it is needed, which minimizes the initial cash investment needed. Hirebase, Speedyservices and HSS are only three examples of companies offering services to hire machines and transport vehicles in the UK and Europe. Considerations on the length of time and when to invest into buying a tool or machine either new or used need to be carefully done, soon after start-up.

Buying used equipment is a bootstrapping way to reduce initial investment cost. There are many places to buy used equipment – from auction sites (eBay), online market places (Amazon, Gumtree) to using ways to gain free goods through networks such as Freecycle and Gumtree again. Freecycle is an international movement to reduce waste by encouraging members of local networks to offer unwanted electrical items or furniture to others before sending them to the landfill area. The takers of an offered piece pick up the item at their own cost and items are offered for free. Non-essential items such as tables, shelves or chairs, and even some office equipment such as printers, can be brought in at low cost.

The next section discusses the money you need to get up and running. How much do you think you need? Banks in as much as investors want to have a clear overview of how much money is needed, how much will be generated by the business and how it will be spent.

9.7 Concluding remarks and application of new insights

Chapter Nine discussed in detail financial literacy skills, from personal survival budgets and simple banking to various types of cost. It then discussed in detail a large variety of sources for monetary funding, from personal savings to loans from friends, debt finance, equity finance, crowdfunding, peer-to-peer lending to funding circles. Plenty of examples from the UK and other countries showed that most funding sources are available in many countries in relatively similar forms. Additionally, three ways to leverage non-monetary resources showcased ways that the co-creation approach can add value for all stakeholders. The last section offered advice on how to select funding while balancing the limitations of legal form, personal goals and track record in business and carrying out a commercial activity successfully.

Revision questions and further applying the learning to your *sustainable start-up*

1 What is the difference between the minimum and living wage?
2 What happens if you are under 18 and want to open a bank account?
3 What is the definition for debt financing? What forms can you identify?
4 How does crowdfunding work?
5 What two basic types of cost are there?
6 What is salary on-cost?
7 List and explain at least five different sources of monetary funding.
8 What are the advantages of equity finance compared to bank loans?
9 Activity 9.1 and 9.2 allow you to apply the discussion of funding sources to your own venture. Carry them out now, if you have not done so already, and add the findings and selection to your start-up diary and business plan.
10 Go to Section 9.5 and answer the seven questions on your preferences for ways to run the business. Note your answers in your start-up diary.
11 Create a list with all the equipment you think you need, and all the office materials – your start-up shopping list. Add it to your start-up diary. Imagine now that you do not have the cash to spend to buy any of the items on the list; what can you do to get each of those items? For those items you cannot come up with an alternative way of getting access to, think again and go back to the shopping list – how essential are all of those items you put on the original list for getting the business up and running?

10

SHOW ME THE MONEY – FINANCIAL PLANNING AND PRICING

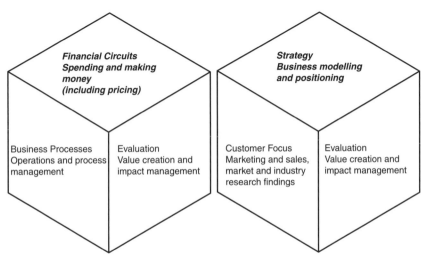

Figure 10.1 The Cube Financial Circuits and the Cube Strategy
Source: © Hill, 2012.

Summary

This chapter discusses ways to establish how much money you actually need to get up and running. "Show me the money" is meant literally: Where is the money coming from and what is it going to be used for, what are the Financial Circuits (Figure 10.1)? Banks as much as investors want to have a clear overview of how money is generated and what it is used for. And even if you do not use external finance, it is vital to monitor your financial performance on a regular basis. The chapter introduces important financial planning tools needed to stay in control of your money, from start-up budget to cash flow and sales forecast and balance sheet. Understanding them and being able to at least read them yourself is essential in order to create and maintain a sustainable new venture. Once all costs have been identified in their distribution over the year, it is appropriate to identify pricing strategies and discuss again market positioning. In the context of the market research findings on how much customers are actually willing to pay for a new solution to their problem, the *sustainable start-up* can draw conclusions on how feasible the new venture is from a financial perspective. The book's companion website offers templates for cash flow, start-up budget and balance sheet to download and use (see www.palgrave.com/hill-start-up).

CONTENTS

10.1   Start-up budget

In order to get up and running you need to spend some money, how much varies greatly. If you manufacture, you need a lot more money to buy stock, machines, get staff in place, find premises, etc. or to pay a company that manufactures on your behalf. If you start an online business, you need to invest a lot less up-front.

Funders and banks will want to see how much money you think you need and how you intend to spend it in order to check if you calculate or estimate it wisely and do not spend money unnecessarily.

How do you know what you need? Some costs are common to all businesses. These are listed in Table 10.1. If you need more information on any of those, go to the companion website for this book (www.palgrave.com/companion/hill-start-up).

Research on the financing of start-ups has shown that underfinancing is one of the biggest barriers to growth and can be a factor in failing during start-up. Remember, about one-third, or about 33%, of all start-ups fail during year one. Even more importantly, not considering all necessary costs is a reason for start-ups not doing as well financially as they thought they would and can even be a reason for failing. Table 10.1 lists some start-up costs you need to consider. Some might not apply to your venture (for example for online businesses) whereas some others might be missing. Consider whether you can sort the costs listed in a better way.

Table 10.2 illustrates the start-up costs for Jones Associates Ltd, a marketing training consultancy, as an example. Peter Jones works from home and does not need business premises.

The start-up budget by Peter Jones is a very simple example of a business started from home, as about 75% of all businesses are. In order to get up and running he has considered marketing costs, fixed costs for company set up and tax return, infrastructure costs for communication (phone, Internet, computer and accessories such as a printer), professional updates and protection (insurance and professional memberships). When you compare this budget with the empty list of potential costs you can see how easy it can be to put costs together. The next section explores sales forecasting. While predicting the future is difficult, your research on industry and market will give you some indicators on how much you can

Table 10.1   Start-up budget

Start-up expenses	Cost £
Machines needed for production? Purchase or hire cost	
Rent for premises, premises insurance, deposit	
Car insurance, car or van hire	
Professional indemnity and public liability insurance/product liability insurance	
Phone line rental (with minutes)	
Mobile phone rental with minutes	
Utility bills (some vary by amount)	
Laptop and computers	
Printers and faxes	
Transport – mileage, public transport	
Subscriptions to membership organizations and professional magazines	
Office furniture	
Start-up stock	
Website/domain name/hosting space	
Stationery/stamps	
Marketing cost	
Wages	
Business rates	
Tax (income tax for self-employed, corporation tax, VAT)	
Professional services, accountant, lawyer, designer	
Licenses	
Permissions	
Raw materials	
Duty where applicable	
Goods you buy in to sell on	
Interest rates on loans	
Other: suppliers that produce on your behalf	
TOTAL	

sell in the first years, and what possible seasonal variations there might be. Funders and banks will look out for indications of research carried out in the way the sales forecast is done.

10.2   Sales forecast

A sales forecast is the attempt to predict the number of units you are going to sell in a defined time period, per month, quarter or year for example. This has to be based on all

Table 10.2 Start-up budget for Peter Jones trading as Jones Associates Ltd

Peter Jones, consultant, trading as Jones Associates Ltd, Start-up costs Core services: marketing training and developing marketing strategies	£
Website domain and hosting, website development	915
Marketing cost	800
Legal costs for company set up	100
Accountancy costs	950
Company return	25
Mobile phone contract (with 600 inclusive minutes per month, for a year)	420
Telephone landline rental and broadband (for a year, without phone calls)	180
Professional liability and public liability insurance	250
Capital expenses (PC, accessories)	2500
Professional membership and subscriptions	250
Total	**6390**

available research that was hopefully gathered in the activities you carried out while working your way through the other chapters, in particular Chapters Four and Five on industry and market conditions. The sales forecast is an essential basis for your cash flow. If your assumptions about the number of units you will sell are too high, and you sell a lot less, this will create a negative cash flow and a "hole" in your bank account. This might mean you cannot pay suppliers, staff or utility bills, and that very quickly can lead to the need to close the business unless you can bridge the gap with loans or other debt finance at short notice.

 The 80/20 rule is known as the Pareto principle. In the context of sales it indicates that 80% of the desired sales outputs are achieved with 20% of the clients/inputs; similarly, 80% of all profits come from 20% of all services or products. While this does not need to be taken literally, it gives the idea that in many cases small businesses make their income with a limited number of clients. Or with a more positive spin: a small proportion of your efforts provides most of the results. For the *sustainable start-up* this means you need to focus in your sales on the customers that actually buy the product.

What can you do to predict these sales figures when you have not even started trading? This is where the market research you already carried out and in particular target customer research provides the data you need. Look again (using Key Note and Mintel, for example) for data on:

- Sales of products in that subsector and region you are in (where applicable);
- Sales per customer groups;
- Profitability of customer groups (willingness to pay higher prices);
- Profit margin of your product(s);
- Findings of your own market research.

Identify the primary customer group you will be selling to and how much they spend currently on the type of product you intend to sell. Hopefully, you decided to enter the market with the most profitable product and are targeting customer(s) that have the money to buy it. Which are the most effective and profitable channels for marketing that lead to actual sales?

Sales forecasts can be based on three types of market information:

1) What customers say about their intentions to continue buying products in the industry.
2) What customers are actually currently doing in the market, their buying behaviour.
3) What customers have done in the past.

But how does that apply if you are offering a totally new product or service? There a number of ways to calculate sales forecasts if your product is unique. Below are some simple steps:

1) Prepare a macroeconomic forecast – what will happen to overall economic activity in the relevant economies in which a product is to be sold.
2) Prepare an industry sales forecast – what will happen to overall sales in an industry based on the issues that influence the macroeconomic forecast.
3) Prepare a company sales forecast – based on what the founder(s) expect based on primary research to happen to the company's market share.

The question then remains, what methods will be useful to fill these steps with information. In Chapters Four and Five we discussed in detail how to generate information for the above three steps on industry and market, and by now you should have identified the target customer(s). We had discussed that for start-ups and focused marketing on a shoestring (with only a very small amount of money to spend), one segment that is most likely to buy it needs to be targeted first for market entry and inspire other segments to do so at a later stage. For the sales forecast you should focus on the first (or only) product/service you plan to sell.

Once you have summarized your findings, you can start engaging in sales forecasting. Unfortunately, many new venture plans use the forecast method "guess what", which shows a lack of evidence and argument for the numbers presented. It is, at best, based on gut feeling and "guestimates" of what other sellers in the market sell to their customers, seen through the eye of the innocent outsider. While gut feeling is one useful component in making judgements and decisions, it should not be the only rationale used for deciding on market fit and customer behaviour, as there is plenty of information available that is reliable.

There are a number of established *evidence-based* methods, which include surveys, observation, statistical methods, analogy and market tests. In practice, a combination of some of those is useful to gain a reasonable evidence base for an argument on how much money you can make.

Statistical methods use the above-mentioned numbers for the recent three to five years for projecting the future sales, assuming factors remain stable or including some change in factors influencing the sales figures. If you have a unique product this will be difficult; however, many start-ups open a business with an existing product/service in a different location, such as a retail outlet, IT or design consultancy or restaurant-type business.

For new products in consumer markets there are two methods for forecasting worth mentioning, one is mathematically modelling the process of diffusion for consumer durables (for those many start-ups without the needed mathematical or statistical skills this might mean getting a professional to do it, which is a cost you need to include in the cash flow). The other one is a method for forecasting how different combinations of attributes can impact on consumer demand, called conjoint analysis. In practice, I have rarely seen a start-up applying statistical methods for fine-tuning the value proposition and sales forecasts.

Limitations of the statistical approach are that it is difficult to project what factors will influence the conditions in the future and adjust the forecast for those factors. What is often done is that price increases, salary increases and inflation increases are factored for with percentages for buying power and number of buyers. But what if demands change due to a product recall of one large supplier in the market? One example: in summer 2014 the charms for the loom bracelets, the latest wave of creatively making bracelets using rubber bands, were found to contain chemicals that could cause cancer. As the young boys and girls making these bracelets were known to be likely to chew on them, the danger hit hard. One UK-wide toy company had to recall all charms after tests had shown them to contain the chemicals. This affected sales of not only charms but also looms. This kind of damaging factor is difficult to predict.

Observation is another method: this involves gathering real-time information on consumer buying behaviour in the market segment you want to enter. There is secondary data available on actual buying behaviour that was mentioned in Chapter Five on market research. In order to verify if the data apply to your local area, if you want to open a retail outlet or restaurant for example, it is helpful to actually go near shops and restaurants and count at different times of the day the number of customers and map their buying behaviour: what products do they actually buy, in what numbers and who are these customers (age, gender, etc.). This could be combined with a survey.

Similarly, online surveys could establish online actual buying behaviour using online user groups or Facebook groups.

Surveys are commonly used to gain some data for estimating market potential. The survey has to focus on buyers' intention to actually buy the product. However, the data achieved cannot be taken at face value that in reality consumers will *actually buy* the product in those numbers. Most consumer product manufacturers use some deduction factors to calculate those results (Dolan, 1990a and b). One of those methods is illustrated below in Table 10.3 and with data in Box 10.1.

Imagine you intend to open up a new smoothie and milkshake bar in a local suburb, where there are only coffee shops offering a limited range of smoothies. This seems to be a popular choice for student projects. Your survey results on purchase intent show the results in Table 10.3: 35% would definitely buy a smoothie at least once a week, and 45% indicate that they would probably buy one, 20% are not sure yet, and 5% simply do not like any smoothies or milkshakes. Experience from large corporates having seen the differences between expressed buying intention and actual buying after market launch would suggest multiplying the first two answers with a factor less than 1, and ignoring the results for the last two answers completely.

Table 10.3   Adjusting results from surveys measuring buyer intentions

Survey purchase intent	Response in %	Rule of thumb reduction factor for forecasting	% Estimated to be actually likely to buy
Would definitely buy	35	0.75	26.25
Would probably buy	45	0.35	15.75
Unsure about buying	20	0	
Probably or definitely not buying	5	0	
TOTALS	100		42.0

Source: After Dolan (1990a).

Dependent on the product type, the "definite" buying intention answers would be multiplied with anything between 0.7–0.8 and those given as "probable" with 0.25–0.35. The results given are using a factor of 0.75 for those saying they would definitely buy and a factor of 0.35 for those probably buying. Applying those numbers turns the results into 42% of respondents that might buy the product. This is the result that has to be used for all forecasts, in particular sales forecasts.

There are many reasons for the differences shown:

▶ Many survey respondents who actually do take part seem to want to "help" the survey processor and say they "definitely" would buy to please the "nice" person asking the questions even if they are not quite sure about their buying intention. This is called *social bias*.
▶ The product/service used for testing is very likely to be different from the one used in the survey or the market testing, and for that reason the actual number of potential buyers purchasing the product is smaller.
▶ Survey respondents might not know enough about the product/service in order to clearly assess their actual buying decision.
▶ Some purchasing decisions are made on impulse and difficult to capture.

For new products for which no similar product is yet in the market, sometimes *analogy* is used, as statistical methods or observation or survey cannot achieve reliable insights. For example, before tablet computers were in the market, testing or statistical methods would not have generated useful results. The only way to use secondary data was to look for the most similar product available, which at the time were netbooks, other portable smaller devices and the data on their market introduction. However, it was so different to a tablet that these figures had to be adjusted. Additionally, market conditions have to be checked for similarity and differences and factored into the analysis and projections. For these reasons, survey, observation and/or analogy need to be combined with actual market tests and other methods to get a closer estimate of the actual units that would be bought. Whatever factors are used, they have to be explained reasonably for investors or funders to be convinced.

I have mentioned *market testing* before in Chapter Seven on business modelling. It is most commonly used for new products or services where a prototype is available or a taster of a service can be offered, for example an eBay store is created to see if the goods sell online. Have you seen a small stall in a supermarket near the entrance or the tills? This is one way the market for a new consumer food product can be tested. Or samples, such as for ice cream or a drink, are given out near shopping centres and you are asked up to five questions about the product. It is very useful to gather additional socio-demographic data during these market-testing phases about who the respondents are in order to establish to what extent they are representative of the target customers you are trying to reach.

There is the well-known story how Innocent founders tested their smoothie: they went to a festival and offered tasters of their smoothies for free and simply asked consumers to put the empty cup in one of two containers: YES for going ahead with producing more of the smoothies, and NO for recommending them not to go ahead with it. This method is well known and tried, and might be useful for your *sustainable start-up*; it proved to be useful for one of our case studies.

Picture 10.1 shows how our case study start-up **Ben Smith** used market testing to get some consumer insight about his fruit jelly: he was inspired by the way Innocent tested to what extent customers liked their fruit smoothie, and adapted that exercise to his needs. You can see that in the box on the left there is only one pot by a consumer who had tried his jelly and did not like it (the box has the label "Erm, not for me"); the box on the right

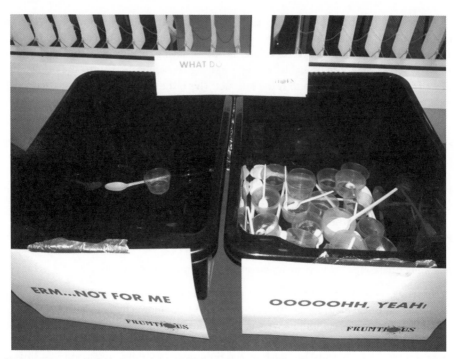

Picture 10.1 Ben Smith's approach to establishing if customers liked his fruit jelly
Source: © Ben Smith, 2014.

Table 10.4 Simple sales forecast

Time period (month / quarter) Example: Peter Jones Associates Ltd	Units sold Training days	Price/unit	Revenue per time period in £ / monthly sales
Month: December	2	£400/day	800.00
TOTAL			

is full of empty jelly pots and spoons. This box has the label "ooooh, yeah", indicating that customers liked the jelly.

The next step is to see how representative the people were who did this kind of product testing, and to what extent for that reason these data can be scaled to the whole population. In the case of Innocent, they had not collected any other data on those testing their products.

Table 10.4 shows a simple way to put down the units you intend to sell, the unit price(s) and the revenue you can generate based on these prices. Include entries for large volume sales when you might offer a discount. Remember to consider seasonal variations.

In the cash flow section 10.3, Table 10.5 a row entitled "units of sale" shows you the sales forecast for Jones Associates Ltd. You can see a seasonal adjustment for August, as in the UK little training activity happens in August, as so many staff are on holiday: sales go down from six training days in July to two in August and up again to six training days in September.

The next section discusses one of the most important financial planning tools, the cash flow forecast. It allows *sustainable start-ups* to stay in control of their money and gives you an overview that each month you can pay your bills (and salaries to staff where appropriate). When applying for funding and to banks for a loan, cash flow is an essential forecast to present to them.

10.3 Cash flow forecast

 Turnover is vanity,
Profit is sanity,
Cash flow is survival.

The above nicely summarizes that positive cash flow is essential for a healthy business, and that means for a *sustainable start-up*. Some professionals call it the banker's mantra.

A cash flow statement shows the amount of cash generated by a company through sales, loans, grants and investment and the amount of money used by it (spent on expenses) in a given time period. Imagine water flowing into a tank at one end, then being swirled around and mixed with some objects and other liquids and flowing out at the opposite end of the tank.

Looking at it practically, it is the difference in amount of cash available at the beginning of a period (opening balance) and the amount at the end of that period (closing balance). There is a positive cash flow if more money comes in than goes out in a particular time period; it is negative if more money goes out than comes in.

This forecast or projection is used to predict as precisely as possible how much money is needed in every time period, often a month. The main reason for doing it is to avoid cash flow problems. Cash flow problems indicate that you cannot pay your debts, such as loan repayment or interest, or pay your suppliers, utility bills or a salary to staff.

Ultimately, if these financial demands cannot be met, the business becomes insolvent and has to close. Predicting whether this might possibly happen, allows the business owner(s) to plan to get additional finance.

A cash flow forecast is carried out on a monthly basis, and usually done for three to five years from the month of starting to sell. The entries used in the first column list all the expenses that need to be catered for each month in the month they occur. As the business owner you need to be able to either build reserves for that month or get additional finance in if the expense is large or many are occurring in a particular month. This is likely to happen towards the end of the financial year or at the start, when you take out insurances, buy a car, rent premises, etc. A summary by quarter/every three months is not a good idea, as this hides the particular month an expense occurs.

The items to consider include all of those from the start-up budget and several important other ones. These other items include:

▶ Reserves for extra unexpected business expenses;
▶ Payments for tax to pay (in the UK to the HM Revenue and Customs (HMRC) for corporation and/or income tax dependent on the legal form);
▶ VAT payments to the HMRC if you decide to register for VAT;
▶ On-going expenses for stationary, marketing, transport, and materials;
▶ Professional services (accountancy, legal services);
▶ Depreciation of capital expenses, such as machinery, including computers, cars, and manufacturing machinery.

Table 10.5 shows an example of a cash flow for the first year for the marketing consultancy Jones Associates Ltd we discussed in the previous section when looking at the start-up budget. What you can see is the simple method for calculating the first opening balance of £145. This is achieved by deducting TOTAL 1 from TOTAL 2, income minus expenses. As the expenses are £145 lower than the income generated in that month, the cash flow is positive and has a value of £145 (£3500 minus £3355).

In the first month, the director Peter Jones pays in cash to the value of £2500 and gains a start-up grant of £1000 (that adds up to £3500); the sum of that makes up the first total, TOTAL 1, cash in. While he sells two days of training for the value of £800, the money gets only paid 30 days later, that is, towards the end of the next month. It is normal practice in business that payment is made up to 30 days later, or even six weeks. For that reason you can see that in the row entitled "sales" the value of the training days reflects the volume of the previous month, not the same month's.

The expenses each month are put in and added up at the end of the month to create TOTAL 2, or cash out for each month. The closing balance is the subtraction of TOTAL 2 from TOTAL 1 plus the opening balance. You can see that the results of the sales forecast have been included in the cash flow. The opening balance for the start-up was £0, as no money was available. Further explanations of the cash flow are found in Box 10.1.

Box 10.1 outlines the steps that need to be taken to calculate the cash flow forecast and the meaning of the headings.

Box 10.1 Steps to calculate the cash flow for each month and at the end of the year

If you look at the cash flow in Table 10.5 in column one, you can see that after "grants" there is the first total, called TOTAL 1. This is the sum of all money coming into the business. As explained above, the cash balance at the bottom of the table is the result of deducting TOTAL 2, expenses, from TOTAL 1, money coming in. As there is no opening balance at the start of the month, the opening balance is £0. For that reason, the closing balance is identical with the cash flow in that month.

For the next month, the closing balance of the previous month becomes the new opening balance, as shown in Table 10.5 The cash flow in that month is negative with −£35, as there were many expenses but less income. Now, in each month, cash flow is added to the opening balance to obtain the closing balance. For month two, or December, the closing balance is £110, the sum of £145 plus −£35. This closing balance of £110 becomes the opening balance for January; cash flow of £265 is added to that to get to the closing balance of £375. After 12 months, there is a closing balance of £4325. This means Peter Jones has £4325 cash in the bank.

Keeping on top of your start-up's cash flow can be managed practically with *bookkeeping*. Ideally do it yourself, or employ a bookkeeper by the hour to do it for you. Simply by noting down daily your expenses and income in a cashbook (for retail brick-and-mortar as well as online, simple services), which can be kept online, you can keep on top of your expenses, and money coming in. Such a cashbook will have two main parts:

One column for receipts for expenses, and one for payments received (with note of how: bank account, credit card, cheque or cash).

Table 10.5 Cash flow for year one for marketing consultancy Jones Associates Ltd

Month	Nov	Dec	Jan	Feb	Mar	Apr	May	Jun	Jul	Aug	Sep	Oct	Total
SALES													
Units of sale	1	2	2	2	3	5	7	7	6	2	6	8	51
Earnings	400	800	800	800	1200	2500	2800	2800	2400	800	2400	3200	20900
Money coming in and going out													
Money coming in													
Sales		400	800	800	800	1200	2500	2800	2800	2400	800	2400	17700
Capital invested	2500												2500
Grants	1000												1000
TOTAL 1	3500	400	800	800	800	1200	2500	2800	2800	2400	800	2400	21200
Expenses													
Wages	10	120	20	20	20	20	20	20	20	20	20	20	330
Rent *													
Heating*													
Marketing	250		200	100	150	150		150		150		150	1300
Insurance	250												250
Travel	10	20	20	20	30	50	70	70	60	20	60	80	510
Telephone	55	55	55	55	55	55	55	55	55	55	55	55	660
Stationery	130	30	30	30	30	30	30	30	30	30	30	30	460
Repairs of equipment		200						150					350
Sundries	150	10	10	40	10	10	10	10	10	10	60	135	465
Capital purchases	2500												2500
Dividends taken			200	200	600	900	950	1200	1200	1300	1500	2000	10050
TOTAL 2	3355	435	535	465	895	1215	1135	1685	1375	1585	1725	2470	16875
CASH BALANCE													
Cash flow	145	-35	265	335	-95	-15	1365	1115	1425	815	-925	-70	
Open bal		145	110	375	710	615	600	1965	3080	4505	5320	4395	
Closing bal	145	110	375	710	615	600	1965	3080	4505	5320	4395	4325	

Note: * not applicable to this business.

 Activity 10.1   Cash flow calculation and exercise

Go to the companion website (www.palgrave.com/companion/hill-start-up) and download the cash flow template with data for a crafts business.

Read the associated short description of expenses and transfer them to the cash flow.

What has the business owner not addressed that needs consideration?

The next section discusses how to find the break-even point – that is, the point in time when your income equals your expenses for the first time.

10.4 Break-even

Why is it important to discuss and calculate the break-even point? And what is the break-even point? The break-even point is reached if your business activities can generate sufficient cash to at least cover the costs (including your salary). This happens when the amount of sales equals the total cost required to produce the product. The month that happens is the break-even point. If the business makes sales after this point it generates a profit or surplus.

It is important to know this point in time for deciding on price strategies and setting prices as well as setting a sales budget. It also helps to identify how many sales units you need to sell so that you can make a profit and how low sales figures can be before you make a loss and no profits, but still cover your costs. Similarly, it helps to identify how much you have to increase a price and volumes of sales when a fixed cost goes up.

How do you calculate that point? There are several ways of doing it; we will focus on one simple form that is sufficient for early calculations. Let us look at the example of the same marketing consultancy we have been discussing, Jones Associates Ltd: the yearly fixed costs are £6620. On average, the unit of marketing training costs the client £400; each unit has variable cost of £200 per training day, so the remaining £200 makes a contribution to cover the fixed cost. The break-even point is reached when 34 of those training packages of one day have been sold.

Why? Deduct the variable cost from the selling price (£400 minus £200 = £200), and then divide the total yearly fixed cost by the £200 contribution per unit (the result of the subtraction above) to gain a value of 33.1 units, that means 34 days. Box 10.2 briefly outlines the steps to take for this simple calculation.

Box 10.2   Calculating the break-even point for Jones Associates Ltd.

Step 1 Contribution margin to fixed cost per unit of sales

Deduct variable cost per unit from the unit sales price:

Unit sales price (£400)

– Variable costs (£200)

Contribution margin to fixed cost per unit of sales (£200)

Step 2 Break-even point: fixed costs divided by contribution margin

Fixed cost (£6620)

÷ Contribution margin (£200)

Break-even units, that is days (33.1 rounded to 34)

 Case study

There are some start-ups that will not break even within the first or second year of operating and sometimes only at the end of year three. This applies often to those manufacturing a new product themselves in the UK or technology related businesses. Frinter Ltd, one of our case study companies, did break even only in their first year, as they had an investment of £50,000. Should you not break even and rely on loans, for example, this time period needs to be covered by either start-up loans or grants, loans from family members or personal savings. Some technology and manufacturing start-ups do not break even for the first two years.

On the other hand, some start-ups make a profit within three months of starting trading. These include retail offerings of homemade craft goods or complementary health services and business services, to name a few. Serratomo, founded by **Vivek George** (see Section 1.8.7 in Chapter One) had very little start-up cost and was profitable within three months; the same applies to Lantyx Ltd, the tennis consultancy by **Lewis Barnes**.

The next section discusses profit and loss forecasts and balance sheets. These financial tools are not necessarily required for the feasibility study, but are useful for a business plan that is presented to banks or funders.

10.5   Profit and loss forecast and balance sheet

A profit and loss forecast can show you how much profit or loss you make in a given time period, indicating the expected revenue or income and expenses for your start-up. This means, it can show how much profit is likely to be generated from a planned level of trading. It is a guide for your thinking and planning, as at the end of the day you need to make a profit, however small, in order to survive. While you cannot predict the future, as the environment all businesses operate in is so unpredictable, you need to forecast financial performance of the start-up in order to make appropriate decisions on purchasing materials, spending on marketing, to name only a few areas you need to decide on how much money you can afford to spend and when.

As we pointed out before, forecasts as much as goals, need to be SMART (S stands for *specific*, M for *measurable*, A for *achievable*, R for *realistic* and T for *time-bound* or *time specific*) and contain specific numbers based on all the available information you can get hold of on market and industry trends.

You need a cash flow forecast as well as profit and loss to identify your company's financial position. Why? Because it is possible that you can have a positive cash flow while making a loss. This is how: a seasonal business that sells a lot before Christmas has to pay for materials and goods in advance before they are being sold. This means in the months you pay for those goods/materials, you have a negative cash flow, and need extra investment to cover the outgoings. If the loan, for example, exceeds the expenses, you can have a positive cash flow. Yet, you have not sold any of those newly purchased goods and materials.

A profit and loss forecast has usually two sections: one for income or revenue (1) and one for expenses (2). The top section is also known as a trading account for a business, in particular for retail-type businesses.

(1) The most important section is total sales, followed by figures for interest on current assets, that is money in bank or saving accounts, dividends from shares, etc. and grants and loans bringing money into the business. If you plan to sell more than one product, divide the sales by product to see what product might sell better than another.

(2) Expenses from all areas of the business, from cost of sales to labour and losses made. The cost of goods sold (all direct costs, such as labour, materials, etc. that are used to produce or import and package the goods/services; suppliers or associates) are the most important set of expenses, followed by operating cost (all indirect costs such as indirect

labour – needed even if no goods are sold, such as managers, secretary to you as the CEO and other costs not directly linked to the production of goods/services).

The profit and loss forecast can be used to calculate your profitability. Banks and investors are keen to see these figures:

▶ Gross profit: revenue – (minus) cost of goods sold.
▶ Gross profit margin: (gross profit + revenue) × 100.

(These figures shows how much money you retain from each dollar or pound of revenue generated; in other words a gross profit margin of 30% means that from each £/$ you take, 30 pence/cents are profit.)

▶ Operating profit: gross profit – operating expenses.

(That is profit that is generated from core business activities. It excludes expenses from interest and is often also called "earnings before interest and tax".)

▶ Net profit: operating profit – (taxes and interest).

(This type of profit is often referred to as the "bottom line", the total profit after deducting all imaginable expenses.)

Table 10.6 shows an example of a profit and loss account for the marketing consultancy.

Table 10.6 Profit and loss account for marketing consultancy Jones Associates Ltd for 12 months of trading

Revenue	Amount £
Product sales (51 training days)	20,400
Grant	1,000
Bank interest	25
TOTAL REVENUE	21,425
LESS expenses	
Webhosting, domain and website design	900
Drawings and salary	10,380
Associates	2,000
Marketing	1,300
Insurance	250
Travel cost	1,065
Communication (landline and mobile phone line and calls)	660
Capital expenses	2,500
Business services (accountant, company set up)	1,050
Capital purchases (PC, laptop, projector)	2,500
Sundries	150
Repairs of PC	350
Stationary	460
TOTAL Expenses	18,875

Note: Net profit in year one: £2550

In the cash flow there was no entry for associates; however, as it turned out over the year, Peter Jones could not take up all the training days himself, as he had other client commitments and was ill for two training days.

A *balance sheet* is a financial statement that summarizes a company's assets, that is what a company owns, its liabilities (what the company owes to other parties) and shareholders' equity (amount invested by the shareholders) at a specific point in time, also called financial position statement.

The balance sheet has three different sections:

(1) Assets

What are assets? These are all the items a company owns which have current and future economic value that can be measured. These include costs paid in advance such as prepaid advertising or insurance or rent. Assets are usually presented in groups in a classified balance sheet: current assets, investments, property, plant and equipment, intangible assets and other assets.

Current assets include cash and other resources that are expected to turn to cash or to be used up within one year of the balance sheet date. Current assets are presented in the order of liquidity, that is, cash at bank and petty cash, temporary short-term investments, accounts receivable or trade debtors (people who owe the business money), inventory or stock, supplies and prepaid insurance.

Investments include funds held for construction, the cash surrender value of a life insurance policy owned by the company and long-term investments in stocks and bonds.

Properties, plant and equipment are one category and usually include land, buildings, leasehold improvements, equipment, furniture, fixtures, delivery trucks, and cars, etc., often called fixed assets.

Intangible assets include for example intellectual property (IP) rights (copyrights, patents, trademarks, designs), goodwill, mailing and customer lists. Goodwill is less well known as a term, but it refers to the amount you would pay for the reputation and performance of a business if you buy one, sometimes called "business value".

(2) Liabilities

This section includes current liabilities, that need to be paid back within the next 12 months from the date of the statement, such as overdrafts and short-term loans, and long-term liabilities such as longer loans with a payback period of over 12 months, mortgages and secured bills.

(3) Owner's equity

When you deduct the liabilities from the value of the assets you gain the owner's equity. This is also called shareholders' equity, if there are more partners or external shareholders.

The next section discusses simple price calculation methods and pricing strategies that enable the *sustainable start-up* to become profitable as soon as possible.

10.6 Pricing strategies and market positioning

10.6.1 Price setting – an introduction to its context and place in the *sustainable start-up*

Why do so many start-ups think they have to charge less than their competitors do in order to get into the market? This decision is often fear based. Being the "newbie" amongst seemingly harsh experienced competitors seems daunting and can lead to questioning the right to be there for many start-ups. But why? I will leave that for you to ponder, as I am not a psychologist.

Value creation starts with the value you create for yourself as a founder, which is also but not only measured in pounds. If you have a well-researched and fine-tuned value proposition that meets the needs of target customers, or even better you can exceed customer expectations, why should you not charge a reasonable price? By now, you should know your production cost in full (including your salary) and have decided on a profit margin you desire. This will have created a minimum line for the price per unit you have to charge. If not, go back to the operations chapter, Chapter Six. The *sustainable start-up* does not fail within the first year (one of the "milestones" we plan to pass by). Once you have gathered all your costs, you can have a look at some pricing strategies, keeping in mind that you are selling an overall value proposition, and not just simply a phone case or a haircut or a website.

For the *sustainable start-up*, pricing is part of the strategy (Cube area "Strategy: Business modelling and other strategic activities") and an important part of the cost structure (when applying the business model canvas). It not only has the function of covering the costs when selling the products, but also indicates a perceived value of a product and a brand.

The next section discusses the main important pricing strategies and gives some pointers on how to select one. Keep in mind that as a new start-up you have to cover your costs, which includes your salary, and need to create a profit to be a *sustainable start-up*. And just looking at the price for the product alone is cutting it too finely. What other services or associated goods can you offer to create a unique value proposition that is convincing and might even create a Turquoise Lake? Go to the market research chapter, Chapter Five, to the section on market positioning and read it again. If you re-segment an existing market to create a low-cost niche, as the low-cost airlines have done for flights and Black Circles has done for buying car tyres, then a low price is an important part of the positioning. If you create a completely new market for new products that did not exist before, a low price is not so important in the positioning process. In both cases we assume that fixed and variable costs are well covered by the price charged.

10.6.2 Pricing strategies

Technically speaking, there are numerous pricing strategies, that is, ways of setting a price, based on the above-discussed considerations. The most common ones are listed and briefly explained below. In addition to covering your costs as just outlined above, you need to consider what expectations customers have of the kind of value proposition you offer. Do they simply expect your product to be at a certain high price?

Penetration pricing means setting a relatively low price to boost sales. This is often used when a new product is launched or a firm's main objective is growth. Satellite television companies set a low price to get subscribers then increase the price – SKY is one company using that approach.

Price skimming means setting a relatively high price to boost profits. This strategy is often used by well-known businesses launching new, high quality, premium products. They start by charging a premium at product or service launch and move to a lower price near the end of the product lifecycle.

Loss leading refers to a strategy where the price is set below unit cost. The aims can be to gain sales and market share and also attract customers to buy other more expensively priced products from their product range. Have you ever entered a shop or supermarket because they had a special offer of your favourite chocolate or beer? And then while you were there, you bought some other products as well.

Economy pricing illustrates a low-price strategy: costs of marketing and promoting a product and operations cost are kept to a minimum.

▸ Supermarkets – most have economy brands for soups, spaghetti, etc.
▸ Budget airlines – Ryanair and EasyJet ensure that planes stay on the ground as little time as possible.

Value pricing refers to a strategy to offer basic products, such as bread, potatoes or milk, at low prices to enable people on very low incomes to survive. External factors such as recession or increased competition force companies to provide value products and services to retain sales. "Value meals" at McDonald's and other fast-food restaurants suggests to the buyer that for the price that you pay you are getting a lot of product. Yet, it does not mean added value is offered.

With *premium pricing* the price set is high to reflect the exclusiveness of the product. Examples include Harrods, first class airline services, Porsche or Apple products. Can you imagine seeing a "buy one get one half price" offer for an iPhone? This is most unlikely for companies choosing a premium pricing strategy.

Competitive pricing means a firm decides its own price based on that charged by rivals.

Setting a price above that charged by the market leader can only work if your product has better features and brand value, for example a fancier appearance (bright colours for shoes).

Cost plus pricing is when the price charged eventually covers the costs of making an item and you add a percentage for your profit and overheads. As an example, adding a 50% mark up to a sandwich that costs £2 to make means you price at £3. The drawback could be that this price may not be competitive.

Going-rate pricing describes a strategy where you match what you charge with going prices in the marketplace.

Bundle pricing is when a business bundles a group of products so that buying more units means a reduced unit price is paid. Have you heard of BOGOF? "Buy one and get one free" promotions or "buy one get one half price" or "buy two and get a third free". Supermarkets often use bundle pricing strategies to convince the buyer to spend more money, as per unit they will save, yet overall they spend more.

Psychological pricing. The seller using this strategy will consider the psychology of price and the positioning of price within the marketplace. Research has shown that buyers consider a price just under a full pound or dollar or £10 or £100 as lower than the 1p or 10p, etc. more. For that reason, you see so many prices as 99p instead £1 and other numbers respectively. Buyers will still be able to say they purchased their product under £10, etc.

The next section assists you in selecting a pricing strategy based on your goals and findings from market research.

10.6.3 Selecting a pricing strategy

Market research should have addressed what kind of price for a specific product with what features and value proposition target customers are willing to pay. If the market research did not address that, you need to carry out additional research now that it is clear what the costs are and what goals for profit during years one to three you aim to make.

 Your market testing and associated research will be able to identify when customers cannot appreciate the value proposition in relation to the price they have to pay. Then you have at least four possible options:

a) You check on how the value proposition will be sold, and if all the benefits and unique added values are understood. If not, there is a task to communicate the value and the benefits much better.
b) You check if you can save cost by taking something out of the value proposition without compromising it.
c) You reduce the selling price once you have checked on your production cost and profit margins, provided that the reduced selling price still allows you to reach your financial goals.
d) You check the cost cannot be reduced and you consider seeking a new target customer group who are willing to pay the price for the value proposition.

Guess what the *sustainable start-up* decision should look like? You check option a) is not applicable, as you do want to get the message across as clearly as possible. Then you follow option d): You check the cost cannot be reduced, and then you consider seeking a new target customer group who are willing to pay the price for the value proposition you intend to offer.

The next section brings the findings on prices and possible pricing strategies into the context of positioning your service and product within the value chain and the competition. It gives pointers on how to make a decision on where to position your new venture based on the money-related information analysed so far.

10.6.4 Decision on market positioning with price setting

Positioning is the process of packaging a value proposition and creating a marketing mix that creates a competitive advantage in the minds of customer targets relative to competitive offers. Positioning involves the development of a strategy for positioning and its implementation through the marketing mix.

 Here is again the point in time to re-consider Blue and Red Oceans and Turquoise Lakes. This was discussed in Chapter Five, at the end of Section 5.7 on market positioning. In a nutshell, if you can, create a value proposition and a new target segment in a new market so that there is no competition; this is what I call the Turquoise Lake, a small market with unique customers. Develop that position further while selling and fine-tune your value proposition and theory of change accordingly.

An example: we mentioned before the strategic alliance between Samsung and DreamWorks Animation where buyers of the new Samsung 3D TV sets got free copies of selected DreamWorks 3D Blu-ray versions of two films in 2011 (including *Kung Fu Panda 2* and *Megamind*), which were included in the starter kit for the 3D television Samsung was selling. There was no competition possible to this package, as DreamWorks are the sole distributor. This offer by Samsung is an example of the "Blue Ocean"; another term for the same issue is to create a unique small niche.

The "Red Ocean" is the normal situation where many companies sell very similar products or services and you have to differentiate themselves in a number of ways through service, price, etc.

The next section sheds light on how to draw conclusions from the above financial analysis and projections for the decision to start a venture based on the business idea you are currently investigating.

10.7   Financial feasibility of a potential new venture

Financial feasibility is a conclusion of all the financial analysis carried out so far: can you make sufficient money with the product or service that allows you to cover your costs and make the profit you want to make in a reasonable time period?

If there are no customers willing to pay the price you need to sell at to reach your financial goals, then the business opportunity is not feasible, at least not with the target segment and value proposition you explored. If that is the case, go back to the business modelling chapter, Chapter Seven, check what you can change, and do some more research. Chapter Eleven has some more detailed support to offer for drawing conclusions on financial feasibility.

If it will take a few years to make a profit, you have to make a decision. If the costs cannot be covered within the first two or three years, you have to consider for how long you can afford to pay money out instead of making sufficient money to pay for your outgoings. You will need investors or grants/loans to be able to cover the period of time. Will you find investors to back you? Will loans from family members support you? Do you want to do that? The answer is a personal one based on your values and goals, nobody can make it for you.

When we talked about opportunity and personal decisions in Chapter Three, we indicated that not every business opportunity is suitable for everybody. Personal values, life goals and norms must come into play when making a decision, in addition to cost.

If the costs *can* be covered and a small profit can be made, but never more, you need to ask yourself the question whether this is what you want to achieve and do. The answer to this question might be "yes" or "no", and it might be different for different people even if the numbers are the same. If someone intends to become rich quickly and earn a specific amount of profit each year, on top of a salary, but cannot do that based on the financial analysis of a given venture, then it is very likely that the decision is no, if only small profits can be achieved in year two. Someone aiming to serve a particular community, such as disadvantaged young people, might be able to make a small profit only with the same service, which is sufficient to create reserves. The decision for the same venture might be "yes, it is financially feasible". This is discussed further in Chapter Eleven on opportunity modelling.

The next section builds on the assessment of your skills and attitudes started in Chapter Two. Do you have gaps in your financial skills? If so, you might want to add some training, reading or mentoring into your personal development plan.

10.8   Update your personal development plan

Can you carry out all of the essential activities this chapter has discussed? If not, make a note in your diary, in the personal development plan section, on what finance-related knowledge and skills you need to develop/acquire. Box 10.3 lists the skills and knowledge areas you need to address in order to be successful on the finance side of the new venture.

Box 10.3   Skills and knowledge related to finance

These are the skills that you need to have:

▶ Basic maths skills: adding, subtracting, multiplying, percentages and rounding – for calculating your costs, unit price, overheads, etc.;
▶ Using MS Excel or similar software – the basic functions for creating an easy-to-use cash flow template or adapting an existing one;
▶ Effective Internet research – for identifying reliable and unreliable sources;
▶ Analytical skills – to analyse promises made by banks and suppliers, by Internet sources.

These are the knowledge areas you need to develop or have:

▶ Start-up budget development;
▶ Sales forecast development, cash flow calculation and forecast;
▶ Profit and loss account and balance sheet;
▶ Funding sources for pre-start-up and start-up.

 Activity 10.2   Assess your financial skills

In Chapter Three we discussed already an assessment of your skills and knowledge, and financial skills was one of the areas we explored. Check with your start-up diary, what did you score your skills at back then? Now that you have worked your way through Chapter Nine and this chapter, what is your assessment? Use the star introduced in Chapter Two, section 2.5 for financial skills again and add the results to your start-up diary.

The website for this book offers a test so that you can assess your financial skills further (www.palgrave.com/companion/hill-start-up).

Do not forget to set some milestones and SMART end goals with a date for your personal development and venture development process and note them in your start-up diary.

10.9   Concluding remarks and application of new insights

This chapter discussed important financial planning tools assisting you to identify how much money you can make with the business idea and emerging business project. The tools discussed included:

▶ The start-up budget, outlining how much money you need to get up and running;
▶ The cash flow forecast – planning ahead how much money will be going out and into the business every month for at least three years; this is important to see if you can pay your bills (suppliers, utility bills, salary) every month;
▶ Break-even point – the month when the money coming in through sales covers your core expenses;

▶ The profit and loss forecast – a projection that sets expenses against core income through sales and is the basis to calculate a number of profit types, including net profit;
▶ The balance sheet – a juxtaposition of assets with expenses that shows you the owner's equity.

All of these financial planning tools were illustrated with a case study of the marketing consultancy Jones Associates Ltd.

We then discussed a number of pricing strategies, and concluded that for the first product entering the market for the first time, the best solution is to focus on one single pricing strategy or a maximum of two combined, such as value pricing and psychological pricing. Pricing was also discussed as a tool for market positioning.

For conclusions on the financial feasibility of the venture you are exploring, we discussed a number of possible conclusions if the potential profit that can be achieved is small; one possible conclusion is that there might be an opportunity for a social enterprise, where the profits are sufficient to build up reserves. The final conclusion about financial feasibility needs to be based on your personal values and goals, as much as the financial viability of the potential start-up. Further help in drawing conclusions about financial feasibility is offered in Chapter Eleven.

The last section invited you to reflect on your finance skills, re-assess them using the financial skills star (see WAASSIP in Chapter Two, Section 2.5) and carry out an online test on the Palgrave companion website for this book.

Revision questions and application to your feasibility research

1 Why is financial planning useful? List at least three reasons.
2 What is a cash flow forecast? When would you carry it out in the start-up planning process?
3 What skills do you need for successful financial planning at (pre-) start-up phase?
4 What conclusions can you draw from the cash flow forecast for Peter Jones? Is he taking out too much or too little money through drawings?
5 Apply the learning on pricing strategies to your venture idea: what did you learn from the research on the price buyers are willing to pay? What pricing strategy or strategies are suitable for your market? Why? Note down at least three reasons for the selection of a pricing strategy.
6 Your sales forecast: what is it going to be? What adjustments do you need to make during the year? What events will affect sales? When do you project sales will be at its highest in year one? Why?
7 Carry out a cash flow for your venture idea: have you done all the research needed to do that? If not, start gathering information on the prices of goods you need to purchase. The rule of thumb is to get at least two, better three quotes or prices.
8 When will you break even? Are your sales figures SMART? How many units do you think you will need to sell? Whatever your product, or services, this point in time is important to note. And then imagine you sell 25% less, when will you break even then?

11

OPPORTUNITY MODELLING

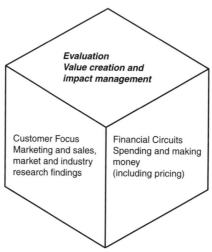

Figure 11.1   The Cube Evaluation
Source: © Hill, 2012.

Summary

This chapter is one of the most important ones in the book, as it assists you in developing a set of conclusions – is there a potential business opportunity for you behind the business idea you explored so far (Figure 11.1)? The chapter addresses the principles and practices of responsibility, resourceful impact, interconnectedness, co-creation and sustainability through the way we create the business opportunity. The chapter discusses four areas of fitness – operational, financial, market and industry, and personal introduced in Chapter Three – and offers guidance on how to draw conclusions and achieve a weighting of the fitness that has been found. Finally, the overall summary of fitness across all four areas needs to be drawn. Having done that, we need to explore if the conclusions are the same for social enterprises.

CONTENTS

11.1   Introduction to opportunity modelling

Chapter Three introduced the idea of a business opportunity as a proven possibility to sell a product or service at an appropriate price to a sufficient number of customers in order to make at least an identified profit beyond covering costs. What have we discussed and researched since then that brought you to this chapter? We explored if the business idea under consideration is actually a business opportunity, a way to earn at least a living, and if it is an opportunity for a for-profit business that offers a high profit margin or a social enterprise.

For the *sustainable start-up* approach this chapter is realizing the evaluation aspect, detailed in the principle and practice of sustainability. Before engaging with business planning you have to be clear as early as possible if the idea is worth pursuing further.

Chapters Four to Ten address the various aspects of business modelling: Chapter Four gives guidance on carrying out industry and competitor research with a co-creation principle, keeping in mind that competitors and other stakeholders are co-creating the environment you will potentially be operating in. Chapter Five provides support and guidance on carrying out market research and analysing results to identify target customers and a value proposition, and we start to discuss the concept and application of market positioning. Chapter Six addresses considerations for operations. For the *sustainable start-up* the idea of test trading with a minimal viable product or test product, which allows you to learn from customer feedback and further develop the product, is also introduced. We focus on imagining and costing, doing whatever possible online and starting with mobile service and/or pop-up shops if appropriate. This involves sketching operational processes, from a business viewpoint and the customer journey.

Chapter Seven then assists in business modelling, the process of linking all functions of a business together loosely and testing the value proposition in the marketplace. Trying selling your services for the first time or engaging in market testing and reassessing assumptions and conclusions drawn previously is part of that discussion. Chapter Eight looks at possibilities to comply with licenses, law and regulations and ways to keep a competitive advantage by protecting the intellectual property in what you create; we also discuss possible legal forms. Chapter Nine introduces you to basic financial tools, from personal budgeting to bank accounts and sources of finance for starting a business, as well as non-monetary sources of finance. Chapter Ten discusses all financial aspects that need consideration when finding out what it will cost to run the start-up as a business, and introduces key financial planning tools.

What is left to do now is to come to a conclusion across the research, test trading and analysis carried out: is there a business opportunity behind the business idea you want to pursue that is personal-ability? The next sections offer a matrix to capture the findings from the previous seven chapters and come to a conclusion if a business opportunity is in front of you that you wish to pursue. We build on the discussions from Chapter Three, considering whether the opportunity fits you or the team that have looked at it, (as the business opportunity is not just about money making but about matching your willingness) if you have the necessary capabilities as well as values matching the business opportunity. All this needs to be done before spending further time on business planning and in particular marketing.

While feasibility is not a new concept, it is one that is difficult to apply practically and come to reasonable conclusions. Even large corporates launching new products get it wrong more often than not and have to take a new service or product off the market. The big question is, why? They might not have asked the most appropriate questions and/or did not interview the most appropriate potential customers. It might also be the case that they have drawn some inappropriate conclusions in one or more of the three areas of financial fit, legal and operational fit or industry and market fit. Personal fit is less important for large companies, as people working in the teams involved in new product development and launch can easily be replaced. For start-ups, the personal fit area can become the most important one that leads to the conclusion that an opportunity should not be pursued. Figure 11.2 shows an overview of the processes for the opportunity identification.

The view I take in *Start Up* is that opportunities are developed – they are not just there ready to be picked. While it is easier for some to see a potential business opportunity, even those individuals still need to carry out research and financial analysis to come to a conclusion that there is a real opportunity to make money that is suitable for them. In the end, for the first start-up, an opportunity to make money in an appropriate way that meets their goals and values is a matter of perception and construction.

Based on the financial figures and findings, it is essential to forecast how much sales can be achieved, in order to decide if there is a suitable business opportunity available. In Chapter Three we discuss the details that the research and analysis needs to find out about for each area. The sales figures then have to be matched to the production cost estimates, as discussed in Chapter Ten.

For drawing conclusions I suggest a combination of a descriptive and percentage fit summary for each area: The percentage value has to be a very close estimate based

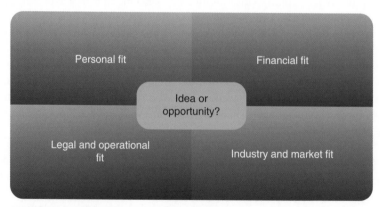

Figure 11.2 Opportunity fit areas
Source: © Hill, 2013.

on the findings from the analysis; then the percentage given fits into the bands of the descriptive fit listed below:

- 90–100% fit means a *perfect* fit;
- 70–89% fit means a *reasonable* fit – consider adjustments to achieve a perfect fit;
- 50–69% fit means a *limited* fit – before pursuing this opportunity this area needs some development; the opportunity should not be pursued straight away, more market testing and/or business modelling is needed to achieve better results;
- Under 50% fit means *no* fit – reconsider the opportunity and what you can possibly change to achieve a fit; or give up on this idea and start with a new one.

The financial fit needs to be nearly perfect; overall, all areas should achieve a value of over 330%. Under this percentage the opportunity should not be pursued straight away, but you need to carry out further research and/or make adjustments.

These opportunity fit areas clearly partially overlap. For example, you might be enthusiastic about the industry and market fit, achieving 100%, and importing the good from abroad is not a problem, yet costly, for example, because duty on wine is rather high. Niche producers often charge a reasonable amount of money for their wines, and you have not included the cost of duty in your calculations. Once you estimate the financial fit, and have included all costs, you could find that your market fit might change, as the selling price you have to charge exceeds what the target segment is willing to pay.

While these above percentages will and can only be an approximation, it is a way of coming closer to a conclusion if this idea is an opportunity at a given point in time for an individual or a team.

The methods suggested below include forecasting and, estimation that is, where possible, evidence based. Forecasting uses many variables that rely on judgement and results are far from accurate. And as with all methods and approaches, forecasting has limitations. As far as individual judgement is involved, they are prone to being too optimistic. Furthermore, the fact that only *X* amount of units were sold in a relatively new industry can have as a reason that simply not enough units were on offer so that demand could not be met. When the iPad was first sold, for example, waiting lists had been in place, and only some of the demand could be met with a product. If someone looks back in 20 years' time to find out about sales figures, the actual figures could be misleading. Tens of thousands more iPads could have been sold in that year, had they been available.

Similarly, sufficient marketing and awareness raising are needed intensely over a short period of time to help some high forecasts to become reality, and the product or service needs to be available in the right places in the right amount and the right quality. This has often been included implicitly in forecasts. Too often these calculations have not been carried out, sales forecasts can only be too optimistic or rather unrealistic.

The next section offers guidance on drawing conclusions on the industry fit.

11.2   Industry and market fit

11.2.1 Industry fit

Ideally, you have essential findings from the industry analysis, applying PESTLE and Five Forces that allow you to carry out a SWOT. S stands for strengths, W for weaknesses, O for opportunities and T for threats. Having done all of that you should be able to answer the following questions:

▸ Is the industry sector you plan to enter growing? For how much longer?
▸ At what point in the life cycle of industries is it?
▸ Is the industry entry and exit costly for you?
▸ How quickly can other new entrants enter the industry?
▸ Can you create a Turquoise Lake, and how long will that blue last before it turns purple or red?

Indicators for answering those questions were already discussed in Chapter Four on industry analysis.

 Activity 11.1 Final analysis of industry findings

Is this a new industry sector? One example is the tablet computer subsector. Indicators include a growing number of sellers and product variations. Refer back to the results of your industry analysis gathered with Table 4.6 in section 4.8.

Summarize the findings here.

Conclusion: What fit does the industry offer? _____ %

11.2.2 Market fit

In order to convince a funder or investor that money can be made you need to be able to answer the following questions:

▸ Is there potential in the market now and for the next three to five years? The answer to this question has to give a reasonable estimate of the number of potential buyers, the number of units, turnover and profit in £ or $ or €, the size of the overall current market and if all buyers in this segment all have a solution.
▸ What market share of this current overall market is it reasonable for you to win? With what kind of products/services?
▸ What drives demand and how likely are these drivers going to change over the next five years? In other words, what makes people buy the products/services?
▸ What is the core need or pain they have, and how likely is that going to change over time? The answer to this question helps to answer the next one:
▸ How competitive is your value proposition and USP: how likely can this USP be imitated by the competition? How likely is the USP of interest to customers the following year after market entry?

Target customers or target segment(s) are discussed at the end of Chapter Four: add them in the first box in row 1 Table 11.1. We discuss in this context that for start-ups and focused marketing on a shoestring, one segment needs to be targeted first for market entry, which is most likely to buy your product and inspire other segments to do so at a later stage.

 The *product(s)/service(s)* that should be sold first to this first segment need identifying. The market research should have identified which one that is and at what price, if there is more than one. Product(s)/services should be selected based on which one offers the largest profit margin versus bringing in large number of buyers that will also buy other products as soon as they are offered.

Table 11.1 Adjusting results from surveys measuring buyer intentions

Survey purchase intent	Response in %	Rule of thumb reduction for forecasting	% estimated to be actually likely to buy
Would definitely buy	35	0.75	26.25
Would probably buy	45	0.35	15.75
Unsure about buying	20	0	
Probably or definitely not buying	5	0	
TOTALS	100		42.0

If you have not read the finance chapters (Chapters Nine and Ten), do that now. Use the forecasts based on the product/service you select to help you draw a conclusion on the industry and market fit. Replace the figures in table 11.1 with your survey results and carry out the calculations in the section on financial tools.

Conclusion: What fit does the market offer? _____%

To make an overall conclusion for industry and market fit you could use a proportion of: 60% of the market fit and 40% of the industry fit.

An example for a wine bar could be: industry fit was concluded to be at 80%, market fit for the type of wines you intend to offer was concluded to be at 60%. For an overall fit:

60% of market fit 60% = 36%
40% of industry fit 80% = 32%
32% + 36% = 68%.
Overall conclusion for market and industry fit: 68% – that is a *limited fit*.

The conclusion for the example is that there is not yet a true business opportunity. The other fit conclusions can be carried out now, yet this one needs further work in order to reach a higher value.

What is your overall conclusion for your potential business venture?

Overall conclusion for industry and market fit:

_____%

11.3 Legal and operational fit

11.3.1 Legal fit

For the legal fit you need to bring together all legal considerations and the ability and costs to comply with them. That has to address the:

▶ Licenses you have to obtain and renew;
▶ Need and/or cost for intellectual property protection;
▶ Cost for company registration;
▶ Ability to meet the requirements of the law;
▶ For importing a product and meeting EU and UK product reliability and health and safety standards, you need to put some time aside for product testing.

The costs will have been added to the cash flow forecast, including the potential training costs and time needed to be able to meet regulatory requirements.

As far as licensing is concerned, can you comply with all regulation and laws easily? Does it cost a lot of money and time to acquire licenses, or can you bring in staff that already have those licenses as far as personal licenses are concerned (for selling alcohol in the UK, for example). The time period needed to meet all required compliance and address IP protection needs to be estimated and added to the time needed before you can trade officially (that is, after business registration).

One example to illustrate fit of a legal form: you have decided to run a social enterprise, with no profits being taken away by shareholders, in a form such as the community interest company in the UK, limited by guarantee. This means you are eligible for funding that is solely for non-profits and can use particular support programmes for the so-called community and voluntary sector (a term used in the UK); in other countries, the term community sector is used or community enterprises. This is a positive fit, as the legal set-up enables you to access different types of funding and support. However, it limits the access to investment funding, should that be something you are interested in within a few years or earlier in order to scale the business. To scale the business means to be able to multiply investments made by you or third parties through growing the business and profits. While the area of social impact investing is growing, it is still relatively small when compared to traditional investment funding.

 Legal fit has to be precise, as either you meet the requirements of the law or regulations or you do not.

Conclusion: What legal fit have you identified? _____ %
For this area, we said a perfect fit has to be found; that means over 90% need to be reached.

11.3.2 Operational fit

The operational fit needs to examine the choice of mode of operation in terms of online or brick-and-mortar with associated temporary forms of face-to-face selling, such as market stalls, craft and other fairs, pop-up selling opportunities, or a combination of some of those options.

You also need to analyse the technological fit – is it only a matter of a few years or even less until a new technological development or product will change your operations? For the technological fit, the industry research and PESTLE should have identified trends in technology. Establish if and in what way they would affect your production and customers. Have you or your partner(s) the skills and training or qualifications needed to run specific business activities, and if not, can you buy in staff who have? Have you got the money to do so? Activity 11.2 will help with that.

 Activity 11.2   Summarize the technological trends that affect your business idea

Differentiate between those affecting (a) your whole operations, (b) your product distribution, (c) production and (d) consumers' lives. Then establish what impact possible changes in technology in each area might have on the likelihood of your product to be bought at the price you decided to sell it at to the target customers.

For the operational fit, the founder(s)' capabilities (skills and resources available) need to be matched to the best way the buyers need to experience or buy the product in order to make a purchase decision.

An example: for some buyers of luxury consumer goods such as high-end shoes or clothes, the experience of trying them on, having them explained in a personalized manner and having questions answered while sitting on a nice sofa in a living-room atmosphere and having a glass of water or a cup of tea is part of the buying experience. While the price they have to pay might be slightly higher than buying the same designer dress online, they are willing to pay that higher price. If the cost for providing the personalized experience in a small room is more than covered by the increased price, and a sufficient number of units can be sold, and renting the premises is possible, a decision needs to be made.

 Management and people fit is important as well: if there is a founding team, do the team members share the same goals for the start-up? Have they got the skills needed, or is there a need to buy some in, or pay for some training for (one of) the founder(s)?

Conclusion: What fit do operations offer? _____%

11.4 Financial fit

The financial fit needs to be nearly perfect; that means a fit of 90% or more. The main, hopefully convincing, reason is that if you cannot get the money needed to make the *sustainable start-up* work, then there is no point in pursuing it. It also means it has to be a close financial and personal fit.

The financial analysis should have identified what amount of money is needed initially through the start-up budget and for the first months and years until the break-even point is reached. It should have also identified what price you have to charge for the product/service in order to sell it to the identified target segment and make a reasonable profit. What a reasonable profit is will be a result of the personal goals set for starting the business.

The operations cost will have been identified clearly in the finance section. This means that decisions were made to either produce the product or import it or have it produced in the UK, the decision on the need for an office space will have been made, as well as the decision on hiring or leasing equipment instead of buying it, etc.

If one target segment is likely to pay only £X for the service, yet you need £X + £5 in order to break even after say 18 months, as you personally do not/cannot live on your savings for such a long period of time, and you can only support a low salary from the business for 12 months, then there is no fit, is there?

Then you need to consider changing one of those elements that do not provide a fit, such as the target segment. Can you re-segment the market and charge a higher price to a different segment? That would address the insufficient fit. Or you might have to reconsider the production cost – can something be done at lower cost without compromising on quality or features essential for changing the consumer experience so that they buy it?

Can you get in external funding to bridge the time? Bank loan? Investors? Other loans? Are they available? How big is the chance of you getting it? What is the success rate of applications, as far as they are being published? Are you willing to give up some ownership in the start-up?

Before you draw a conclusion here, carry out the personal fit and answer the questions raised there.

Once you have carried out the personal fit analysis, draw up a list of financial sources and in what sequence you are willing and capable of accessing them. I have read too many business plans that assume they will get this grant and that loan of a particular amount, all within the first months before and after start-up.

Now you should be able to draw a conclusion about the financial fit as far as your exploration of the business idea goes so far:

 Activity 11.3   Likelihood of obtaining external finance

List the finance sources that you identified in Chapter Nine you aim to get, in the sequence you are hoping to get them, using Table 11.2 below. Then identify on a scale of one to five how likely it is to obtain that finance, based on success rates for example, where one means very unlikely and five means very likely.

Then identify the timelines from application submission to decision and receiving the money in your account (often found in the guidelines). In the last column, list conditions the funders might impose, and if you have to have other finance in place to get this type of finance.

Then consider the findings from the cash flow analysis and profit and loss forecast carried out in Chapter Ten. Having assessed the likelihood of obtaining external funding, consider the findings from the cash flow analysis and profit and loss forecast carried out in Chapter Ten.

Table 11.2   Assessing access to financial resources

Finance source	Likelihood of getting it	Timeline	Conditions to meet and dependencies on other funds

Conclusion: What financial fit is there (over 90 %)? _____%

11.5   Matching opportunity to personal life and career goals

Having worked with so many individual and team start-ups, I can tell you that the personal fit is often not considered at this stage. Later on down the line after start of trading, differences in views on how to run the business and who does what roles become obvious and have destroyed business partnerships and friendships. And for individuals starting a business, what commitment and skills that the venture needs do not meet what the individual is willing and/or capable of offering at a certain point in time? For start-ups, a theoretical business opportunity needs to be turned into a personal viable business opportunity – that is you must be interested, willing and capable to turn your attention, money and skills to executing a business opportunity. Only then there exists a person-ability opportunity. While this may sound strange, this is important to recognize for start-ups. It is your life and work we are talking about here, and most of your lifetime you spend working each year, so this decision needs to reflect what your life is about.

In Section 3.4.1 we talk about matching an opportunity to your own life stage, ambitions, values and interests. Some opportunities are great, yet not for you where you are in life at the time. Check out what two of our case studies say below. This is what our case study **Lewis Barnes** said about his first venture, importing a travel device.

Case study

There was a road safety device, a travel device, [that] an American company had, and I was in talks of getting it over here to be able to distribute it exclusively. [It was a] fantastic idea, fantastic product, but the issue was, it was not me. I was biting off more than I could chew. It was an opportunity but then I wasn't ready at the time to execute it; so the timing wasn't right and where I was with my knowledge and skill-set was nowhere near adequate to fulfil the potential of the opportunity.

Nevertheless, Lewis values this experience highly; he calls it the most beneficial he has had in his life apart from playing tennis at a high level.

Case study

If at this point in time you cannot commit full-time to any business activity, for example, as you are studying or in a carer or parent role, and the opportunity requires you or a team of people to do that, is this opportunity at this point in time for that reason suitable? The answer here might be that this is possibly not the case. Or, as our case study **Richard Rodman** from Crowdentials decided, you might have to consider interrupting your studies for a while, if you think this business idea and the framework of funding and the team you have are so great that they pull you much stronger to change what you were doing, studying for a degree, than finishing the degree is pulling you.

As the brief description points out, the investors Richard Rodman found expected the team of young entrepreneurs to commit all their time to the start-up. And after some consideration, this is what he and his friend and co-founder decided to do. They regarded the opportunity to be able to develop the business idea at this point in time as more important than finishing their studies.

For crafts businesses the time period needed to be able to rely on an income from selling the home-produced craft goods can be up to three years. Do you have the possibility to earn an income through employment part-time, and can you live on the lower income that part-time employment with the little income crafts selling will provide you with? If you have a partner or a child and are the sole earner, the answer will be different than if you have a partner whose income is sufficient for the household.

This means you need to carry out a realistic assessment of your own commitments, time and money available at this point in time and check on your willingness to give up ownership of parts of the company. The *Dragons' Den* television series in the UK with business angels has shown that some owners are not willing to part with 40% of the ownership in the company. Some personal decisions and preferences of "control" come into that.

Activity 11.4   Questions for assessing personal fit

Here are some questions that might help you get closer to what kind of personal fit you need:

What amount of time can you actually realistically spend on the business over the next year, or three years, per week?

How much personal money are you *able* to invest into the business?

How much personal money are you willing to invest into the business?

How much personal attachment have you got to the product/service you offer? Is it just a means to make money? Is there a personal commitment to make a difference?

How passionate are you about the business idea, and to make it work?

What would it mean to lose your personal money/X amount of personal money should the venture not generate sufficient profit?

What would it mean to you personally if you were not successful with the venture? What effect would that have on your life?

For what period of time are you willing to spend very little money and time on leisure and holidays and hobbies? If you do not get sufficient investment and are required to use all or more of your personal assets than you were originally willing to invest, would you want to do that?

Are you willing to accept any co-ownership with an investor?

How much equity are you willing to give up?

Are you willing to share the ownership with peers as co-owners?

Answer these questions honestly, and the answers will give you a realistic insight into your willingness and ability to realize a potential business opportunity behind the idea you were exploring. Go back to your start-up diary and look up all the entries that you made when working through Chapter Three as well.

After having carried out Activity 11.3 you should be able to draw a conclusion on the personal fit:

Conclusion: What personal fit can be achieved? _____%

The next section summarizes the conclusions to all of the four fit areas to come to an overall conclusion for pursuing a for-profit venture. Section 11.7 below outlines considerations that go beyond just personal fit and offers considerations to pursue an opportunity as a social enterprise in the UK model.

11.6   Summary of all findings on fit

Figure 11.3 offers a way to visualize the fit of each area analysed so far. For any co-creation results this should be displayed on a wall for all to see and/or shared online with all stakeholders who worked with you on the feasibility and business-modelling journey.

    The overall conclusion should be easy to draw, as all areas can be regarded as equal and the percentage values simply added. The financial fit needs to be nearly perfect

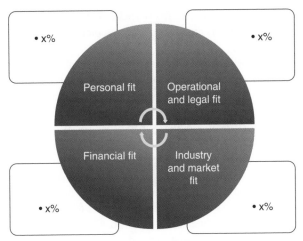

Figure 11.3 Is there an overall fit?
Source: © Hill, 2013.

and the same applies to the legal fit; overall, all areas should achieve a value of over at least 330%. Under this percentage the opportunity should not be pursued straight away but further research and/or adjustments sought.

Overall conclusion: What fit is the business idea? _____%

11.7 Is this an opportunity for a social enterprise?

After elaborative analysis, market testing and business modelling you might have to come to the conclusion that the profit margins are small and might very well remain small. Based on the findings of your analysis, you will always be able to pay yourself a decent salary and put some money into reserves for business emergency. But ... there is no chance to get rich. The yacht, the Lamborghini, the castle or mansion you were dreaming of cannot be financed with the profits of that venture. For many young and not-so-young individuals the journey ends here and they shelve the business idea as not viable for them.

However, it could be a *social enterprise*. Opportunity evaluations, so far, applied in the same way to social enterprise and for-profit. As a reminder, social enterprises do need to make a profit to operate sustainably. However, that profit does not have to be large. I can see the questions coming: but how large?

 It is now up to your personal values, current goals in life and your point in your life course if you pursue this venture at all or not.

Option one is that you say to yourself that you remain optimistic and that further fine-tuning of the opportunity over time might increase the profit margins and you still want to go ahead with the business opportunity. If your analysis has shown it is unlikely it will, then this is still only hope. That venture could be run as self-employed or with a small team as a company limited by shares, for profit.

Option two is that you consider you might want to create a venture not just for you but for making a difference to other people as well. But you might not need the biggest of all profits for a social enterprise. Not many social enterprises as yet have this starting point. And the media, newspapers etc. always draw the picture of the mission-driven social enterprise start-up.

For some social enterprises the profit margins can be smaller, as some balance can be achieved in cost reduction through using volunteers and attracting sponsorship.

The starting point can well be that you are passionate about a product or a service, yet cannot make a lot of money with it in terms of getting rich, profit margins are small and large-volume sales are not possible either. What other social or environmental mission could you add to the venture?

If you are in your twenties, you might care about youth unemployment and those from disadvantaged backgrounds getting into work. Or you care about those with a disability and can offer employment to them? Both could be opportunities for a social firm, an enterprise that offers employment opportunities for those who otherwise could not get them. For example, providing employment for those over 50 who have difficulties in finding a job simply based on calendar age, the year they were born, yet are still very capable in their job and have the balanced experience in how certain business processes work, could add value to society and provide the backbone of a social firm; you could still generate a reasonable income for yourself at the same time. Yet, the enterprise might not make you rich.

Below you will find a reminder of the UK industry sectors social enterprises are operating in (Social Enterprise UK, 2014):

▶ Education;
▶ Consultancy;
▶ Employment skills;
▶ Housing;
▶ Retail;
▶ Culture and leisure;
▶ Health services.

 Activity 11.5 Causes you care about

List the causes you care about, and then check with the list below if there are any you might have forgotten about.

(Human rights, animal welfare, re-forestation, women's equality or empowerment, children's care, ex-offenders, older people, reducing all forms of abuse, war zones, natural disaster zones)

Can you imagine to provide employment for young people or those disadvantaged in the labour market, while still producing the services or product you are passionate about?

After you have done all the summarizing of the findings and the analyses above it is time to summarize the value proposition, the change and benefits statements, business type and distribution channels for your business opportunity.

11.8   Is this an opportunity you are willing to pursue? Yes

11.8.1   Example statement: wine bar and wine retail

I am offering you the chance to relax in style in a unique atmosphere for classy social and business meetings for city professionals while enjoying high quality wines from small European vineyards with a selection of high quality international tapas and bites of food from all over the world. Wines can be bought online from us 24/7 and ordered in the fortnightly wine bar events for personal pick-up during wine bar opening hours. Try our special offer of a selection of wines with nibbles for your personal drinks party at home or invite us to run a wine tasting where you are.

The above statement is an example of a benefits oriented brief business presentation. When you are asked from now on what you are doing, you can say:

_____

_____

_____

_____

Now it is time to go to Chapter Twelve and start putting the business plan together, which you need at least in the form of an action plan.

11.9   Concluding remarks and application of new insights

Chapter Eleven is one of the most important chapters in the pre-start-up process, as it summarizes the research and reflections on the business idea and potential opportunity. This includes personal-ability of the potential business opportunity – how it may fit your personal aspirations and life stage.

For that reason, various sections guide you through the process of drawing overall conclusions for the analysis, market testing and reflections carried out so far. The four areas identified are:

▶ Industry and market fit;
▶ Operational fit (operations, with technology and legal fit);
▶ Financial fit;
▶ Personal fit.

We discussed an assessment for each area that uses percentages for indicating levels of fit from "perfect" with 90% or more, to "no fit" with under 50%. The overall fit should be over 330%.

For a social enterprise opportunity, the levels of fitness might have different results, in particular in the area of financial fitness. For some social enterprises the profit margins could be smaller, as some balance can be achieved in costs through using volunteers and attracting sponsorship and grants.

Once this conclusion is positive, indicating there is sufficient fit for this business idea to be turned into a profitable business opportunity, then the value proposition and change benefits statement can be finalized further.

The next chapters assume that you have identified a business opportunity that is sufficiently profitable and/or that you intend to pursue as a social enterprise or for-profit business. Chapter Twelve discusses the basics of business planning and business policies. Chapter Thirteen discusses in detail marketing strategy and implementation, whereas Chapter Fourteen explores sales planning and practice and PR. Chapter Fifteen summarizes the practical essentials for getting up and running and making the decision on when is the most appropriate time to register a business. Finally, Chapter Sixteen discusses challenges the *sustainable start-up* might encounter when up and running, including risk mitigation, and offers solutions following a co-creation approach, including building networks further and various forms of collaboration to gain contracts.

Revision questions and application of new insights

1 What processes are required to identify an opportunity?
2 What aspects of legal and regulatory issues have to be considered in order to assess the legal fit?
3 What aspects of fit or feasibility are necessary to consider to identify if an idea is an opportunity?
4 What percentage do you need to achieve overall to gain a reasonable fit?
5 When is a business idea possibly an opportunity for a social enterprise?
6 What would you advise a friend to do who has recorded the following fits? Why? Explain your reasons briefly. A new Take-Away for African-style food:
   a) Legal 95%;
   b) Industry and market fit 68%;
   c) Financial fit 80%;
   d) Personal fit 65%.

There are no questions in this chapter that invite you to apply the learning to your venture, as most of this chapter asked you to draw conclusions on your research, market testing and activities, reflection and modelling carried out so far.

12

BUSINESS PLANNING AND START-UP – LAUNCH

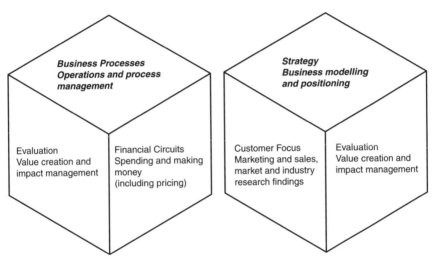

Figure 12.1 The Cube Strategy and the Cube Business Processes
Source: © Hill, 2012.

Summary

Chapter Twelve introduces you to business planning as a process and the formal written business plan report. This chapter realizes the aspect of Strategy and business positioning (Figure 12.1). Style, format, length and content of a business plan vary depending on the audience you write it for. We discuss the expectations banks and traditional investors and programme managers might have and run through the traditional outline and headings of a business plan. Business plans for social enterprises have some differences, in particular outlining the social mission and objectives and the potential beneficiaries they serve. Finally, we explore selected business policies as a tool to realize the principle and practice of resourceful impact for the *sustainable start-up*.

CONTENTS

12.1   Why bother with a business plan, and who for?

12.1.1 Why and how you could write a business plan

Do you have a plan? Do you have to have a plan? "I know so many people who have been successful without a business plan" and, "I do not need a plan, I have it all in my head" or, "I cannot predict the future, I need to be flexible, a plan will hinder that" are all statements I have heard from students and other people setting up a business.

There are many reasons why you should bother – but before we discuss those let us clarify what a business plan is.

A business plan is a structured document that outlines the aim and objectives for a business, defines the value proposition, lists the core products and services and outlines how it goes about achieving them, outlining a business modelling process with key elements, based on a thorough analysis of the environment it operates in. Simple?

In these discussions I am reminded of Hannibal, the lead character from the 1980s TV series *The A-Team*, and hear him in my head saying, "I love it when a plan comes together". Plans can have many shapes and come in different forms. Staying for a moment with the character Hannibal Smith, his plans developed while they went along solving a client's problem and leveraging as well as integrating all sorts of resources with a bootstrap approach. He facilitated the development of the solution using his team members in their areas of strength and linking them together in mini-teams of two ensuring tensions did not affect the outcomes they needed to achieve.

That is a type of practical plan, an action-oriented plan that is developed with the team, we can call them internal stakeholders, and with the input of the client(s) and their contacts. While this plan is not written down, it works for them, and every stakeholder plays their role in the execution; we can call this an *emerging plan*, developed while working practically towards a solution.

Regard the business plan as an action plan for yourself, or the founders and supporters (or stakeholders), that needs regular adjustment, when new insights have been developed and regarded as helpful for solving the problem(s) your customer has. Ideally, it has a condensed implementation plan for each important business area you can enlarge and hang up on the wall for yourself and everybody else to see and look at as a reminder of what to do each week. This plan can be creative in style, with lots of mind maps, the results of brainstorming sessions, hand-drawn graphs, pictures or flip charts around the open Cube. The next section points out practical ways to bring all the discussions you hopefully had already around the business model together creatively using the Cube image – opened up.

For now, let us discuss other roles of and reasons for writing a business plan. Even a traditional business plan document such as the one outlined in Box 12.1 can be a flexible planning tool. For each section, create some objectives with milestones, not just for the overall business performance.

> ## Box 12.1   Traditional business plan headings
>
> ### Executive summary
>
> ### Introduction
>
> (The founder or the founding team; reason(s) for starting the business; vision, mission and objectives; an introduction to the industry subsector and/or location of business; change statement and value proposition (product benefits and features); market positioning.)
>
> ### Industry review with competitor evaluation
>
> ### Market analysis, with findings on market research
>
> ### Marketing and sales strategy
>
> ### Operational plan
>
> (Including purchasing goods/services, organizational structure, management team, rational for choice of premises and location where appropriate.)
>
> ### Legal issues
>
> ### Financial plan
>
> (Including costs and pricing strategy, start-up budget and cash flow.)
>
> ### Risks and rewards
>
> (Keys to success, main risks.)
>
> ### Exit strategy or Plan B
>
> (Some organizations ask for a back-up plan in case the business does not take off.)
>
> ### Appendix
>
> (CV of founder(s), more detail on market research findings, company documents (memorandum of association and articles; letters of intent from potential buyers.)

 One example: craft business start-up Jenny creates bags and jewellery from felt. She intends to sell goods to the value of £200 per week by the end of month six. In order to be able to achieve that goal, she needs to set herself a number of objectives in the various business areas including:

a) Spending time on marketing each week (2 to 2.5 days per week);
b) Creating new pieces of jewellery and bags (1 day per week);
c) Purchasing new stock, finding better suppliers, ensuring quality control;
d) Sending out goods to clients;
e) Managing finances – chasing and processing payments from clients, planning expenses for the following months, checking on cash flow, etc. – 0.5 day per fortnight.

 If you write the plan in a way that it creates a framework for setting monthly/fortnightly/weekly goals, then it becomes a living and working document. A business plan is not static; it needs to be revised every three months, at least. You need to check if you are operating and performing to plan and if not what you can do to address that – adapting either your behaviour and actions, or your objectives, or both.

While you cannot predict the future, you can relate to trends for industry and market you or others identified in the past: you can plan for the uncertain future based on these trends and insights.

In focusing your thoughts and resources on a particular set of actions, identified as appropriate at the time, you focus your energies and can save time and effort, and ultimately money. When you are clear on what resources are needed for achieving a certain business outcome, you can adapt the outcome you are aiming for if conditions change and know what else to put in place to achieve a changed outcome.

Keeping an eye on the finances that should come in to keep your cash flow either positive or when negative during the first months at the lowest possible level, you need to keep track of what money was supposed to come in and has or has not come in. The *financial plan* shows you that information, if done with sufficient detail. Thus, if money is not coming in as planned, a set of actions needs to be carried out: chase the payment, ask for a larger overdraft, get a loan, etc. Money coming in and out of the business should be monitored closely; daily is essential in some businesses in retail services, for example.

You also have to ensure that you actually think about and address everything necessary to get the business up and running and calculate all your costs into your prices. On a couple of occasions I found with start-up clients that they were wondering why they were not making enough money to get a salary from the business. In one particular case for a flower shop by a design graduate I remember that he was certain the pricing he had developed was spot-on and did not want to discuss it. After discussing a number of other business areas, I returned to the pricing and quickly took a look at a rose priced at £2.50. When discussing the pricing it was clear that he had not put in a figure for his salary in the overheads, but was just covering fixed and semi-variable costs (for details on pricing see Chapter Ten).

For some stakeholders, such as banks, investors or funders, it is helpful to have a business plan with a different look and style. This type of business plan is discussed in the next section; additional points for business plans for social enterprises are discussed in Section 12.4.

While the business plan as a living document outlined here is a useful tool for start-up, it helps to understand what a traditional business plan looks like and why it is still useful to have for some audiences. In Section 12.3.1 we discuss what funders are looking for in a more traditional business plan of a start-up.

12.1.2 Who is the business plan for?

There are a number of audiences for whom you might have to have a formally written business plan document. These include:

▶ Banks;
▶ Grant-giving organizations;
▶ Investors;
▶ Shareholders;
▶ Other loan providers such as the Prince's Trust, in the UK, a local council or municipal authority.

Each of them might have a particular expectation regarding the format, style and even headings you have to include. Most of the above organizations will have guidance on the type of business plan they expect, sometimes even in terms of length of the plan in number of pages; increasingly, organizations ask for a short summary of two pages and a longer plan. If you are applying for funding, check out the website and any guidance the organization in question offers.

The potential audiences can be divided into two big groups: those with traditional expectations of how a plan should look (banks, local authorities, investors), and those who are not particular about the headings and style and format, as long as all the important issues are addressed.

 Case study

All case studies in this book did have a written business plan: **Alison Barton**, the photographer, needed a short one for the programme she was on. **Lewis Barnes** had a form of a business plan, even though he did not seek funding. **Vivek George** had a written business plan for his first venture, the wine bar, with particular focus on the investment needed. **Alexandru Damian** had a business plan, as an outcome of his Master's dissertation findings, and he adjusted it while he went along realizing the start-up. **Ben Smith** had a business plan, also because the funding he applied for needed a business plan. Frinter Ltd founders **Shivam Tandon and Muhammad Ali** had a business plan. **Kathryn Kimbley** had a business plan, also because she was seeking funding. **Richard Rodman** and **Lillie Ranney** had business plans for their ventures.

The next section outlines the understanding of business planning for the *sustainable start-up*, using the business planning process as an activity for realizing "strategy".

12.2   Ingredients for the *sustainable start-up* planning process

12.2.1 Using the Cube to organize findings

Many of us are visually guided, and when it comes to important documents such as business reports or plans, they can tend to get too text focused. The *sustainable start-up* business planning process is providing a guide through the six areas we highlighted using the Cube model.

The Cube image was introduced in Chapter One and discussed further in Chapter Seven on business modelling; it works as well for business planning.

1) Business Processes: Operations and process management;
2) Financial Circuits: Spending and making money (including pricing);
3) Frameworks: Internal frameworks (governance) and legal issues;
4) Customer Focus and Environment: Marketing, sales, market and industry research;
5) Strategy: Business modelling and positioning;
6) Evaluation: Value creation and impact management.

Using the opened (or unfolded) Cube as an outline for the internal business plan (see Figure 12.2), we can bring together all the findings from the previous sections. You should have most of the information and insights available through the discussions, research and insight developed in the exercises in previous chapters when doing your research, market testing and business modelling.

For the *sustainable start-up* it is essential to include the most viable business processes as identified during operational exploration as the basis for the operational planning and use as many flexible ways of resource leverage and distribution as possible.

 For the business plan as a living document, flip charts with lots of flow charts, drawings and lists are a useful tool to remind all stakeholders involved in the planning process what happened. Pictures of each of the six areas can easily be shared online with all stakeholders; and they can at any time in any place make contributions to develop any area.

The Cube model reminds us that all business areas are connected, like the six areas of a Cube. One is always directly linked to four others and through them indirectly to the sixth one. And it does not matter which face you are focusing on at any point in time. Should you make changes to one of the six areas, ensure you make the associated changes to the other five areas.

Using flip charts, answer the following questions for each area, focusing on: WHY something should be done; HOW it should be done, with what staff, tools, materials; WHEN it should be done, including a timeline and duration of each activity with starting and end point (using a Gantt chart for example); WHERE it should be done – meeting places, online meetings; WHO should be involved, internal staff and stakeholders, external ones; what RISKS are involved in carrying out an activity and not carrying it out; and the mid- and long-term IMPACT each activity will have.

As this list shows, there is a clear overlap with the building blocks of the business model canvas by Osterwalder we discussed in Chapter Seven; overlap indicates some commonalities but also differences between the two models. The Cube face "Financial Circuits" overlaps with the business model canvas's "cost structure" and "revenue streams", the difference is that we are acknowledging the dynamic changing nature of cost and provide help how to put the financial considerations into practice. Instead of the customer-related building blocks ("relationships", "channels" and "target customers"), the Cube offers "Customer Focus – with environment" – with a wider coverage of secondary market analysis, market positioning and the important area of industry analysis. Instead of the canvas area of infrastructure (with "key resources", "key activities" and "key partners"), the Cube face of "Business Processes" includes operations and covers a wider scope of activities as well as a focus on process management. Two Cube areas, "Frameworks" and "Evaluation", are not addressed by the business model canvas; and strategies for realizing the business model canvas elements are not discussed either.

The canvas is an excellent tool for a snap shot of what is happening within a business at a given point in time, and developing the building blocks further. The Cube, however, is addressing further areas for the dynamic strategic approach to start-up management that go further. In particular, the additional area of "strategy" is going beyond business modelling and addressing the essential market positioning. What you should have identified by now for your *sustainable start-up* (after working through Chapter Eleven) is the external strategic fit of your idea with customers, social and economic trends, industry and technology; similarly, the internal fit we discussed and how to develop it so that personal goals, business needs and customers' needs can be brought together.

 Action plans can be pinned physically or linked visually to each of the six faces and pinned to a wall for each staff member, volunteer and stakeholder to take down and away. Electronically, action plans can be shared as text documents easily accessible for a limited circle of stakeholders.

While this can be turned in a written narrative in report style, the posters themselves ideally tell the story that was developed. For that purpose I recommend to use the flat

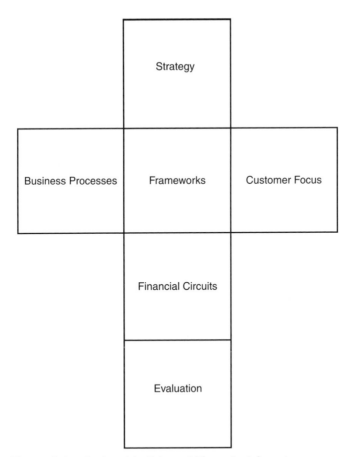

Figure 12.2 The practical application of the Cube model for sorting information
Source: © Hill, 2012.

Cube as a starting point for bringing information together (see Figure 12.2, also used as Figure 7.2 in Chapter Seven on business modelling).

12.2.2 Professional story-telling and report style with infographics

Story-telling is great skill to have for everybody in business, and in particular for a start-up/ founder of a small business. What is story-telling? Are you not too old for the fairy tales you might have enjoyed as a kid or stories like Harry Potter? The easiest way to convince a funder is to tell a professional convincing story of how you are going to make money through addressing unmet customer demands. This story is well evidenced with numbers and some findings from research on industry and market from secondary sources and your own research. The main character(s) is the founder/the founding team. Their experience and education and skills need to be told in a convincing way through previous achievements.

DO's:

- Case studies with clients from test trading or product trials: what did they find, say or do?;
- Quotes from customers/clients and their praise as well as criticism – and for the latter how you addressed the criticism and fine-tuned your value proposition;
- Clear objectives – smart ones;
- Evidence of market demand and intention to buy the product/service once available – ideally with a contract or letter of intent signed, dated and on letter headed paper; list of intended client base;
- Well designed and with clear, easy to follow layout (header, footer, table of contents, lists of tables/graphs, references);
- Well-explained financial projections, in particular for cash flow;
- Well-worded business model with focus on value capturing in terms of money going in and out and profits;
- Clear route to market through a detailed marketing plan targeting new or existing customers;
- (Clear route to beneficiaries for social enterprises);
- Additional forecasts with worst-case scenario well explained;
- Appreciation of competition even in larger corporates in terms of their strengths and weaknesses;
- A clear outline of how much of your own money has been invested or is going to be invested (if you do not risk part of your own money, how committed are you is the question behind that)

DON'Ts:

- Un-credible financial projections;
- Lack of a viable opportunity to make a profit;
- No clear route to market;
- Overestimation of revenues;
- Lack of appreciation of the importance of good cash flow management;
- No clear objectives;
- No evidence of real demand;
- Inconsistencies throughout the report;
- Negative, disrespectful and unjustified criticism of the competition;
- Rushed report full of spelling mistakes, format omissions, no headings, footers, etc.

The publisher's companion website offers one example of the business plan for an online magazine for young people written for a traditional funder (www.palgrave.com/companion/hill-start-up).

The next sections explore traditional business plan content and expectations of bankers and investors followed by outlining the differences in plans for social enterprises.

12.3 Content for traditional business plans

12.3.1 What funders and banks are looking for in a business plan

There is plenty of research that explains what it is that funders of for-profit businesses look for, investors and banks alike. For start-ups they look for a management team/founder that has the appropriate skills and, ideally, sector knowledge or work experience. Ideally, that is combined with financial management skills in particular and an ability to demonstrate the financial side of the business convincingly and a demonstration of a proven evidenced demand for the product or service. Pitching skills can be practised, and the *Dragons' Den* television series often enough has badly prepared pitches by start-ups that cannot present either of the above. Watching a number of *Dragons' Den* pitches for the questions the Dragons ask is a good idea to establish what a pitch should contain and what questions to expect. The DO's listed above should all be considered for a good pitch.

More importantly, investors are interested in what you have learned about the market and the product/services, and yourself. The investors on the television series *Dragons' Den* have a number of emotional reasons why they sometimes go with a candidate: they like the product or they like the candidate (or both). Researching the organization's past funding decisions and successful collaborations will reveal some insight valuable for the application and the business plan and pitch.

If an investor provides some guidelines on what to put into an application, follow these to the letter. If it is not on the website, talk to their office and try to find out what they are looking for.

All the high street banks offer at least a template, often a whole package of information and support including a disc or downloadable forms to use for the business plan. Again, if you want to gain a loan from a bank, follow their guidelines.

The list of DO's and DON'Ts gives you the gist of what most funders are looking for. *Tailor the plan to the funder's requirements* is the most important rule of thumb. Research them on their website; talking to successful start-ups that they funded will get you a long way.

12.3.2 Overview of a traditional business plan structure

Box 12.1 shows you some standard headings for traditional business plan. In Section 12.3.3 the section headings and what has to be discussed in them are explained in more detail. Overall, as this approach to a business plan is featured in many websites and other books, the content overview is kept short here.

There are business plans for sale online, and software out there that promises to do lots of the work for you. However, many of these plans only slightly scratch the surface and do not really explore in depth the challenge of what it means to get the business behind the plan up and running and making it work. Many of the business plans for sale or software from large corporates that promises you a lot of help do not support you in tailoring the given plans to your specific needs.

12.3.3 Business plan content

In a nutshell, the business plan summarizes precisely the decisions made in Chapter Eleven to go ahead with a business opportunity. The plan summarizes and illustrates the decisions and plans of actions with findings from industry and market analysis and financial projections.

The **executive summary** sums up the essence of the findings for each section very briefly and focuses on the USP and the value proposition with clearly outlined target customer(s). Vision and mission statement provide the framework for the goals. The aim is to outline how value is created and captured and maintained over a three-year period. You need to demonstrate briefly how and when you will break even and how profit can be generated. For social enterprises it is essential to add how and why beneficiaries have been selected and how profits will be used; the governance structure and board constitution is summarized as well.

Box 12.1 gives sufficient detail for the content of the **introduction**. Value proposition and USP and even the business model might be explained.

Industry review with competitor analysis is the result of the industry evaluation that Chapter Four offers you support with. It should list some developments in the industry for the last five to ten years and for the next five years, identify success factors and barriers and highlight technology issues where appropriate. For competitors the main players in the industry could be shown with a SWOT analysis.

The **market analysis** chapter summarizes the findings from secondary and primary market research with the appropriate conclusions on selection of target customers and development of market position, this includes the pricing strategy, USP and value proposition(s). The customer target group(s) need to be named, the first customer explained and the persona of this first customer outlined. This section needs to offer findings on the kind of marketplace you operate in, business-to-consumer or business-to-business for example, findings on buying behaviour of the first customer, making a case that they will buy at the price you suggest, based on findings of their buying behaviour in the past where appropriate. If you sell more than one product, there needs to be a projection for each type of product you are selling, and what might be loss leaders or cash cows. You need to provide a rationale for entering the market with only one or several products based on the findings, and which one first. The market demand for the product/service and the route to market need to be clearly outlined and evidenced. The detail of the implementation of marketing and sales is discussed in the next two chapters.

The **marketing and sales** chapters outline the marketing strategy, tactics and marketing implementation plan with a detailed explanation of choices made. The chapters also discuss the sales approach and strategy and tactics, with clear financial projections of sales, either in quarters or for full years, usually for the three years following start-up. We discuss these issues in Chapters Thirteen and Fourteen.

The **operations** chapter summarizes the management structure, if several people are involved in the start-up also the roles and line management arrangements. It summarizes the team members' skills and responsibilities while outlining how operations will work. These differ for online businesses, retail, service industry, and manufacturing and hospitality start-ups. It might present an HR strategy including what staff with what type of skills to employ over the next three years. It might explain choice of location and premises. Ideally, health and safety issues are addressed.

Legal challenges are shorter to address. The company's legal form needs brief explanations with naming directors, executive and non-executive, and company secretary where that applies. Potential licenses the business needs for operating legally and within regulations are outlined with a timeline when they were or will be acquired. If there is intellectual property to protect, that is detailed with a timeline when the application went in or will go in with details what for.

The **financial plan** will discuss the financial sources that will provide the money needed to get the business up and running in as much as finance the first three years of trading.

Various financial statements are discussed, including cash flow forecast and break-even analysis (that is, when profit will be made), management accounts, profit and loss, and any assets that have to be purchased or leased will be represented in the financial accounts. Some funders expect to see a balance sheet as well. Break-even analysis and cash flow forecast are the most important ones. Chapters Nine and Ten on finance outlined these calculations briefly.

Investors might also be interested in a number of financial ratios such as gross margin, net worth, pre-tax return on net worth, return on equity to name a few. As these are well explained by other books and sources, I recommend going to the further reading listed on the companion website for learning more about financial ratios.

Risks and rewards and **Exit strategy/Plan B** are required by some funders. Business risks that can impact on performance or even endanger the continuation of the business are discussed in Chapter Sixteen. Exit strategy refers back to some business goals outlined in the introduction. Some business opportunities are short-lived, due to imminent or current changes in the market or industry. A goal might be to earn for a fixed amount of time while there is still a need for a product, and then close the business down, or better, sell it to a larger company.

The Prince's Trust, for example, wants to know what applicants will do if they cannot make the business work, and so do other organizations, in particular those offering grants.

The **appendix** can contain a number of documents. The most common ones are CV of founder(s) and company documents from company formation (memorandum, articles of association for limited companies). Other documents to attach can include:

▶ A professional adviser report if it was done;
▶ Quotes for buying larger equipment, property;
▶ Details of premises where appropriate;
▶ Letters of support from advisers;
▶ Letters of intent from potential buyers.

12.4 Business plans for social enterprise start-ups – the differences

As a social enterprise, you have different stakeholders and different objectives. The core objective is your social mission, and making a profit is only a means to an end. This is the first vital difference.

All the guidance outlined in the previous section applies here as well, yet additional pointers are needed.

Box 12.2 shows an overview of the headings of a traditional social enterprise business plan. As outlined above, there is no golden rule for what the plan should contain. Dependent on the audience, and in particular funders, it is most helpful to follow their guidance and questions they ask you to answer. Box 12.2 shows the same content as Box 12.1 for the traditional business plan plus additional or different headings marked in italic capitals. This means that several sections will contain very similar content. But there are some significant differences.

Box 12.2 Business plan outline for social enterprises

Executive summary

Introduction

(The founder or the founding team; reason for starting the business; SOCIAL AIMS; vision, mission and objectives; an introduction to the industry subsector and/or location of business; benefits of the suggested products/services.)

SOCIAL PURPOSE (see explanations below) and theory of change

Industry analysis with competitor evaluation

Market analysis, with findings on market research and market testing

SOCIAL PURPOSE (if not placed above)

Marketing strategy

Operational plan

(Including purchasing goods/services, organizational structure, management team, managing staff, *VOLUNTEERS*, rational for choice or premises and location where appropriate.)

Legal issues (*FORMAL AGREEMENTS ON DISTRIBUTION OF PROFITS, DISTRIBUTION OF ASSETS***)**

Financial plan

(Including costs and pricing strategy, start-up budget and cash flow, *RAISING DONATIONS AND SPONSORSHIP.*)

Risks and *SOCIAL IMPACT*

(Keys to success, main risks.)

Plan B/Exit plan

Appendix

The first difference is that the above-mentioned social mission or purpose and the social aims are already indicated in the executive summary.

 An additional section on the **social purpose** can be included either before the value proposition or after the market analysis section. If it is before the value proposition this section should address the following questions:

▸ Who will benefit?
▸ Why is there a need for this social enterprise?
▸ How will running a social enterprise meet the need?
▸ What type of social enterprise is suggested, and how does this type meet the need you have discussed above?

If the section on social purpose is after the market analysis section, the following two questions should also be answered:

- What are the critical success factors?
- What is the strategy to meet the critical success factors?

In the section on **operations** a section on recruiting and managing volunteers needs to be included.

In the section on **legal issues**, it is important for community interest companies in the UK that give out shares to explain how profits will be distributed and when, and how much money will be retained in the organization and what it will be used for, showing percentages. An example is, of those profits retained 40% will be used to build reserves, 30% will be used to provide free services for those most disadvantaged, another 10% will be donated to a named charity while the remaining 20% will be spent on local community projects that involve children (or education about the environment, to name another example). Similarly, it needs to be specified how any assets (machines, PCs, cars, mobile phones, furniture, buildings, etc.) and financial assets (savings, saving contracts) will be distributed and to whom in case of closure of the social enterprise; this section should also contain some information on business continuity which is addressed below in Section 12.5.5).

Management issues are different, as very often, not always, a social enterprise is started with or by a group of volunteers. In Chapters Fifteen and Sixteen we discuss in more detail some aspects of how to manage volunteers. In comparison to the for-profit business that might have the odd unpaid placement student, social enterprises work with more volunteers on a regular basis, often for the lifetime of the enterprise. The HR strategy might detail for social firms ways to integrate disadvantaged people into the labour market and outline a strategy for their recruitment and skills development.

The **marketing** section might have additional details on marketing to gain donations and marketing activities to gain sponsorship from individuals or large corporations. We discuss marketing, PR and sales in Chapters Thirteen and Fourteen.

For the **financial** section, additional ways to raise finance that need addressing include getting donations and sponsorship, and grants for social enterprises. These points were discussed in Chapters Nine and Ten on finance and Financial Circuits.

Risks and social impact is a section that outlines the plans and considerations of how the social venture will make a difference to people's lives or the environment as well as the risks of when the venture cannot reach the financial goals and is not able to achieve the projected differences to people and/or the environment. The latter differences we call social impact; it looks to quantify the differences made (a difference to an individual, groups, situations, the environment, etc.), in terms of soft outcomes for people (in areas of education, and knowledge increased, skills development, confidence increase for example, increasing awareness) and the outputs (which are better to measure) in terms of qualifications, number of participants in programmes, events, etc. The social impact has become significantly more important and is ideally integrated into the planning considerations from the start. These social impact considerations go beyond the achievement of financial goals.

Typical business risks are outlined in Chapter Sixteen; however, it is essential to consider them throughout the planning process, and we have discussed risks in most chapters so far. It will be helpful to go to Section 16.1 now and identify the risks in detail, as addressing business risks needs to be integrated into the planning process.

The next section outlines the most important business policies that are needed.

12.5   Policies a business should have

12.5.1 Introduction to business policies

Policies are broad statements by a business that set out what the business stands for and what its goals are in a particular area, such as environmental issues. Procedures are usually summarized or examples are given that guide the policy's implementation or how to apply it in practice. In the *sustainable start-up* approach we regard selected business policies as a tool to realize principle and practice of "resourceful impact". Put simply, pinning down in writing how you will go about meeting standards of good practice in waste reduction, waste disposal, to name one area, makes business sense, as it assists you in reducing the amount of resources you use and can save you money. At the same time, considering other areas can increase your productivity, reducing time needed for carrying out core business activities. We briefly discussed that in Chapter Six on operational design.

While most of the policies discussed in this section are not legally *required* for a start-up with fewer than five employees in the UK, having them in place will add credibility to the business presence. Policies should implement some well-known standards in doing business for your organization, even if you start by yourself. The most acknowledged standards have been published by the International Organization for Standardization, ISO (there were 19,500 standards by the end of 2014).

Other features adding value include that they can be added when bidding to large corporates for winning contracts. Some public sector bodies require some of those policies as well, in order to give work to a new supplier. It will be a distinct differentiating feature if you can demonstrate these policies are in place and make them accessible to some business customers on request. It confirms the serious approach you take on running your enterprise.

Below we discuss health and safety policy, environmental policy, equality and diversity policy, harassment and grievance policy and business continuity policy. These are the most common ones for external use. Further policies for mainly internal use and operational in focus include customer service and customer complaints policy, social media and IT policy.

Quality policy is not included here, as the standards of quality vary widely for different sectors and trades. This is a statement by the organization's managers or founders that outlines the ways quality is ensured in the processes and products created. While some quality standards are now internationally recognized, such as those in the ISO9000 group, the quality standards published by the International Organization for Standardization, others are very particular to the particular activities carried out.

Practically speaking, there are plenty of examples of policies available to learn from, in books and published on company websites. In my view you should write policies yourself based on a model you like as a *sustainable start-up* so that you are fully aware of what you should and will do. Policies need to be updated once a year ideally, as regulations might change, laws come into force, technology and hazards develop.

12.5.2 Health and safety policy

This policy is legally required if you have five or more employees. The most important content that needs covering includes:

a) Your goals for health and safety and what you want to achieve;
b) Your commitment to managing health and safety effectively;
c) Setting out who is responsible for specific actions to implement the policy;

d) Some detail of what you are going to do in practice to achieve the aims set out in your statement of health and safety policy. In particular, what you are doing to reduce or eliminate risks and hazards at work.

The UK Health and Safety Executive provide a lot of detail and templates for the policy (www.hse.gov.uk).

What you can do includes things like having no cables lying around that can make staff or customers trip, staff training, wearing vests in warning colours such as yellow and green, additional lighting, special equipment, etc.

12.5.3 Environmental policy

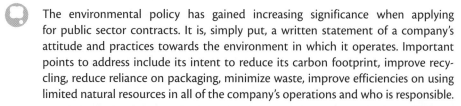

The environmental policy has gained increasing significance when applying for public sector contracts. It is, simply put, a written statement of a company's attitude and practices towards the environment in which it operates. Important points to address include its intent to reduce its carbon footprint, improve recycling, reduce reliance on packaging, minimize waste, improve efficiencies on using limited natural resources in all of the company's operations and who is responsible.

All environmental commitments should be an integral part of the day-to-day activities (they may form part of application for ISO14001 certification). Where there are staff, it needs to document how the policy is communicated to all staff and associates and ensure they implement it.

The policy needs to define the environmental objectives as outlined earlier that the company is following, who is accountable and how these are going to be achieved and by whom. Areas that need addressing include:

▶ Transportation – how to reduce or avoid it, for example by using online meeting facilities where appropriate;
▶ Stationery and supplies – encouraging staff and others not to print emails is a common procedure;
▶ Improved efficiency in using resources – how that is achieved;
▶ Improved recycling and waste minimization – if environmental products are bought for cleaning, etc.

This policy can be a one-page statement for start-ups and micro-businesses that summarizes the main important points.

12.5.4 Equality and diversity, harassment and grievance policies

Within a few months of trading for my first start-up, I had written these policies, really too late in at least one case. I learned through feedback for a contract that while there was no legal requirement to have any of these policies, having included them in my application to the council would have increased my scoring.

Equality and diversity policy is the most important one; often micro-businesses and start-ups combine these policy areas in one.

The policy addresses the need to demonstrate the wish to avoid discrimination and victimization in terms of gender, age, racial origin, religion or belief, disability, sexual orientation and gender reassignment and to implement the codes of practice issued by the Equality and Human Rights Commission and other statutory organizations.

The topics covered have to include:

- A statement of aims and objectives and commitment;
- How these attitudes translate into company practices;
- Who is responsible for its implementation, monitoring and review;
- How it is communicated to staff and stakeholders and suppliers.

Harassment is a term for a behaviour that victimizes staff due to the differences outlined above. In practice that could mean a staff member does not get a promotion because of having any of the above features. Grievance is the process staff can use to complain to the senior management which should be spelt out in a grievance policy.

12.5.5 Business continuity policy and plan (with risk management policy)

This policy sets out what procedures are in place if the business cannot operate, either because access to premises and/or operating equipment is impossible or because the business has to close down. Examples where this recently happened are through flooding, fire or electricity blackouts. Since 2012 there is an international standard in place that sets out in more detail what should be planned for (ISO 22301:2012, see http://www.iso.org/iso/catalogue_detail?csnumber=50038, accessed 30/5/2015). Areas that need addressing include stock, information, data, people, assets and premises.

The most important advantage to having this policy in place is that it demonstrates to clients that you are prepared for emergencies and important known business risks and have procedures in place to act if the emergency arises. This makes start-ups and small businesses more reliable.

The main objective of the plan is to recover all *business critical processes* and minimize the impact on your employees, customers and your reputation.

The plan should at least contain the following:

- Objectives;
- Responsible staff;
- A list of critical functions and their priorities;
- Business impact analysis for each critical function, with effects on operations for each day following the emergency incident; the resources needed to recover for each 24 hours;
- Hazard analysis table with a risk matrix score (see the chapter on risks analysis for more details);
- Emergency response list;
- Key contacts sheet with phone numbers and any additional useful information;
- Monitoring information on messages sent.

The next section briefly discusses an answer to a question that is often asked during the time of business planning: when can I do my launch and celebrate it?

12.6 *Sustainable start-up – the launch event?*

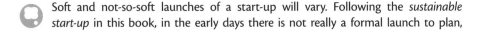

Soft and not-so-soft launches of a start-up will vary. Following the *sustainable start-up* in this book, in the early days there is not really a formal launch to plan, apart from registering the company and continuing the development of the value proposition with selling more and gaining more feedback and customer insight. Opening a restaurant, bar, bistro or retail outlet with an event is always a good idea, as it raises awareness of the business's existence. However, if you start your activities with pop-up restaurants – for example at fairs across the country, or on a monthly basis in a particular location – the formal launch is not necessary.

Having said that, some start-ups throw a launch party to reward their early adopters and co-creators amongst customers and suppliers and other contacts. This is a good idea, as it recognizes and rewards their efforts and input while at the same time is an opportunity for them and you to bring along further contacts who are curious to try out what you have to offer. It will get you further feedback and learning and hopefully further leads you can eventually turn into sales. With a sustainable approach, you do not have to offer champagne and canapés, but focusing on some drinks and nibbles is a good idea. It gives something for people to hold on to (a glass) and talk about to other people at the event. This event or party you could call a formal launch, but does it really matter what you call it? None of our case studies in this book has done a formal launch event.

The question you might ask is: do I need a fully-fledged written document of a business plan before I launch or register? If you use your own money and do not want a loan through a programme or from investors, no, not necessarily. You silently register and then move on continuing to write a plan in report form, if you need one. As outlined under Section 12.4, the living wall-pinned detailed plan (with goals and actions, and the rationale for what you are doing) might be all you (and your partner or team where appropriate) might need. This assumes that you nevertheless have thought through all the aspects that a business plan in report format would summarize.

12.7   Concluding remarks and application of new insights

This chapter introduced you to the process of business plan writing. For social enterprises we highlighted the differences including the separate section on the social mission and objectives and the rationale for trading. The business plan needs to be written in different ways for each audience. Banks and traditional funders expect a certain format and focus on how money is being generated and used, so they get an understanding that money will be invested wisely and not spent on unnecessary items. Those social enterprise start-ups applying for grants need to ensure that the social mission and objectives as well as potential beneficiaries are highlighted; where appropriate, the use of profits and shares needs to be detailed and that in case of closure of the social enterprise any remaining cash or assets will be going to another social enterprise, for example. Stakeholders have not much interest in a long document to read and often prefer a visual summary using mind maps and pictures.

For the actual planning process we outlined practical ways of using visual tools and involving your stakeholders in the planning process where possible. This interactive planning process is realizing the principles and practices of alertness, interconnectedness, resourceful impact and co-creation.

The chapter then explained the most important business policies a *sustainable start-up* should develop. While no legal requirements exist for all the policies discussed, when wishing to deliver services on behalf of a local authority, for example, these policies might be required. However, once employees are employed, some policies become a requirement in some countries. Even the sole trader is advised to consider writing these policies, as they require the *sustainable start-up* to consider most effective ways of addressing many of the issues. Policy areas discussed included health and safety, equality and diversity, harassment and grievance, environment, risk and business continuity. The last section briefly discussed the often asked question about a formal launch event, which in many cases is not applicable.

Revision questions and applying the new insights to your own *sustainable start-up*

1 What can you gain from engaging with business planning?
2 What do banks and funders look for in a business plan?
3 What are common mistakes in a business plan?
4 What are the main differences in a business plan for a social enterprise?
5 Which policies do you have to have?
6 When should you do a launch party? And why?
7 Write an outline of your business plan with headings. Then gather some stakeholders, such as an adviser and a volunteer and family member or friend and bring together what you have learned so far using flip charts (when working face-to-face) or an online tool (when you are located too far apart). Only the outcome of that process will be populating the written document business plan.
8 There will be some gaps, as we have not considered in detail marketing strategy and timing, for example. Write a list of the gaps and a time plan for when you can work on them.
9 Write an action plan for the next weeks: what can you actually do and when? Keep that plan visible for all team members where applicable and yourself. Share it online with the stakeholders so that they can support you when they wish to. What support might you need to do any of those tasks? Note the decisions in you start-up diary.

13

MARKETING PLANNING AND IMPLEMENTATION

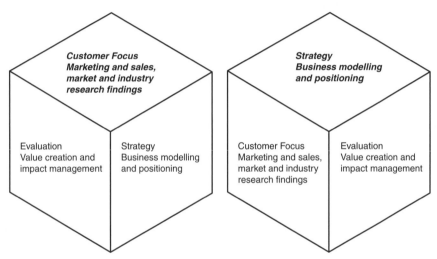

Figure 13.1   The Cube Customer Focus and the Cube Strategy
Source: © Hill, 2012.

Summary

This chapter talks for the first time about marketing in the pre-start-up journey. The main reason for its late appearance is that for the pre-start-up phases, the actual practical marketing planning is not necessary. Rather, outlining the marketing to establish its cost for the financial planning is essential for establishing the viability of the business idea we are exploring (Figure 13.1). This costing should be done as part of business modelling, in the cost structure section, Chapter Ten for financial planning. Table 13.1 in Section 13.1.4 offers an overview of what data needs to be collected to establish the cost of the considered marketing activities, while Table 13.2 in Section 13.7.2 shows an example. Marketing basics are discussed as well as marketing using social media and bootstrap marketing. Branding is introduced here in a basic way, as there is specialist literature on start-up branding; rather, its nature is introduced to the newcomer and advice on its importance for the *sustainable start-up* explained.

For social enterprises and businesses addressing a social problem, two particular types of marketing are discussed: social marketing aiming at behaviour change and cause-related marketing or sponsorship marketing, where a for-profit company donates a small amount of money from each unit sold to a social cause (Figure 13.1).

CONTENTS

13.1 Marketing for start-ups

13.1.1 Timing of marketing in the start-up process

Why is this chapter so late in the book? As we said in Chapter One, the chapters do not need to be read and used in the sequence they appear. However, the *sustainable start-up* process is aimed at helping you to focus on the most important challenges that enable you to first make a decision if money can be made with your idea. And that includes finding out if there *is* a market before you waste time and money on activities you will not need, if you decide not to start a business with the particular service or product you researched. At earlier stages when finding out if there is a market and when estimating your potential operating cost, it helps to outline what marketing you might do and what it might cost. Funders and award-giving organizations want to know you spend your money wisely. In essence, this means investing early on into TV adverts that cost a fortune will not get you funding from third parties.

Thus, while marketing is exciting and creative and colourful, considering how to market your value proposition, your package of service(s) and product(s), is amongst the last tasks to carry out once you know there is an opportunity.

While the business plan outline discussed the marketing section very briefly in Chapter Twelve, this chapter discusses in more detail what you need to consider and what to do around marketing, whereas Chapter Forteen explores PR and sales.

The next section discusses some fundamentals you need to understand about marketing and introduces some classic marketing tools.

 In practice, as a start-up you are marketing nearly all the time, often without knowing it. Why you might ask? When you do your research, you are alerting potential customers and those people that might know people who would want your service or product that you are working on something of interest to them (or their contacts). When you talk to potential suppliers, friends, advisers, banks, etc., you are developing a network of people who know about what you plan and learn about your presence. Keeping that in mind is essential for the co-creating approach in *Start Up*. This important insight is also the key to making sure you are using your time and resources most effectively when you are finally out there selling.

13.1.2 What is marketing, really?

Now that you have decided on the package of products/services, the question is what marketing is and what it involves. The first insight is that marketing is *not* the same as advertising. Some marketeers (those actively involved in marketing) say that advertising and selling are part of the broad field marketing, and some include PR (public relations).

There is no single agreed definition of marketing, which comes as no great surprise by now. Marketing covers a huge area of interest to all organizations, large and small. Because organizations and those doing marketing are all so different, it is not possible to develop a single definition.

There are a number of questions to answer. Firstly, not all organizations are designed to make a profit and not all organizations would consider themselves to have "customers". Does this mean that marketing does not apply to charities and not-for-profit organizations? Do political parties not utilize marketing techniques to communicate with the electorate? Marketing does apply to them; however, it does depend upon how we define profit. If we consider profit to mean a surplus, then charities can benefit from the use of marketing techniques by increasing support and donations for example.

Secondly, what do we mean by a customer? If we consider a customer to be individuals or organizations with whom we interact, then by stretching the point the definition does apply to all organizations.

Thirdly, is marketing just a management process or are all employees in an organization involved in marketing? Can marketing activities be carried out by an organization for example who has no marketing department?

The Chartered Institute of Marketing (UK) has had this definition since 2010 in their publications:

> The strategic business function that creates value by stimulating, facilitating and fulfilling customer demand.
>
> It does this by building brands, nurturing innovation, developing relationships, creating good customer service and communicating benefits.
>
> With a customer centric view, marketing brings positive return on investment, satisfies shareholders and stakeholders from business and the community, and contributes to positive behavioural change and a sustainable business future. (CIM, 2010, p. 14)

The next section introduces some models that can help to manage marketing communications and guide the actions in the context of entrepreneurial marketing. This concept has been defined as an entrepreneurial approach to marketing issues, "the innovative, proactive and risk taking approach to the processes of creating, communicating and delivering value to customers" (Sole, 2013, p. 29). This marketing concept has two aspects: tactics and strategy of entrepreneurial marketing. After introducing two models of traditional marketing, the practice is briefly outlined.

The AIDA model

It is helpful to remind us of the purpose of marketing. Put simply, the aim of marketing is to convince a potential buyer to purchase the product/service. For marketing communications and consumer response to them we can view this as being a four-stage process (AIDA):

Attention → Interest → Desire → Action

What do these terms mean?

Attention: Marketing communication in particular has to attract the attention of a choosy audience, suffering from overload of information. For that reason, advertising often adopts humour or shock tactics in order to attract attention. Sometimes marketeers push the boundaries of this approach to the (un-) acceptable limit.

Interest: Interest will only be generated if there is some perceived value in the mind of the potential customers. Does the product or service have a relevance to them? This will vary with the viewer's position regarding purchase. This is expressed through the change and benefits statement and the overall value proposition. An individual thinking about buying a car will pay more attention to advertisements for cars.

Desire: Does the perceived value offered in the advertisement create a desire to own or participate in the minds of the individuals in the audience? Even if a desire is kindled, are the viewers able to purchase? Children cannot purchase many things before they reach 18 years of age.

Action: If all of the above hurdles have been overcome, we still need the marketing recipient to actually part with their money and buy.

The AIDA model is a very simple and basic approach to understanding communications. More complex models have been developed on buying decisions (see the list with further reading on the companion website on marketing).

 Activity 13.1   Analysing an advertisement

Answer the following questions related to an advertisement of your choice

Consider examples of advertising that you have seen recently (or look for examples on www.palgrave.com/companion/hill-start-up). How did the advertisements apply the AIDA model? Were you influenced by these advertisements? If you did not actually buy, did they influence your perception of the product or organization concerned? How have your perceptions changed?

The seven (or more) Ps

A traditional view of marketing communication management was, and for some people still is, that marketeers practised their craft by managing and manipulating a mix of factors, called the *marketing mix*. No factor should be considered by itself, as they all form part of the marketing experience and plan. Depending on the academic or practitioner you talk to the marketing mix consists of five to eight (or even more) elements, all starting with P, therefore called the seven (or eight) Ps.

Product: The actual goods delivered to customers, this can be services or a mix of products and services or a tangible product. We have called it value proposition with a customer-centric view so far in *Start Up*. Ensure that the quality the customer wants is what you sell, and not more – if a simple glass is fine for wine glasses, do not try to sell crystal glasses to this customer. Consider the product look, feel and design.

Price: This is the amount of money you charge both customers and other intermediaries such as a wholesaler or retailer and includes discount structures. We discussed pricing strategies in Chapter Ten: it needs to cover your costs and allow you to make a profit; it needs to allow you to be competitive, not the cheapest and needs to reflect the value you create. The price chosen has an impact of the choice of distribution channels (see *place* below).

Promotion: This P addresses how you communicate the value proposition to customers and other stakeholders and promote trial and adoption of your product or service, ideally by engaging in a dialogue with the customer. Promotion must follow AIDA, use coherent branding and transmit a consistent message, and focus on the benefits.

Place: Where do customers buy the product? Channels of distribution to the place of purchase and the customer location, sometimes their home, are important to consider. Are the goods delivered in a timely manner and do they deliver the expected quality and quantity? Can that be done at a reasonable price? Do we sell from vending machines, online or shops, and if so which type of shops? How is the product displayed and showcased in that place? Do you sell through sales agents/telemarketing agents?

People: All staff market your product, even if they do not work in marketing. When talking to their friends, they market your business and product. And when talking to customers, staff and sales agents need to have the appropriate attitude, skills and company and product knowledge. Nothing is more disappointing when in a restaurant the staff do not know what the food on the menu actually is. In particular for after-sales support this is important. Often customers do not differentiate clearly between product and company: you might really like the food at Pizza Hut, but if you have more than one bad customer experience with staff, you might stop going; after all, there are other places to get good pizza.

This mix was extended by two further elements to incorporate the concept of a service. These additions were *process* and *physical evidence*, and finally, *packaging* was added by tangible product marketeers.

Process: We discussed this element under customer journey in business modelling and operations. You need to ensure through excellent customer service that the customer experience from being interested in the product to having bought it and living with it is satisfying. Ensure there are no unnecessary or unexplained waiting times. All of this is relevant for products and services.

Physical evidence: This aspect addresses how the product is presented. As a service is intangible and cannot be seen, for that reason you need to demonstrate in other ways what quality a service user can expect. This starts with the physical premises, where they exist: organized, clean, tidy, with friendly staff, well presented, evidence of qualifications or testimonials by satisfied customers. This can be transferred to printed and online information. The physical evidence needs to mirror the value proposition made and the assumption the customer makes. It also addresses the way the packaging of a tangible product such as a drink continues to make the message of the vision and mission statement. An ethical, green company would be advised to use sustainable package materials, or even recyclable ones to reduce the carbon footprint.

Packaging: This term is often used instead of physical evidence by product marketeers. It focuses on the tangible packaging of a tangible product, such as the packing of chocolate. Sometimes, it is used to refer to the same wider areas as outlined for physical evidence.

While this is a good starting point for supporting the mechanics of marketing, co-creation of a *sustainable start-up* needs more than that. As pointed out before, it is essential to have the customer-centric long-term view in mind when planning and developing your start-up. Otherwise, your start-up is a flash in the pan, starts with a bang and flashes and then cannot survive longer term. There are a number of overlapping areas between the seven Ps and the business model canvas: "customer relationships" partially overlaps with *promotion*, "customer channels" with *place* and "value proposition" with *product*; the business model canvas takes a more customer-focused view of the same aspects whereas the seven Ps offer the view of the company.

Entrepreneurial marketing (EM) tactics focus on proactiveness, creativity and innovation enabling entrepreneurs to bring a new product more quickly to market as the practice of developing a minimal viable and most marketable product outlines (see Chapters Five and Six). The above tools can help to structure the marketing communications. The next sections assist you in focusing on those aspects of the start-up work that are essential to consider when co-designing the marketing for your *sustainable start-up*.

13.1.3 Summarizing the market positioning, value proposition, USP and target customers

Chapter Ten helped you to decide on the selling price and pricing strategy, based on the costs you have, the market position you intend to take, the first customer illustrated through the identified customer persona and the price you are selling your value proposition at, while Chapter Eleven allowed you to draw overall conclusions that there is a viable business opportunity you are looking at. The value proposition you are making needs to influence the market position "choice", based on your capabilities, that is, what you can deliver. All of them need to mirror your vision and mission, and your motto, which we discuss below in Section 13.2.1. These links are illustrated in Figure 13.2.

 Activity 13.2   Deciding on your USP and value proposition

In the form below fill in your USP(s), your target customer(s) for the first customer only, and the value proposition. Limit the value proposition to 50 words.

Target customer profile – customer persona:

Unique selling point:

Value proposition:

Theory of change:

Story of change:

13.1.4 Deciding on your marketing efforts in hours and pounds

As a *sustainable start-up* you need to decide on what you will spend your money. And if you try to gain start-up funding from investors or the bank or even a grant-giving body, they want to have a clear idea that you plan to spend the money wisely. TV advertising is expensive and not effective for a start-up, but you guessed that anyway by now.

In Chapter Ten, we summarized some of the expenses and promised they will be looked at later in more detail. It is essential to consider all expenses, including staff time and its cost as many activities are needed for the co-creating approach for start-up development. Table 13.1 lists a way of ensuring you get your marketing activities considered with their associated costs so that you can arrive at an overall marketing cost.

Some start-ups fail, as they have not considered the time and costs needed to market their business appropriately; and they very often do not market it sufficiently. In Box 13.1, there is a little story out of my adviser basket of insights.

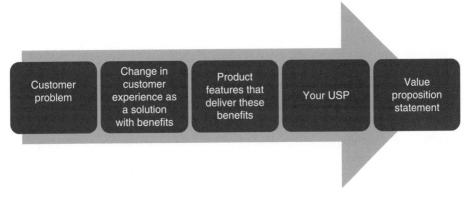

Figure 13.2 From customer pain to value proposition statement

Table 13.1 Marketing expenses

Marketing activity	In-house	Lead staff	Resources	Cost in £	External
Social media	X	Partner/associate; placement student	Pictures, text; staff time	££	
Printing folders / brochures / business cards		Marketing staff/ owner/supplier	Staff time	£££	Quotes from local providers
Designing business cards, folders, brochures, create branding		Marketing staff/ owner/supplier	Vision and mission statement, objectives,	££££	Quotes from trusted designers
Networking meetings		CEO to delegate to staff	Membership organisations	£	Council, Chambers etc.
Membership fees for associations / networks		CEO to delegate to staff	Memberships	££	X
Exhibition stands / banners		Marketing staff/ owner/supplier	Pictures, text; staff time; logo, branding	££	Quotes from local providers for design and print
Trade fair fees		CEO to delegate to staff		££££	Trade fair organizers
Advertising in magazines / newspapers		CEO to delegate to staff, marketing staff	Logo, branding; text, pictures	££££	X
Sponsorship with appropriate sports clubs / other causes		CEO	Contacts, Logo, branding; text, pictures	£££	X
Other?					

Note: £ means 1 o 50 pounds
££ means 51 to 100 pounds
£££ means 101 to 200 pounds
££££ means over 200 pounds

Box 13.1 Start-up marketing needs effort

I once had a discussion with one of my clients, a crafts business. I had asked a contact in a local gym, the catering and event manager, if there was a chance she could help this client of mine in some way, after all, she was a local business start-up. She was more than happy to do that and I introduced the two. She was then invited to offer her lovely handmade crafts products on the same day The Book People were on site selling their books, collections of books and individual books. Great, you might think?

Well, so did I, *but* the argument ran as follows: "I have no access to a car that day so cannot make it, and I do not know if it is worth the effort." My point was she could get there in just under an hour by public transport, and market her work for six hours. As she normally transported the goods in a box, she complained it was too heavy to carry the box to a bus stop, and change buses and then walk from the bus stop to the gym. I suggested to think of other ways of carrying it, such as rucksack and bags, or to consider a combination of bus and taxi. As sales this third month of trading had been very low via the website and directories she was on, she did not want to spend any money on a taxi. Her argument was she was not sure she would sell anything, and then the expense would be too big (£12). There was no fee to pay for the stall, she was provided with a table and a place to sit.

She had so far attended six fairs, for most of which she had had to pay a fee to be there. At one she had sold really well, and at two for which she had paid to have a stall, she sold nothing in one case and made less than £10 in another case. She had given up believing she would sell at fairs after attending six, of which one was very successful.

The opportunity I had facilitated was free of charge, apart from transport costs, and she could sit and produce goods, to demonstrate her work was handmade, and be productive, while waiting for customers to pass by and then communicate with them. Her final decision was on this occasion not to use the opportunity. Instead, she sat at home creating some more goods.

 My rule of thumb for all start-ups is *at least a day and a half* has to be spent on marketing activities, ideally more when your week is six days long, or even seven. As nobody knows you exist, you have to ensure the word gets out. Use a multi-channel approach that allows you to choose the most appropriate ways to reach your target customers, and those that might know your target customers. Networking face-to-face is still a great way to build a profile and get a customer base; so are social media and pre-existing networks on social media. Making a phone call to a contact to catch up on what they are up to is always a good way to remind them of what you do, and so is email.

In the co-creation approach, ideally you have ambassadors that do part of the work for you. But first of all, you need to create these ambassadors. Building ambassadors for your value proposition needs time not included in this day and a half, so add another half day per week for that.

Have we discussed what ambassadors are? Ambassadors in this context are people who believe in your theory of change and value proposition and are happy to share that belief and experience with others in an organized way. Enthusiastic early adopters are a type of customer (they were discussed in Chapter Five) that might share their experiences for free, and for others you might just need to offer some free goods if they bring in new customers that buy from you. In other chapters we discussed how Frinter founders Muhammad and Shivam created brand ambassadors and recruited a number of student volunteers to spread the work about the location and use of Frinter printers, rewarding them with iPads and free printing/copying for the rest of their studies and other goods, but no money.

13.2 Practical essentials

13.2.1 Vision and mission statement and motto

It is essential to develop a vision and mission statement early on and include it in the business plan, ideally. The list of content in Chapter Twelve indicated to include these two statements in the introduction and executive summary.

Even for the start-up by one person, I suggest involving others in the development process (applying again co-creation practice and principle). The main reason for that is that the statement needs to convince others immediately what your start-up is about, its goals and objectives. The message needs to be clear and simple, and create a positive effect when heard or read the first time. To achieve this effect, it is helpful to have input from a number of different individuals with different viewpoints early on.

The *vision statement* focuses on the future: what does the venture aim to achieve, and where does it aim to be? The vision should be a source of inspiration and motivation for stakeholders, in particular employees and customers. It often summarizes simply the kind of change for the world or society the venture aims to contribute to and sums up why the company exists.

The message needs to be simple and clear, showing a bright future, easy to understand, memorable and engaging, and needs to be in line with the values of the founder(s). Good vision statements have a timeline and indicate a way to get there.

For start-ups this statement is the first you write, as the mission statements only specify the detail around it.

Here is one example:

 Case study

Richard Rodman, co-founder of Crowdentials, US, one of our case studies, has this vision statement on his website:

> Crowdentials strives to grow our economy by helping every company and investor focus on raising and investing capital in a safe and cost effective manner. In the next 10 years, companies won't view regulations as cumbersome but rather a necessary step to protecting all parties involved in a transaction. (www.crowdentials.com, accessed September 2014)

The positive aspiration is coming through "grow our economy", appealing to the listener by indicating with "we" that they and Crowdentials' staff are aiming for the same improvement. It is specific in setting a timescale and goals for what they aim to achieve within the next ten years and highlights the overall benefit for the key clients – investors – offering them safety and protection.

Mission statements specify in more detail how the company intends to achieve the stated vision, and name some of the goals and the purpose it was created for. They can also point out what makes the company stand out from the competition.

The best statements identify the clients and the role the venture seeks to have in the clients' lives and how the venture will add value. They focus on the benefits the clients gain from the offered product/service.

Crowdentials also has a mission statement on the website:

> At Crowdentials, our mission is to help companies raise capital and ease the burden of complying with the JOBS Act with automated solutions. We believe that those raising funding shouldn't be blindsided by laws they didn't know existed and shouldn't pay hefty fees and spend countless hours to stay compliant. (www.crowdentials.com, accessed September 2014)

This mission statement qualifies further how the venture is assisting companies with a focus on the benefits – getting capital for start-up and reducing effort in complying with a particular law. The idea of protection raised in the vision statement is detailed further, such as avoiding paying fines for making mistakes and doing what a particular law requires them to do.

Mottos (or slogan) focus on one simple message on what the start-up is about and/or what the one key benefit is the customer gains from working with the venture, expressing the spirit and main purpose. Well-known examples include "Play on" (Lego) and "Just Do It" (Nike). Mottos can be serious, funny, light-hearted or aggressive. The message needs to be very simple and expressive, easy to grasp the first time. Ideally, they relate to the core product or business area, such as Ford managed to do. "Built for the road ahead", using the double meaning of the physical road ahead and the figurative meaning of the way to the future.

 Activity 13.3 Do you know the mottos?

1) List the company names behind those mottos. (The solutions are available on the companion website at www.palgrave.com/companion/hill-start-up.)
- Impossible is Nothing;
- THINK;
- I'm lovin' it;
- Just Do It;
- At the heart of the image;
- Hello Moto;
- Vorsprung durch Technik;
- Think different;
- Forged in Industry, Striving for Glory.

2) What do you need to know in order to write a motto or strap line?

The motto or strap line is very important, and both logo and strap line form part of the branding. Tesco's "every little helps" is so strong now that most people in the UK will identify the motto with Tesco without naming the company – what a great effect!

13.2.2 Company name and logo

Essential for branding and establishing a memorable impression with contacts and potential clients is a company name that is easy to remember, a compelling logo that tells part of the story of your business and a motto or strapline. Both need to mirror your vision and mission statement and tell a story of you and the business in a very small space.

Hopefully, the company name was well chosen, is not protected by someone else, or already registered with Companies House. For the UK, check Companies House for business names already in use.

In my experience, it helps to engage a professional in getting the logo designed. After all, the company name and logo are aiming to stick with the business and you for the rest of its lifetime, ideally. Changing a logo comes at a high cost, as it will have been used everywhere, from packaging to website to marketing material. While it is possible, it comes at a great cost in terms of expenses, and might confuse clients for a while.

Practically viewed, your business cards and branded communication materials (website, flyers, brochures, etc.) should showcase at least the motto or the vision (or both) to reinforce the clear simple message.

13.2.3 Business cards and other print materials

We live in a digital world – so do we need anything on paper? You might be right here, and in some sectors such as creative industries and in particular digital media a few might agree.

The answer to what marketing material you need can be answered like this: whatever feels right to you, and then try it out. As you want to stand out in the crowd and differentiate yourself from others, it needs to work for you *and* the customers. It is great to have business cards handy in some of those nice boxes or folders with pockets for them, and at networking events this still works great.

High quality business cards go a long way at events. Yet, there are digital cards that have a small disc with the paper card. Other start-ups only use pens or a coaster to spread the word. In a B2B context it might be different again.

For a cost-effective *sustainable start-up*, in particular for the B2B sector, a high quality professionally designed folder with company details in A4 is a useful investment. If and when services and products develop and change, you only need to insert factsheets and promotional flyers or brochures, which are much cheaper to print.

Postcard size flyers can work very well for events and special offers. The sky is your limit, and promotion companies offer hundreds of products from pens, coasters, T-shirts, mugs, memory sticks to bags and carpets.

Having e-brochures and promotional materials is really important, as they can easily be shared within a company when your enquiry is passed on to other staff in a quick way.

For retail businesses, services (including beauty, hair dressing; less so for professional services such as letting agent or accountant), hospitality outlets such as take-aways, pubs, restaurants and bars, the "good old" billboard on the pavement outside is well worth investing in, and so are posters in the window for cars driving past offering the core value proposition and the contact details readable to take note of. They raise awareness and often bring in footfall customers passing by.

13.2.4 E-marketing or digital marketing

The topic of e-marketing has been the subject of many books recently (see for example El-Gohary, H., 2012, Riyad and El-Gohary, 2013). We discuss it under practical essentials, and only mention it under marketing on a shoestring, as no business can really thrive today without some form of digital marketing. This section is meant as an introduction only to the practical issues in e-marketing. We assume in this decade everybody knows about the essential role and importance of a website and discuss a small selection of digital marketing tools to consider. For small businesses, using e-marketing tools has a positive effect on pre-sales and after-sales activities and marketing performance (Riyad and El-Gohary, 2013).

Getting the message across in the best possible way needs compelling writing, in style and choice of words. Writing for the web is different from writing newspaper articles or brochures. While there is free easy-to-get guidance via the Internet and books, it might help to engage the services of a copywriter. This often helps start-ups to clarify what their core benefits for customers are. Good copywriters will first ask lots of questions before they start writing based on the interviews and written copy from you.

Websites have been around for so long, and clear guidance exists. They need to be:

- User friendly, clearly structured, intuitive to use;
- Easy to use, offering a quick way to find information, applying the 3-click-rule (only three clicks needed to find the information someone searches for, as after that they might stop using the site);
- Interactive, such as offering a poll (a one-question "survey" you can do and then see the answer of others);
- Easy to read, web-style writing, offering the appropriate key words early on;
- Search engine optimized, useable on smartphones and tablet computers.

They need to offer:

- Video and audio, very short, maximum of 3 minutes;
- A CEO blog and a news section;
- Big enough contact details on every page;
- A "contact us" page to leave questions/queries;
- Some free information to download in the company's area of expertise;
- Links to your social media.

Search engine optimization or SEO is a word used by nearly everyone, yet not many professionals and business people understand it. Essentially, it means to ensure that in web searches your website comes out at the top or on page one of the results page. This can be done through "optimizing" the words you use in your copy, and a few other technical details I cannot go into.

Spending money on an expert to do it for you provided that your website copy is written well, and you had fully carried out the development of the benefits-oriented value proposition and your USP, which was built into your copy for website and social media profiles, may be worthwhile. Searching for keywords you can carry out by yourself and identify the most used ones; these should have been built into your copy. Too often that is not the case, and money is spent on SEO (search engine optimization) that cannot bring the return on investment needed, as the owner's clarity was not there on what the value proposition was supposed to be (see "The Beginner's Guide to SEO",

Moz.com, http://moz.com/beginners-guide-to-seo, accessed 1 January 2015). However, with the importance social media have, and the amount of paid advertising that brings up these paying companies, it loses its impact and importance. Social media optimization is rising, as a recommendation by a "friend" or contact counts for more (see Section 13.5 below on social media).

Provided you or someone else has written good copy for the website, you can start considering a number of e-marketing tools. Some are free of charge for all services, some offer a free basic service, and others offer a free trial for a month and then ask for payment from the start. My advice is to start simple and build up to more sophisticated tools while you build the business for consumer markets. In the B2B market, it might be useful to start with a more sophisticated tool that looks the part, such as LinkedIn and maybe Google+.

Here is what our photographer **Alison Barton** has engaged in (see Box 13.2). The entries represent a selection of Alison's digital marketing and include examples of online and face-to-face networks, of which some are free, general business directories that are free of charge with a short entry, local websites promoting local businesses, and affiliate marketing (free of charge). The various channels are explained in the next paragraphs. Which ones do you think are the most effective ones, bringing in the most clients? The list gives you the ones she is using now, at early start-up she concentrated on networking and word-of-mouth and affiliate marketing through her website; she added social media much later.

Box 13.2   Marketing channels used by Alison Barton

Business networks, online and face-to-face

http://www.netmums.com/sandwell-dudley/local/view/local-services/photographers/alison-barton-photography – an online network for mothers.

http://www.bobclubs.com/Photography/West-Midlands/Alison-Barton-Photography/company – Business over Breakfast, a network that meets at breakfast time for local businesses.

http://www.thebiponline.co.uk/bip/bringing-entrepreneurism-into-focus-alison-barton/ – an online newsforum for entrepreneurs.

General business directories online

http://gb-companies.com/biz/stourbridge-general-photographers-alison-barton-photography,263667

http://www.freeindex.co.uk/profile%28alison-barton-photography%29_168271.htm

http://www.misterwhat.co.uk/company/2271923-alison-barton-photography-stourbridge

Affiliate marketing

http://funkyconcepts.com/themes-ideas/alison-barton-photography/

http://www.griffiths-pegg.co.uk/links/ – there is a link to her website on there

---

Professional websites for photographers

http://www.photographycentral.co.uk/photographer/468346/alison-barton-photography

Directories for local businesses

http://www.tuugo.co.uk/Companies/alison-barton-photography45/0300003614839#!

http://www.freeindex.co.uk/profile%28alison-barton-photography%29_168271.htm

http://www.citylocal.co.uk/Stourbridge/Photographers---General-in-Stourbridge/Alison-Barton-Photography/DY8-5JL/b-19lj1/

http://www.yell.com/biz/alison-barton-photography-stourbridge-6009165/

Directories for people with a special interest, such as wedding or pets

http://www.thegooddogguide.com/west-midlands/stourbridge/dog-pet-photography-portrait-artists/alison-barton-photography/9954

http://theweddingsearch.co.uk/supplier-profile/277/Alison-Barton-Photography.html

---

The question remains as to which of Alison's channels are the most effective; have you come up with an answer? The following three online directories increased her position on Google during the first year of trading: Yell.com, Netmums and Business over Breakfast. Of secondary importance are specialist online business directories such as for weddings.

Online directories

Regionally as well locally and nationally there are 1000s of online business directories, going beyond Yell.com and Thomson.local.co.uk, for the UK, the digital versions of the *Yellow Pages* and similar directories. Some of these directories are for certain professions only, others are for tradespeople (www.tradespeople.com), and as pointed out in the research chapters (Chapters Four and Five for industry and market research, respectively) there are several for social enterprises. It is worth getting listed in as many online free directories you can think of. Yell.com has a free one-line entry, and paid-for larger entries with web address and full contact details. It depends on the profession and trade if it is useful to pay for those: when looking for a service provider to go to, or retail, many consumers do not want to spend too much time travelling.

Apps

Applications, or more often "apps", are a good way to stay in consumers' minds, in particular if there is a fun game that only advertises you and related complementary businesses. There are apps that allow you to create an app and might be useful for consumer markets. Unless a huge budget for marketing is available, the expense of hiring a designer to create an app is not yet creating in many cases the expected return on investment. You can advertise on third party apps or bring out your own.

Pay-per-click advertising (Google AdWords)

With Google AdWords and similar services you can create ads and choose keywords, words or phrases related to your products or services. When people search on Google using one of your keywords, your advert may appear next to the search results. This means you are advertising to an audience that is already interested in your product. You can use text, image and video formats to get your message across. A fee is only payable when someone clicks your advert, not when it is just displayed. You can set a daily limit of payments and do not have to commit a minimum spend.

Affiliate marketing via website links

Alison Barton is listed on the links pages on the websites of a number of businesses local to her (see above in Box 13.2), such as a locally based but nationally operating promotional gifts company, Funky Concepts, and a local solicitor. Her networking has allowed her to build these contacts, and they appreciate her as a reliable local provider and are happy to feature her business on their website.

One success factor is that the recommended business, called recipient, must be of genuine benefit to the customers of the linking business, also called referrer, Funky Concepts Ltd in our example. This means that the recipient needs to be in the same industry or complement your offerings. The affiliation can take many forms including:

▶ No fee to referrer;
▶ Commission to referrer for sales made or leads gained.

Monitoring the referrals can be done by an affiliate network provider to keep track of any commission or through questioning each new enquiry where they learned about you. Advantages include higher hit rate and higher conversion rates as links come from trusted sites.

Email marketing

Email marketing can be very effective when you have mastered the style and copy as well as learned which headers work best. There are numerous tools available that help to set up email campaigns. Yet the tools provide only the technical support and infrastructure, the actual content still needs to be created. It is helpful to use the available guides on copywriting for email marketing. Online infrastructure is offered for example by Mailchimp (www.mailchimp.com) or Campaign Master (www.campaignmaster.co.uk/). Email marketing has been found to be one of the most effective tools for SMEs (Riyad and El-Gohary, 2013).

QR codes

Quick Response Code is the trademark for a type of two-dimensional barcode, a machine-readable optical label with information about the item to which it is attached. A QR code consists of black modules arranged in a square grid on a white background. They can be read by an imaging device (such as a camera) and processed so that a direct link to a webpage is created and the webpage opens, thus shortening the customer journey.

QR codes have become common in consumer advertising, as they allow quicker access to a brand's website than by manually entering a URL. The impact is that their use increases the conversion rate bringing the viewer to the advertiser's website immediately.

The use of QR codes is free of any license, yet patented widely in the US, EU, Japan, by the company Denso Wave, which chose not to exercise their IP rights.

Case study

Our case study **Ben Smith** used QR codes to market his first start-up, an online magazine, as an effective way to bring potential buyers to the advertisers in his e-magazine and thus created a route to market for them to customers they would otherwise not have reached. It is also an example of a co-creation practice and principle. Here is how he describes it:

> The reason I used QR codes was as a way of keeping it lean whilst also keeping engagement. I found through research that people picked up and engaged with a magazine more if it was physical – but this obviously incurred large costs. If it's only online, then people don't engage, and ignore it, it's difficult to find a channel to attract people to read it. I'd been working with N. H. on one of his earlier ventures called Ark, which used QR codes on business cards to download information directly to your contacts on your phone. So I created a small credit card-sized branded card, which contained a QR code. If you scanned it, then the magazine would download directly to your smartphone or tablet.

Integrated events marketing (Eventbrite.com)

Eventbrite is an online platform that offers support in events marketing and online registrations for events, with or without payment. For events that do not charge a fee, the use is free of charge. For events that charge a fee, Eventbrite takes a fee for managing the payments, which can be done via PayPal, using a credit card or via cheque to the organizer. The system easily links with Mailchimp so that all contacts can be imported from there. The platform offers help with designing email invites and informs you of every registration and payment made. Before the event, registration lists are created and sent to the organizer. Ownership of data remains with the event organizer.

Added value includes the time that can be saved in event administration and on using a CRM system. Cost is reduced for staff time and software for CRM and event management. The data and information are held online in a central space so that wherever you are you can access it and share access with other co-organizers. It also creates a sense of familiarity for users, as so many organizations use it today.

Limitations include that the design is not very sophisticated, and you cannot differentiate yourself using it as many organizations already use it.

The next section discusses branding for start-ups.

13.3   Building a brand from the start

13.3.1 Everyone talks about "brand" – in different ways

What is a brand then? Many people use the term in different contexts with different meanings, and for that reason alone there are many definitions. Here is a definition that captures different aspects of its meaning.

> A set of associations that a person (or group of people) makes with a company, product, service, individual or organisation.
>
> (Design Council, www.designcouncil.org.uk/news-opinion/power-branding, accessed 19 August 2014)

A successful brand is an identifiable product, service, person or place, augmented in such a way that target customers perceive relevant, unique added values, which match their needs most closely. Furthermore, the brand's success results from being able to sustain those values in the face of competition.

Brands transmit perception about the product or service offered. Commercial organizations invest heavily in protecting their brand image and use legal protection (design right and trademark legislation) to prevent copying by others. Brands work by creating particular associations in buyers' minds, with symbols, colours, shapes or trying to evoke an image and sound.

Brand image influences the desirability of products and services, and this in turn affects the demand for those products and services.

When popular brands, such as Apple, bring out a new product they are sold out quickly, as buyers strive to gain products according to their *perception* of them, even if they might not have used or tried them. Different individuals will use different criteria to identify the most attractive option from their own perspective. It therefore follows that we can use communications to influence the perceptions of potential "customers".

No company can gain complete control over its brand, as it is subject to outside influences (changes in technology, extreme weather, to name a few), intelligent use of design, product/service proposition, organizational culture, etc.

Over the last two decades, the customer voice has become louder through social media, the Internet and mobile devices, including smartphones and tablet computers. As many consumers share insights on websites such as TripAdvisor and other online forums and on company Facebook pages they have gained much more influence on brands than ever before. This can have a big effect on the brand and the way it is perceived.

13.3.2 How to develop and manage your brand as a start-up from the start

Branding is an attempt to capture, create, influence and, ideally, control these associations to help the business perform better. The brand needs to make a company or person distinctive, trusted, exciting and/or reliable, to name a few attributes; naturally, these attributes need to be derived from the mission statement, vision and company objectives.

Branding helps start-ups nobody has heard of stand out from the competitor crowd and remain in people's minds. If you do not start a business with a unique product, but start another restaurant/consultancy/nursery/retail store with unique gifts, etc., then you have to work hard to differentiate yourself. The brand can help you a long way down that road and lift you out of the crowd if done well. Branding also creates an emotional link with customers if done well.

Typical elements in a brand can include:

- The company or product name;
- Colours;
- Graphics;
- Motto or tagline;
- Shapes.

Many of these elements are protected by trademarks for large companies; but it helps to protect a name when you start-up and have come up with a great name you would like to keep to your own business.

Brand building for SMEs has been found to consist of two stages and five steps (Centeno et al., 2013): during the first stage the brand identity is created, whereas in the second stage it is developed. The first phase is creating the brand as a person, where the brand has a lot of similarities to the features of the owner(s) or founders. During the brand as a product phase, owners develop the product as well as the brand with more focus on the product features than themselves. In the third phase, brand name, logo and colours are identified (as discussed above). Finally, when building the dimension of brand as an organization, the founder's wider values for how to run the business are codified in a vision and mission statements.

Let us learn from Frinter, Frumtious, as an example of product branding, and the personal brand Alison Barton Photographer: Boxes 13.3 and 13.5 illustrate how three of our case study companies realized their branding. The photographer Alison Barton uses the approach "I am the brand" where she and her story and skills are at the core of the successful brand.

Frumtious founder Ben Smith uses branding in a more traditional way. Box 13.4 shows his logo. The logo is the name "frumtious" and the strawberry replacing the letter "o", indicating that real fruit is in the products he sells. Both, he and Frinter founders, apply extensively social media channels to build and maintain the brand.

Box 13.3   Alison Barton's logo and self-presentation

Alison Barton has even used her initials to create her logo. She is her brand, crystallizing her passion, skills and professionalism in her logo. She realizes two of the levels of meaning discussed below: utilitarian function of the logo and company name is Alison Barton, Photographer; and naming the profession indicates the commercial level of meaning.

Source: © Alison Barton www.alisonbartonphotography.co.uk, accessed 1/1/2015

Source: © Ben Smith, 2013

When I was meeting our case study Frinter's co-founders Muhammad Ali and Shivam Tandon for the second time, they gave a presentation to students focusing part of the presentation on branding the venture from day one to become so recognizable that the brand name is eventually used as the generic term for the kind of product they provide. Box 13.5 shows their printer, the logo is next to the name "Frinter station" on the machine. "Frinter" is a play on printer and replacing the first letter with "f"; this attracts attention.

Box 13.5   Frinter's branding on the printer and copy machine

Brands have four levels of meaning to potential consumers:

▶ Utilitarian sign – an indication that this product or service does what it says or claims;
▶ Commercial sign – values of the brand such as value for money, quality;
▶ Socio-cultural sign – social effects of buying or not buying the product or service;
▶ Mythical value – heroic images about the product or service such as James Bond's Aston Martin.

It is the brand associations which are the most influential. Consider the social group requirements of teenagers. They have a need to belong to their social peer groups and actively seek "acceptable" brands and images such as Nike trainers to demonstrate belonging. We need to identify whether we can apply the brand concept and manage perceptions of others about your organization.

The next section outlines practices for marketing on a shoestring, on top of using social media and online directories.

13.4   Marketing on a shoestring

13.4.1   Tangible product and intangible product marketing – is there a difference?

There are some clear differences in marketing dependent on market type: B2C, B2B, B2G or C2C or C2B. Communication with different market segments needs to relate to their needs and use their language in order to be successful: when communicating and marketing to young people marketeers use language different to a women-only market. Similarly, different approaches apply to a student market or a social enterprise marketing to private sector large corporates.

Service marketing is different in several ways, as the product is not tangible and the quality for that reason is much more difficult to measure. Lovelock et al. (2009) identified the following common differences between goods and services:

▶ Most service products cannot be stored or registered in an inventory.
▶ Intangible parts most often dominate how value is created for customers, thus the customer needs help in distinguishing your service from that of competitors.
▶ Services are often abstract and their quality is difficult to grasp.
▶ Customers can be involved in co-production.
▶ People can be part of the service experience, thus affecting quality perception.
▶ Quality can be varied, as it is more difficult to maintain consistent service quality.
▶ Customer demand for a service and actual capacity to deliver it do not always match in terms of time.
▶ Distribution can be easier, as for information-based services it can be via electronic channels.

These differences have implications for services marketing. In particular, the people involvement aspect means that training staff to certain standards is much more important than when selling tangible goods. Similarly, customers may need to be educated to understand the service quality and its effect on their lives. The story of change is essential to include in marketing communication to ensure the difference the service makes is understood.

Applying the co-production principle for the *sustainable start-up* requires you to listen to customers to be able to optimize service quality and design on an on-going basis.

The next section discusses one key tool for marketing for start-ups, the contacts you already have and can develop.

13.4.2 Networking and word-of-mouth marketing for start-ups

Discussing networking again in the context of marketing shows the essential function of networking for start-ups; it has a function within strategy as well as marketing.

Word-of-mouth marketing is probably the most powerful of all channels because:

▶ You are always marketing your business, whether you want to or not.
▶ It is an interactive discussion between two individuals although the organization cannot control what is said.
▶ It allows for feedback and confirmation of the message.
▶ The source (friend) carries greater levels of credibility that an advertisement.

The power of appropriate networking cannot be underestimated. Our case studies **Vivek George**, Hong Kong, **Lewis Barnes**, UK, and **Richard Rodman**, US, illustrate how they used networking strategically for gaining customers and growing their start-ups.

 Case study

Vivek George has a large family network with family members living across the world, from India, to the UK, other Asian countries and the US. He decided early on that his only marketing tool, apart from social media, would be word-of-mouth. This meant that members in his worldwide family network checked their contacts to identify businesses, which might need his services, and created a link so that he always talked to potential customers to whom he had been recommended. This powerful focused networking brought clients rather quickly, so that in month two he was making a profit.

Lewis Barnes was also making a profit within a few months, as he used his wide-reaching tennis contacts to gain contracts for building tennis academies. All his contacts had been developed over years while playing tennis in international tournaments. This meant he had access to potential clients from day one.

Richard Rodman, however, had to start with no contacts when he came to university. He actively engaged early on in networking, becoming president of the student entrepreneurship society, amongst other things. He learned during his first start-up that without contacts no business development is possible. He has developed networking skills in many contexts and gained a reputation as an expert in crowdfunding.

13.4.3 Shared approaches to marketing

Affiliate online marketing is illustrated by the named local businesses recommending Alison Barton's services as a trusted local business on their websites (in Section 13.2.4 above). This is one example of a shared approach to marketing. Linking to each other's websites is often the most successful way of co-creating leads for each other.

When two businesses are sharing a printed flyer or postcard to market their products or services together is another example of shared marketing. This approach reduces printing costs significantly, as the higher the number of printed output, the lower is the unit cost. One side could be a designer offering his or her services whereas the other side could be a promotional items provider offering a special offer on flyers or mugs, for example.

13.5   Social media marketing for business

13.5.1   Introduction to social media for business

Most of you use social media daily. What really are social media? The term *social media* refers to the use of web-based and mobile technologies to turn communication into an interactive dialogue. Put simply, they are different types of Internet-based applications that allow creation and use of content by users. In this context we talk about the shift from a buyer-centred logic to a customer and user-centred logic of buying (Smith and Zook, 2011).

But are these media useful in the same way for all types of businesses at all times? Naturally, the answer is no. The key lies in selecting some and engaging in their effective use on a regular basis.

 Case study

Explore what **Alison Barton**, our photographer case study has chosen to use: a mixture of online directories as discussed above and the following social media channels:

Facebook: https://www.facebook.com/alisonbartonphotography

Instagram: http://instagram.com/alisonbartonphoto

Google+: https://plus.google.com/112724982039715047599/about

LinkedIn: http://uk.linkedin.com/pub/dir/Alison/Barton

Twitter: https://twitter.com/alison_barton

Flickr: https://www.flickr.com/photos/thebiponline/sets/72157625112382297/

The online directories were explained in Section 13.2.4 on digital marketing. In order to select some of the many social media on offer, it helps to briefly reflect on their different nature and core purposes. All social media have in common the one advantage for businesses that they can reach out to thousands of potential clients within minutes at no fee, and in 2013, 89% of all advertisers used free social media tools.

In 2013, worldwide the most used social media by business was Twitter, followed by Facebook and LinkedIn, then YouTube and with a gap Google+. Large businesses are increasingly paying for adverts on social media, as the effectiveness of placed adverts can be evidenced (Nielsen, 2013).

Social media sometimes are differentiated by their key purpose:

▸ Sharing – photos and videos (for example Flickr, YouTube), slides and books (Slideshare, BookCrossing);
▸ Social networking – keeping in touch and sharing news and activities you attend/create (for example Facebook, LinkedIn, Xing, Instagram, Pinterest, Google+);
▸ Social news – interaction via votes and comments on articles;

- Micro-blogging sites (best known is Twitter);
- Wikis – interaction via writing and adding articles and editing existing ones.

The key social media we will look at briefly for business use include:

- Twitter;
- LinkedIn;
- Facebook;
- YouTube;
- Instagram and Pinterest;
- Unltd World.

Kaplan and Haenlein differentiate social media by social presence/media richness and self-disclosure (2010, p. 62). Social media with high levels of self-disclosure and presentation as well as social presence are virtual social worlds, and there are companies making real money in those virtual worlds (Second Life is the best-known example). Low on social presence and media richness as well as self-disclosures are collaborative projects, such as all types of wikis (*Wikipedia* as one best-known example). Blogs and micro-blogs such as Twitter are high on self-disclosure yet low on media richness and social presence, whereas social networking sites are classified as having a medium level of media richness yet high level of self-disclosure (Facebook and Instagram as examples). Content communities sharing resources can be classified as low on self-disclosure and medium for media richness (examples are YouTube, SlideShare). This differentiation is useful, as it helps in choosing social media for the purpose they are built and can be applied in business marketing.

The next section outlines ways to use social media for business success.

 Case study

Here is what our case study **Alison Barton** says about two of the social media she uses:

Facebook is great for me as my client base is mostly all on Facebook and love sharing images through it. Instagram I initially set up for personal use but found clients were finding my account and following me and I like that they can see other images, which I snap on a daily basis.

13.5.2 Social media examples for business use

Twitter's info on Google highlights the instant communication you can have …

"Instantly connect to what's most important to you. Follow your friends, experts, favourite celebrities, and breaking news."

This quote highlights one important value added by social media. There are others:

- It is free of charge (yet it costs a business, as staff time costs money).
- Quick instant communication is possible.
- It is accessible from wherever you are – via smartphone, Wi-Fi, outside of the office, etc.

Limitations include:

- The time needed to update the news section/information regularly;
- The effect on working time as employees use them during work for private purposes;
- The risk of unfocused use that does not generate results for many businesses (as yet).

It has been pointed out that using social media effectively and wisely is still an issue. For that reason, many companies as well as individuals offer free (and paid-for) training or guides. (For an example see *The Twitter Guide Book: How To, Tips and Instructions*, by Mashable, http://mashable.com/guidebook/twitter/, accessed 4 August 2014.)

Micro-blogs like Twitter allow 140 characters to share some insight or news. You need to create a personal profile to be able to use it. Many CEOs of companies use blog pages or websites to share insights with their employees and key stakeholders; remember, the level of self-disclosure makes blogs the ideal tool to do so. Many TV or film stars have blogs, and so have politicians.

The limitations include:

▶ Customers might not like the blog content and comment badly on it on the net.
▶ Employees might voice their dissatisfaction about the company and the products/services.

LinkedIn is clearly a business networking site (B2B) that allows users to share their news with clients, staff and followers. You need to create a profile and can include photos, video, audio files, blogs. You can share up to 200 characters on news that are then sent to your network or the public.

Facebook is one of the world's largest networking sites. Founded by Mark Zuckerberg to keep in touch with fellow students once he had left university, it is now used by over a billion people worldwide. Increasingly, it is used by companies to target potential customers directly. You need to create a profile and decide who can have access to it, and who can write on "your wall". This is most effective when selling to consumers, sharing news and updates and appointments for services.

Content sharing sites – content communities

YouTube, and **SlideShare**, are content sharing sites. You do not need to create a profile for sharing content. In 2010 **YouTube** showed 100,000 million videos per day. You can publish a video visible for the whole world or create a link that you then send on to selected users. The latter way is used within other social media to limit the access to a video. This function enables you to have some level of control over who has access to it. Since 2006, Google owns it.

Businesses have used **YouTube** in different ways. Some PR departments of large corporates share keynote speeches by the company leading management and press announcements. Others use it for recruiting employees. And Procter & Gamble used it to invite consumers to upload a short video of themselves singing about a particular product.

Instagram combines sharing of photos and videos with social networking services. One feature is that all photos can only be a square shape, like the old Polaroid images, although most mobile phone pictures are rectangular. Founded only in 2010, it has become popular very quickly and has far more than 130 million users worldwide. Interestingly, the majority of users are women. The Instagram hashtag acts like a keyword and can offer a way for customers to find your company through engaging pictures.

Pinterest is a free visual discovery tool, the founders point out, and others talk about an online scrapbook or pinboard. Launched in 2010, it grew exponentially.

The Internet-based service focuses on users storing and sharing photos, called pins. A personalized media platforms can be created, which many use to find ideas and get inspired; others use it for collaboration on projects. Registration is necessary. As with Instagram, the majority of users are women worldwide, although not in the UK. Pinterest stores copies of all photos on their cloud server, and other users can copy your photos to create boards of their own. Businesses can create pages and promote their products and brands with pictures as a virtual storefront for a retailer, for example.

The big advantage is the visual appeal through using infographics, videos and pictures to convey an atmosphere and image of a company. Search engine optimization is important for users to find the content and needs attention.

Google+ was originally meant to be a competitor to Facebook and LinkedIn, yet it is much more than a social networking site. All Gmail users have to have a Google+ account. Since its launch in 2011 (as a web and app service) it has gained hundreds of millions of users. Its key advantage is the integration of many services and the search engine Google.

Google+ is competing with other providers of a number of services offered separately such as event marketing (Eventbrite), LinkedIn and Skype by providing these services all under one Internet "roof", Google. There is:

- Google Hangouts for video conferencing, integrated with other Google services, such as Google apps.
- Google Event for Google+ users to easily send out event invites not only to other Google+ users, including for Google Hangout meetings. Photos can be uploaded instantly and shared in a folder.
- Google+ Communities for discussions and Google Pages for a page with fans, Google My Business.

13.5.3 Social media optimization – the trend?

Social media tools and sites have mushroomed, and still new ones are on the rise. In order to keep on top of what you do and analyse what is said, social media monitoring for business is an important tool, before you engage with social media optimization.

Social media monitoring looks at when and where your company name or product name has been mentioned on the web. Even for the start-up using social media widely, it is important to find out by whom and where you and/or your product have been named. Take note on where, by whom and with what content and emotions and associations it has been mentioned. Do you need to respond to the post? And has your response been commented on again?

Plentiful tools exist, and those that are free include Google Alerts and Social Mention; others charge a variety of fees, such as Brandwatch and Webtrends. It needs some careful comparison before paying a fee as a start-up – these tools focus on different social media (Brandwatch has less coverage of LinkedIn, for example) – why not do it yourself using free tools to manage the process?

Social media optimization is then the next step, once you know which ones work for you and which ones do not. While mentioned earlier, it is essential to keep the tone and communication style the same across all social media, as it contributes to your brand image. If the tone is always corporate and formal do not suddenly just because you are using Facebook change the language to "all streetwise" and use very colloquial language.

The next section discusses marketing particular to social enterprises, yet not used only by them: social marketing and cause-related marketing. Section 13.7 then discusses the need for a marketing plan.

13.6 Cause-related marketing and social marketing

13.6.1 Cause-related marketing – an example of co-creation?

Have you ever bought a product that promises in the advertising and on the packing that 10% or 15% of its profits or a fixed amount such as £2 goes to a named charity or a particular cause, such as aid to a war zone? Examples include Cadbury Ltd partnering with the charity Save the Children to raise funds for the charity's work. Similarly, volunteers for Age Concern, the charity for supporting the elderly in the UK, knitted little hats that were added onto the lid of Innocent smoothie drinks. From all bottles sold with a knitted hat 25p was donated to Age UK. In this way, over £1.75 million was raised. These are examples of marketing partnerships that can be either corporate led or social enterprise/charity led. However, most of the research views this type of marketing from the perspective of the corporate, and not the social enterprise or cause (Steckstor, 2012). The effects of cause-related marketing on customers' attitudes and buying behaviour have been researched with some contrasting findings on the effect of this type of marketing on consumer buying behaviour. Some findings suggest a gain of new customers whereas others could not find any evidence for that.

The key goal for the commercial partner is to maximize the sales of the carrier brand (that is, the product or service they sell within this partnership) – and research shows that for-profits gain the most out of those partnerships in value from sales and the positive PR effect. It reduces the risk that the sum donated exceeds the financial return achieved by the promotion. There are many benefits for the commercial partner for this type of marketing, including the ability to differentiate itself from competitors and generate publicity, often resulting in increasing sales by existing buyers.

This type of marketing is increasingly becoming a way of achieving some corporate social responsibility goals across the world. There is evidence that it attracts new customers; some studies found that over 80% of interviewed consumers would switch brands if there were two products on offer with very similar features, quality, price and benefits. However, other studies looking closer at actual buying behaviour find little evidence of brand change (Cone Communications, 2013, Steckstor, 2012).

Benefits for the social enterprise partner, in particular the start-up, include raising awareness of the product or service and the organization, and differentiating itself as trustworthy and reliable by being selected by the established commercial company as a partner, provided the commercial partner is not violating the values and norms of the social enterprise. What does that mean? When a social enterprise promoting healthy eating, for example selling fruit jellies, chooses KFC as a partner, this would not raise the brand of a healthy eating company. Other benefits are clearly fundraising in a short period of time and increased publicity.

Challenges in this type of partnership working well for social enterprises can be:

▶ Partnership working requires resources that may not be available – staff in small organisations have multiple roles and cannot donate sufficient time to make the relationship a true partnership and often lack marketing skills to make it work best for them.
▶ Different cultures and unequal power and resources may lead to the social enterprise not gaining what they need in terms of publicity.
▶ Compromise and a collaborative approach is necessary.
▶ Decision processes take time – internal committees, board wishes and decisions, senior management team decisions, etc. can delay the start of such a partnership to bring in money.
▶ Mission can constrain ability to deliver on all aspects.

Done well, both partners benefit from reaching out to different audiences and increasing their reputation. And then co-creation works at its best.

13.6.2 Social marketing

Social marketing is not social media marketing but a distinct approach in marketing that aims to achieve behavioural change with the target customers. While it is used a lot by social enterprises in the health sector, it is not limited to non-profit organizations, in as much as the NHS uses it, so do private sector companies devoted to a particular cause, such as giving up smoking through buying a particular product such as electronic cigarettes or eating more healthily.

Social marketing is a conceptual framework or an approach to creating social good by solving social challenges through promoting behaviour change (Hastings et al., 2012). An example is programmes to quit smoking. The marketing needs to achieve two behaviour changes: to participate in the programme and to give up smoking.

In social marketing, the *core product* is conceptualized as the benefits the new behaviour will generate; in the case of giving up smoking these benefits include spending less on cigarettes, better health and fresher smell of clothes and the flat/house. The actual product is the new desired behaviour itself – in the case of smoking, not to smoke. The *augmented product* includes all tangible objects and services employed to support behavioural change, which could include free counselling or coaching and electronic cigarettes or patches that release small amounts of nicotine into the human body.

Market research needs to identify *barriers* to that behaviour change, often looked at as "cost of change", benefits and competition to behaviour change. Language, values, norms and how the current behaviour fits into daily lives as "normal" need to be identified.

Barriers tend to be the costs of adopting a different behaviour; it involves an understanding of what moves and motivates the target audience. Market insight is also concerned with internal drivers and competing behaviours – the factors which are perceived as "cons" to behaviour change. Costs can be psychological, time and effort related or financial in nature.

Benefits are something your target market wants or needs. They can be perceived in the desired and current behaviour and may include short-term benefits of continuing their current behaviour, and potential benefits of changing behaviour.

Benefits of an activity or behaviour may not be obvious to outsiders and require considerable "unpicking" before the insight is found. For example, stressed mums may attend smoking cessation meetings because there is a free crèche and therefore an hour of free childcare. Insight will come from understanding the perceived benefits of behaviours from the target consumer's point of view.

Competition may not be obvious. It may come from:

a) Behaviours the target audience have been "doing forever", such as smoking while watching TV;

b) Behaviours your target audience would prefer over the one you promote, such as smoking with friends as part of or after a night out;

c) Organizations which send messages out to counter or oppose the desired behaviour, such as the tobacco industry in relation to giving up smoking programmes.

Box 13.6 shows an example of a social marketing approach.

Box 13.6   Example of a social marketing approach

Childhood dental health is becoming increasingly poor in some parts of Dembridge town. Children aged between four and ten are having more teeth extracted than ever before, causing them to face the risks associated with general anaesthetics, as well as missing school and experiencing pain and distress.

This dental hygiene problem is due to several factors, including the cheapness and ready availability of sugary drinks and snacks, and parents being increasingly busy and not able to supervise their children every time they brush their teeth. Also, children's toothbrushes are often more expensive than adults' brushes.

There are five target groups for campaigns:

A – Parents;

B – Children aged 4–10;

C – Teachers;

D – Manufacturers;

E – Local shop owners selling children's toothbrushes.

The costs that are important in this context for each stakeholder group include:

A – monetary cost for regularly buying toothbrushes for children, the effort to supervise children when brushing teeth – costs time; changing shopping behaviour – buying less sugary drinks and snacks – costs time and money; extra travel to different shops costs time; learning about where to find new information about different food and reading new information on healthier eating – costs time and requires psychological effort; packing children's lunch – costs time and effort; taking children to the dentist or hospitals – costs time, effort; consoling them when they have toothache is challenging – costs effort and time; convincing children to change their buying behaviour might need incentives for behaviour change.

B – changing buying behaviour of snacks paid for with pocket money – costs time and effort, as healthier snacks might not be attractive; learning information about healthier eating and thinking about it requires time and effort creates a psychological cost and needs time – going shopping elsewhere, standing out from their peers when not having sweet drinks costs time and effort – they might be facing ridicule and mockery from peers.

C – informing children, giving information sheets, designing extra exercises – it costs time and psychological effort.

D – lowering recommended selling price is not in their economic interest, new design of toothbrushes costs money, finding ways to reduce costs time, money and effort production costs;

E – lowering selling price for kids brushes – monetary cost, extra campaigns – costs for material, signing, etc.

13.6.3 Social impact marketing or social difference marketing

The most recent form of marketing is not yet fully established, and I call it social impact marketing. This is a marketing style and approach aimed at showcasing to potential buyers what difference to society or environment has been made in the past with the product/service bought and will be made. This is for the whole organization and all its products and services, for an unlimited period of time. While this kind of marketing is not new (Cone Communications, 2013), its quantity has risen over the last decade.

For some social enterprises and charities there is increasingly the dilemma: do they market the social difference made when purchasing a product/service or do they focus on that the product stands by itself? The answer needs to be different for different types of products and services. A cafe run by a social enterprise working with ex-offender staff to rehabilitate them into the normal working environment might not want to make this public, or a clothing and accessories business having staff that are recovering from some mental illnesses will want to protect their staffs' right to privacy. These two examples show that the decision on the marketing approach again needs to be linked to the vision and mission of the organization. If the mission is to raise awareness about an issue as well as generating income to improve the situation of those people suffering from a condition or being affected by a situation such as having been in prison, then the decision to use social impact marketing is more likely to be "yes" than if the mission is to empower these individuals by providing them with employment they might otherwise not find.

Similarly, the fair trade movement created the question for some shop owners if they focus their marketing on the fact that the products are fairly traded, that is, producers from countries in development get a fairer share of the profit generated from raw material to finished product, or do they focus on the benefits the products have alone. The answer to the question is the same, that is has to be mission and vision led.

Since the discussion of social impact and social return on investment grew bigger in the US and Western Europe, Australia, before the UK had a law (Social Value Act, 2013 (or Public Services Act)) asking public authorities to engage with social enterprises and show social impact, the need to showcase social difference made has become more important. Highlighting social impact can help to attract donations, funders and contracts from government agencies and local government to be able to compete either with other social enterprises or with private sector for-profit businesses, including large corporates.

There is a good argument to use some metrics that make the social difference visible, without necessarily mentioning all the various beneficiaries, where that does not feel appropriate.

If £1 spent/invested can create £3.50 in value that can be used in different ways to create value for the community, this is a useful tool to use for demonstrating social return on investment. Additionally, using compelling case studies and stories combined with facts illustrating the above figures of added value can bring evidence to life in a different way and position the social enterprise and every other organization so that it stands out from the competition.

Thus, instead of only highlighting the unique selling points of products or services sold to a customer, the social projects and their outcomes, which are financed with the profits generated, are featured simultaneously. This can be the difference made for a particular group of people (young disadvantaged or the elderly) or the environment or a particular possibly disadvantaged area. Secondly, the social value created is put at the forefront of the marketing approach: improving health of a disadvantaged group, reducing the carbon footprint, etc.

A recent survey with social enterprises in the UK in 2013 revealed that there is an increasing confidence amongst social enterprises using their status for PR and marketing: 78% used the social enterprise status for marketing to a greater extent than in previous years. Amongst recently started social enterprises, 88% use their status for marketing (Social Enterprise UK, 2014).

The next section argues that the *sustainable start-up* benefits from some form of marketing planning.

13.7 Do I need a marketing plan?

13.7.1 Advantages of a written marketing framework

A written marketing framework enables you to identify better which activities are effective and under what conditions. When you know what works best, the *sustainable start-up* process can be optimized. If you read other textbooks or online advice, different terms are used for planning marketing activities, often interchangeably: marketing plan and marketing strategy. We use *marketing plan* for the report that outlines objectives, targets for the activities and financial performance measures from the marketing budget.

There are many benefits of planning your marketing: identifying risks and weak points, knowing about potential costs, and budgeting for them. Marketing practice is never a linear process, but rather spiral in nature, as you will have to go back to doing something else in the Ps once you have considered what works and what feedback customers gave you. But, planning it out encourages strategic and forward thinking. Sharing a plan with others is of great value, particularly when key partners are involved, to ensure shared goals and understanding of key objectives.

An integrated marketing communications planning process requires a link from the organizational start-up strategy (what the organization wants to be or be seen to be), mission and vision and financial business targets to the marketing strategy and plan.

It often includes the six key aspects outlined below to ensure that a consistent message reaches the required audience(s). The planning process itself works in different ways in different organizations; however, one of the most common models is the SOSTAC model explained below.

▶ *Situation analysis*
  Where are you now? This requires you to analyse the current situation and the existing perceptions of your target audiences.
▶ *Objectives to be defined*
  Where are you going? What do you wish to achieve with your communications plan?
▶ *Strategy*
  How do you get there? What approach will you adopt to achieve these objectives?
▶ *Tactics*
  What will you actually do? What types of marketing communications vehicles will you use and why? When? The marketing implementation table addresses most of these aspects in Section 13.7.2.
▶ *Action*
  Who will do what and when? Delegating responsibility within the organization is needed.
▶ *Control*
  How will you know you have succeeded? How can you measure if perceptions have changed? You have to monitor and evaluate what you do.

Situation analysis: You need to consider a number of aspects, which we gathered in the previous chapters: operational aspects in Chapter Six, and market research findings in Chapter Five.

You need to summarize the goals and objectives of your start-up. Where do you want to be in a few years' time? What are the organizational ambitions? Are they realistic? What resources are available in terms of money and staffing? Who would be involved? What skills does the staff have? What is the likely level of budget available?

Secondly, do you understand the marketing environment in which you are communicating? What factors will have an influence? Can you identify political, economic, social and technological factors that could make a difference to the way in which we operate? What about legal issues?

Thirdly, you need to make sure to understand your target audience(s). All the previous chapters have provided plenty of insight into these aspects.

Smart objectives: What means would you use to achieve your objectives? Would you conduct a public relations campaign? What about a newsletter? Perhaps you would conduct an advertising campaign? What about posters or brochures delivered door to door? You need to have clear ideas about what is the correct approach allowing for the issues and constraints (lack of money, staffing and expertise) that we have identified in our situational analysis.

Strategy/implement with good tactics: This is the detailed implementation part of your plan. What message do you want to communicate? How will you do this in detail? What specific marketing communications activities will you need to implement? We discuss this below in Section 13.7.2 under Marketing Action Plan.

Actions: This will be a detailed listing of all the activities that will be needed and an allocation of responsibilities to individuals with timescales and budgeted costs to complete the activities.

Control/Evaluation: How will you measure how successful you have been in achieving your objectives? How would you know whether this was due to your marketing communications or other external factors? You need to devise specific means of measuring your achievements.

There is a lot of literature about managing impact and return on marketing; for suggested books and resources see the Further Reading on the companion website to this book.

13.7.2 Marketing action plan

The marketing action plan, then, is a to-do list that helps you (and your team) to put planned activities into action. It takes all its information from the marketing plan and strategy. Table 13.2 gives you an example of entries in a marketing action plan. It lists the person leading on the marketing activity, the resources needed with associated costs, what milestones and goals there are to reach and by what point in time.

Important is to note that the co-creation process builds on the contacts and interested parties developed during the planning and research phase.

Table 13.2 Marketing action plan

Marketing activity	Who leads it	Milestones and goals	Dates for milestones	Resources: time and other input	Cost in £ / $
YouTube: Create videos for YouTube	CEO/ owner	First video created and uploaded about the owner; second video about the clients (2) with greatest benefits	First video by March 31, 201x; second one by June 30, 201x	Make video 1/2 hour; read guidelines on good videos – 1 hour	CEO time 1.5 hours; checking the video by IT associate and editing it – 1 hour of his time
Facebook: Set up social media page and discussions	Placement student	Set-up and three messages	Set-up done – May 15, 201x, three messages May 30, 201x	Pictures, text from CEO for set-up; message text/content from CEO	2.5 hours; hourly rate for placement student
Develop ambassadors for your product	CEO/ owner, marketing director	Develop at least 5 people to ambassadors in 3 months; develop another 10 the next two months	[Specific dates]	Time and marketing materials paper and online	Printing of materials; hourly rate for CEO/ marketing director
Network wisely	All staff	Gain at least 10 leads for potential business per week in month one; gain at least 20 leads in the following weeks	[Specific dates]	Time, marketing materials, phone, travel time; membership fees; fees for attending networking events	Phone cost; marketing material printing cost; travel cost; membership fees; fees for attending networking events

As pointed out in previous sections, writing this marketing action plan down, and ideally hanging this up on a wall, helps you to keep focused on what you want to achieve. When working with associates/placement students remotely, share this action plan via e-sharing platforms such as Dropbox folders or Google documents, etc.

You can download a template for the marketing action plan from the Palgrave website (www.palgrave.com/companion/hill-start-up).

13.8   Concluding remarks and application of new insights

Chapter Thirteen discussed for the first time in a focused way marketing processes and issues. Only when a viable venture opportunity has been identified does it make business sense to start considering the practical details of marketing and branding we discussed. For business modelling and cost structure, marketing costs of suggested marketing activities had to be outlined in order to establish all the costs and the potential viability of your business venture. Table 13.1 helped with that evaluation. The fact that you read this chapter hopefully means that you are working on a viable business venture opportunity and planning its launch.

This chapter introduced the newcomer to marketing to some essential concepts, such as AIDA – attract attention, interest, create the desire and action to buy. It discussed branding in a basic way to create an understanding of its goals and nature and pointed to further reading on how to deepen the understanding and apply it to your own venture opportunity in development, the *sustainable start-up*. Marketing planning and implementation were discussed in sufficient detail to get the *sustainable start-up* beginning on its marketing.

For social enterprises, a number of particular marketing types were discussed: cause-related marketing takes the viewpoint of the for-profit business that uses the fact that it donates a very small amount of its income generated through product sales to a social cause. For the social enterprise this can mean that it generates funds through its work and beneficiaries being mentioned in the marketing activities of a for-profit business.

Social marketing was introduced as a particular form of marketing that at its core attempts to change behaviour, such as giving up smoking, eating more healthily, etc. This form of marketing follows a step-by-step process that has been well established, researched and practised worldwide. Other marketing types more common to social enterprises include benefit-focused marketing that highlights the social difference buyers make through purchasing a service or product.

Revision questions and applying new insight to your *sustainable start-up*

1   Define marketing. Why is it important to consider what it really means?
2   What is AIDA? Explain the term behind each single letter.
3   List some practical marketing essentials.
4   What are the four levels of meaning that brands have for customers?
5   Define social marketing and cause-related marketing and differentiate these two types of marketing from each other.
6   Use the example of Table 13.2 and select the marketing activities you plan to carry out; additionally, go back to the activity in Chapter Seven on business modelling and the results you gained there, and to Chapter Twelve on business planning.

7 Draw up in detail responsibilities for marketing activities, and their timing, using a Gantt chart. As a rule of thumb, you alone should spend at least one and a half, better two, days per week on marketing.

8 List the social media you choose, and focus on two or three as a maximum. Note your reasons for selecting them, and their dis/advantages in your start-up diary.

14

PUBLIC RELATIONS AND SALES

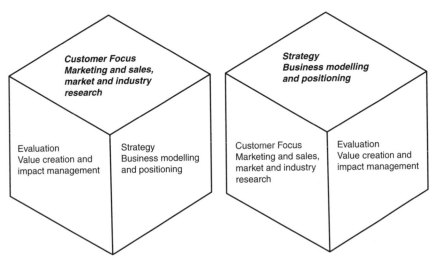

Figure 14.1 The Cube Customer Focus and the Cube Strategy
Source: © Hill, 2012.

Summary

Chapter Fourteen discusses public relations as an important tool for the *sustainable start-up* (see Figure 14.1). The focus is on practical tips and the rationale for using a variety of PR tools, from press release to sponsorship even the start-up can use. Sales is introduced as a process of co-creation, providing a customer relationship is struck that genuinely values the customers and their needs. Based on the developed theory of change for the customers' experiences, the story of change is a simple convincing story based on the research findings for customers' wish for change. Sales for social enterprises differs depending on what business model they follow and the kind of products they offer. This might differ for different services or products and thus may differ slightly, or significantly, from selling.

CONTENTS

14.1   Public relations

14.1.1 Introduction to public relations

> Using yourself to get out and talk about it is a lot cheaper and more effective than a lot of advertising. In fact, if you do it correctly, it can beat advertising hands down and save tens of millions of dollars.
>
> (Richard Branson, *Strategy+Business Magazine*, 2013)

> It takes 20 years to build a reputation and five minutes to ruin it. If you think about that, you'll do things differently.
>
> (Warren Buffett)

What is PR? There are many definitions. What many have in common is that it is an organized and planned on-going effort to establish and maintain mutual understanding between an organization and its stakeholders in society. It is also about reputation, what others perceive about you and say about you and your business.

Generally speaking, public relations makes use of media for its own organized reputation management. This does not mean that PR is free, yet it can save a lot of money (as Richard Branson's quote points out). A business may sponsor a local children's football team in order to build a positive image of its interest in the local community as part of a PR campaign. Although they have not paid for any media, this engagement would help to try to make sure that they gained some free coverage in the local paper communicating a very clear message to the readers.

Your reputation is also built by others, whether you want it to be or not. For that reason it makes sense to have a strategy and a practical approach to manage your reputation yourself as much as you can. Warren Buffett's quote highlights how important reputation management is.

Public relations can focus on external and internal communications.

External PR

External PR works in conjunction with the media. Press and television media constantly seek newsworthy items to bring to their audiences. PR professionals can utilize this to communicate messages about their organization and communicate with their public (see Section 14.1.2 on press releases below). If there is a **major** news story about your Start-Up it may be possible to organize a press conference for a number of publications' reporters, such as winning a grant or a competition. This will require careful planning and the founder(s) will need to be prepared to answer difficult questions. Most newspapers are more than happy to feature a successful start-up.

Word-of-mouth: This is probably the most powerful of all channels:

▶ It is an interactive discussion between two individuals, although the organization cannot control what is said.
▶ It allows for feedback and confirmation of the message.
▶ The channel (friend or contact) carries greater levels of credibility than an advertisement.
▶ It works as a channel for marketing in terms of marketing a particular event, tangible product or service as well as creating a reputation for the owner or a founding team of a venture.

Internal PR

Internal PR is about communicating within an organization, including outside stakeholders, such as beneficiaries. Staff members have a psychological need to feel part of the organization and be recognized for their contribution to the organization's success. When organizations expand beyond one or two individuals it becomes increasingly difficult to make sure everybody is informed about what is going on within the organization. And for teams working remotely, this is even more important, as so much information can get lost.

There are a number of approaches that can be used:

▶ Internal newsletters – these need to be regular and informative. They also need to be interesting.
▶ Staff meetings – possible for small numbers of employees, but sometimes organizations have key relationships with individuals who are not staff members but have a close link (for example parents of children at a school, volunteers and suppliers).
▶ Electronic media – emails, intranets (internal organizational private networks), blogs (online open diaries) and chat-rooms (interactive electronic chat facilities usually subject based).
▶ Online meetings on a regular basis, sharing documents online using appropriate platforms such as Dropbox, Google documents, Instagram and others.

The next section briefly discusses some of the most used PR tools start-ups can use effectively: press release, media interview, crowdfunding, participation in start-up competitions, sponsorship and the PR spin on market research (see Figure 14.2). These six approaches have in common that they are easy to do, do not cost a lot of money or time and can have a large effect to raise awareness of your business.

14.1.2 Press releases

The press release is a well-established tool to raise awareness free of charge through online and print newspapers in the local and regional area. It is a short text you write yourself and send off to online magazines or newspapers with the focus on telling them about something interesting to their readers that is innovative and possibly makes a difference to the local area or someone's life.

Online businesses that do not have a local base can still use it to create a more direct following in the area where the founder(s) lives or the warehouse office premises are.

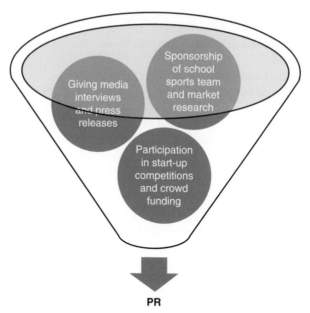

Figure 14.2   Easy-to-use start-up PR tools

According to Blythe (2012) good press releases can be more effective than advertising for the following reasons:

▶ The space in the medium is free so there is better use of the promotional budget.
▶ The message credibility is enhanced because it is in the editorial part of the paper.
▶ The message is more likely to be read because readers buy the newspaper to read the news stories.

DO's for getting a press release published include:

▶ Inform the journalist, but stories must not be thinly disguised advertisements. There is a limit to what you can include in the story about product features and benefits. Provide the wider context for your business, including information on the competition.
▶ Stories must be newsworthy. Newspapers will not publish information about your prices or discounts, but they will publish a write up on your whole organization running the London Marathon for charity.
▶ Have a case study ready that illustrates the effect your product has on a user.
▶ Write in accessible language and use as little jargon as possible; if you have to use a technical term, explain it immediately.
▶ Create a flow and storyline that keeps the reader wanting to read to the end.
▶ Use direct quotes from customers, and yourself, the founder.
▶ Write in the third person about yourself.
▶ Stories must fit the editorial style of the magazine or paper to which you send it. Different publications have different readers and you need to tailor the press release for the individual style used. Online newspapers have different styles than those that exist only in print.

14.1.3 Giving interviews

Many journalists are interested in a new start-up that makes a difference or does something different, as it can provide the basis for a great story. Finding out who the relevant business or news editors are helps to prepare for the email and phone contact with them; find out who they are on the newspaper's website and professional networks like LinkedIn or Google+.

Journalists can do at least two kinds of interviews with a start-up: a news interview and a profile of the (co-)founders that is of interest to local people/businesses or has some newsworthy angle to it. To get the most out of the interview, it is best to prepare thoroughly on what you want to get across and practice that, as you will be challenged to show some insight into yourself or the business you might not want to share.

The journalist might want to get something different out of the interview than you do, so you need to be able to direct the conversations towards the messages you want to get across.

DO's include:

▶ Be well prepared on the facts you want to get across.
▶ Practise talking about what you want others to know about and going back to those topics.
▶ Research the kind of information they might be interested in for the newspaper's target audience through reading interviews that were published in the past.
▶ Research the style of articles written, so you can offer something that fits the style.
▶ Be careful about what you say, even about what has been said "off the record", as it might still go into the article.
▶ If you do not know an answer to a question, say so and offer to get back to the journalist with the answer; ensure you do that within 24 hours, ideally.

When to contact a journalist in the start-up process needs careful consideration. You need to have enough to say that is newsworthy yet want to use the interview to get attention and leads for your business. Ask for interviews for launching the start-up, a great success such as a contract won or an award won. Keep in mind to *practise co-creation*: you want to be featured in the newspaper or magazine and the journalists want a great story, so do enable them to have an easy way to gain a good story for their work.

14.1.4 Competitions and crowdfunding

There are plenty of start-up competitions, as outlined in Chapter Nine on finance. Participation with either IP-protected goods or even only slightly innovative value propositions that work allows you to raise the start-up's profile in many ways.

Using any crowdfunding platform to gain some funding is also a great PR activity: even those who might not fund the venture learn about what it does and if they like it might become customers. Those who do fund it, will talk about it positively in their networks, thus spreading the word and providing free PR. Should the capital raising goal be too unrealistic in either amount or time period set, this might create some negative publicity. A list of crowdfunding platforms in the UK, US and a number of other countries were discussed in Chapter Ten.

14.1.5 Sponsorship

Sponsorship is a great way of raising awareness of your brand and company, even as a start-up. While the initial investment might seem daunting as a one-off expense, the pay-off can be of great value when done appropriately. Sponsorship for start-ups can be done in many ways and needs to focus on where the target customers might spend time in their leisure activities, sports activities, travel, and what they would regard as an appropriate vehicle for such a product. Examples include:

▶ T-shirts and/or bags for a school's sports team for games with other schools, or a local rugby or football club;
▶ Free branded goods to a local charity event;
▶ Mugs, branded, for the above and many other promotional items that are branded.

A luxury good seller, such as for handbags, might not gain much out of sponsoring the local rugby club, if the club is not yet famous. There is also no ideal strategic fit with rugby fans and luxury handbags.

In particular, when the sponsorship enables an organization to do what they otherwise would not have been able to do due to lack of equipment or time; this can make good news features.

14.1.6 Market research

Chapter Five discussed in detail why initial and regular market research is important. From a PR perspective, initial market research is an important activity to get the company name and product/service into circulation, that is, to raise awareness. Interesting findings from this research are also worth mentioning to a journalist for a local/national newspaper.

Regular market research has the same effect and can be used to distribute the news that, for example, a product has changed or a brand new taste, size or material is being developed, while researching customer and public perception of it. Presenting these findings is interesting to networks and their events, and professional associations and press releases; it is worth including them in a newsletter or in an update on social media, such as LinkedIn.

The last four suggestions illustrate again the co-creation approach to a *sustainable start-up*. A good quality good or service will remain in the market, if the change in customer experience is sufficiently important, so that people believe in it, even if they personally might not purchase it, yet know people who do. Taking part in competitions, ideally being shortlisted, crowdfunding and sponsorship all create a following that provides plenty of communication for the business and input to develop it so that it meets the customer needs even better.

The next section discusses sales and ways to organize it for the *sustainable start-up*.

14.2 Sales processes and sales practice

14.2.1 What sales really is and when to consider it

Selling is an old established trade. It got a bad name in the past through sales people who were dishonest about the product's quality and features they were selling. This often

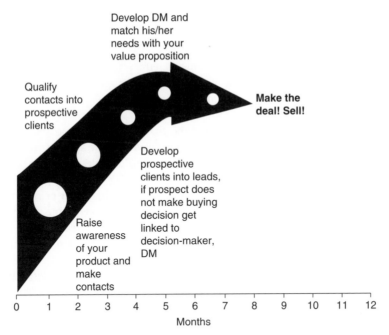

Figure 14.3   The simple 5-step sales process

misleading product-led sales practice, which ignored the person of the buyer, could and can be found in the business-to-business (B2B) or the business-to-consumer (B2C) markets.

The traditional process of selling included the following five or seven steps (see Figure 14.3):

- Raise awareness and make contacts.
- Qualify contacts into prospective clients.
- Develop the prospective client – into a lead.
- If a prospect cannot make the buying decision, get linked to the person in the organization that can make the decision (decision-maker) (this step is left out if the contact is also the one who makes the purchasing decision).
- Establish if that decision-maker (DM) is sales ready.
- Develop the opportunity and match the DM's needs with the change you can make.
- Make the deal successfully and sell the product/service.

Raising awareness (often carried out by marketing (and PR) activities) is the first step that can be realized through all forms of networking already discussed. Then, you have to find out if the contacts you made are interested in buying the product, and if not, if there is someone they know, in their organization, that might. This is often called qualifying the contact into a prospect. If you then have a prospect, you need to establish if they make the buying decision.

If that is not the case, you need to get linked to the person in the organization that can make the decision, but work with the interested prospect how to convince the decision-maker to actually make the buying decision. The areas to explore include asking when do they need the change your product offers to happen? Rarely that is right away. Nevertheless, keep telling the "theory and story of change" to the interested prospect and buyer. When the buyer is sales ready, they might even talk to you in person.

More often, they are not sales ready when you meet them – most prospects are not and need to be further educated and nurtured.

This is where the real sales process starts; develop the opportunity that matches the lead's needs with the change you can make, only then the actual sales can be made. Use the theory and story of change, how and why the change will happen, as part of the story you tell. The last step is when the deal has been made successfully.

This deal costs money, and this is where the theory and story of change need to explain in detail the whole value proposition around the change, from free updates, helplines or information services, warranties, training or costs of delivery where appropriate.

This process can take months from the first contact to the sales, and in particular can take longer for higher value goods or service contracts in B2B markets. Figure 14.3 shows the length of the process as about eight months, yet it can be longer or much shorter. As a newcomer, the start-up can expect an even longer development time, as possibly no relationship exists that can be developed and contacts have to be developed. As a practical rule of thumb, the higher the price of the good, and the higher the sophistication, the longer is the sales process on average.

At what time in the start-up process should you start thinking about sales? Depending on which type of market you are entering, this should be as early as possible for B2B markets. The general and administrative cost of sales need to be considered as early as possible, in the feasibility stage at least, as an estimate of the cost should be established. More generally, sales needs to be considered already in the market research phase, as research establishes named contacts in phase one of the sales process. Similarly, during the secondary market research as well as industry research, information on trends in sales over the previous years ideally needs to be gathered, as the sales forecast for feasibility study and business plan needs to be based on the most realistic figures and numbers that exist at the time of forecasting.

Some of you might ask: where does PR stop and sales start? There is clearly an overlap, as PR is focused on raising awareness – more so for the start-up as a whole as well as the founder(s), and much less for an individual product, whereas raising awareness of the product is much more at the focus at the first part of the sales process. Yet, at all times sales also raises awareness of the company behind the product. Similarly, PR is included by some authors under marketing, and thus marketing and sales clearly overlap. Marketing is the overall process of communication between the start-up and the external environment (and there is internal marketing to staff, board members, etc., as well). Sales is much more relationship driven; it is focused on each client and on their perceptions and needs and adjusts the story and theory of change to their particular needs. Then the above-discussed total cost of ownership or total value proposition develops into a partnership discussion on how best to realize the biggest change in the customer experiences that is worth the price written on the tag.

The next few sections offer some tools that help the *sustainable start-up* to manage the processes without restricting them and to enable a customer-centred start-up.

14.2.2 Sales forecasts, budgets and the 80/20 rule

 Sales forecasting is the attempt to predict the amount of units you are going to sell in a defined time period, per month, quarter or year, for example. This has to be based on all available research that was hopefully gathered in the activities you carried out while working your way through other chapters. Chapter Nine on finance sources and Chapter Ten on financial forecasts outlined the need for a sales forecast in detail. If you are not familiar with forecasting, go to these two chapters.

The 80/20 rule is known as the Pareto principle that applies in many areas. It indicates that 80% of the desired sales outputs are achieved with 20% of the clients/inputs; similarly, 80% of all profits come from 20% of all services or products. While this does not need to be taken literally, it gives the idea that in many cases small businesses make the largest amount of income with a limited number of clients. Or with a positive spin: a small proportion of your efforts provide most of the results.

What can you do to predict that when you have not even started trading? This is where your already carried-out market research, and in particular target customer research, provides the data you need. Look again for secondary findings on (using Key Note and Mintel, for example):

▶ Sales of products in that subsector and region you are in (where applicable);
▶ Sales per customer groups you identified as target or you created;
▶ Profitability of customer groups (willingness to pay higher prices) right now;
▶ Profit margin of your product(s).

Identify the primary customer group you will be selling to and how much they spend currently on the type of product you intend to sell. Hopefully, you decided to enter the market with the most profitable product and target customer(s) that have the money to buy it now. Which are the most effective and profitable channels for marketing that lead to actual sales your test trading and customer exploration has shown you.

Carrying out sales costs money, naturally, and the cost of sales activities should be included in the marketing budget. The sales budget is the amount of money estimated to carrying out sales. You might want to consider using a sales agent, buying in services of a leads generator or buying databases from companies whose customers have purchased in the past similar products or services where that applies. For truly unique products the latter will not apply.

The next section discusses sales planning for the *sustainable start-up*. As outlined in Chapter Twelve on business planning, the flexible approach is essential, yet using practical tools such as flip chart and Gantt charts will be of great advantage to visualize the information for all stakeholders to share and contribute.

14.2.3 Sales strategy and implementation plan

The sales strategy brings together the tactics, activities and the resources needed to achieve successful sales (see Figure 14.4). The *sustainable start-up* needs to keep a bird's-eye view on the optimal combination of those three areas in order to achieve the objectives most efficiently.

In Figure 14.3 we discussed the idea of the sales process, though in a linear model. The last two steps were identified as the actual sales process. The sales implementation plan usually starts in the previous phase when qualifying prospects and identifying leads, that is, company staff with decision power and the budget, developing the need to buy the product soon.

The sales plan needs to be regarded as a to-do-list that helps in keeping an overview of what needs doing and by whom as well as monitoring the customer journey from

Figure 14.4   Sales strategy elements

Table 14.1   Simple sales plan template

Sales activity example:	Who does it?	What resources are needed?	When/how often is it done?
Keeping in touch with contacts who have not yet bought – via email or phone	CEO/sales consultant	Database with contact details; phone/email	Monthly or bi-monthly

enquiry onwards to ensure best quality attention and prospect building. It needs to be guided by smart sales goals and actions needed to reach them, broken down to weekly and monthly goals with associated activities. Table 14.1 outlines a possible way to account for the required sales activities with time plan; an Excel sheet or Gantt chart can illustrate the activities in a simple way.

14.2.4 Sales for social enterprises

The sales process can differ for social enterprises, dependent on several factors:

▶ Has the chosen business model a focus on the financial model profit generator/trade-off model or trading to generate profits?
▶ Who are the customers the social enterprise is selling to – B2B, B2C, B2G?
▶ Are the customers paying the full price or a reduced price?
▶ Is the trading activity itself having a social impact?

If the business model is the profit generator model (see Section 7.4, Chapter Seven), for the whole organization or for one service or programme, then generating as much profit as possible through the trading activity is a key overarching goal of the purpose of the organization. The profit generator model's purpose is to make as much money as possible with any trading activity; profits are rather called surplus and used to provide free-of-charge or low-cost services to those who cannot (fully) pay for the services or products they need.

In this case, the services and products will be sold at the best possible surplus. Marketing, PR and sales approaches will be similar to those discussed earlier in the context of for-profit ventures. What may be different is the style and content of marketing as outlined in the marketing chapter, Chapter Thirteen. The social impact of the profits gained could be highlighted in the marketing message, and the social change that can be achieved with individuals, using case studies, could be a marketing message. The deal making should focus on the last two points as a rationale for not lowering prices and link to the value of the social change element the business clients can use for their own marketing.

If the customers are government departments of publicly funded organizations, then the wider benefit to society and possible savings in public expenses need highlighting – that is, a change in the marketing message; yet the profit-making is as important as for commercially focused enterprises. This is unfortunately an aspect often overlooked by government departments, and commercial enterprises alike, when dealing with social enterprises; the assumption is made they do it for less and do not want and need too much of a profit. Social enterprises need to highlight that the profit is called surplus and is much needed, as it is being used to provide services for free or low cost to those who cannot afford them. Trading itself has not a direct social impact, but the surpluses have, so an indirect social impact. If those purchasing services or products know that the price they pay means that those in need can have the same product cheaper, this can make the deal for those customers with a philanthropic attitude. One example is that with every ten pairs of shoes that are being bought, one young person in a country in development gets a pair of shoes for free.

For social enterprises working towards the trade-off model, when the trading activity itself has a direct social impact, then this would mean that more social impact can mean less financial organizational surplus. A social enterprise employing staff from disadvantaged backgrounds might have less effective staff for a while and can only make a lower profit. This is an internal balance the managers have to strike on how many staff with this background they can afford to use. For the sales process this does not necessarily have an impact on the sales steps or the deal making as such. It can influence the deal making and thus the total product price setting; if the management decision is to make a deal in order to bring money in, then the price can be reduced.

If the model is a member- or staff-owned organization, where members gain a share in the profits dependent on their purchases from the organizations they are members of or work for, and the customers are predominantly non-members, then the message for the deal with non-members needs to reflect that. The sales argument for deal negotiation can only point out the social benefits of the deal for the members or staff owning the organization, thus having a weaker case than those working with the profit generator or trade-off model with a sliding price scale.

The next section looks at the practice of selling and the small steps for making a successful deal.

14.3   The practice of selling

14.3.1   General insight from practitioners

At the start of my own sales activities I discovered how easy sales can be when you truly believe that what you offer is of value to others. From the start of the contact with a potential buyer you need to be comfortable with the role you are in and happy to take control of the process.

The seven-contact rule is an experience-based rule that suggests you need to have had seven contacts with a potential buyer or prospect until you can be certain that the prospect cannot be turned into a buyer before giving up.

Here are some Do's to consider for making selling easy and successful for you:

1) Have a genuine interest in the client/potential client.

Most people get a sense if someone is insincere or dishonest, and why would they buy from such a seller? Listen to what their needs and pains are and find out what they tried to do to address them. Show a genuine desire to help. Customers have to be the focus of every conversation, after all – when they buy from you they keep you in business.

2) Have a genuine total belief in the value of the product you sell.

While indicated under 1), just doing a job and selling because you have to is an attitude people pick up on. If you cannot be passionate or enthusiastic about your product, then why are you selling it? Both of these emotions are highly convincing to any listener and in particular for a potential buyer. Focus on those aspects/features of the product that make a real difference to your buyers' lives. While there might be a few, or even just one aspect that is not as good as the competition, you do not have to mention it. When asked, be honest and explain why this really does not matter that much in the big scheme of the overall benefits the product offers.

3) Be knowledgeable about the market and industry you are operating in – be the "expert".

Ideally, become an expert in the niche market, or the wider industry segment. This creates credibility and confidence in the perception of the potential buyer.

Show authority in the way you talk about the customers' pains and other solutions in the marketplace weaker than what you offer. Combine confidence in talking about what you know with a relaxed attitude to the situation; it does not matter if they buy today or tomorrow, you have already a good number of clients in your portfolio. No need to push anybody to become one, is there?

4) Decide to spend more time with prospects who can make the purchasing decision.

While networking is great, it is ok to spend only little time with some attendees, and much more time with others. Concentrate your efforts on the ones who have the authority and resources to make a purchasing decision, and who have the interest in your products because they have a need/pain that needs addressing. If they are willing to listen and open to starting a relationship, that is all you need. Ideally, they also have an urgent need that compels them to act.

5) Build rapport and develop a relationship.

Rapport can be developed over the phone, online and face-to-face in a few minutes. It means you need to find out quickly how to connect with a prospective client, and as pointed out in 4), find out if the person you are talking to is a prospective client. If that is the case, it helps to search the Internet before or while talking to the lead or prospective clients on the phone to find out more about them, using social media platforms that publish profiles (Google+, LinkedIn and others) and the company website. This information will help to build a relationship based on mutual understanding. Similarly, revealing selected personal interests and motives in business and hobbies as part of the conversation can help to develop a genuine exchange of information and experiences that help to develop trust necessary for building a relationship that can lead to a purchase decision by the buyer.

6) Become a trusted adviser.

Building on what we discussed under 3) and 5), you advise clients on an optimal solution to their problem, with your service/product. As you are competent, an expert, and have a relationship, and genuine interest and concern for their needs, you can ask difficult questions to evaluate the need and urgency further, and you truly believe in your product – all that makes you credible. You also need to demonstrate reliability, which can be done with feedback and testimonials by other clients.

This last point is important for all types of customers, yet is particularly useful for business and public sector customers. To ensure this message is clear, include prospects in a regular newsletter in which you share insights on events, a book, articles you publish and interviews you give. Blogging is another easy and quick way to share insights and links to important news and documents, Twitter is one tool to use, and/or the blog section on your website. This links clearly to the need for regular PR activities that support the establishment of yourself as a trusted knowledgeable professional.

14.3.2 B2B selling – additional insights

The social media and Web 2.0 changes have also changed B2B sales, as prospects have more time to research for information on products and potential suppliers worldwide, and use their networks actively when sourcing products. This means that companies encounter potential buyers earlier in the sales process than decades ago.

Building trust with prospects is even more important than before, as the external (economic crisis, lower turnover of companies, increasing competition from low-cost countries, etc.) and internal pressures such as job insecurity create personal pressure situations that lead to even more risk-avoiding behaviours. The risk an employee might face in engaging the wrong supplier needs to be addressed by newcomers to the B2B market. They need to have the patience to develop the relationship and trust that gives the buyer the assurance that little can go wrong in the working relationship. Point 5) in the previous section about relationship building is even more important.

Selling is much more based on relationships than a decade ago due to the amount of product and other information available to buyers via the Internet and social media. The pre-purchase process also needs to be an educational process in that the buyer needs help to understand, filter and analyse the wealth of information that can be found. Listening to customer needs becomes even more important.

Establishing thought-leadership is even more important for the B2B seller now, which can be achieved longer term through publications, including White Papers with feedback from readers, articles in leading trade magazines, high level newspapers, blogs, presentations at networking meetings and taster workshops free-of-charge. Proven thought leadership is a big factor in building trust with prospective customers.

Even as a start-up you can offer insights valuable to others through a blog. Box 14.1 gives an example of a blog by our case study start-up **Ben Smith**. His aim is to get his fruit jellies into large supermarkets, and for that and other reasons he is writing his blog on the business and himself, creating the image of a reliable knowledgeable partner.

Box 14.1   Blog by Ben Smith

An Entrepreneur's Guide to the Galaxy

https://benpfsmith.wordpress.com

On this blog, every two or three months Ben writes a longer article on his insights and learning on starting his own businesses.

The next chapter starts with helping you to assess if you are ready to launch the venture, offering a checklist (and a badge!).

14.4   Concluding remarks and application of new insights

This chapter shed light on the significance of PR and the sales process. To start with we discussed the various channels for PR that are available free-of-charge, including selected social media and blogging. Press releases, giving interviews with local media, sponsorship and market research were amongst the soft tools discussed to raise awareness.

We then discussed the sales process and identified five simple steps from raising awareness to actual deal making and identified the long time it can take to turn a contact into an actual sale. Practical sales tips offered insight into the importance of relationship development and genuine interest in the client, supported by your passion and belief in your product. The 80/20 rule applies to the sales process, in which in business reality often 20% of clients bring in the large amount of the income; 80% should not be taken literally. Sales forecast was discussed as a financial planning tool in Chapter Ten so that here we only remember the key points. Potential differences for social enterprises in sales were discussed alongside the various models differentiated by the balance of financial return and social impact focus.

Revision questions and application of the learning to your *sustainable start-up*

1 Define public relations. Then list the most important tools you can use as a *sustainable start-up*.
2 What are the most important steps in the sale process? Outline them briefly.
3 List the most important practical Must-Do's in selling to consumers.
4 Plan your PR activities: what channels will you use before start-up? And after start-up?
5 Outline your sales processes using activity lists and a flow chart outlining the sequence of activities essential for your *sustainable start-up*. How long will it take? What are the starting points? Note the findings in your start-up diary.

15

GETTING UP AND RUNNING

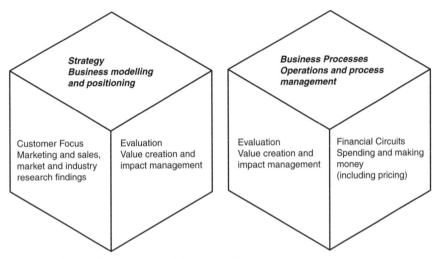

Figure 15.1 The Cube Strategy and the Cube Business Processes
Source: © Hill, 2012.

Summary

Chapter Fifteen sheds light upon the timing of market entry in the course of the calendar year, adjusting to potential seasons that industries and marketplaces have. These considerations realize aspects of Strategy in our Cube business model (Figure 15.1). There is a section detailing what practically should ideally be in place when starting trading and the practicalities of registering a business, with a focus on the UK and relevant links for what to do in the countries the case study companies operate in, from the US to Hong Kong and the already discussed EU countries, including the Netherlands, Norway, Sweden, Finland and Romania. These reflections realize further aspects of business processes, another important Cube area. It then discusses many of the practicalities that are needed to be a *sustainable start-up*, including business insurance and legal protection. This chapter also sheds light on what is or is perceived to be different when running a social enterprise.

CONTENTS

15.1   Introduction to the notion of getting up and running

When shall I run the first trial? This is a question that I am rather rarely asked by first time start-ups when we discuss the significance of market testing. More often, it is the statement that "I am not yet ready, sort of" when I suggest to "give it a go" in a safe environment. "Giving it a go" here means to offer services and products for the first time to people other than your own personal contacts, using the minimal or most marketable product. This is an essential part of the customer development process, as discussed in Chapter Five.

It is not rocket science – with all preparation, research and planning, gathering the customer voice and insight and appreciating industry and competition, at some point you just have to start to sell your service(s) and product(s) – on a small scale, in a selected area of the Turquoise Lake. Chapter Five on market research and positioning discussed the significance of selecting a narrow and focused market segment to start trading in, ideally with one product or service.

And many start-ups do exactly that – they offer the new service or product (or not-so-new service in case of established service types such as beauty, web analytics, marketing, etc.) to people they know, family, friends and open-minded others and like-minded links they have. This experience in selling to willing customers should be regarded as market exploration and research. Why you might ask? The willing buyers or users should ideally give you detailed feedback about what they like about the product/service and what they do not, and why. These insights should be used to adjust the value proposition and fine-tune the product features, again. This behaviour is practising co-creation and being alert for creating the *sustainable start-up* (the latter is principle and practice one, see Chapter One, Section 1.4 for more detail).

Once you have done this type of selling and gaining feedback, it is time to sell to other customers, be it as part of a trial and free-of-charge to them or at a reduced price. This type of selling is still part of the exploration and should be used to gather more insight on how customers perceive and use the product/service, perceive the marketing and price you sell at.

 Case study

This is what three of our start-up case study entrepreneurs did: **Lewis Barnes**, Lantyx Ltd, first sold his services to contacts he knew in the tennis community in the UK. Similarly, **Vivek George**, based in Hong Kong, used his wide range of family members and their contacts selling his online marketing services to clients across the world from Brazil, the US and the UK to other countries in Asia. **Lillie Ranney**, based in the US, used her start-up and student contacts to sell online portfolio services, and developed a client base through that.

All three of them used a network approach to develop the client base, relying on word-of-mouth to some extent. Vivek George intentionally only used word-of-mouth marketing, supported by his social media presence, as he only wanted to talk to clients he knew were interested in his services at point of contact; this worked very well for him, due to the large size of his family and personal contact network. This approach of using networks, both informal, as in the case studies, and formal business networks, is well researched and has proven to have a positive impact on start-up and SME performance and growth (Eisingerich and Bell, 2008, Parker, 2008, Pirolo and Presutti, 2010, Schoonjans et al., 2013).

 Case study

Our case study **Richard Rodman**, in the US, did not know anybody when he came to study at Ohio University. He built up his networks through engaging in student entrepreneurship societies and used those to sell his first online service aimed at students to save study time, and took part in an incubator programme that linked him with investors and potential business partners. His example illustrates the well-documented significant impact of developing networks, often called social capital, and their impact on start-up success (Pirolo and Pirutti, 2010).

Some start-ups intentionally do not sell to people they know but jump immediately to selling to people they do not know. One reason is that they prefer to gain customer reactions that are more honest about the potential flaws of the product than friends and personal contacts might be. Other reasons are that their product is for a very small niche market so that they do not know sufficient potential customers. Similarly, selling to businesses might mean that you only have a small number of contacts or none yourself; however, your investor team or business mentors have more you can build on.

 As pointed out when discussing market positioning, first in Chapter Five on market research, this market positioning will need several readjustments to get it right. Similarly, when discussing the business modelling process we highlighted that this is an on-going circular, or rather, spiral, process from having the experience of interaction with customers, first via research, then via test trading with friends and family and open-minded potential customers from the shallow small Turquoise Lake approach (see Chapter Five).

In case of business-to-business markets, by this point in time you should have developed some keen interested business contacts willing to try out a prototype of a tangible product or a version of the minimal viable service.

 Case study

The question remains, when are you up and running? That is matter of your judgement and feeling, and the understanding of the market and the customer. It looks different for everybody, and it feels different for most of us. You need to feel ready to go beyond the circle of friends and family and their contacts and do a real-life test with your offer or value proposition.

Our social enterprise case study founder **Kathryn Kimbley** points out that even after start of trading and official business registration she did not feel she was up and running. It still felt new and unusual for months that what she was doing was running a social enterprise, more than just counselling.

Some academic sources based on high growth start-ups identify the employment of the first staff member as the sign of the actual trading. But that approach is too narrow for the large majority of start-ups, as many micro-enterprise start-ups do not employ a staff member for a few years, or not at all (GEM, 2014a).

Carrying out test trading is like an ice-skater learning to do a pirouette. If you then fall on the ice, it is regarded as normal, part of the package of "learning by doing".

Acknowledging that for ice-skating, when do you feel you can do "it" by yourself, and do it a few times? "It" meaning selling the product or service to buyers that are not part of your friends' networks a few times, learning from the experience and adjusting the value proposition and your practices. Not selling anything is hard, and yet it is an experience that you can learn from if you ask for honest feedback and can understand it and adjust your pirouettes, that is, your business practices. Then you can tell yourself the *sustainable start-up* is up and running. These are the co-creation principle and practices for judging you are up and running.

15.2 When shall I start trading officially?

By now everything should be sorted, and you know that you have clients lined up. You have done some trading and tested the minimal viable product sufficiently – online or for free or paid-for tasters and a more fully-fledged package or have tested a prototype and know it is fit for purpose and loved by your potential customers? Have you got at least a minimal marketable product? Can you make a decision if the minimal or exceptional marketable product is best for your target segment and for you to start with?

As a reminder, the minimal viable product is the product or service that you developed with minimal cost and time investment, yet that can be sold to the target customers you identified to test and explore the market, which we introduced in Chapter Five. This is an agreed learning tool today for a cost-effective way to find out if there is a market for a product or not. Manufacturing companies use a prototype for learning what potential customers like and to gain funding for further product development.

The minimal marketable product (MMP) is a saleable product with the minimal amount of features meeting the most important customer needs that make the biggest difference in the customer experiences and that customers are willing to pay for; this implies the smallest amount of features possible to reduce costs yet still making the important difference to the user experience.

And then practitioners and entrepreneurs differ on what you start selling to larger numbers of customers, the minimal marketable product (MMP) or the exceptional marketable product (EMP). How do you make a decision to offer the minimal or the exceptional marketable product? My answer to that debate is that it depends on the resources available, the type of product and market it is sold to, and the likelihood of other companies entering the market with this new product or service in the next few months.

The MMP is the product that can be sold to a larger group of customers, which has the most important features that make a difference to their lives, and the route to market is much quicker. The point in time after MVP testing and development can be reduced to months or weeks, dependent on the product. One example: Groupon, the online voucher service to bring income to businesses with vouchers that reduced customer prices, was developed over time with customers, who fed back. The developer added features to a minimal marketable product he had started with that according to users was neither easy to use nor looked very nice online. He then developed a more suitable website that attracted many more customers offering the same features in a nicer looking way.

A provider of online training services to businesses decided that MMP was not good enough for him and he developed the exceptional value service (the EVP), which took more time and money. His market testing and research had shown to him that his customers wanted a quality product from the start with some extras, and he decided to do that and not offer a cheap online version that might cost him some time and money and might scare off some target customers.

 When you have a list of at least a handful of clients urging to buy from you – does that mean and feel right to start registering the business activity? Do you feel ready to face the ups and downs? Are you all excited to go for more? And are you sure you have got the costs sorted, calculated so that you charge enough to become a sustainable start-up?

You can register the business, as self-employed (or sole trader or sole proprietor) rather quickly (within a day), or as a company limited by shares, within a few working days. But that is the how. How do you know you are ready?

Here is a checklist in Activity 15.1. You should be able to say "yes" to 80% of the questions on the list, or if number 8 applies, just go for it and consider number 9).

 Activity 15.1   Checklist for start-up readiness

Read through the questions and answer them truthfully.

1) *Can you summarize your USP and value proposition in two sentences and say them convincingly to any stranger?*
(If not, use the voice recording app on the phone and do it a few times until you are convinced it is convincing; then do it to a few friends, and record it, and then do it at a train station to someone in a queue, note your feelings and experiences in your a start-up diary.)
2) *Can you outline your benefits, customer pain/needs and your features in a convincing way that would convince an investor, such as a TV Dragon or business angel?*
(If not, follow the advice above under number 1.)
3) *Can you summarize your target customers and their profile, and where in their daily/ working lives your value proposition fits?*
(If not, go to Chapter Five and do Activity 5.5 in Section 5.9 and Activity 13.2 again.)
4) *Have you got an action plan for when and how to market your value proposition?*
(If not, go to Chapter Thirteen, revision question six and do the marketing action plan.)

5) *Have you tested a minimal viable product long enough to gain sufficient customer insight to decide on the priority minimal features your end product should have? And have you sufficient resources to build this minimal marketable product? Have you made a decision if the MMP or the EVP are the appropriate product for your target customers?*
6) *Have you registered as either self-employed or a company or any of the other forms?* (If not go to Chapter Eight and read about legal forms and Section 15.4 for practical essentials about registering for self-employment or a company or a social enterprise with a different legal form.)
7) *Have you got business cards?*
8) *Do you feel ready to go?*
9) *Have you got a handful of customers who want to buy from you?*
10) *Have you got business insurance in place?*

Figure 15.2   Ready to start up badge
Source: © Hill, 2014.

You need many ticks to be able to award yourself the READY TO GO badge (Figure 15.2). This badge is for you to tell at least yourself that you are ready to register your business and trade officially.

The next section briefly discusses considerations for timing the start of trading.

Chapter 12.6 discussed considerations about a formal launch with an event versus continuing to learn from trading. This kind of launch event needs to happen soon after you have officially registered as trading. The next sections discuss the timing of registering the business activity and the actual steps in registration.

15.3   Timing of registering a business activity for the *sustainable start-up*

The next question to answer is: when is the most appropriate time to register the business? There is no one clear answer or checklist for it. In the UK, you are allowed to do some trading activities for at least a few weeks without any government organization minding that trading behaviour, yet you are expected to register formally as soon as possible after start of trading.

Within the law and tax regulations of each country, there might be a requirement to register after a certain amount of time of trading. In the UK, you should register business activity as outlined above with the HMRC or Companies House soon after starting trading. This means in practice after a few months at the latest; many regard three months as the acceptable period of trading without official business registration.

Ideally, for the *sustainable start-up* several things come together:

▶ You have developed a minimal marketable product that will generate sales for a while.
▶ You have at least a handful of customers lined up willing to pay you and/or a contract lined up.
▶ You have spent some time business modelling through co-creation considering the twelve Cube elements and have evidence that there is some market fit for your value proposition, including an estimate of the market share you can gain with the minimal viable product.

There are some limiting factors that externally influence the timing of official registration. Two examples are:

▶ If your start-up costs are high, for example, you are producing a prototype for a tangible product and need to spend a lot of money, there is a need to claim VAT back in the UK to reduce expenses; for that reason, from a practical viewpoint you should not spend years and years planning and preparing, and test trading, as otherwise you cannot put some expenses down against the income you generate later.
▶ If you have a grant or loan lined up, but should not have started trading when you obtain it, you get ready but wait until the money has hit your account before you register the business and start trading officially.

Having registered the business, however, does not mean you have to be trading. Registration is a good milestone to indicate to the HMRC in the UK (the government department dealing with tax and duty in the UK) that you are serious about starting trading, and that expenses you have incurred so far and from the day of trading are expenses that will balance your profits. Otherwise, if you plan and spend for too long before registration, you might not be able to put them down in the first tax return as business expenses. Figure 15.3 summarizes briefly the steps before the official business registration.

It is also helpful to consider trading seasons: when do you think companies purchase goods such as gifts, or plan events for Christmas? Some start in August, and that is late. Others start in spring or immediately after the previous winter season. If you have a seasonal winter or Christmas related product that you want to sell to other businesses, you need to be ready to go long before the actual season it is for, so you should be up and running even before that, as you need to market your product/services to potential buyers.

Some sectors have an even earlier start, such as fashion. Decisions on what to buy are made much earlier in the year for the winter season.

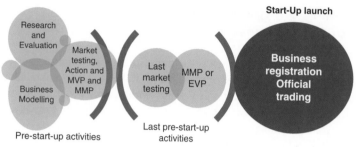

Figure 15.3   The last steps in the *sustainable (pre-)start-up* journey
Source: © Hill, 2013.

If you miss the season when businesses buy (B2B) for your sector, then your first year of trading could be much lower in turnover. Your industry and market research should have identified the seasons and given you a clear indication when the best market entry times are for your subsector. Figure 15.3 showcases two of the last important steps before official start-up launch and business registration.

Box 15.1 illustrates what some of our graduate case studies put in place or what made them feel they were up and running. These examples illustrate how different the experience and personal perception of being up and running might be. The actual business registration was a formal step, but it was not significant for the perception of being up and running.

Lewis Barnes put into practice the learning from his first start-up and did a few things before he started trading with his second business: he brought in staff straight away in month one to do the routine administrative work while he focused his time and energy on customer acquisition and service delivery. For him the service he offers is the exceptional valuable product.

Damian Alexandru in Romania felt he was up and running when he had the first paying client who came through to contact them via the new just-established website. He had registered the business three months before that event.

Box 15.1   What some of our graduate entrepreneur case studies did

Lewis Barnes, Lantyx Ltd, UK

From registering ... it coincided with having the first employee. The lease would have started ten days from registering, we had a location all up and running ready to go. All the planning was all done prior to setting up. I know it sounds quick but there was a lot of scouting round and everything was in place before we registered the company and then we just put the action into place.

Damian Alexandru, AMD Nobel, Romania

Damian regards having the first paying customer the essential experience that made him feel he was up and running.

My first paying customer. My first end-user paying customer I got through the Internet. We were searching for a solution, we just finished our website, somehow he got to it even though it was a new website. We made the first order, we celebrated the whole night! My first paying customer we got by promoting it to doctors, to private clinics, which have the ability to sell directly, so we don't need to go through the pharmacy to sell the product, we can also sell through the private clinics. We have a kind of an optic shop.

Well we started more seriously taking the promotion into account in January. And it took about two weeks, I think. Our product needs high volumes. It's not one, two, that's not a lot. We're talking about in years, thousands of units per month. So having a ten-unit order is not much but it was a psychological incentive for us, seeing that it can work. So that's [the] important start. ... So since January – three months.

15.4   Registering a business activity – practical essentials

The UK is one of the countries that allows citizens to register a business activity for self-employment online or on the phone: registering with HM Revenue and Customs to become self-employed can be done online or via phone in less than 30 minutes, provided you have a National Insurance number and an address. This does not cost anything.

Registering a company limited by shares or guarantee can be done online as well, yet with Companies House and takes more time. Provided you accept the standard documents online, for £15 (in spring 2015) you can register online a company limited by shares; within a week the paperwork should arrive with you. Or you can ask an agent or a solicitor to do it on your behalf, with particular wording in the documents. The fees for that go up rather quickly: small changes are not so expensive, but fees can be from £150 onwards then; the more changes you make the sky becomes the limit for the fee a solicitor might charge.

Table 15.1 lists some of the things needed for *business registration* in the countries our case studies are located in, and additional countries in Europe. What can be gathered from this table is that registering a business activity is relatively simple in most countries, and does not cost a lot of money.

For measuring how easy it is to start a business, four indicators are used: the number of procedures required, the time it takes to register a business (in calendar days, from filing the application to receiving formal documentation, such as tax number or company certificate), the cost of registering a business (official fees and taxes) and the minimum capital that has to be paid or deposited prior to company registration.

The indicators attempt to identify – when taken together – how easy it is to deal with regulations to start a business. The assumptions made include that the company registered is a limited liability company (so the time for registering as a sole trader or sole proprietor is not addressed), located in the largest business city in the country, that business premises are rented, the core business activities are production or sale of products or services to the public, and the business does not perform activities that need special permission, such as the sale of alcohol.

It is important to note that in the US and the UK six procedures have be undertaken until a company registration is completed, more than in many other countries, including Romania. The cost of registration is lowest in the UK and New Zealand. Most countries in the table do not require a deposit for company registration, apart from Denmark and Sweden.

Table 15.1 Starting a business: practical essentials in selected countries

Country / Indicator for doing business	Number of procedures	Time in calendar days to register a business	Cost of registration – fees and taxes (measured in % of income per head in the country)	Capital to be deposited for business registration (measured in % of income per head in the country)
Denmark	4	55	10.2	14.5
Finland	3	14	11	7
Hong Kong SAR, China	3	2.5	1.4	0
Netherlands	4	4	5	0
New Zealand	1	0.5	0.3	0
Norway	4	5	0.9	5
Romania	5	9	2.1	0.7
Sweden	3	16	0.5	12.8
UK	6	6	0.3	0
US	6	5.6	12	0

Source: World Bank Group, 2014.

Table 15.2 Country rankings for starting a business and doing business

Country / Ranking	Starting a business	Doing business
New Zealand	1	2
Singapore	6	1
Hong Kong SAR, China	8	3
Netherlands	21	27
Norway	22	6
Denmark	25	4
Finland	27	9
Sweden	32	1
Romania	38	48
UK	45	8
US	46	7

Source: World Bank Group, 2014.

Table 15.2 offers a ranking of how easy it is to do business and to start a business in selected countries. Singapore is the country it is easiest to do business in, whereas it is easiest in the world to start a business in New Zealand. A project run by the World Bank ranks 189 countries: the UK is in place 45 and is one place before the US with rank 46 for starting a business, whereas for doing business the US leads before the UK with rank 7. Are you surprised? Hong Kong is high up on the ranking with a place of 8 for starting a business, and even better in place 3 for doing business. All Scandinavian countries and the Netherlands are much better business environments for starting a business than the UK – with the Netherlands leading (21) before Norway (22), Denmark (25), Finland (27) and Sweden (32). Even Romania is better positioned than the UK and the US, in rank 38. The main reason why the US and the UK rank relatively low on the list of countries for starting a business is the number of procedures (6), the relatively high cost in the US for registering a business and the number of days it takes from filing to receipt of tax number or company documents.

The interesting question is what these rankings are based on: for the ranking of doing business, 31 indicators capture ten different topics. These ten topics are:

Starting a business, paying taxes, registering property, getting credit, protecting minority investors, trading across borders, getting electricity, dealing with construction permits, enforcing contracts, and resolving insolvency.

"Starting a business" is one of the ten areas, and the four indicators used are the number of procedures required, the time it takes to register a business (in calendar days, from filing the application to receiving formal documentation, such as tax number of company certificate), the cost of registering a business (official fees and taxes) and the minimum capital that has to be paid or deposited prior to company registration (World Bank Group, 2014).

For social enterprises, registering a company limited by guarantee in the UK is nearly as easy or costly as the company limited by shares. Registering a development trust, a community interest company or a registered society can take much more work if you make changes to the standard documents. In the UK, most local Councils for Voluntary Service offices offer services advising and supporting the development of those documents free of charge. In most other countries it is similarly easy.

You have to be clear by this point in time that you have the legal right to open a business as a student or professional, based on your visa conditions, where that applies.

The next section discusses the important aspect of business insurance and legal protection in practical terms.

15.5 Have you got it covered? Legal protection and business insurance

15.5.1 Introduction to business insurance and legal cover

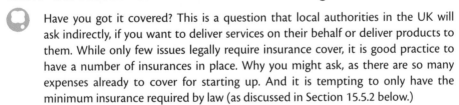

Have you got it covered? This is a question that local authorities in the UK will ask indirectly, if you want to deliver services on their behalf or deliver products to them. While only few issues legally require insurance cover, it is good practice to have a number of insurances in place. Why you might ask, as there are so many expenses already to cover for starting up. And it is tempting to only have the minimum insurance required by law (as discussed in Section 15.5.2 below.)

However, there are at least two reasons why this expense makes business sense for the *sustainable start-up*. Having more than the legally required insurances in place gives some business clients in particular the idea that you are serious about being in business and if something goes wrong, that you are covered, so that they are covered themselves for the risk of you not being able to deliver due to – for example – fire destroying access to data and offices or staff illness. Consumers and end-users are very unlikely to ask you if and what insurance you have got in place; often they do not know themselves what is useful or required by law.

Business insurance is clearly a tool to minimize the appearance of being a risk to clients, even if it is not required by law in many cases. For the *sustainable start-up* it is an expense, yet one I can recommend. Secondly, increasingly clients and customers question the service or product they received, and sometimes, the materials or parts you use might simply be faulty, without it being your fault. This risk of faulty supplies can be covered (see below for product liability insurance).

Practically speaking, many professional membership associations and lobbyist organizations for small businesses such as the Federation for Small Businesses (the largest body in the UK) have special arrangements in place with insurance providers for their members to gain reductions in insurance premiums. It is still worth comparing various insurance offers before buying one to compare cover and fees.

Similarly, most membership associations have free legal advice helplines in place. This means you can call a number 24/7 to arrange a solicitor to call you back within one or two hours to discuss any legal aspect of business. They also provide sample contracts, terms and conditions and many other documents. While this is only advice, you can gain a lot assurance and confidence from discussing a query with a legal professional.

The next two sections explain the most important insurances.

15.5.2 Legally required insurances

The moment you take on a staff member you have to have employer's liability insurance in place in the UK. You can be fined if you have employees, apart from yourself as a director of a company, and have no adequate cover in place. This insurance is required to protect employers from liabilities arising from the actions of their employees, in case they gain injury or disease arising out of their employment practices.

Public liability insurance is not legally required in the UK, but expected to be in place as good business practice. As business owner/director and self-employed you are legally liable to pay damages for any bodily injury, illness or disease contracted by any other person, other than employees, or loss of or damage to their property caused by your business, that is, caused by you and your staff when carrying out work. Public liability insurance covers you for claims made against you by members of the public or other businesses. The damages can become big rather quickly, such as spilling coffee over a client's desk and keyboard that destroys a paper document or by accident leads to someone deleting a file.

15.5.3 Insurances to consider

While not a legal requirement, in particular start-ups wanting to sell to the public sector and in some cases wanting to supply to larger corporates (B2B), are well advised to put in place insurances for:

a) Professional indemnity;
b) Product liability;

c) Business content cover;

d) Buildings and property.

Professional indemnity – for services received by clients/customers

Increasingly, a culture of complaints and suing has reached the UK and other countries in Europe. Businesses can be sued, rightly or wrongly, for vast damages over a range of complaints. This type of insurance provides protection against any claims by clients who believe they received bad or negligent services, and incurred a loss as a result.

Anyone who supplies advice or services such as consultancy, legal services, accountancy, as well as health-related services, hair and beauty should consider professional indemnity.

Product liability

An example: a hairdresser uses on client request a hair colour. The client complains later that he got a skin infection from this hair dye. An investigation then finds out that actually the skin infection could not have come from hair dye, but it came from wearing a bonnet constantly that used fibre the client was allergic to and which he did not know about. Without insurance cover that paid for the costs to investigate the possible victim's skin and engage a solicitor to sort the case out, the hairdresser would have gone bankrupt.

Product liability is your legal liability to pay damages that happen as a result of a defective product being used. Businesses that supply products to other businesses or the public, from software to machine tools, are at risk if a faulty product causes damage or injury. Manufacturers of a product are usually at risk if things go wrong, but the liability can fall on a supplier if the maker of the product goes out of business.

Business content cover for assets and equipment

Your business stock (the goods or merchandise kept on the premises and are available for sale) should be insured for its cost price. Plant and business equipment can be insured in two different ways: either to have it replaced as new (which is more expensive) or on an indemnity basis; the latter includes wear and tear (reduction in product lifetime through usage), which will reduce the amount you will get (the fee for it is cheaper). This means that in case of loss in equipment value you do not make a loss.

Electrical or mechanical breakdown for most machinery, including computers, can be insured. By law, many items of plant such as boilers, lifts and lifting machinery must be inspected regularly by a qualified person. Insurers can arrange to provide this service.

Contents are usually covered against theft provided there has been forcible and violent entry to or exit from the premises. Damage to the building resulting from theft or attempted theft will also normally be covered.

Buildings and property

Buildings can be insured against fire, accidental damage through lightning, explosion of gas, riot, malicious damage, storm and flood, impact by aircraft, road and rail vehicles, escape of water from tanks or pipes and sprinkler leakage. Ideally, business premises should be insured for their full rebuilding cost (including professional fees and the cost of site clearance) when you own them, and not just for their market value.

Other insurance worth considering for those transporting valuable and/or fragile goods is for "goods in transport". This covers the time a good is being transported and is still your property. Some issues of business interruption beyond the owner's control can be covered with business interruption insurance: even minor interruptions such as rain coming through the building roof can prevent you being able to deliver a product or service on time. The loss of business income and extra expenses can be compensated for to bridge the shortfall in gross profit as well as paying any increased working costs, again through a particular insurance policy.

 Activity 15.2   Check out insurances

In your country, go to the website of one of the main insurance providers and check out what business insurance they offer, and if they offer some insurances for small businesses. What are these insurances? List them and provide some bullet points what each of them covers. Then include the notes in your start-up diary.

The next section briefly outlines what might be different when starting and running a social enterprise.

15.6   Running a social enterprise – what is different?

15.6.1   Introduction to differences when running a social enterprise

While research in the past found that an 80/20 rule applies, that is, that 80% is the same as running a mainstream for-profit business, and 20% is different. In practice, that is often not applicable, as the differences can be bigger, such as 30–35% different versus 65–60% the same or very similar to for-profit businesses. The difference depends very much on the chosen organizational form, type of business (manufacturing or non-manufacturing), industry sector and social mission. Figure 15.4 summarizes the areas visually. They are:

▶ Staff management;
▶ Governance and strategic management of the social enterprise;
▶ Marketing and PR;
▶ Financial management and fundraising;
▶ Customers;
▶ Sourcing of materials and procurement.

15.6.2   Staff management

If you have volunteers as well as staff, they need a very different management style, as they give their time for free and possibly want to learn new skills. You need more time to manage and motivate them than traditional staff.

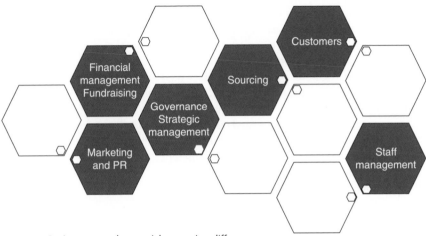

Figure 15.4 Business areas where social enterprises differ
Source: © Hill, 2013.

And if you employ those men and women who have difficulties in getting a job in the mainstream labour market, as is done by social firms, then a different skills set is required, dependent on what constitutes their disadvantage. The required management style can be significantly different, such as for people with an intellectual disability, or adults with learning difficulties.

15.6.3 Governance and strategic management

Dependent on the legal form, governance can be very time-consuming and require a lot of skills going beyond what business schools call management and governance skills. Membership organizations require the consent of members for certain types of decisions affecting the whole organization, and they need to be informed and guided differently. Meetings need to be held, information sent out in a different way. Some of the formal requirements are discussed in Chapter Eight on governance and legal issues.

Most social enterprises have at least a management committee and/or a board of directors. Directors can be residents in an area or beneficiaries, and information needs to be presented and managed so that it can be easily understood without commercial knowledge and experience.

Many social enterprises engage all stakeholders in decision-making processes, which requires various forms of consultation. These processes take time, cost money and require different skills than traditional management.

Dependent on the governance requirements, many operational decisions might also need board approval. However, boards rarely meet on a monthly bases, rather every quarter or bi-monthly, and sub-committes have to make decisions that then will need board approval before they can be implemented. This process can take weeks if not months. All those tasks require more time, different skills and additional expenses. The annual meeting of all members is an important decision-making body to approve financial accounts and significant changes to the organization. The adoption of new board members needs to be accepted by the annual meeting, for example.

Many operational decisions in community-led or focused enterprises are made based on consensus or votes, including staff in the decision-making process, and service users or beneficiaries of services. The latter are often referred to as beneficiaries. The participatory nature of service and organizational development means that a lot more time and resources are needed to gain decisions and move processes on. However, there are person-centred social enterprises, where similar to a founder, business decisions are made mainly by one person.

Vision and strategy are closely related, as social enterprises are in most cases mission driven. The mission and vision statements are ideally developed collaboratively with staff and beneficiaries and sometimes even funder representatives, and the board. This is often done through wide consultations, often with beneficiaries, online and through face-to-face meetings and focus groups.

15.6.4 Marketing and PR

The big advantage social enterprises can use when marketing their services and products is that the company uses the profits it generates for creating social good and social benefits or environmental benefits, which are often not met otherwise.

Many social enterprises are applying marketing principles and techniques alongside other techniques to creating "social good" with clearly defined actions. Important is the "selling" of the social outcomes you create with the enterprise activities.

Thus, instead of only highlighting the unique selling points of products or services sold to a customer, the social projects and their outcomes, which are financed with the profits generated, are featured simultaneously. This can be the difference made for a particular group of people (young disadvantaged or the elderly) or the environment or a particular possibly disadvantaged area. Secondly, the social value created is put at the forefront of the marketing approach: improving the health of a disadvantaged group, reducing the carbon footprint, etc. In other words, the value proposition needs to highlight as well how through purchasing this service or product a social difference is made. Further details were discussed in Chapter Thirteen on marketing.

A recent survey with social enterprises in the UK in 2013 revealed that there is an increasing confidence amongst social enterprises using their status for PR and marketing: 78% used the social enterprise status for marketing to a greater extent than in previous years. Amongst recently started social enterprises, 88% use their status for marketing (Social Enterprise UK, 2014). The argument more often used now is that buying goods or services from a social enterprise means supporting them in fulfilling their social mission, while receiving as professional and good quality a service/product as you will elsewhere. This purchase is then counted towards a company's corporate social responsibility or sustainability.

In PR activities even more so, social enterprises can highlight the social/environmental gain and benefit they create while demonstrating the functional benefits of their services and products. They can also use supporters'/sponsors' names to add value to their message. Corporate social responsibility of large corporates follows the opposite flow of information, in that it highlights the social engagement in company PR to improve the company's image. There are some marketing techniques for non-profits including cause-related marketing and social marketing, which were discussed in more detail in Chapter Thirteen.

15.6.5 Financial management and fundraising

Banking in ethical and socially responsible ways is important for many social enterprises. There are a couple of banks specializing in working with and for the third sector in the UK, some are social enterprises themselves, and offer tailored products, such as the Charity Bank, Triodos Bank, Unity Trust and the Co-operative Bank. For many social enterprises, working with an ethically operating bank is very important.

Working with European Funding programmes and delivering services for the disadvantaged or in in disadvantaged areas has some practical impact on financial management. To start with, more often than not, the contract requires providing match funding, that is, that the amount of money asked for in the grant or contract to deliver needs to be matched by funds from your own organization. While this request can be matched by time provided and not charged for by staff in some cases, this is not always possible.

Reliance on short-term funding for many services and projects is a key challenge to financial sustainability. Staff contracts may have to be limited to funding awards and for that reason are fixed term in many cases. This impacts on business goals and continuous growth and strategic development.

Demands for accountability and transparency are common to all forms of social enterprises, and even small organizations publish their financial data in annual reports, either on the website or on request on paper. At annual membership meetings all members receive a short report on the activities and successes/challenges the organization faced.

15.6.6 Customers

The word "customer" alone is understood differently by different types of social enterprises. One reason is that often the mission is to provide free services to those in need, and many managers would not use the term "customer" for those beneficiaries of these services, such as care and training. They are more familiar and comfortable with the term "stakeholder" or "beneficiary".

As pointed out previously, social enterprises often have more than one customer group: they sell goods in charity shops for example to the wider public, who is one customer group. The money generated is used to provide services free of charge, for example to those with sight problems or elderly in need, referred to as beneficiaries.

Often, the term customer is used with a different meaning by social enterprises. It can be used solely to describe those who pay for goods or services provided, which is similar to the notion for for-profit businesses. It can also be used for the community as a whole, be that regional or local to the organization.

Some social enterprises would not use it at all. When providing services for local authorities, social enterprises often refer to the contract manager in the contracting organization as a funder, not customer, or the main stakeholder, and those receiving services as beneficiaries, or stakeholders in the narrow sense, or service users.

15.6.7 Sourcing of materials and suppliers

Many social enterprises focus on using suppliers that are social enterprises themselves, or charities, and/or trade ethically, using as few resources as possible. In that way they often differ from most other small enterprises, which are not yet exclusively sourcing that way.

The next chapter discusses ways to grow the early business activities, including using a number of approaches following the principle and practice of co-creation not only suitable for the *sustainable start-up*, but also established micro- and small enterprises.

15.7   Concluding remarks and application of new insights

After discussing the various considerations when planning the start of trading after test trading or market testing, this chapter discussed business registration. After some detail on what to do in the UK, a brief comparison of the case study countries was made, using an existing international ranking for business start-up conditions and practicalities.

Then we introduced a variety of insurances and how they offer protection for and against risks, faulty products and equipment and protection when you or your staff make a serious mistake with consequences for your clients or the public. It is important to be aware of the types of insurances available so that you are not surprised when local governments/municipalities require insurance cover when applying to deliver to them or on their behalf. Public liability is an important requirement in the UK for all start-ups, yet not a legal requirement.

We then discussed the main important areas that are different when getting a social enterprise up and running, with focus on finance raising, strategic management and governance, PR, marketing and staff management. Most importantly, the social difference made to society is an important marketing message that not only consumers increasingly look out for but also the public sector and private sector companies.

The activities below from question five onwards invite you to apply the learning to your venture planning process.

Revision questions and applying the new insights to your *sustainable start-up*

1 What factors might influence the time you register your business?
2 Why should seasons be considered when deciding when to start your business?
3 List some reasons why legal protection and insurance are important.
4 Outline the differences between a for-profit business and a social enterprise.
5 Using the checklist in Activity 15.1 above, establish where you are in your readiness journey with your *sustainable start-up*. Include the notes in your start-up diary.
6 Go to your national or regional business support agency or central government department and check if there is any legal requirement for any business insurance in your country. Take note of the answer in your start-up diary.
7 Include the results of your insurance research in Activity 15.2 in your start-up diary.
8 Start to plan your official business registration. How many days will you need just for that process? Based on the results of doing question five, you have a clear understanding of where you are in the pre-start-up process. Fix a week in the near future when registration might be suitable.

16

JUST STARTED – RISKY?

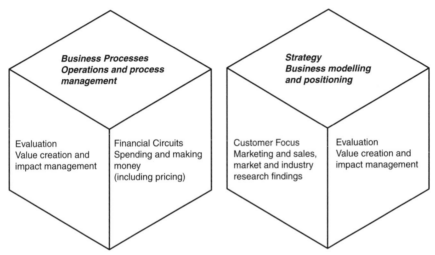

Figure 16.1 The Cube Strategy and the Cube Business Processes
Source: © Hill, 2012.

Summary

This last chapter addresses in detail start-up risks the *sustainable start-up* needs to address early on and points out ways to manage them, applying the principles and practices of alertness (1) and co-creation (5). It then discusses briefly the challenges in using volunteers to increase capacity temporarily and addresses challenges first-time employers face. Ways to create short-term, temporary focused alliances is explored in detail, implementing the Strategy aspect of the Cube (see Figure 16.1) and applying practices of responsibility (2), resourceful impact (3), interconnectedness (4) and co-creation (5). The activities and the chapter end tasks invite you to engage in applying this learning to your *sustainable start-up*. You are now equipped to create and maintain a *sustainable start-up*, wherever you are based in the world.

CONTENTS

16.1　Pitfalls and risks in the first year of trading

16.1.1　Reasons why start-ups fail

> There are a number of reasons why entrepreneurs see their fledgling businesses falter. "They haven't done the research, they don't know where to go for the right funding ... it's rarely one thing." However there is a common theme, argues the retail magnate. "The reason people fail is because they don't do their homework." You wouldn't sit an exam without doing any preparation, he points out. "A business is no different." (Theo Paphitis, interviewed in *The Guardian* online, http://www.the guardian.com/small-business-network/2014/jul/08/theo-paphitis-startups-dragons-den, accessed December 2014)

The ability to manage risks is a core competence of successful business people, and that is no different for the *sustainable start-up*. On the contrary, those using the *sustainable start-up* approach have the skills and appropriate attitudes to imagine what could go wrong and flexibly develop the position as part of the described on-going re-adjustment processes through co-creation. If principles and practices one to five are applied, then the failure for those reasons Theo Paphitis points out need not apply: they cover alertness, responsibility, resourceful impact, interconnectedness and co-creation, and are addressed in the sixth Cube area "evaluation".

There are still many so-called high growth start-ups that are backed by venture capitalists or business angels, and have a board with board members who have started and run their own successful ventures. And yet, so many of those ventures fail as well. Why is that the case you might think?

In Chapter One we had outlined the most important reasons why start-ups fail. What is a risk then? Put simply, a business risk is an unintended yet often unavoidable consequence of activities or an event or unforeseen circumstance that might happen outside of the control of the business. The *sustainable start-up* has to deal with those effects and prepare for their occurrence so that the least possible impact interferes with its business activities.

Two examples for these events are floods that affect business premises and travelling to client sites, and an economic recession. Other business reasons for start-up failures include:

- Insufficient market research was carried out before and after start-up.
- Market research was superficial, including not asking the appropriate questions.
- Forecasts for sales were too high.

▶ Not all essential costs were considered.
▶ Too much stock was bought.
▶ Skills needed were not in place.
▶ Cash flow was negative for too long with insufficient funds to cover it.
▶ Insufficient marketing activities were carried out.
▶ A commitment to long-term premises that were not initially needed was made, thus having to deal with high fixed costs.
▶ Other fixed costs were too high.
▶ Staff was taken on too early.
▶ Lack of effective management.
▶ Money was spent on inessential items where other solutions might have helped (see Chapter Ten), also called insufficient cost control.
▶ Insufficient money was invested into essential items or activities, such as market research or branding.

The above list of possible reasons for failures addresses the outcomes of business activities that were either not carried out at all or insufficiently or with underdeveloped competence.

And there are reasons relating to the person who carries out the business start-up: over-confidence, over-estimating their own skills, misjudging the market situation, and for that reason not carrying out sufficient market research, insufficient skills in an important business area, lack of management skills.

While we cannot predict the future, we can look at possible events that might happen and how they affect our own business activities. As a *sustainable start-up* you then do everything in your power to reduce the likelihood of the effects having any or a large impact where that is within your control. For example, staying on top of the most likely events to happen based on research and being alert about economic and techno-logical developments allows business owners to anticipate potential risks outside their control.

Professional associations and small business lobbyist organizations (such as the Federation of Small Businesses in the UK) do a lot of that work for their members. An effect a law or change in regulation can have for some SMEs in a sector is well discussed before it actually happens so that business owners can prepare for any changes. This was the case for example when the duty for employers to pay for employees' pensions in the UK in 2013 was put in place.

The next section discusses business risks and what can proactively be done to address these to ensure you build a *sustainable start-up*.

16.1.2 Business risks

The main important risks a start-up business could face are listed in Table 16.1, applying the principles of alertness, responsibility, resourceful impact and co-creation. They are differentiated by those that have little effect and can be ignored (1), risks that can be addressed with simple measures (2), those that are fully out of the area of influence of an individual, some of which can be covered by an insurance and not been addressed with own actions (3) and risks that can actively been identified, monitored and addressed (called mitigated) (4). Furthermore, risks are differentiated by business areas, such as IT and

Table 16.1 Risks start-up businesses face

Risk type	Identified risk
(1) Minor risks that can be safely ignored	Examples: • Roadworks on the normal daily journeys to clients/to work; • Delays of public transport; • Getting a flat tyre.
(2) Annoying bad timing risks	Examples: • No toner/printer cartridge when you need to print a client report for the deadline on the same day; • Laptop/desk top fail, all work of the last two days is gone, and not saved externally, you have to deliver to the client the next day; • Your printer falls ill, and you need to find another printer/your normal suppliers cannot deliver the one key component you need and you never looked for a possible replacement supplier, so you are delayed in delivering the output on time.
(3) Risks that can be insured against and/ or are beyond your control	• An unsatisfied client sues you – professional indemnity insurance covers that risk; • Your product is faulty – product liability insurance covers that; • You made a mistake and a client sues you – professional indemnity insurance covers that; • A client slips and breaks a leg, even though the floor in your premises was not wet – public liability; • A concert has to be cancelled, as the main star has fallen ill – and you are the event manager; • An employee makes a gross mistake – employer's liability insurance.
(4) Big business risks	Some examples are listed that give insight into the types of risks that are involved; further risks can be identified following the train of thought developed.
IT	• You PC/laptop breaks down completely; • Your back-up drive breaks down; • An associate/employee has not backed up their work; • Broadband breaks down for hours; • Your phone/laptop gets stolen on a train; • Your systems are hacked; • Your access to the Internet is interrupted due to flooding, fire, etc.; • You have a computer virus that destroys your work; • Software is outdated and breaks down.
Operations and technology related risks	Office premises or your private office on fire/flooded – you cannot access the premises for days. Technology related: New technology comes to market that reduces production cost, yet you cannot buy it as you have not sufficient capital to pay for it: your prices get too high compared to the competition; Your machines break down/the machines of your supplier break down and you cannot deliver on time; You cannot take payments, as your tills are down/payment provider is down.
Transport	Are you relying on fuel intensive industries? What other ways of transport could you use, as oil prices will keep going up? Your logistics company has overpromised, your delivery is late; The mail company staff goes on strike; trains are cancelled and/or delayed.

(continued)

Table 16.1 Continued

Risk type	Identified risk
Finance	***The examples below all have an effect on your cash flow:*** • Your clients delay payments and you relied on that income to pay your supplier's bill; one specialist supplier for an expensive part always wants to be paid in advance; you have a cash flow risk and cannot pay this supplier. • The bank rejects your loan application and you need to find further finance to bridge the finance gap, quickly. • You cannot find investors that invest the amount of money you intend to raise, or no investors at all. • When importing/planning to export, currency exchange rates are an important risk factor. • Change in interest rates, going up significantly, makes borrowing money more expensive. Can you actually produce at the estimated cost? In the time you planned to? You have not sufficient investment/capital to buy the latest technology, thus your production cost are too high.
Staff and people risks	Flu epidemic – all key staff are taken ill and you cannot meet the deadlines. Staff have not got the skills to do the job; staff leave suddenly; management does not manage staff properly. The staff member doing the client presentation falls ill and has not backed up his work (he is in hospital for a while). Staff/associates working from home fall ill and have not stored their work on a shared drive.
Client related	• A deadline is put forward. • Goals are changed half-way through the project. • Staff managing the project change and have different views on how it should be done. • Client does not pay on time at half-way point.
Market risks	Change in demand influences the buying behaviour of clients. Potential target customers are not buying at the price you sell the product.
Competitive risks	The competition reduces prices, uses cheaper materials that are hard to spot; competitors sell products that offer more useful benefits for customers etc.
Legal and regulatory risks	Changes in taxation affect your cash flow. New regulations come into force rather quickly that increase production cost. New laws affect how you can operate.
System risks	Events affect a whole industry or market: banking crisis, increase in fuel prices due to increase in oil prices.

operations. These business risks apply to for-profit and social enterprises in all countries the case study companies cover, from the US to Hong Kong and Europe.

Category (1) risks can be explained as minor – in the likelihood of occurring when referring to statistics. Getting a flat tyre – how often does that happen to you and others? No need to prepare for it in any other way than complying with the guidelines of having at least a spare wheel in the car. Similarly, delays in public transport can happen, and stations and train companies work hard to avoid that and have statistics about their trains being on time above 80%. Leaving early enough for a meeting is good professional practice anyway, as it is unprofessional to let anybody wait for a meeting.

Category (2) risks can be addressed with simple behaviour changes. I call them "annoy-ing" and they are often related to bad timing and preparation. Some can easily be avoided with some planning and stock building, and applying some common sense in advance.

Category (3) risks are those that happen despite all measures put in place to reduce their occurrence. While you should train and supervise your employees, mistakes do happen, and for that reason employer's liability insurance covers that risk, unless gross negligence was at play.

Category (4) risks are the big risks endangering a business's survival. The most important ones are listed in detail in Table 16.1. While the stolen laptop can be replaced (insurance cover applies), the data on the laptop for the client presentation cannot be reproduced that quickly for the meeting. They are hopefully stored safely in several places, yet I have seen it often that they are not.

Table 16.1 gives sufficient detail with examples of what risks can affect your start-up, yet without discussing solutions or activities you can engage in to reduce the risk from occur-ring or ways to manage the effect of events discussed. The next step business owners of start-ups need to address is how to manage those risks. This is discussed in the next section.

16.1.3   Risk management – a simple pragmatic way

Risk management is one of the important project management tools all businesses should use. Risks are usually assessed on how likely they are to occur/happen and what level of impact they will have on the business activities. A simple way of assessing the risk is to set a scale of either one to five or one to ten for each, and assess each risk on this scale for its likelihood to occur and its possible impact on the business.

When you multiply the likelihood number with the impact number you obtain the risk factor. Using a scale of one to five for both, the highest risk factor can be 25 (5 for likelihood × 5 for impact), the lowest 1 (1 × 1).

Table 16.2 indicates an example of how this risk can be calculated. The next step then is to identify reasons why this risk could occur and any possible activities that can minimize its occurrence and impact or even prevent it if this is possible. The latter activities are

Table 16.2   Pragmatic risk management

Risk	Likelihood 1-5	Impact 1-5	Impact detail and cost	Risk factor	Responsible staff	Mitigation	Cost of mitigation
IT collapses	2	5	No work possible, loss of data if not backed up; loss of client work; days / weeks of work might be lost.	10	CEO	Back up on external hard drive every day; keep external hard drive in different building; back up via cloud technology.	Daily rate for staff to redo the work; buying new hardware.

called *mitigation* of the risk. Ideally, in an organization you identify the person responsible for monitoring the risk. For the self-employed, all the risks need to be managed by the owner or passed on to a supplier. Finally, you need to identify the costs associated with risk mitigation and dealing with the consequences of this risk occurring.

> ### Activity 16.1   What could go wrong? Analysing risks for your *sustainable start-up*
>
> On the companion website www.palgrave.com/companion/hill-start-up you will find a form to download. Explore the risks for your start-up.

The next section illustrates some approaches to increasing capacity to produce and/or deliver, including employing staff.

16.2   Employing and managing staff

16.2.1 Recruitment and selection for first-timers

 Many first-time employers seem to make similar mistakes. These include:

- Treating staff as friends instead of employees to start with;
- Not having a clear job description with skills listed and tasks for candidate selection;
- Being led by the first impression and not engaging in sufficient due diligence – for example, checking details in a CV for accuracy, asking for certificates of qualifications.

The *sustainable start-up* can invest in staff where and when it makes business sense to have someone else take on jobs that either are of a routine nature and/or need specialist skills the owner does not have. Examples include asking someone to do the administrative tasks and on-going customer contact while the start-up founders focus on the tasks that create value with higher return using their expertise, such as seeing clients and engaging in production. If you have money or seed funding to do that, this makes a lot of business sense. Similarly, asking a designer to create a logo and branding instead of spending hours or days trying to do it yourself applies the principle of resourceful impact in managing your resources, time, money and skills, in a cost-effective way.

 Case study

Consider what our case study **Lewis Barnes** did. He took on the first employee within two weeks of the start of trading. He needed a staff member to look after administration, keep in touch with enquiries and clients, and ensure that information was sent out promptly. This freed Lewis to focus on what he is best at, working with clients and building up a tennis academy infrastructure. At the time of the interview Lewis had six employees apart from himself, of whom two were part-time and four worked full-time for him. Similarly, **Lillie Ranney**, Ohio, US, employed a staff member while working through the accelerator programme, as she did not feel her time was used the best possible way in working her way through financial issues; finance is not her area of expertise.

Where do you go to find employees? If you cannot find the right skills in your personal networks, there are a number of possibilities that do not cost you a fee:

- If you are a student and are keen to employ other students, liaise with your employment or placement office. You can ask a staff member to send the job offer round in your school/department or faculty if that is where you would like your students to come from.
- You can go to the job centre and put a job advert through the system there.
- You can use your social media contacts and websites to put up the job advert.
- You can put up the job advert on your website.

For a fee there is no limit: you can place a job advert in a local newspaper, use online or brick-and-mortar recruitment agencies.

As a graduate start-up you might also want to consider offering some work experience or placements to students. Section 16.3 shows you an example of an advert our case study founders **Shivam and Muhammad** from Frinter Ltd sent out.

Recruitment and selection are areas well researched and published. The section with further reading on the companion website lists some useful books in that area.

However, it is worth considering carefully, do you really need employees? Applying the principles and practices of resourceful impact (3) and of sustainability (6), it is worth considering working with freelancers and volunteers or consultants. Committing to an employment contract is a great responsibility that should not be taken on too soon, as it might not be sustainable, in particular when the financial projections are too high. Using the above flexible options is also applying the principle of responsibility (3) and sustainability (6), as having to close down due to fixed costs being too high is a risk that can be avoided.

If you take on employees, there are a number of duties and responsibilities the next section discusses.

16.2.2 Employers' duties for first-time employers

It was an uphill journey for the two case study start-ups that took on staff very early on their journey. Where do you find out about what you have and could and should do? Here is what Lewis says:

Asking around, speaking to people, Internet, yeah it was a lot [of research]. National Insurance, insurance, health and safety, all these different things that you don't realize need to be addressed ... If I was a little bit unsure, I made it crystal clear, whether it would be through Internet reading, to make sure I ticked the box, I wasn't liable or doing something unethical. So yeah, a lot of reading.

And when he considers what he could do differently if he were to start-up again, one important area is recruitment.

[I would] do the recruitment a little bit more stringent[ly]. The first person I employed now we didn't necessarily work with anymore; I looked for the wrong things in an employee that I look for now so that'd be nice to know back then, but c'est la vie, it's done.

The duties an employer has can be summarized with the term *duty of care* in many ways. Employers have to take out employer liability insurance we discussed in Chapter Fifteen;

they have to protect employees from harm and inform them about their rights. There are further issues to address:

▶ Ensure that the person you employ has the legal right to work in the UK/your country.
▶ Identify the number of hours you want to employ them for.
▶ Carry out a check of their criminal records with the Disclosure and Barring Service (DBS, formerly known as CRB) if you work with vulnerable adults or children.
▶ Decide on and pay a wage (at least minimum wage, this type of wage was discussed in Chapter Ten).
▶ Send a written statement with employment details (including terms and conditions) to any employee working with you for more than a month.
▶ Register as an employer with HM Revenue and Customs before the employee starts.
▶ Pay National Insurance contributions for the employee and take off the tax to pay before paying the salary into their account.

One important recent duty for the UK is the workplace pension employers have to provide. In the UK, in 2012 the Pensions Act 2012, a law, came into force so that many employers must automatically enrol workers into a workplace pension scheme over the next few years if they have at least one staff member aged between 22 and State Pension age, earning at least £10,000 a year and working in the UK. This is an additional cost every employer has to put down on his start-up costs and cash flow. For further information check out the Pensions Regulator (http://www.pensionsregulator.gov.uk).

The **length and hours of contract** need some consideration: part-time to start with is a good idea as you do not know how the business will develop, and a full-time salary is a fixed cost you have to pay out whatever the income. You might want to combine that with a fixed-term contract that allows you to finish the employment after the fixed amount of time or renew it if you want to.

Learning and development makes business sense, and many employers that follow a co-creation process in ensuring their staff can attend training in all sorts of forms and provide the necessary on-the-job training themselves. Training is an important aspect of working life, in particular with so many aspects of work changing (IT, funding and social media, to name only a few). It is an important part of increasing staff job satisfaction and staff retention. For bite-size training delivered at reasonable prices online, LearnDirect is a useful source (www.learndirect.com, see also www.alison.com for free online training in business skills).

Free training is still available for employers offering apprenticeships and taking on young people as employees in the UK. It needs some local research to find out if local colleges can offer that support and training to small local business, often with support of EU funding.

16.3 Recruiting and managing volunteers for your sustainable start-up

Managing volunteers is not only important for social enterprises and charities; it also applies to for-profit start-ups who take on student placements on a short-term basis, which they cannot or do not pay. Many social enterprises, however, work a lot more with volunteers in all phases of their development, from pre-start-up to maturity.

 Volunteers decide to offer their time for a purpose they believe in. This offer is temporary, as at any point in time they can decide not to offer their time and do something else. This means the purpose needs of their role to be clear to them, the benefits they gain from carrying out this role and the difference they can make. While a clear goal or outcome is not always important, it helps for many volunteers to know "where this is all going". It is possible that a volunteer, as pointed out earlier, is an individual who might also be in paid employment, part-time or full-time, or working unpaid either in the home or for another organization.

Box 16.1 shows an advert for placements for our case study company **Frinter Ltd** to find enthusiastic volunteers as brand ambassadors, current undergraduate students. Notice the incentives offered in kind, such as an iPad. An incentive "in kind" is a good or service (but not money) offered in return for services provided or time spent.

Box 16.1   Advert for volunteer brand ambassadors for Frinter Ltd

BRAND AMBASSADOR for FRINTER

Your Personality:

- ☐ *Excellent time management*
- ☐ *Innovative and creative*
- ☐ *Reliable*
- ☐ *Sociable*
- ☐ *Goal oriented*
- ☐ *Confident public speaker*
- ☐ *Comfortable with social media (Facebook, Twitter)*
- ☐ *Relationships builder*

The Brand Ambassador role:

This is a part-time role running throughout your first and second term. Your main responsibility is to promote Frinter on your campus and encourage more students to use Frinter.

Duties:

- ☐ *Network with societies to promote Frinter*
- ☐ *Run competitions*
- ☐ *Promote Frinter in lectures via public speaking*
- ☐ *Deliver one campaign per term*
- ☐ *On-going Frinter support, progress review and networking with other Frinter Brand Ambassadors via conference calls*
- ☐ *Attend Fresher's fair with another Frinter employee*

Benefits:

- ☐ *Guaranteed work for majority of the year*
- ☐ *Amazon vouchers*
- ☐ *Free Frinter VIP membership*
- ☐ *Lots of prizes to be won throughout the year*
- ☐ *Bonuses on achieving targets*
- ☐ *Free promotional material*
- ☐ *Excellent experience for your CV*

To apply:

Send your CV and cover letter, including why you want this job & why you are the best person suitable for this job.

This is a volunteer position but comes with a lot of benefits such as free Frinter VIP membership and priority access to deals and offers. The role also comes with a number of prizes such as paid holiday packages and iPads on achieving targets.

CONTACT hello@frinter.co.uk

 In recent years, policy-makers and volunteers themselves have taken a more strategic view of volunteering. This means that volunteering is not just carried out to support a cause, but also to develop a skill or a skills set. Students volunteering want to be able to show to an employer what skills they developed while volunteering. The unemployed are encouraged to volunteer and are often interested in developing skills in a particular area that allows them to prepare for a paid job in this or a related area. Just these developments alone have meant that volunteering roles have to be managed carefully and handled like a paid job, with clear responsibilities and skills profile needed and/or that can be developed.

Social enterprises that develop from a group of like-minded people who share a commitment to helping a particular disadvantaged group of people or share an interest in developing a project, such as a community centre or a local nursery or a Hub (a shared workplace) face slightly different challenges to start with:

From a group of equal voices some will move into:

▶ The role of director/trustee of the organization with more formal responsibility;
▶ Others will become executive directors and or managers and paid staff, while others remain as volunteers.

They will need to delegate tasks to volunteers, as there is no money to pay someone to start with.

 Case study

Having been part of such a community group that attempted to build a social enterprise around a local shared workspace for the self-employed and home-based businesses to meet other entrepreneurs, I witnessed the challenges the two co-founders had with each other and some volunteers who had their own priorities. In the transition from a group of equals to some becoming formal directors while others remain volunteers, relationships change and can break. This means that several of the formerly equal individuals move into a leadership position, maybe even into a paid job, part- or full-time, that requires them now to manage their peers and ask them to carry out specific tasks.

In my start-up support practice, I have seen it happening in four cases very recently that this can lead to frictions and that volunteers leave, as they do not want to be asked to carry out the less important tasks, at least less important in their perception. And partnerships and friendships that seemed to be sound broke over the development of the social enterprise, as views about direction and who does how much actual hands-on work were incompatible. The task division and role management need to be carried out carefully, so that unpaid and paid roles remain interesting enough for volunteers to continue to commit.

The next section discusses the essential activity for the start-up of managing relationships with customers, followed by a brief outline of the similarly important management of contact with stakeholders, as co-creation with stakeholders is important for the *sustainable start-up*.

16.4 Customer service and customer retention for the *sustainable start-up*

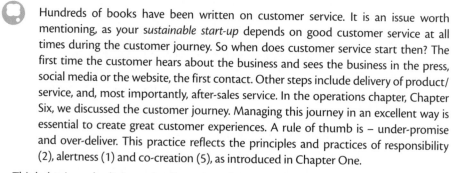

Hundreds of books have been written on customer service. It is an issue worth mentioning, as your *sustainable start-up* depends on good customer service at all times during the customer journey. So when does customer service start then? The first time the customer hears about the business and sees the business in the press, social media or the website, the first contact. Other steps include delivery of product/service, and, most importantly, after-sales service. In the operations chapter, Chapter Six, we discussed the customer journey. Managing this journey in an excellent way is essential to create great customer experiences. A rule of thumb is – under-promise and over-deliver. This practice reflects the principles and practices of responsibility (2), alertness (1) and co-creation (5), as introduced in Chapter One.

This behaviour also links to the discussion of the MMP, the minimal marketable product, and the excellent marketable product, EVP (started in Chapter Five and discussed further in Chapters Eleven and Fifteen). It is easier and quicker to start trading with a MMP to generate income, which then can finance the development of the excellent marketable product, applying the co-creation principle and practice.

Put simply, customer service is an organization's ability to supply the customers with what they need and want and *ideally more* than that. Customers need to feel satisfied so that they come back to buy from you again. Good customer service is an essential part of customer retention, that is, keeping customers who buy from you again and again. It reflects the principle and practice of responsibility never to engage in promises that you cannot deliver on, but instead exceed when and where you can. This is a successful effective way customers remember you, come back and recommend you. This way, customers having had an excellent experience will act as your ambassadors and bring in new customers as they are spreading the word for you just talking about their great experience. Similarly, it is well known that bad ratings and experiences are shared much more often than good ones. Bad press is bad for business.

These effects also apply to online businesses, where there is little or no human interaction. Sometimes, human interaction only happens in the online buying context if something has gone wrong. Experience and research have shown over and over again that exceeding customer expectations creates the impression of excellence.

Here are some insights on what makes excellent customer experiences (they implement principles and practices of alertness, responsibility, co-creation and resourceful impact):

- Personable services with a personal touch;
- For online automated services –
  - Create automated emails that include the name of the customer, not just "Dear customer", to have some personal touch.

○ Gather searches/queries a customer makes over time so you can send offers related to them.
> For retail and hospitality –
○ Ensure that staff always wear a name badge and make an effort to introduce themselves to customers when approaching them.
> Reliable and consistent service quality;
> Patience with customers, whatever they do or say;
> Going the extra mile and being proactive;
> Speed in dealing with queries and complaints;
> Flexibility on returns and complaints;
> Positive attitude and tone reflecting that everything is possible within reason.

The *sustainable start-up* knows by now that having contacts is a great starting point, and that some can be turned into paying customers, if they are true leads, you keep in touch and develop a relationship (applying principles and practices of resourceful impact, co-creation and responsibility). Practices are: Give free information on your website that inspires and make visitors want more. Give out little nuggets of information relevant to them, and remind them what your value proposition is. Use newsletters sent online and the occasional colourful printed letter. Create interaction through polls, surveys and prizes to win. We can only touch on these issues here, and recommend the further reading provided on the companion website to this book at www.palgrave.com/companion/hill-start-up.

16.5 Building and maintaining the *sustainable start-up* with ongoing practical co-creation

16.5.1 Introduction to business building with co-creation for B2B markets

For start-ups and even established micro-businesses it is difficult to get contracts bigger than their own turnover from the public and private sector, the business-to-government and business-to-business markets. In particular, many local authorities use a rule of thumb to only give a contract to a company where the contract value is matched by five times the company's turnover, for example. Some large corporates apply similar rules, or use three to four times the turnover as a rule of thumb. While this is not written down anywhere, the term "track record of similarly sized contracts" is often used to hide this assessment factor.

For that reason, to create and maintain a *sustainable start-up* there are a number of ways to increase in size and gain track record virtually through co-creating the virtual larger organization, practically and operationally. All partners gain in this process. Naturally, while working together to gain one contract, at the same time these businesses will compete to get other smaller contracts. These modes of collaboration are briefly outlined below. They apply to all types of businesses, from electricians to carpenters to designers and consultants and architects or childcare providers, and are being used in all European countries, as well as in Hong Kong and the US. In Romania, however, it seems that the practices discussed below are less common, in particular competitors working together temporarily.

The important practice underlying all discussed business practices illustrated in Figure 16.2 below is to collaborate temporarily for particular projects in a focused way, while at the same time competing in other contexts and projects.

Figure 16.2   Co-creation approach towards gaining contracts

16.5.2 Working as an associate or subcontractor for larger organizations

If you have a niche business with a particular expertise with certain materials, technology, skills or knowledge, working with a larger business or large corporates might be a starting point for the start-up. The advantage is that the other business might get a contract through adding you to the team, thus you can gain work experience and the ability to develop a track record. The disadvantage is that the other larger business gains financially a lot more, as you will only be paid either a lump sum or a daily delivery fee. Key in those relationships is not to reveal too much about your niche skill or knowledge in the process. The choice has to be yours. This is in no way an equal partner relationship.

16.5.3 Lead business and associates as subcontractors

A more equal partnership can be achieved with a loose form of an association between established micro-businesses and start-ups and the self-employed through bidding as a team of businesses together; competitors as well as complementary businesses then create a unit dependent on the contract. This type of arrangement is regarded as riskier than the next mode, the consortium arrangement. Yet, for less risky business activities this can be successful.

Some large corporates or government departments do not like the loose arrangement and expect a more formal arrangement between suppliers delivering on one contract. This can be addressed by building a consortium, which is discussed in the next section.

16.5.4 Consortia building for bidding for contracts

Consortia are built and exist for all types of trades, from plumbers to designers to research consultancies and recruitment agencies.

For the reason of gaining larger contracts, an alliance between competitors to reach this track record of similar value contracts is a way to move beyond the small contracts. A consortium is expected to have a lead company for dealing with the client, and often it is expected that a written agreement is in place between consortia members for roles and regulating delivery and non-delivery challenges. This formal contractual arrangement reduces the risks of such a delivery partner as it has been fixed in writing what will happen if one partner does not deliver on time or to specification.

16.5.5 From strategic alliances to building a new organization with others

Strategic alliances are known from large corporates, which form strategic alliances with non-competitors to gain a competitive advantage. Samsung and DreamWorks formed an alliance in the following way: the 3D Blu-ray version of *How to Train Your Dragon* that was exclusively available through DreamWorks became part of the Samsung 3D starter kit bought together with the Samsung 3D TV. The same practice can be applied to the *sustainable start-up* strategies. For example, a web designer can build a strategic alliance with a printer to offer a full package of branding for start-ups or companies rebranding themselves and market the services together.

The three most important value-adding features of this strategy include:

▶ Gaining in economies of scale and optimizing resource management;
▶ Reduction of risks and uncertainties for gaining sales;
▶ Gaining new particular resources and networks/buyers.

 Activity 16.2 Strategic alliances

List at least six strategic alliances each for the following four start-ups:

Fusion restaurant

Student bar

Social media consultancy

Second-hand furniture retail

In some cases there is business sense in building a third organization, a joint venture, for example, as a company limited by shares, where two or three or four equal partners form a new company to access or penetrate one particular market segment collaboratively.

16.5.6 Finding and selecting temporary alliances

While the above good business practices for start-ups work well for some start-ups, they do not work for all.

To find businesses or individuals who might qualify as potential temporary business alliance partners, the following channels are suggested:

▶ Regular attendance at business networking meetings;
▶ Taking part in online networking via social media and online discussion groups.

These are two of the most important ways to meet like-minded professionals and competitors. Finding business network meetings was discussed in Chapter Two, Section 2.6.

Similarly, attending business fairs and trade exhibitions allows for easy access to established businesses of all sizes, and free workshops and tasters as well as talks give further insight into the business philosophy and practices of an organization.

Selecting one or more of them requires first clarifying what you expect from an alliance partner, a list of criteria, and your goals for engaging in such a temporary partnership. Ideally, you will find a close match of goals and criteria from the alliance partner. Virtually, every project and product, and even a client, might require a different set of alliance partners; however, often, some partners are suitable for working with you on more than one project. The following list gathers some generic features of possibly suitable partners:

- A track record/experience in this type of work;
- Ability to double your skills sets;
- Ability to provide skills/products additional to your set of skills and products required by the client or project;
- Reliability – delivers on all promises made in terms of time, quality and cost;
- Quality – delivers promised quality;
- On time – keeps to deadlines at all times;
- On cost – manages costs well and keeps below or at promised spending needed.

Goals for working with alliance partners often include:

- To increase capacity – the ability to deliver larger quantities of services or products at the same time;
- To widen diversity of services/products offered, more similar and different ones;
- To extend the track record in doing this kind of work;
- To increase virtually the organizational turnover.

Those start-ups with a truly unique and innovative product or service might want to consider strategic alliances to get access to established distribution channels, for example, or marketing channels.

This was the last chapter of this book. You are now fully equipped to start and run a new venture in your first year.

Good luck with your *sustainable start-up*!
Inge Hill

16.6 Concluding remarks and application of new insights

This chapter allowed you to explore in detail the risks of business failure in the first year of trading. It identified the reasons for this failure referring to business activities and personal traits and behaviour of the business owner(s). We then differentiated business risks in two ways, by the impact they can have on the business, categories (1) to (4), from no impact to very high impact, and the areas in business they can occur in, from staff related to technology, IT, finance and transport. We applied a simple scale of one to five to measure the likelihood of an event occurring and the potential impact it can have on business activities.

Multiplying these two numbers leads to the risk factor, which can have a maximum value of 25. Risk management is an important activity that all businesses should carry out regularly, and many actually do. Listing a number of activities that can be carried out to be prepared for if a risk should occur, and having lined up activities that can reduce the impact of an event, is called risk mitigation. The *sustainable start-up* is advised to carry out some risks assessment before start of trading and to update their risk table on a regular basis, ideally every six months.

Those start-ups employing staff and/or working with volunteers need to be aware of the legal duties employers and managers of volunteers have, in terms of employer's liability insurance that is compulsory in the UK and challenges in recruitment and selection.

The co-creation approach to working with others during start-up and the first years was discussed in detail outlining a variety of ways to create successful short-term temporary alliances with others, be they individuals or businesses.

Revision questions and applying the new insights to your *sustainable start-up*

1 What have been the main reasons for start-ups failing?
2 Explain the four risk categories and give two examples for each of them. Which ones apply to your *sustainable start-up*?
3 What types of practical risks are there? Give one example for each of them. Which of those risks will apply to your *sustainable start-up*? While they were briefly discussed in each chapter of this book, it is important to bring them all together in one table.
4 For your *sustainable start-up*, create a risk table and include a column in which you list activities to engage in to reduce the impact of a risk or the likelihood of it occurring.
5 What must you do when you become an employer?
6 Outline the modes of collaboration the *sustainable start-up* can create with others.
7 For your own *sustainable start-up* – what would be useful collaborations for the following areas: marketing, finance, supplies, getting new work/clients. Outline them now and make an action plan for how and when you will realize them. Note these considerations and decision in your start-up diary.

Coventry University London

REFERENCES

A

Aidzes, I. (1988) *Corporate Lifecycles*. Englewood Cliffs (New Jersey: Prentice Hall).

Al-Debei, M.M., El-Haddadeh, R. and Avision, D. (2008) Defining the Business Model in the New World of Digital Business. In: *Proceedings of the 14th Americas Conference on Information Systems held 14–17 August 2008*, Toronto, Ontario, Canada, pp. 1551–1561.

Amit, R. and Zott, C. (2012) Creating value through business model innovation, *MIT Sloan Management Review*, 53 (3), pp. 41–49.

Ashoka (2014) *Mission*, Arlington: Innovators for the Public: https://www.ashoka.org/visionmission (accessed July 13, 2014).

Austin, J.E., Leonard, B., Reficco, E. and Wei-Skillem, J. (2006) Social Entrepreneurship: It's for Corporations, too. In: Nicholls, A. ed. *Social Entrepreneurship, New models of Sustainable Change*. Oxford: Oxford University Press, pp. 169–180.

B

Baden-Fuller, C., MacMillan, I.C., Demil, B. and Lecocq's, X. (2010) Business models and models (editorial), *Long Range Planning*, 43 (2–3), pp. 143–145.

Baldwin, C., Hienerth, C. and von Hippel, E. (2006) How user innovations become commercial products: A theoretical investigation and case study, *Research Policy*, 35 (9), pp. 1291–1313.

Baron, R. A. and Tang, J. (2009) Entrepreneurs' social skills and new venture performance: mediating mechanisms and cultural generality, *Journal of Management* 35 (2), pp. 282–306.

Battilana, J. and Lee, M. (2014) Advancing research on hybrid organizing – Insights from the study of social enterprises, *The Academy of Management Annals*, 8 (1), pp. 397–441.

Battilana, J. and Dorado, S. (2010) Building sustainable hybrid organisations: The case of commercial microfinance organisations, *Academy of Management Review*, 53 (6), pp. 1419–1440.

Bhave, M. P. (1994) A process model of entrepreneurial venture creation, *Journal of Business Venturing*, 9 (3), pp. 223–242.

Birley, S. and Westhead, P. (1994) A taxonomy of business start-up reasons and their impact on firm growth and size, *Journal of Business Venturing*, 9 (1), pp. 7–31.

Blank, S. (2006) *The Four Steps to the Epiphany. Successful Strategies for Products that Win*, 3rd edition (Wahroonga: K & S Ranch, Wheelers).

Blythe, J. (2012) *100 Great PR Ideas* (Singapore: Marshall Cavendish Business).

Bowman, H. and MacInnes, I. (2006) Dynamic Business model framework for value webs. In: *Proceedings of the 39th Hawaii International Conference on System Sciences (HICSS), 4–7 January, 2006*. US: Hawaii, pp. 43–53.

Burke, A. and Hussels, S. (2013) How competition strengthens start-ups, *Harvard Business Review*, March, pp. 24–25.

Bryman, A. and Bell, E. (2011) *Business Research Methods*, 3rd edition (Oxford: Oxford University Press).

C–D

Cardon, M., Vincent, J., Singh, J. and Drovsek, M. (2009) The Nature and Experience of Entrepreneurial Passion, *The Academy of Management Review*, 34 (3), pp. 511–530.

Carter, N.M., Gartner, W.B., Shaver, K.G. and Gatewood, E.J. (2003) The career reasons of nascent entrepreneurs, *Journal of Business Venturing*, 18 (1), pp. 13–39.

Cassar, G. (2007) Money, money, money? A longitudinal investigation of entrepreneur career reasons, growth preferences and achieved growth, *Entrepreneurship and Regional Development*, 19 (1), pp. 89–107.

Centeno, E., Hart, S. and Dinnie, K. (2013) The five phases of SME brand building, *Journal of Brand Management*, 20 (6), pp. 445–457.

Chan, J.K.L. and Baum, T. (2007) Motivation factors of ecotourists in ecolodge accommodation: The push and pull factors, *Asia Pacific Journal of Tourism Research*, 12 (4), pp. 349–364.

Chell, E. and Karatas-Ozkan, M. (2014) *Handbook of Research on Small Business and Entrepreneurship* (Cheltenham: Elgar Publishing).

Christiansen, J. (2014a) *What do Founders get from Attending an Accelerator Program* (Brussels: Accelerator Assembly).

Christiansen, J. (2014b) *The European Seed Accelerator Ecosystem* (Brussels: Accelerator Assembly).

CIM (Chartered Institute of Marketing) (2010) *Shape the Agenda, Tomorrow's Word – Re-Evaluating the Role of Marketing* (Maidenhead: Chartered Institute of Marketing).

Cone Communications (2014) *2013 Cone Communications Social Impact Study* (New York: Cone Communications).

Culking, N. (2013) Beyond being a student. An exploration of student and graduate start-ups (SGSUs) operating from university incubators, *Journal for Small Business and Enterprise Development*, 20 (3), pp. 634–649.

Curedale, R. A. (2013) *Service Design: 250 essential methods* (Topanga, CA: Design Community College Inc.).

Davidsson, P. (2006) Nascent entrepreneurship: Empirical studies and developments, *Foundations and Trends in Entrepreneurship*, 2 (1), pp. 1–76.

de Bono, E. (2009) *The Six Thinking Hats* (London: Penguin).

Dees, J.G. (1998) *The Meaning of Social Entrepreneuship* (Stanford: Stanford University, mimeo).

Defourny, J. and Nyssens, M. (2012) *The EMES Approach of Social Enterprise in a Comparative Perspective* (Liege and Louvain, Belgium: EMES European Research Network asbl, Working Papers Series, WP no. 12/03).

Delanoe, S. (2013) From intention to start-up: the effect of professional support, *Journal of Small Business and Enterprise Development*, 20 (2), pp. 383–398.

Department for Business, Information and Skills (BIS) (2014a) *Business Population Estimates for the UK and Regions 2014* (London: BIS).

Department for Business, Information and Skills (BIS) (2014b) *Small Business Survey 2012: Businesses with No Employees* (London: BIS).

Department for Trade and Industry (2002) *Social Enterprise: A Strategy for Success* (London: Department for Trade and Industry).

DeTienne, D.R. (2010) Entrepreneurial exit as a critical component of the entrepreneurial process: Theoretical development, *Journal of Business Venturing*, 25 (2), pp. 203–215.

Dobbs, M.E. (2014) Guidelines for applying Porter's five forces framework: As set of industry analysis templates, *Competitiveness Review*, 24 (1), pp. 32–45.

Doherty, B., Haugh, H. and Lyon, F. (2013) Social enterprises as hybrid organisations: A review and research agenda, *International Journal of Management Reviews*, 16 (4), pp. 417–436.

Dolan, R.J. (1990a) *Conjoint Analysis: A Manager's Guide* (Boston, MA: Harvard Business School Publishing).

Dolan, R.J. (1990b) *Concept Testing* (Boston, MA: Harvard Business School Publishing).

Dorado, S. and Ventresca, M.J. (2013) Crescive Entrepreneurship in complex social problems: institutional conditions for entrepreneurial engagement, *Journal of Business Venturing*, 28 (1), pp. 69–92.

DTI, Department for Trade and Industry (2002) *Social Enterprise: A Strategy for Success* (London: Department for Trade and Industry).

E–F

Eisingerich, A.B. and Bell, S.J. (2008). Managing networks of interorganisational linkages and sustainable firm performance in business-to-business service contexts, *Journal of Services Marketing*, 22 (7), pp. 494–504.

El-Gohary, H. (2012) *The Impact of E-Marketing Practices on Marketing Performance. A Small Business Enterprises Context* (Saarbruecken: Lambert Academic Publishing GmbH & Co. KG).

European Commission (2003) *Commission Recommendation 2003/361/EC* (Brussels: Official Journal of the European Union L 124, 20/5/2003).

European Commission (2006) *The New SME Definition. User Guide. And Model Declaration* (Brussels: European Commission).

European Commission (2011) *Communication from the Commission to the European Parliament, The Council, The European Economic and Social Committee and the Committee of the Regions: Social Business Initiative. Creating a favourable climate for social enterprises, key stakeholders in the social economy and innovation* (Brussels: COM(2011)682 final / SEC(2011) 1278 final).

European Commission (2014) *A Partial and Fragile Recovery. July 2014. Annual Report on European SMEs 2013/2014* (Brussels: European Commission).

Fayolle, A. and Matlay, H. (2012a) Social Entrepreneurship: A Multicultural and Multidimensional Perspective. In: Fayolle, A. and Matlay, H. eds. *Handbook of Research on Social Entrepreneurship*. Cheltenham: Edward Elgar Publishing, pp. 1–14.

Fayolle, A. and Matlay, H. eds. (2012b) *Handbook of Research on Social Entrepreneurship* (Cheltenham: Edward Elgar Publishing).

G–H

GEM, Global Entrepreneurship Monitoring (2014a) *Global Entrepreneurship Monitor 2013 Global Report* (Santiago, Kuala Lumpur and London: Jose Ernesto Amoros, Niels Bosma and Global Entrepreneurship Research Association (GERA)). (see www.gem.org.uk)

GEM, Global Entrepreneurship Monitoring (2014b) *Global Entrepreneurship Monitor. United Kingdom Monitoring Report 2013* (Glasgow and Birmingham: Strathclyde and Aston Universities). (see www.gem.org.uk)

Ghosh, S., Surjadjaja, H. and Antony, J. (2004) Optimisation of the determinants of e-service operations, *Business Process Management Journal*, 10 (6), pp. 616–636.

Gooding, P. (2014) *Consumer Price Inflation: The Basket of Goods and Services* (London: Office for National Statistics).

Granovetter, M. (1985) Economic Action and Social Structure: The Problem of Embeddedness, *American Journal of Sociology*, 91 (3), pp. 481–510.

Hastings, G., Bryant, C. and Angus, K. (2012) *The Sage Handbook of Social Marketing* (Hastings: Sage).

Haeflinger, S., Jaeger, P. and Krogh, G. von (2010) Under the radar: industry entry by user entrepreneurs, *Research Policy*, 39 (9), pp. 1198–1213.

Haeussler, C., Harhoff, D. and Mueller, E. (2009). *To be financed or not...-The role of patents for venture capital financing*. Centre for Economic Policy Research (CEPR) Discussion paper 7115. London, UK: CEPR.

Hockerts, K. (2010) Social Entrepreneurship between market and mission, *International Review of Entrepreneurship*, 9 (2), pp. 188–198.

Humbert, A.L. and Drew, E. (2010) Gender, entrepreneurship and motivational factors in an Irish context, *International Journal of Gender and Entrepreneurship*, 2 (2), pp. 173–196.

I–K

IFPI (International Federation of the Photographic Industry) (2014) *IFPI Digital Music Report 2014* (London: IFPI).

Jayawarna, D., Rouse, J. and Kitching, J. (2011) Entrepreneur motivations and life course, *Small Business Journal*, 31 (1), pp. 34–56.

Kaplan, A.M. and Haenlein, M. (2010) Users of the world, unite! The challenges and opportunities of Social Media, *Business Horizons*, 53 (1), pp. 59–68.

Kauanui, S.K., Thomas, K.D., Rubens, A. and Sherman, C.L. (2010) Entrepreneurship and Spirituality: a comparative analysis of entrepreneurs' motivation, *Journal of Small Business and Entrepreneurship*, 23 (4), pp. 621–635.

Ketchen, D.J., Short, J.C. and Combs, J.G. (2011) Is franchising entrepreneurship? Yes, No, and Maybe So, *Entrepreneurship Theory and Practice*, 35 (3), pp. 583–593.

Kim, W.C. and Mauborgne, R. (2005) *Blue Ocean Strategy: How to Create Uncontested Market Space and Make the Competition Irrelevant* (Boston: Harvard Business School Press).

Kirkwood, J. (2009) Motivational factors in a push-pull theory of entrepreneurship, *Gender in Management*, 24 (5), pp. 346–364.

Klapper, L.F. and Parker, C. (2010) Gender and the business environment for new firm creation, *Worldbank Research Observer*, 26 (2), pp. 237–257.

Klyver, K., Nielsen, S.L. and Evald, M.R. (2013) Women's self-employment: An act of institutional (dis)integration? A multilevel, cross-country study, *Journal of Business Venturing*, 28 (4), pp. 474–488.

Kozinets, R.V. (2002) The field behind the screen: Using netnography for marketing research in online communities, *Journal of Marketing Research*, 39 (1), pp. 61–72.

Kyrgidou, L.P. and Petridou, E. (2013) Developing women entrepreneurs' knowledge, skills and attitudes through e-mentoring support, *Journal of Small Business and Enterprise Development*, 20 (3), pp. 548–566.

L–M

Lafontaine, F. (2014) Franchising. Directions for further research, *International Journal of the Economics of Business*, 21 (1), pp. 21–25.

Leyden, D. P., Link, A. N. and Siegel, D. S. (2013) *A Theoretical Analysis of the Role of Networks in Entrepreneurship*, Working Paper 13/22 (http://bae.uncg.edu/assets/research/econwp/2013/13-22.pdf, accessed 13/5/2015) (Greensboro: Department of Economics Working Paper Series, University of North Carolina at Greensboro).

Liao, J., Welsch, H. and Tan Wee-Liang (2005) Venture gestation paths of nascent entrepreneurs: Exploring the temporal patterns, *Journal of High Technology Management Research*, 16 (1), pp. 1–22.

Lord Young (2013) *Growing Your business. A Report on Growing Micro-businesses* (London: Crown copyright).

Lord Young (2012) *Make Business Your Business* (London: Crown copyright).

Lovelock, C.H., Wirtz, J. and Chew, P. (2009) *Essentials of Services Marketing* (Singapore: Prentice Hall).

Low, M.B. and MacMillan, I. C. (1988) Entrepreneurship: Past research and future challenges, *Journal of Management*, 14, pp. 139–161.

Mair, J. and Marti, I. (2006) Social entrepreneurship research: a source of explanation, prediction and delight, *Journal of World Business*, 41 (1), pp. 36–44.

Markova, G., Perry, J. and Farmer, S.M. (2011) It's all about the data: Challenges and solutions in the study of nascent entrepreneurs, *Journal of Developmental Entrepreneurship*, 16 (2), pp. 169–198.

McCline, R. and Bhat, S. (2012) An exploratory investigation into the role and importance of networking partners of South Asian entrepreneurs in the venture creation process, *International Journal of Entrepreneurship*, 16, pp. 37–62.

McKeever, E., Anderson, A. and Jack, S. (2014) Social embeddedness in entrepreneurship research: The importance of context and community. In: Chell, E. and Karatas-Ozkan, M. eds. *Handbook of Research on Small Business and Entrepreneurship*. Cheltenham: Elgar Publishing, pp. 222–236.

Mendez., M.T., Galindo, M.-A. and Sastre, M.-A. (2014) Franchise, innovation and entrepreneurship, *The Service Industries Journal*, 34 (9–10), pp. 843–855.

Miller, D. and Friesen, P.H. (1983) Strategy-making and environment: The third link, *Strategic Management Journal*, 4 (3), pp. 221–235.

Mintel (2014) *Social and Media Networks UK* (London/New York: Mintel).

Moore, D. and Buttner, E. (1997) *Women Entrepreneurs: Moving beyond the Glass Ceiling* (London: Sage).

Morris, M., Miyasakik, N., Wattters, C. and Coombes, S. (2006) The dilemma of growth: Understanding venture size choices of women entrepreneurs, *Journal of Small Business Management*, 44 (2), pp. 221–244.

Mullins. J. (2012) *The New Business Road Test: What Entrepreneurs and Executive Should do before Launching a Lean Start-up*, 4th edition (Harlow: FT Publishing).

N–P

NatWest / BFA (2014) *Franchise Survey 2013* (Abingdon: British Franchise Association).

NESTA (2014) *Impact of Mentoring. How Creative Businesses Have Benefited* (London: NESTA).

Nielsen (2013) *Paid Social Media. Industry Update and Good Practices 2013* (New York: Nielsen Consulting Group).

OECD, Organisation for Economic Cooperation and Development (2014) *OECD Statistics on International Trade in Services*. Volume 2014, issue 2 (Paris: OECD).

OECD, Organisation for Economic Cooperation and Development (2013a) *The Missing Entrepreneurs: Policies for Inclusive Entrepreneurship in Europe* (Paris: OECD).

OECD (2013b) *The App Economy* (Paris: OECD Digital Economy Papers, No. 230).

Office for National Statistics, ONS, (2009) *UK Standard Industrial Classification of Economic Activities 2007* (SIC 2007) (London: Office for National Statistics, http://www.ons.gov.uk/ons/guide-method/classifications/current-standard-classifications/standard-industrial-classification/index.html, accessed 30/5/2015.

Office for National Statistics (2014) *Business Demographics 2013* (London: Office for National Statistics).

Office for National Statistics (2013) *Business Demographics 2012* (London: Office for National Statistics).

Osterwalder, A. and Pigneur, Y. (2010) *Business Model Generation: A Handbook for Visionaries, Game Changers, and Challengers* (Hoboken: Wiley).

Padley, M., Valadez, L. and Hirsch, D. (2015) *Households Below a Minimum Income Standard: 2008/09 to 2012/13* (London: Joseph Rowntree Foundation).

Parker, S.C. (2008). The economics of formal business networks, *Journal of Business Venturing*, 23 (6), pp. 627–640.

Patel, P.C. and Thatcher, S.B. (2014) Sticking it out: individual attributes and persistence in self-employment, *Journal of Management*, 40 (7), pp. 1932–1979.

Pirolo, L. and Presutti, M. (2010). The impact of social capital on the start-up's performance growth, *Journal of Small Business Management*, 48 (2), 197–227.

Plunkett, J., Hurrell, A. and D'Arcy, C. (2014) *More than a Minimum: The Review of the Minimum Wage – Final Report* (London: Resolution Foundation).

Porter, M. (2008) The five competitive forces that shape strategy, *Harvard Business Review*, January, pp. 78–93.

Porter, M. (1980 and 1985) *Competitive Strategy: Techniques for Analysing Industries and Competitors* (New York: Free press, Republished with a new introduction 1998).

Preece, J., Nonnecke, B. and Andrews, D. (2004) The top five reasons for lurking: Improving community experiences for everyone, *Computers in Human Behavior*, 20 (2), pp. 201–223.

PricewaterhouseCoopers (2011) *Millenials at Work. Reshaping the Workplace* (London/New York: PricewaterhouseCoopers).

R–S

Rassenfosse, G. de (2012) How SMEs exploit their intellectual property assets: evidence from survey data, *Small Business Economics*, 39 (2), pp. 437–452.

Reynolds, P. and Miller, B. (1992) New firm gestation: Conception, birth and implications for research, *Journal of Business Venturing*, 7 (5), pp. 405–417.

Ries, E. (2011) *The Lean Start-up. How Constant Innovation Creates Radically Successful Businesses* (London: Penguin).

Right Management, Manpower Group (2014) *The Flux Report. Building a Resilient Workforce in the Face of Flux* (London: Manpower Group).

Rindova, V., Barry, D. and Ketchen, D., Jr (2009) Entrepreneuring as Emancipation, *The Academy of Management Review*, 34 (3), pp. 477–491.

Riyad, E. and El-Gohary, H. (2013) The impact of E-marketing use on small business enterprises' marketing success, *The Service Industries Journal*, 33 (1), pp. 31–50.

Roomi, M.A. and Harrison, P. (2011) Entrepreneurial leadership: What is it and how should it be taught?, *International Review of Entrepreneurship*, 9 (3), pp. 1–44.

Royal Bank of Scotland, RBS (2013) *RBS Enterprise Tracker, 2nd quarter* (Edinburgh: Royal Bank of Scotland).

Saunders, M., Lewis, P. and Thornhill, A. (2012) *Research Methods for Business Students* (London: Pearson).

Scheiner, C., Sarmiento, T., Brem, A. and Voigt, K. (2007) *Entrepreneurship in the United Kingdom and Germany: Educational concepts and their impacts on intention to start-up*, 17th Global IntEnt Conference Proceedings, Gdansk, Poland. 8–11 July, Internationalising Entrepreneurship Education and Training Conference, Germany.

Schoonjans, B., Cauwenberge, P. van, Bauwhede, H.V. (2013) Formal business networking and SME growth, *Small Business Economics*, 41 (1), pp. 169–181.

Schumpeter, J.A. (1982) *The Theory of Economic Development: An Inquiry into Profits, Capital, Credit, Interest, and the Business Cycle* (original edition 1911 with the same title). Social Science Classics Series (Book 46) (New Brunswick: Transaction Publishers).

Seelos, C. and Mair, J. (2007) Profitable business models and market creation in the context of deep poverty: A strategic view, *Academy of Management Perspectives*, 21 (November 1), pp. 49–63 (available at doi:10.5465/AMP.2007.27895339, accessed 4 August 2014).

Servaes, H. and Tamayo, A. (2013) The impact of corporate social responsibility of firm value: The role of customer awareness, *Management Science*, 59 (5), pp. 1045–1061.

Shafer, S.M., Smith, H.J. and Linder, J.C. (2005) The power of business models, *Business Horizons*, 48 (3), pp. 199–207.

Shah, S. and Tripsas, M. (2007) The accidental entrepreneur: The emergent and collective process of user entrepreneurship, *Strategic Entrepreneurship Journal*, 1 (1–2), pp. 123–140.

Shane, S., Kolvereid, L. and Westhead, P. (1991) Exploratory examination of the reasons leading to new firm formation across country and gender, *Journal of Business Venturing*, 6 (6), pp. 431–446.

Sivakumar, A. and Schoormans, J. (2011) Franchisee selections for social franchising success, *Journal of Nonprofit and Public Sector Management*, 23 (3), pp. 213–225.

Smith, P.R. and Zook, Ze (2011) *Marketing Communications: Integrating Offline and Online with Social Media*, (Philadelphia, PA: Kogan Page).

Social Enterprise UK (2014) *The People's Business, State of Social Enterprise Survey 2013* (London: Social Enterprise UK).

Sole, M. (2013) Entrepreneurial marketing: conceptual exploration and link to performance, *Entrepreneurial Marketing*, 15 (1), pp. 23–38.

Steckstor, D. (2012) *The Effects of Cause-related Marketing on Customers' Attitudes and Buying Behaviour* (London: Springer Gabler).

Stewart, W.H. and Roth, P.L. (2007) A meta-analysis of achievement motivation differences between entrepreneurs and managers, *Journal of Small Business Management*, 45 (4), pp. 401–421.

Stickdorn, M. and Schneider, J. (2014) *This is Service Design Thinking: Basics – Tools – Cases* (Amsterdam: BIS Publishers).

T–U

Taormina, R.J. and Lao, S.K.M. (2007) Measuring Chinese entrepreneurial motivation, *International Journal of Entrepreneurial Behaviour and Research*, 13 (4), pp. 200–221.

Teasdale, S. (2010) *What is in a Name? The Construction of Social Enterprise* (Birmingham: Third Sector Research Centre, Working Paper 46).

Teece, D.J. (2010) Business Models, Business Strategy and Innovation, *Long Range Planning*, 43 (4), pp. 172–194.

Tracey, P. and Jarvis, O. (2007) Towards a theory of social venture franchising, *Entrepreneurship: Theory and Practice*, 31 (5), pp. 667–685.

V–Z

Venturesome (2008) *The Three Models of Social Enterprises. Creating Impact Through Trading Activites*, Part 1 (London: Charities Aid Foundation).

Vestrum, I. (2014) The embedding process of community ventures: Creating a music festival in a rural community, *Entrepreneurship and Regional Development*, 26 (7), pp. 629–644.

Volery, T. and Hackl, V. (2012) The Promise of Social Franchising as a Model to Achieve Social Goals. In: Fayolle, A. and Matlay, H. eds. *Handbook of Research on Social Entrepreneurship* (Paperback). Cheltenham: Edward Elgar Publishing, pp. 157–181.

Wang, J. (2014) RD activities in start-up firms: What can we learn from founding resources? *Technology Analysis and Strategic Management*, 26 (5), pp. 517–529.

Weill, P. and Woerner, S.L. (2013) Optimizing your digital business model, *MIT Sloan Management Review*, 54 (3), pp. 71–78.

Wills, J. and Linneker, B. (2013) In-work poverty and the living wage in the United Kingdom: A geographical perspective, *Transactions of the Institute of British Geographers*, 39 (2), pp. 182–194, (available through http://onlinelibrary.wiley.com/enhanced/doi/10.1111/tran.12020/, accessed 4 August 2014).

Worldbank Group (2014) *Doing Business 2015. Going Beyond Efficiency* (Washington: Worldbank Group).

World Council of Credit Unions (2014) *2013 Statistical Report* (Madison/Wisconsin: World Council of Credit Unions).

Wright, K.B. (2005) Researching internet-based populations: Advantages and disadvantages of online survey research, online questionnaire authoring software packages, and web survey services, *Journal of Computer-Mediated Communication*, 10 (3) (no page numbers), (available at http://online library.wiley.com/enhanced/doi/10.1111/j.1083-6101.2005.tb00259.x/, accessed 4 August 2014).

Wu, S., Matthrews, L. and Dagher, G.K. (2007) Need for achievement, business goals and entrepreneurial persistence, *Management Research News*, 30 (12), pp. 928–941.

Yunus, M. (2010) Building social business: the new kind of capitalism that serves humanity's most pressing needs (New York: Public Affairs).

Yusuf, J.-E. (2012) A tale of two exits: Nascent entrepreneur learning activities and disengagement from start-up, *Small Business Economics*, 39 (3), pp. 783–799.

Zafeiropoulou, F.A. and Koufopoulos, D. (2013) The influence of relational embeddedness on the formation and performance of social franchising, *Journal of Marketing Channels*, 20 (1–2), pp. 73–98.

Zarah, S. et al. (2009) A typology of social entrepreneurs: Motives, search processes and ethical challenges, *Journal of Business Venturing*, 24 (5), pp. 519–532.

INDEX

This index intends to help the readers amongst you to be able to quickly find a topic you are interested in. My first suggestion is to read the list of chapter headings to identify in which chapter it might be dealt with. Then go to the actual chapter and read through the subheadings offered at the start of each chapter with page numbers to ease your searching. If that does not give you the result you are seeking, the index can point you to specific page numbers, where the term is discussed as well.

As the word business precedes many complex words and concepts in business, look for an entry under the first letter of the second word: an example is that you find "business launch" under L "launch" and not under the letter B. The exceptions are concepts like "business model", "business support" and "business planning", as they are technical terms and mean something different when not preceded by "business" and when talking about the Cube face Business Processes.

The index lists specific words you are familiar with and that are used in the running text. If the word is only mentioned in the text in passing, this entry will not be added here in the index.

The nine case study businesses have their own entry so that you find quickly where else in the book I discuss their story. You find ten names, as Frinter was founded by two individuals. Look for their first names in the index to find them. Similarly, you search for the name of the country such as Finland or Hong Kong to find where this country's issues are discussed.

For particular concepts or topics you will find that subthemes are listed under the overarching theme – let's say finance – to be found under F, so that when you look for start-up budget you will find a recommendation under S "start-up budget" to go to the finance entry under F: *see* Finance / start-up budget.

Cross references are made to other topics with the following:

"*see also*" points you to other related concepts or themes in the index;

sometimes you find a word you are looking for, but there are no page numbers, instead you find a recommendation under what term you find the page numbers (*see xxx*);

"*see under*" points you to related topics whereas

"*compare*" links to contrasting or not so obviously related terms.

Start-up is a term used nearly on every page, being the title and the main topic of this book, and for that reason there is no entry just for this term.

Printed and bound in Great Britain by
CPI Group (UK) Ltd, Croydon, CR0 4YY